D1414597

'E DUE

The Wound of Dispos

Telling the Palestinia

Whenever seven or Palestinians get together,
en minutes pass before they begin
to talk about the wound of dispossession.

A Palestinian American

Perceptions of Palestine: Their Influence on U.S. Middle East Policy

THE WOUND OF DISPOSSESSION

Telling the Palestinian Story

KATHLEEN CHRISTISON

Sunlit Hills Press
SANTA FE, NEW MEXICO

OCEAN TREE BOOKS

Please direct inquiries to:
Sunlit Hills Press
23 Camino Sudeste
Santa Fe, NM 87508
(505) 983-2883

Available to the trade through:
Ocean Tree Books
Post Office Box 1295
Santa Fe, NM 87504
(505) 983-1412   www.oceantree.com

The author may be reached at: kathy@christison-santafe.com

First edition, 2002

Printed in the United States of America

Library of Congress Control Number: 2001118212

ISBN 0-9712548-0-X

To
Bill
and the interviewees for this book, from whom I learned so much

Israel and territories occupied by Israel since June 1967.

Contents

Preface

The ten years since I completed this book in 1992 have seen momentous developments in the Palestinian-Israeli conflict but no improvement and in most ways significant deterioration in the Palestinian condition. The Oslo agreement signed in September 1993 brought Israeli recognition of the Palestine Liberation Organization and international recognition of the legitimacy of the Palestinian struggle. Palestinians are widely seen to have a reasonable national claim to part of Palestine and a right to establish an independent state. But, despite these developments, the lives of Palestinians in the occupied West Bank, Gaza, and East Jerusalem are measurably worse.

Another *intifada* rages in the occupied territories. Palestinians there live under siege conditions, enduring a nearly total blockade around every town and crippling economic stoppages, as well as continual Israeli tank and helicopter-gunship attacks on civilian areas. Even before this new *intifada*, Palestinians in the West Bank, Gaza, and East Jerusalem had continued to live with many of the administrative encumbrances of the Israeli occupation and had watched as Israeli settlements expanded, Israeli settlers multiplied, roads accessible only to Israelis criss-crossed the territories, and Israelis confiscated Palestinian land and demolished Palestinian homes. Despite seven years of a peace process that had promised them independence, these Palestinians still lived without the ability to govern their own lives, determine their own fate, travel freely, run their own economy, or any of the other rights that independent peoples around the globe enjoy. Israeli occupation authorities and settlers were still an insistent presence in Palestinian lives.

There has also been little improvement in the lot of the vast majority of Palestinians scattered elsewhere around the world. The Palestinian people are still stateless, and there seems less prospect than ever of a peace settlement that would bring a viable independent Palestinian state or a resolution of the refugee problem. Millions of Palestinians still live in desperate straits in refugee camps in Lebanon, Jordan, and Syria with no prospect of relief. The pain and distress of exile, although eased for some who have returned to the West Bank since Oslo, remains for most Palestinians.

Despite the much greater prominence of the Palestinians and their struggle, the vast majority of the American people and of people around the world are still ignorant of the Palestinian story. I had hoped by writing this book to help publicize some of that story, telling it in the words of Palestinians who live it, but for various reasons—having to do precisely with the difficulty of getting that story across—the book was never published.[1] I am therefore publishing it privately for the benefit of those many Palestinians who are its heroes and heroines.

Chapter 1, which was written a year after the Persian Gulf war and shortly after the opening of the Madrid peace conference in October 1991, is the chapter that most obviously does not reflect the changes of the last ten years, but I have left it as is because it is still a very apt description of Palestinian attitudes, particularly of Palestinian frustration and discouragement. The cynical Palestinian view of the United States and U.S. policy as described in the aftermath of the Gulf war, for instance, is still widespread. There is still, as I wrote in 1992, "palpable gloom and pessimism" throughout the Palestinian community. Palestinians still feel the sense of vulnerability that was so evident when the San Francisco teacher Amal T. told me a decade ago that any predator, including other Arabs, "can buy us and sell us overnight....The U.S. can buy us and sell us overnight."

Some differences should be noted. There are considerably more Palestinians today than the five million figure I gave in 1992 and no doubt considerably more than 200,000 in the United States. The worldwide figure now is probably something closer to 7.5 million.

Hamas is much more numerous and has become a far greater factor in internal Palestinian politics than was the case in the early 1990s, when it constituted perhaps twenty percent of the West Bank-Gaza population and hardly had a presence in the United States. The widespread fear expressed in Chapter 1 that militant fundamentalism was gaining strength among Palestinians, and would continue to do so, in direct proportion to the frustration of Palestinian political goals, has proved to be all too true. Palestinian-American intellectual and scholar Fouad Moughrabi is quoted in Chapter 1 as predicting in 1991 that, if the conflict continued to fester, a deep and widespread sense of alienation was likely—"the kind of alienation that could only be mobilized by Islamic groups and that could turn the region into a very, very difficult place." Although his grim vision was briefly interrupted by the start of the Oslo peace process, the emptiness and stagnation of this process are rapidly bringing his predictions to fruition.

The principal message of this book was that Palestinians are ready for peace and coexistence with Israel. As I wrote in 1992, "Palestinians have so internalized the need for peaceful coexistence that they talk even among themselves not about retaking all of Palestine but about compromising with Israel to secure a small state in the West Bank and Gaza." Although it may not have seemed necessary to put this message across during the years when the peace process was widely thought to be moving along healthily, the collapse of the process, for which Palestinians are wrongly blamed, has again revived the belief among a majority of Americans, certainly among the overwhelming majority of commentators and pundits in the United States, that the Palestinians are incapable of living peaceably with Israel and want to see it destroyed.

I believe this book puts the lie to that ignorant assumption. In Chapters 6 and 7, the heart of the book, Palestinians carry on a deep and thoughtful discussion of what coexistence with Israel, peace, and the peace process, mean to them and their own existence as a nation. There is no sloganeering here, no bravado, no false expectations, only careful self-analysis and a heartfelt search for a way for Palestinians to exist. The underlying assumption throughout the chapters, among all but a minuscule number of Palestinians, is that Israel will and should continue to exist, that Palestinians have no capability and therefore no hope of ever dismantling the Israeli state and retaking all of Palestine. Palestinian thinking is infinitely more complex and nuanced than the simplistic thinking of commentators who characterize them as still pursuing irredentist dreams against Israel. The commentators who propagate this notion would do well to read what Palestinians have to say in these chapters. I am struck by how very much more sophisticated than most of their American antagonists Palestinians actually are. It is tragic that, despite nearly a decade of so-called peacemaking, most Americans and most Israelis still know little about the Palestinians and have little depth of understanding about the Palestinian viewpoint or the Palestinian condition.

Much has changed for the individual Palestinian Americans who appear in this book since I completed it in 1992. Sadly, Sibyl Belmont died shortly after I interviewed her, of an illness from which she was suffering when I met her. In her zest for life and enthusiasm for the Palestinian cause, she never let on to me that she was ill. Ibrahim Abu-Lughod died as I was preparing this preface. Although he once told me he would not return to Palestine until the Palestinians had a state, he did move to the West Bank in the mid-1990s and taught at Bir Zeit University. Appropriately, he is buried in his hometown of Jaffa. I liked him quite a lot.

Many of the interviewees have married, or remarried; many have had children, or more children. Most have advanced in their careers; many have retired. Several have returned to one or another country in the Arab world to live. Many who had previously been unable even to visit Palestine have visited or lived there for brief periods since the Oslo agreement was signed, or live there permanently now. Salah Ta'mari, who now serves in the Palestinian legislature, has finally returned to his hometown of Bethlehem, where the buildings are after not very tall, but where he does belong.

Much more has been written by and about Palestinians, including about Palestinian Americans, since I completed this book—all works that would have added immeasurably to my knowledge and thinking had they been available earlier. Most of the intellectuals in Chapter 11 have written new books themselves that I would have noted were this book newly written.

I've read and reread this book many times over the years, and I still believe it is filled with valid insights into the Palestinian situation—insights that cannot be gleaned from books but that come only from being with Palestinians, in close conversation listening to their thoughts and experiences. Thanks to the countless Palestinians who freely told me their stories, I feel I know Palestine in its human aspect far better than I ever did during my years of government service. So many Palestinians welcomed me into their homes for this project without knowing who I was or what I wanted beyond the fact that I had an interest in their experiences. That was enough for most people. I was fed, sent Christmas cards, even in some instances housed, and in all cases greeted with a warmth and genuine hospitality that are refreshing in an American society growing gradually more aloof. My thanks to all of them.

Several people read all or parts of the manuscript and gave me valuable comments. I am particularly indebted to the scholars Ann Lesch, Philip Mattar, and Fouad Moughrabi for their insightful remarks. During the year, from mid-1990 to mid-1991, that I tried to market the book to commercial publishers, I had the pleasure of working with an agent, John Ware, who devoted endless hours to an energetic marketing effort and to providing me with sharp comments, as well as stern but always very apt directives to rewrite this or that passage. My special thanks to John for his dedication, for continually spurring me on, and for his faith in the book.

I especially thank my husband Bill for putting up with all this—for living with my long and frequent absences during the years that I conducted the initial interviews; with the financial strain the project put on our bank account; with my chronic bouts of worry that the project would go nowhere or was not going fast enough or was going too fast; with my anger and frustration when my hopes for publication finally died in 1992—and for his wonderful support throughout.

I must add the usual caveat that any errors of fact or interpretation are mine alone, along with the additional cautionary note that the views recorded here are as expressed to me in the late 1980s and early 1990s and do not reflect any changes that might have occurred in any individual's thinking in the years since then. If I have misrepresented anyone who has experienced a change of heart or of fundamental viewpoint over the last decade, I offer my apologies.

Kathleen Christison
February 2002

NOTE

[1] The story of my failure to find a publisher is a reflection of how difficult it is to get the Palestinian story across. Several commercial publishers rejected the book because, as one said, the Palestinian perspective was not "the path to commercial success." One university press came close to publishing it but allowed it to be suppressed by those who object to airing the Palestinian story. This episode was instructive. After two peer reviewers and, on the basis of their advice, the editor-in-chief recommended publication, a faculty board that oversees the press cautioned that the reviewers might be perceived as "too pro-Palestinian" and instructed that the book be reviewed by two pro-Israeli readers. These two readers both strongly condemned the book and urged that it not be published. When it was decided that their objections had no basis in scholarship, the book was given for review to a fifth reader, described to me as "pro-Israeli but more objective" than the two previous readers. This final reader, claiming that the book as written simply rehashed old grievances previously covered "by many others...over the last forty-five years," recommended a drastic alteration. Rather than describe a broad sampling of Palestinian-American political views, he recommended dropping almost all of the book's 124 interview subjects, concentrating on only ten interviewees, and writing in-depth and largely non-political profiles of their lives in the United States. Only in this way, the reader said, would the book be of any interest to American Jews. I chose not to make these changes and, after a nine-month review process, withdrew the book from consideration.

Introduction

Whenever anyone asks me where I'm from, I have to go into twenty minutes of history.

Karim Dajani
Student

I feel impelled to bring logic, history, and rhetoric to my aid, at tedious length. We need to retell our story from scratch every time, or so we feel.

Edward Said
After the Last Sky[1]

Some years ago, a Jewish friend of mine picked up a book about Israel and the Palestinians from my bookshelf and took it home with him. Although my friend had never been very much involved with Israel, its existence is of surpassing importance to him, and he thought he knew the story of Israel's creation as well as most American Jews. The book he borrowed was written by a Palestinian about the origins of the Palestinian-Israeli conflict. It was not a particularly good book, not one I would necessarily have recommended, but it did happen by coincidence to be the first book I had read on the subject twenty years before.

Some while later my friend called, having finished the book. He thought it too full of distortion, but it had, he said, opened his eyes to one thing: although he had always looked at the issue as involving Israeli land being coveted by Arabs, he was now able for the first time to focus on the fact that Palestinians see it the other way around—that they believe the land was theirs before Zionism was ever conceived and that it is actually Jews who have coveted Palestinian land.

My friend's insight opened my eyes as well—to a perspective too often ignored in discussion and study of the Palestinian-Israeli conflict. He finally understood, and made me focus on, the crux of this bitter conflict as Palestinians see it. My friend had not turned on Israel; he still loves Israel and believes indeed that its continued existence is intricately linked with his own. But he had become able to look past the common perception that Israel has an inherent right to the land of Palestine and that Palestinians have

1

unjustly contested this intrinsic Jewish right. He had become able to see the issue as Palestinians see it.

Israelis and Palestinians can probably never reach a true meeting of the minds on the fundamental issue of "right" that confronts them—the issue of which of them has the first or the higher claim to the land of Palestine. Such a meeting of the minds is not actually necessary for a peace settlement, but if peace is ever to be achieved, it is absolutely essential that each side know and understand where the other stands and why. No such understanding of the Palestinian position yet exists, either in Israel or in the United States, and I fear that without it there is little hope of finding a genuine solution. So long as Israel is regarded as the only party in this conflict with a reason for hostility toward its enemy, and so long as Palestinians are regarded as without a legitimate cause, as a ruthless people with no good reason for enmity toward Israel, all efforts to reach an equitable solution will be half-hearted and any settlement achieved will be unbalanced and therefore short-lived.

Throughout my work on this book, I encountered confusion among Americans as to what exactly a Palestinian is. To the extent that there is an image of Palestinians at all in the United States, it is primarily of terrorists, and few Americans have ever conceived of these people as a national entity, a people one could easily separate from "Arabs" in the aggregate. For purposes of clarity, then, a Palestinian Arab is any person, Muslim or Christian, who traces his roots to the area that today includes Israel, the West Bank, and Gaza.

It has been quite common in recent years to call Jordan a part of Palestine, but it is important to emphasize that this is an Israeli construct; Palestinians themselves do not consider Jordan to be Palestine, nor do Jordanians. The Palestinians in Jordan, who have made up the majority of the population there since fleeing Palestine in 1948, trace their roots to the area west of the Jordan River, like all other Palestinians throughout the world.

The principal basis for this book is a series of interviews conducted with Palestinians since late 1987. Although the interview sample is composed of Palestinians resident in the United States, both citizens and non-citizens, the attitudes expressed reflect Palestinian viewpoints everywhere. Palestinians in the United States remain an integral and active part of the Palestinian world community. Fully eighty-five percent of the interviewees in this sample are immigrants to this country who maintain contact with family and friends in the West Bank and Gaza and in the Palestinian exile community scattered throughout the world. These immigrants were once themselves members of the much-discussed Palestinian "street" in the West Bank, Jordan, Lebanon, and elsewhere in the Arab world, and they remain highly attuned to the attitudes of the street today.

Several of the interviewees, although citizens or residents of the United States, continue to divide their time between the United States and the Arab world. A few, although U.S. citizens, were living and working in Kuwait when Iraq invaded in August 1990; they have endured the same terrors as have all other members of the once sizable Palestinian community in Kuwait. A few others, also U.S. citizens, have left the United States to live permanently in the Arab world since I interviewed them. Others travel back and forth frequently. One works part of the year in Jerusalem; some others have wives and children who remain in the West Bank or Gaza. Several interviewees have arranged marriages for their children with young men or women from the West Bank. The ties remain extremely close.

It is a striking indication of just how close those ties are that six people in the interview sample are either members of or close relatives of members of the Palestinian and Jordanian delegations to peace negotiations. One interviewee is a member of the Jordanian negotiating delegation; another is on the delegation advising the Palestinian negotiating team; four are close relatives of either Haidar Abdul-Shafi, head of the Palestinian delegation, or delegation spokesperson Hanan Ashrawi.

A dozen Palestinian Americans sit on the Palestine National Council, the PLO's legislative arm, and are therefore involved in PLO policymaking. Seven past and present members of the PNC are among the interviewees for this book. In addition, several of the most prominent Palestinian intellectuals, who are leading opinion molders—in a sense the moral and political vanguard—of the worldwide community, live in the United States and are included in the interview sample.

Another interviewee is and has been since its founding a member of the PLO inner circle—in his own words, one of "the core of the core of the core." He is a former military commander and, although resident in the United States since 1986, he remains in constant close touch with Yasir Arafat and others in the PLO hierarchy. Large numbers of the interviewees espouse the policies of one or another of the factions that make up the PLO; although not formal members, many are loyalists of the main faction, Fatah, or of the more leftist Popular Front for the Liberation of Palestine or the Democratic Front for the Liberation of Palestine.

Probably the best evidence of the indivisibility of Palestinian views in the United States and Palestinian views in the West Bank or Gaza or Jordan or Tunisia is the fact that the range of political thinking expressed throughout the several years in which these interviews were conducted—a period that spans the *intifada*, the PLO's formal acceptance in late 1988 of coexistence with Israel, the period of U.S.-PLO dialogue, the Persian Gulf crisis, and the opening of the Madrid peace conference—is virtually identical with the sentiments expressed by the so-called Palestinian street and the range of positions advocated within the PLO.

3

There are some minor differences between Palestinians in the United States and the worldwide Palestinian community. Palestinians here tend to be somewhat better educated than the generality of Palestinians; they are not a rural or peasant population, as much of the West Bank population is; and they tend to be somewhat more secular than the Palestinian population in general. These are differences only of degree, however, and none results in a significant divergence of viewpoint among Palestinian Americans from the mainstream.

On educational levels, for instance, although Palestinian Americans tend more often to have a university degree, education for Palestinians in general is extremely important, and they are one of the most highly educated peoples in the world. Estimates in the mid-1970s indicated that twenty out of every one thousand Palestinians worldwide were attending universities.[2] As of 1970, the corresponding figure for the United States was higher at thirty per thousand, but the figures for the Soviet Union, France, and England were lower at eighteen, nine, and eight per thousand, respectively.[3]

Similarly, although Palestinians in the United States are not peasants, large numbers do come from rural, agrarian families. It is not at all unusual to find a Palestinian in the United States with a doctorate who grew up in a small village and whose parents are illiterate, another indication of the importance of education for all Palestinians. There are also many Palestinians in the United States who grew up in refugee camps.

The religious difference is also small. One does not find many Muslim fundamentalists among Palestinians in the United States (although I did encounter one Christian Palestinian whom I would have to label a religious fanatic), but such fundamentalism, although a growing phenomenon in the West Bank and Gaza as political aspirations are frustrated, is fairly rare among Palestinians anywhere. The number of practicing but non-fundamentalist Muslims is probably smaller here than in the worldwide community, but a fairly strict Muslim upbringing, even in the secular United States, is not by any means a rarity. The same is true for Christian Palestinians; many have given their children as conservative and traditional an upbringing in this country as they would have back home.

The book is based almost exclusively on interviews conducted with a total of 124 individuals in Palestinian-American communities throughout the country—in California, New Mexico, Texas, Illinois, Michigan, New York, New Jersey, Massachusetts, Vermont, and Washington, D.C., and its Maryland and Virginia suburbs. The bulk of these interviews were conducted between October 1987 and May 1989; I reinterviewed many people in the winter of 1991 in the aftermath of the Gulf War, and again in the winter of 1992 after the start of peace negotiations. I maintained informal contact with many of the interviewees throughout the more than four years of this project.

Although most interviewees gave permission to use their names, a few did not. In some instances in which a person expresses particularly hostile views about Israel or about other Arabs, I have myself chosen to protect him or her by not using a real name. Every full name appearing in the book is a true one; false names appear as a first name and a last initial.

Of the 124 interviewees, thirty-two are women. Forty-one are Christian Palestinians, one is a Druze, the remaining majority are Muslim. Ages at the time of interview ranged from fifteen to sixty-eight. The vast majority are immigrants to the United States; only nineteen were born in this country. Of the immigrants, approximately seventy percent are now American citizens. As for origins within Palestine, sixty-seven are from the West Bank; five are from Gaza; forty-four left or are from families that left areas that became Israel in 1948; another eight are from families that remained in Israel in 1948. Some of these last were born before, some after Israel's creation, but all spent a major portion of their lives as Israeli citizens, and all but one retain Israeli citizenship.

This is not a strictly representative sample. There is nothing scientific about the way I chose interview subjects and nothing quantifiable about the results. This is a study of individuals and of individual political viewpoints rather than a sociological treatise. Because of the unscientific selection process, some categories of interviewee are over- or underrepresented. Exiles from 1948—that is, people who themselves fled or whose families fled the area that became Israel in 1948—are undoubtedly overrepresented. Probably as many as half the Palestinians in this country immigrated from the West Bank after 1967, and 1948 exiles in the United States do not make up anything like the one-third proportion that is represented in the interview sample. I deliberately sought out people from 1948, however, in the belief that if I were to find uncompromising views, it would be among this group. This did not prove to be true.

Women are underrepresented in the sample. I regret this, but I do not believe this fact skews the results. Palestinian society has made great advances in educating and recognizing the abilities of women; Hanan Ashrawi, the spokesperson of the Palestinian negotiating delegation, is a striking example of the capabilities of Palestinian women and the freedom they enjoy to demonstrate those capabilities. The women I counted in the interview sample were almost all articulate and highly politically conscious. But the society is still largely a traditional one, even in this country, and many women remain reluctant to express their political views openly to anyone outside the family. I frequently encountered women who listened intently to their husbands being interviewed but would not participate themselves. This is not to say that women do not have political views—indeed, one

5

study has shown that women are seen as the principal preservers of Palestinian culture and therefore of the Palestinian political identity[4]—but I do not believe women in Palestinian society yet play a role outside the family in formulating Palestinian viewpoints that is proportionate to their numbers.

One-third of the interviewees are Christian. This is high for the Palestinian population in general, which is probably only twelve to fifteen percent Christian, but it more accurately reflects the Palestinian population in the United States. Although at least half the Palestinians here have immigrated since 1967 and the majority of these are Muslim, most Palestinians who came to the United States before 1967 were Christian. The proportion of Christians among Palestinian Americans is therefore probably still higher than the proportion among Palestinians in general. I do not think this makes a significant difference in the results presented here. Contrary to the popular conception and despite the tragedy of violent confessional divisions in Lebanon, there is little tension between Christian and Muslim Palestinians, and I found Christians to be neither more moderate nor more radical than Muslims.

Although based primarily on interviews, this book is not an oral history. Historians are properly suspicious of the history that emerges from the often faulty memories of individuals, although some excellent books have been produced in this genre; Cornelius Ryan's classics on World War II, *A Bridge Too Far*, *The Longest Day*, and *The Last Battle*, come to mind, as do two similar books on the 1948 Arab-Israeli war, Dan Kurzman's *Genesis 1948: The First Arab-Israeli War* and *O Jerusalem!* by Larry Collins and Dominique Lapierre. This book is not intended, however, as the reconstruction of an event, but rather as a presentation of a people's attitudes toward a current political issue. It relies not on their memories but on their ability to articulate feelings and attitudes. Chapter 2 does depend in some measure on individual memories of events four decades ago, but I have tried to supplement those memories with a factual account of the events taken from Israeli historian Benny Morris's book *The Birth of the Palestinian Refugee Problem, 1947-1949*. What is important here in any case is less the events themselves than the political outlook that these events shaped. Palestinians see themselves as a displaced people, and dispossession is a central reality in their lives.

It is worth repeating that what cultural differences exist between Palestinians here and Palestinians everywhere else are not great enough to cause notable differences in political outlook. The well educated are no more or less radical or moderate than villagers on the West Bank; nor do the views of Palestinians raised in comfort in the United States differ from those of Palestinians born and raised in refugee camps. Women are no different in their politics from men; Christians are no different from Muslims; Palestin-

6

ian Americans do not differ from non-American Palestinians. During a speech in 1991 to an Arab-American conference, Hanan Ashrawi told the group, "I will tell you what I told the State Department: There are no Egyptian Palestinians, Jordanian Palestinians, Israeli Palestinians, American Palestinians. There are only Palestinian Palestinians."[5]

NOTES

[1] Edward W. Said, *After the Last Sky: Palestinian Lives* (New York: Pantheon Books, 1986), p. 75.

[2] Muhsin D. Yusuf, "The Potential Impact of Palestinian Education on a Palestinian State," *Journal of Palestine Studies* 32 (Summer 1979): 79.

[3] Muhammad Hallaj, "The Mission of Palestinian Higher Education," *Journal of Palestine Studies* 36 (Summer 1980): 76.

[4] Louise Cainkar, *Palestinian Women in the United States: Coping with Tradition, Change, and Alienation*, Ph.D. Dissertation (Evanston, IL: Northwestern University, 1988).

[5] Hanan Ashrawi, banquet speech to the American-Arab Anti-Discrimination Committee National Convention, Arlington, VA, May 5, 1991.

1 Eternal Guests

All I want is my own country where I can live freely. You can't imagine what it is not to have a state, to be an eternal guest, threatened and humiliated wherever you go.
Tawifk
Palestinian in Kuwait,
speaking after the Gulf war[1]

The American media is saying the Palestinians lost everything [after the Gulf war]. What did we have before the war? The Palestinians in 1988 gave Israel everything that she needs. [But] the Americans stopped the dialogue with the Palestinians, the Americans weren't putting any pressure on Israel, the Americans and the Europeans did not do anything to solve the Palestinian problem. What did we lose? Did we have anything in hand? Nothing.
Fouzi El-Asmar
Israeli-Palestinian
writer and poet

The most evocative story in the large body of Palestinian exile literature created since 1948 is Ghassan Kanfani's "Men in the Sun." The story tells the tale of three Palestinians, exiled from their homeland in 1948, who are smuggled in an empty water tanker across the Iraqi desert into Kuwait to find work and who suffocate in the searing heat while the truck waits at a border checkpoint. Written more than a decade after the 1948 exodus but before the birth of the Palestinian revolutionary movement, the story is an indictment of Palestinian helplessness. But more particularly, the relentless sun and heat that kill these men symbolize the relentless, destructive indifference of the world, and especially the Arab states, to the Palestinians' plight.

Kanafani's 1963 story was eerily prophetic in many ways. It is a unique irony of the crises of recent years—Iraq's 1990 invasion of Kuwait, the 1991 Persian Gulf war, the Palestinians' reaction to these events, and the uncertain start of peace negotiations—that the Palestinians' fate may in the end be determined by events that took place under the hot sun of the Arabian desert, by their own inability to control or respond effectively to those or subsequent events, and by Arab governments indifferent to Palestinian needs and aspirations

It is another unique irony of the Palestinian situation that, although the Palestinian-Israeli conflict is being formally addressed in peace negotiations for the first time in four decades, there is palpable gloom and pessimism in the Palestinian community and a widespread feeling that the Palestinians' current situation is worse than at any period since 1948. The sense is pervasive that Palestine and the Palestinians are being overwhelmed and slowly swallowed by rapidly expanding Israeli settlement in the West Bank and Gaza, by the massive immigration of Jews from the former Soviet Union and, despite the start of U.S.-led peace negotiations, by U.S. indifference and the lack of a firm enough U.S. effort to stop this Israeli envelopment.

Palestinians feel an utter powerlessness to affect their own situation or move it to a resolution. The demise of the Soviet Union, their only superpower patron and the only counterweight to the U.S.-Israeli alliance, leaves them at the mercy of the United States. If the administration of President George Bush pursues the peace process and presses Israel to make territorial compromises, this will, of course, be to Palestinian benefit. But the Palestinians cannot seem to influence this possibility one way or the other, and if the Bush administration chooses not to pursue this course, or if an administration more willing to accommodate Israel takes office, the Palestinians have virtually no power to keep the peace process on track or to influence its course.

Nor is there an Arab patron for the Palestinians. The Arab states have never, from the Palestinian standpoint, provided adequate support or used their diplomatic leverage with the United States to Palestinian advantage, and in the aftermath of the Gulf crisis the Arabs have felt little need even to pay lip service to the Palestinian cause. The Arab states like Saudi Arabia and Kuwait that were pro-American and disinclined to exert pressure on Washington before the Gulf war now owe the United States a debt of gratitude and, most Palestinians feel, are comfortably ensconced in the American pocket. None of the large or militarily strong states can help the Palestinians. Iraq is devastated, Egypt long ago forfeited its military and diplomatic leverage and, with the end of the Cold War and the clear assertion of U.S. hegemony in the Middle East, Syria has signed on with the United States.

"It all depends on the good will of Bush and [Secretary of State James] Baker," notes Anthony Sahyoun, a Boston surgeon originally from Haifa. His statement captures the frailty of the Palestinian position, depending on U.S. good will. "Never," he says, "has the Arab world been more flattened, completely wiped out, than it is now." The Arab states "are being just dragged behind the United States"; the United States is the only power in the world; the United Nations is "just the new handmaid for the United States' power." So why, he wonders, should the United States or Israel want to give anything? Palestinians are acutely aware of the truth behind Secretary of State Baker's repeated admonition to the Palestinians during the lead-up to the October 1991 Madrid peace conference that the train won't stop here again. They are also all too well aware that the United States and Israel are the engineers.

To understand the Palestinians' anxiety about depending so totally on the United States—and to understand their response to the attempt by Iraq's Saddam Hussein to link the Israeli occupation of the West Bank and Gaza to the Iraqi occupation of Kuwait—it is important to recall that a mood of near despair about the peace process prevailed among Palestinians at the time of the Iraqi invasion in August 1990. Indeed, it is a measure of the deep frustration virtually all Palestinians felt over their inability to make progress toward their goal of establishing an independent state, and more urgently of gaining relief from the Israeli occupation, that they responded so strongly to a leader they knew to be using them and their plight cynically, not to advance their cause but to relieve the pressure on himself. They responded to Saddam Hussein's attempt at linkage because they saw it as their only hope of refocusing world attention on the Palestinian-Israeli situation.

In late 1988, the Palestine Liberation Organization had made what Palestinians consider a major concession—what they characterize as a peace initiative—by formally agreeing to coexist with Israel and accepting Israel's right to exist. Palestinians experienced a measure of euphoria in the immediate aftermath of this initiative. With the *intifada*, the uprising in the West Bank and Gaza, still in progress and still in the news, the United States about to start a dialogue with the PLO as a result of its concessions, a new U.S. administration taking office, and clear evidence before the world that the Palestinians were seeking peace and making compromises to achieve it, many Palestinians felt that independence and statehood were inevitable, and soon.

By the spring of 1990, just over a year later, the euphoria had virtually disappeared, and many were reassessing their predictions of statehood anytime in the foreseeable future. By this time, there seemed few reasons, from the Palestinian standpoint, for great optimism: the *intifada* no longer made headlines, no longer aroused worldwide sympathy, and no longer seemed to be moving Israel toward compromise, although Palestinians were still being killed and imprisoned; Israel was still unwilling to make territorial concessions and, although Prime Minister Yitzhak Shamir had, after U.S. prodding, put forth a proposal for West Bank and Gaza elections, he allowed his coalition government to collapse rather than proceed with implementation of the plan; a massive influx of Soviet Jewish immigrants to Israel was underway, presaging a further squeezing of the Palestinians in the West Bank and Gaza; the Bush administration had for all intents and purposes stopped making significant efforts to move the peace process along; and the U.S.-PLO dialogue had produced only four meetings in a year, none above ambassadorial level.

Palestinian frustration at Israel's unresponsiveness and at the U.S. failure to move the peace process forward was markedly increased in May 1990 when the United States vetoed a UN Security Council resolution that would have sent a UN inquiry commission to the occupied territories to report on Israeli practices there. Palestinians saw the resolution, which was drafted in the aftermath of the massacre by an Israeli gunman of several Palestinians from the occupied territories working in Tel Aviv, as a step toward gaining some measure of international protection against the occupation. Palestinians read the veto as an indication that the United States was so much interested in protecting Israel from criticism that it would not even allow Israel's occupation practices to be investigated. The sense of betrayal that most Palestinians felt was intense.

Three weeks after this UN vote, in June 1990, the Bush administration suspended the U.S.-PLO dialogue altogether after PLO Chairman Yasir Arafat refused to condemn, although he did dissociate himself from, an abortive terrorist attack carried out by a PLO Executive Committee member. The incident, launched by the Palestine Liberation Front, a small Iraqi-supported group led by Abul Abbas, a renegade PLO member who had been responsible for the 1985 *Achille Lauro* cruise ship hijacking, involved a seaborne attack on a Tel Aviv beach. The terrorists were killed or captured before they could mount the attack.

Because the attack was thwarted and had never been a PLO-authorized operation, most Palestinians regarded the incident as a tempest in a teapot and felt that Arafat and the Palestinians in general were unfairly penalized. To Palestinians, who feel that the United States never takes action against Israeli policies of which it disapproves, suspension of the dialogue because of this incident appeared to be another case of U.S. willingness to excuse Israeli but not Palestinian missteps. The U.S. veto and the suspension of dialogue, taken together, appeared to Palestinians as a final clear indication that U.S. and Israeli interests were so inextricably intertwined that the United States never intended to work seriously for a peace settlement that involved territorial concessions by Israel.

11

Iraq's Saddam Hussein was not unaware of the depth of Palestinian frustration and appears to have consciously attempted to capitalize on it and manipulate it. He had been openly wooing Arafat since the conclusion of the Iran-Iraq war in 1988, a period coinciding with the PLO's peace initiative and dialogue with the United States, and was providing the PLO with financial support and facilities in Iraq.[2] Observers widely believe that Saddam Hussein instigated the Tel Aviv beach attack in a deliberate attempt to interrupt the peace process, and most analysts agree with Middle East scholar William Quandt that "it is difficult to imagine [Saddam] making such an audacious move as the invasion of Kuwait if Israelis and Palestinians had been engaged in peace talks."[3]

Fouzi El-Asmar, a poet who lives in Washington, D.C., and writes a daily column on the Israeli press for a Saudi Arabian newspaper, expresses the widespread Palestinian viewpoint when he says that if the United States had pressed Israel to respond to the Palestinian initiative, there would now be a Palestinian-Israeli peace and Saddam Hussein could not have capitalized on Palestinian despair. Saddam, he notes, "tried to jump on the Palestinian problem and on other problems in the area because these problems were not solved. If any of these problems had been solved, he would not have had the opportunity to use them."

The degree of Palestinian despair in the aftermath of the stagnation of the peace process and the U.S. veto and suspension of dialogue with the PLO cannot be overstated. The situation in the summer of 1990 left the Palestinians, in their view, with no options. Thus, when Iraq, the only Arab state with anything like military parity with Israel, came along with an offer to exert diplomatic pressure on the Palestinians' behalf, they responded warmly. Saddam "threw us a line when we were sinking," explained one young man who strongly condemned Iraq's invasion of Kuwait but welcomed the hope Saddam presented to the Palestinians.

Hanan Ashrawi, a professor of English literature at Bir Zeit University on the West Bank and spokesperson for the Palestinian negotiating delegation, explains the Palestinian response to Saddam in similar terms. "Look," she says,

> the peace process we worked so hard to build collapsed in the spring of 1990....In June...the U.S. broke off its dialogue with the P.L.O. *You stopped even talking to us!* In August, Iraq invaded Kuwait and promised the Palestinians, who had lost hope, the faint possibility of liberation. Many knew it would not work. But if they dreamed of an Arab liberator on a white horse, if, in their despair, in the absence of any semblance of a peace process, they clung to this reed, can you really blame them?[4]

In fact, most Palestinians had little hope that Saddam Hussein could or would accomplish anything for their cause, but he seemed a better possibility than anything else facing them at the time. Najat Arafat Khelil, a nuclear physicist and political activist living in suburban Washington, D.C., explains the Palestinians' response as a desperate grasping at even the weakest reed. "It's like someone who's drowning," she says. "If you are drowning and you see a little twig passing by, would you say, 'Oh, this is a twig, it won't carry my weight'? No, you would say, 'I'll try it, it could help. It could be a miracle, maybe it will help me reach a larger twig.' That was the situation for the Palestinians under occupation. To them, they were drowning."

It was also, she says, the reaction of a victimized people toward someone they also perceived to be a victim. Palestinians felt themselves to be the victims of U.S. indifference and of a U.S. double standard in mobilizing the world against Iraq's occupation of and human rights violations in Kuwait but ignoring Israel's occupation of the West Bank and Gaza and its human rights violations there. "Sometimes," Khelil notes, "you just go for the underdog"—regardless of the morality or immorality of his actions. "It was more a voicing of their frustration, the way their situation was dealt with and the double standards and the hypocrisy of the rest of the world dealing with the [Iraq] issue, more than it was a full acceptance or support of what Saddam did."

Palestinians differ widely on the wisdom both of the popular outpouring of support for Saddam Hussein and of the official PLO stance. Although virtually none sanctioned the Iraqi invasion or Iraq's actions in Kuwait, most have been reluctant to voice open criticism of Iraq and Saddam Hussein or to criticize the PLO leadership for its stand during the crisis.

In general, the Palestinian intellectual community has been at the forefront of those who straightforwardly denounce Iraq's behavior and its own leadership for not more clearly distancing itself from Saddam Hussein. Walid Khalidi, perhaps the leading Palestinian scholar, wrote a widely circulated rebuke of Saddam's actions shortly before the outbreak of war in January 1991, noting that the "principles violated by Saddam in his invasion of Kuwait were the very principles from which the Palestinian cause drew its moral strength." Khalidi termed Yasir Arafat's apparent solidarity with Saddam perhaps "his greatest strategic blunder since the foundation of Fateh,"[5] the main PLO constituent organization formed by Arafat in the late 1950s.

Other Palestinian intellectuals have been equally critical, and some few individual Palestinians have been forthright in censuring Iraq's actions and the PLO's apparent support. Khalil Barhoum, for instance, a senior lecturer in linguistics at Stanford University, says without hesitation that he feels the invasion of Kuwait hurt the Palestinian cause by diverting attention from it and also by "dredg[ing] up unnecessary and painful images of the blood-thirsty Arab wanting to destroy Israel." Omar Kader, a security consultant in the Washington, D.C., area, wrote in October 1990 that Saddam Hussein's attempt at linkage demeaned the Palestinian cause. Palestinians could only maintain the integrity of their position against Israel's occupation, he said, by maintaining a single standard and opposing all occupation. "If it is wrong when Israel invades and occupies Arab land, then it is wrong when Iraq invades and occupies Kuwait."[6]

Such criticism, however, tends to be the exception rather than the rule. Palestinians most often dodge commentary on either Iraq or the PLO, attempting to explain away the PLO position and focusing instead on what for them is the more important issue of the inconsistency of the U.S. reaction to Iraq's capture of Kuwait on the one hand and Israel's occupation of the West Bank and Gaza on the other.

Whatever their feeling about the wisdom of the Palestinian response to Saddam Hussein, Palestinians across the board are outraged at the notion that their stand on this issue should be taken to reflect on the legitimacy of their cause or their right to participate in negotiations. Rights are intrinsic, the poet Fouzi El-Asmar says, and must be supported unconditionally. Someone who supports the rights of blacks in South Africa cannot retract those rights even if blacks massacre whites. Rami Khouri, a Palestinian author and publisher in Jordan, points out that achieving a settlement of the Palestinian-Israeli conflict is not like "a television quiz game in which one setback sees you out of the game for good."[7]

Some PLO leaders, including Salah Khalaf, who was assassinated in January 1991 apparently by Iraqi agents, openly opposed Iraq's invasion of Kuwait. In addition, leading Palestinian personalities in the West Bank issued a statement calling for the withdrawal of Iraqi forces and supporting Kuwait's right to self-determination.[8] But whatever the fine points and nuances of the Palestinians' posture, the fact that the PLO did not as an organization more clearly distance itself from Iraq, and did not make a point of its opposition to the invasion and pillage of Kuwait, effectively constituted support for Saddam Hussein, in the eyes not only of the West and the Gulf Arabs but of Palestinians as well. Yasir Arafat's embrace of Saddam became the literal and the figurative symbol of the Palestinian position for his own people as well as for the world in general.

The Gulf crisis crystallized many old resentments among Palestinians, not only against the United States and its policies, but against the Arab states that had for decades failed to use their military leverage or their oil wealth to aid the Palestinian cause. Palestinians were seldom hesitant to criticize the Arab states before the war, but the criticism was somewhat muted and cautious, and almost always anonymous. The war, however, and the depth of resentment it sparked against corrupt and dictatorial governments ready to fight for Kuwait, another corrupt and dictatorial government, but not for the Palestinians, have unleashed a stream of open and very bitter criticism. Palestinians are deeply disappointed both in the leadership throughout the Arab world and in the Arab people's tolerance of this leadership and style of government, which they recognize to be precisely what gave rise to the likes of Saddam Hussein. More significantly, there is deep concern about what impact the serious estrangement from Arab states like Saudi Arabia, Kuwait, and Syria will have on the Palestinian diplomatic position.

In the immediate aftermath of the war, the Stanford linguistics lecturer Khalil Barhoum described his mood—typical of the temper of most Palestinians at the time—as angry: not only anger and frustration at the United States, but "anger and frustration at the Arab governments, which are unpopular, unelected, and unrepresentative. And I include in that, of course, Iraq, because I think that Saddam Hussein would not have been able to get away with what he got away with if there was a democratic system of government in Iraq with checks and balances, because I doubt that many Iraqis would have supported him in his power grab in Kuwait."

Palestinians no longer make excuses for Arab dictatorships, as was often the case before the war. "The Arab world at this point is the only place where we still have total dictatorial, authoritarian regimes," says Samir Abed-Rabbo, who runs a small publishing house, Amana Books, in Brattleboro, Vermont. "Everywhere else you have at least a semblance of democratic institutions being created, except in the Arab world." Like many Palestinians, Abed-Rabbo foresees a time when popular Arab discontent will well up into uprisings against these dictatorial governments. He recalls that popular discontent with the Egyptian monarchy began to crystallize during the 1948 Palestine war but did not lead to revolution and Gamal Abdul Nasir's overthrow of the monarchy for another four years.

Muhammad Siddiq, a professor of Arab literature at the University of California, Berkeley, believes that when Saddam Hussein invoked other issues such as the socioeconomic split in the Arab world between the "haves" and the "have nots," he tapped a particularly strong sentiment that already existed beneath the surface. "The fact that even someone like Saddam Hussein, who is not a popular hero, could raise this," Siddiq observes, "shows how strong the sentiment is. If he had been a popular leader, this would have caught fire throughout the Arab world." Siddiq, too, foresees some kind of popular uprising in the Arab world. It is impossible to predict when such sentiment will boil over, but, he says, "to assume that people will endure oppression forever is very dangerous."

The United States is widely perceived to have a vested interest in preserving the undemocratic, socioeconomically unbalanced Arab order as it is and, as a result, it earns considerable Palestinian opprobrium for propping up Arab dictators. The scholar Walid Khalidi notes that the widespread sense of alienation toward the United States at the popular level in the Arab world derives not only from U.S. support for Israel but from a perception that the West in general and the United States in particular benefit so greatly from Arab oil that they have acted as "the guardians of the hated socioeconomic status quo and of the rulers who benefited from it."[9]

Although popular discontent is a very real phenomenon throughout the Arab world, including among Palestinians, their bitterness is to a great extent a projection of their own frustration at the Arab states' and the Arab peoples' perceived abandonment of the Palestinian cause. Noting that the Palestinian left has always believed that the Arab people support the Palestinian cause but are held back by their corrupt leaders and that ultimately the people will rise up in support of the Palestinians, Amal T., a teacher in San Francisco originally from Bethlehem, says she and her family had all thought such a revolt would occur when the war against Iraq began. She is deeply disappointed that nothing happened and says the crisis proves that the Arab people are not ready to face their problems and the need to act for themselves. "It means," she says bitterly, "that people like Saddam Hussein can buy us and sell us overnight. It means the U.S. can buy us and sell us overnight. We're always waiting for someone else to come and save us."

At this point, Amal's mother, who is listening in on the conversation, interjects a word about the *intifada*, noting that this uprising will teach everyone else how to do it—how to revolt and how to be self-reliant. Amal and her husband Rafiq agree, and everyone hastens to point out that "the *intifada* isn't over yet." But their final words carry a note of false bravado, and Amal's melancholy recognition that Palestinians are always waiting for someone else to save them points to a tendency to seek answers outside themselves and to cast blame on others for their setbacks that has plagued Palestinians throughout their history. One thing above all that the *intifada* at its height did for Palestinians was to demonstrate that they could be self-reliant; it provided clear evidence that, although they were militarily weak, they were no longer powerless to affect their situation. The Gulf crisis and the decline of the *intifada* have revived the tendency among many Palestinians to imagine plots being woven against them and to seek an explanation for their failures outside themselves.

To whatever extent Palestinians may tend to rely too heavily on the other Arabs, it nonetheless remains true that the Arab states are an essential source of diplomatic leverage for the Palestinians, and in practical terms what the Gulf crisis has meant is that most of the Arab states have effectively turned away from the Palestinian cause. Palestinians are deeply concerned that the most powerful Arab states, in their anger at the Palestinian response to Saddam Hussein and their scramble to align themselves to gain

16

maximum advantage from the U.S. position of dominance, will leave the Palestinians behind.

Palestinians are sharply aware of the irony of having to work so closely with the United States in peace negotiations after so strongly opposing U.S. intervention during the Gulf crisis. The recognition that only Washington can induce Israel to move toward a peace settlement has not diminished the deep resentment toward the United States that the Gulf crisis and the events immediately preceding it brought into focus, and there is real skepticism among all Palestinians about U.S. intentions and U.S. resolve. Walid Khalidi believes that the reason Palestinians were so hasty in opposing the United States during the Gulf crisis and were able so easily to ignore the immorality of Saddam Hussein's actions in Kuwait was the deep erosion of "U.S. moral credibility in Arab eyes" caused primarily by its policies toward Israel since 1948. Writing at the height of the crisis, he summed up the Arab and Palestinian view of the U.S. posture in the Middle East:

> Fair-mindedness, even-handedness, impartiality, and non-partisanship; championship of the occupied against the occupier, the weak against the strong; espousal of the principle of self-determination, of the sacrosanctity of Security Council resolutions, and of the right of return of refugees to their homes; dedicated pursuit of justice; resistance to the violation of international frontiers and territorial annexation, to the seizure of the lands of others and their colonization, to the forcible displacement and replacement of peoples, to disregard for human rights in the form of collective punishment, deportations and the carpet bombing of civilian targets—these and other germane principles are rightly or wrongly *not* associated in Arab consciousness...with the practice of the American administration and Congress in the Arab world. Thus, when all these principles suddenly and concurrently are invoked by the United States with such uncharacteristic zeal and vigor, the reaction is not only one of deep skepticism and defiant and reflexive anger at such moral selectivity, but of an equally deep fear and suspicion of ulterior motives, despite the obvious merits of the Kuwaiti case.[10]

Cynicism about U.S. motives, and ulterior motives, is pervasive. The notion that the United States launched a major war and wreaked such devastation on Iraq only for oil, however important that may be, seems so disproportionate to most Palestinians that other, deeper motives, generally centered on Israel, are taken for granted. Not everyone subscribes to the idea put forth by a San Francisco librarian, Samira F., that Israel and its American supporters pushed the United States into the war specifically so that

17

Israel would have a free hand to suppress the *intifada,* but it is not merely coincidental to most Palestinians that the forty-day curfew Israel imposed on the occupied territories throughout the war was economically ruinous and virtually destroyed the political and economic infrastructure built up by Palestinians during the *intifada,* badly crippling the uprising.

Far more Palestinians subscribe to the idea that the United States went to war primarily for Israel's benefit, to destroy the only Arab state that posed a serious military threat and, more importantly, was a serious military deterrent to Israel's perceived expansionist aims. Despite the widespread perception in the United States of Israel as a small state always under siege by large Arab armies, to Palestinians Israel has always appeared overwhelmingly strong and unstoppable, expanding its territorial reach with each war, no matter who the aggressor, and guaranteeing its military superiority through massive U.S. assistance and an area-wide monopoly on nuclear weapons.

As Walid Khalidi has noted, Palestinians generally believed that Israel would never be brought to the negotiating table unless it felt some military pressure from the Arabs. In the period leading up to the Gulf crisis, most Palestinians felt that the need for such pressure was becoming more urgent for a number of reasons, having primarily to do with the growth of uncompromising maximalism in Israel: the Israel government flatly rejected the land-for-peace formula embodied in UN Security Council Resolution 242; confiscation of Palestinian land and the construction of Israeli settlements in the occupied territories were rapidly increasing; the concept of "transfer," the expulsion of Palestinians from the territories, was gaining political acceptability; the right-wing Israeli proposition that "Jordan is Palestine" and that Palestinians should seek fulfillment of their national aspirations in Jordan was gaining credibility; and the massive influx of Soviet Jewish immigrants, like previous waves of Jewish immigration, threatened to displace Palestinians from the last remnant of Palestinian territory. To many Palestinians, because Iraq stood as the only deterrent to complete Israeli hegemony in the Middle East, the U.S. effort to destroy Iraq's military capability and its technological and industrial infrastructure promoted what Khalidi calls "the not altogether far-fetched suspicion" that the United States was attempting to preserve Israel's dominance and its nuclear monopoly in the area.[11]

Still more prevalent among Palestinians is the belief that the United States went to war to assert its own hegemony at a time when the Soviet Union was in decline and not able to offer competition and when U.S. power was being threatened by Iraq. Abdur-Rahim Jaouni, a Berkeley, California, geochemist, sees the issues of U.S. hegemony and Israeli dominance as interrelated, one being the instrument of the other. "As long as energy resources, which is oil, are still the driving force of the economy of the world," he says, "then that part of the world is going to be important. You have to have control over it, from a very pragmatic point of view." He tries to look at the issue from a U.S. viewpoint. "If I were the superpower of the world, I would do what the United States is doing. I don't find it morally correct now; as a Palestinian, I believe it is moral cowardice because I am on the receiving end." But he believes that the United States has vital national security interests that from its standpoint dictate maintaining control over the Middle East "for the coming fifty years, until the oil ends." Anyone or any state that becomes "a little bit strong," he says, "must be put down. Just look what happened to Saddam. The war shows you how much that area is important to them."

Israel, Jaouni believes, is a tool of U.S. policy. Colonial powers throughout history have used minority groups as pressure points against the majority, and he sees this as Israel's role in U.S. thinking. He does not believe that Israel's importance to the United States derives merely from the pressures of the pro-Israel lobby but from its intrinsic value as an agent of U.S. policy. He rejects the notion that the United States might view a peaceful resolution of the Palestinian problem through creation of a Palestinian state as a potentially stabilizing factor both for itself and for Israel in the Middle East. "If the United States cared for stability in the area," he observes wryly, "they wouldn't have gone into such a huge war. I don't think these people look at it from that point of view. Don't you think having a strong state like Israel, in their minds, is more stabilizing for the area than the Palestinians, from their point of view?"

Jaouni touches on a belief widely held among Palestinians and the primary reason for the general skepticism and cynicism about U.S. intentions. The United States does not want to see a Palestinian state created, it is widely felt, because such a state would be hard to control and would disrupt the U.S. effort to dominate the Middle East. "The U.S. has always viewed the Palestinians as trouble-makers," says the San Francisco librarian Samira F. "Palestine is the one place probably that would have been democratic, representative, possibly socialist—the things the United States does not want—and therefore not controllable by the U.S., not a client state, not maneuverable, manageable, couldn't be pushed around quite as easily as the other states."

How democratic a Palestinian state would have been or might be in the future is a moot point, but U.S. policymakers since the Truman administration have indeed always opposed Palestinian self-determination and statehood, largely because this was seen as a source of radicalism and increased instability in the area. Since 1948, notes the Stanford linguistics lecturer Khalil Barhoum, the Palestinians have been "a shadow type of entity. People talk about them in the sense of being refugees or even much worse, being terrorists, but not in the sense of a political entity, not in the sense of a nation to contend with. We've been talking around them, talking with the Egyptians or the Jordanians but never with the Palestinians. So the minute you establish a Palestinian state, you are opening a Pandora's Box."

How do cynical Palestinians explain that the United States is now, since the beginning of the Madrid peace process, addressing the Palestinian problem in negotiations and has exerted pressure to bring Israel to the table? Khalil Barhoum believes that "the Americans have been trying to get the Palestinians under these conditions for a long, long time"—that is, without PLO representation, without a commitment to address long-range Palestinian issues such as statehood or the right of return, and with the Palestinians weak and politically emasculated. "At this point," he says, "the Palestinians are in such a weak bargaining position politically that they simply have no leverage over either the United States or Israel."

The United States likes it this way, Palestinians feel. In the aftermath of the Gulf war, they generally believe, the United States had to address the Palestinian issue in some way, for three principal reasons: in order to insure some measure of stability for its so-called new world order by preventing the issue from boiling over into a renewed *intifada* or an upsurge of terrorism or of Muslim fundamentalism; in order to paper over the glaring disparity between its readiness, on the one hand, to go to war to rid Kuwait of Iraq's occupation and its indifference, on the other hand, to the fate of Palestinians under Israeli occupation; and in order to provide a cloak of legitimacy to those wealthy Arab states that by cooperating with the United States and indirectly with Israel in the destruction of Iraq appeared to have violated Arab unity and abandoned the Palestinian cause.

But few Palestinians believe that the Bush administration's effort to start and maintain a peace process amounts to more than damage control in the pursuit of its own interests. The United States does not care about justice for Palestinians or redressing wrongs done in 1948 or 1967, it is widely felt, but only about the smooth functioning of the new U.S.-dominated world order. Palestinians have a role to play in this new order, as far as the United States is concerned, only to the extent that they go along, that they cooperate quietly in the effort to put a lid on the Palestinian-Israeli conflict. If this means a high level of tension in the U.S.-Israeli relationship, heavy U.S. pressure on Israel to stop construction of settlements, possibly an eventual end to total Israeli dominance over the West Bank and Gaza, so much the better as far as Palestinians are concerned, but no Palestinian believes at this point that the United States has any intention of seeing negotiations through to a conclusion that they would find satisfactory, that would give them as a permanent arrangement anything more than autonomy under Israeli or Jordanian control. More than this, they believe, would be viewed by the United States as too disruptive of the status quo.

The Bush administration, Khalil Barhoum observes, "has submitted to the Israeli formula that [the Palestinian problem is] an administrative matter, wherein an ethnic minority is not happy with the extent of freedoms and rights that they enjoy within their own country, as if the Palestinians were like the Afro-Americans in this country asking for more civil rights or like the Hispanics, which is not the case."

"The Americans," he says, "are simply trying to make everybody miss the point." The great fear among almost all Palestinians is that the United States is succeeding in this effort.

The question of whether and to what extent the Palestinians should allow themselves to be pulled along on this perceived U.S. scheme—of whether in fact they have a choice, whether Secretary of State Baker's dictum that the train won't come around again is an accurate description of reality or merely a tactic designed to frighten the Palestinians into making concessions—has been perhaps the most critical question facing the Palestinians at any time in their history.

The number of Palestinians who remain unreconciled to Israel's existence, who would reject and try to disrupt or overturn a peace agreement that created a small Palestinian state in the West Bank and Gaza and recognized Israel within its pre-1967 borders, is quite small. Only Hamas, the Muslim traditionalist organization in the West Bank and Gaza, which represents perhaps twenty percent of the population there and only ten percent of the worldwide Palestinian community, presents any organized opposition to accommodation with Israel. Despite the Gulf war, despite Palestinian support for Saddam Hussein and expressions of pleasure when Iraqi Scud missiles fell on Tel Aviv, the PLO and the Palestinian mainstream both inside and outside the occupied territories remain committed to the November 1988 Palestine National Council initiative accepting coexistence with Israel. No matter how angry and frustrated at the United States, at Israel, at the general situation—no matter, indeed, whether they agree that Palestinians should have entered negotiations under the conditions laid down for the 1991 Madrid conference—Palestinians almost all reaffirm the 1988 initiative and the commitment to making peace with Israel.

There is, however, a minority within the mainstream that, although not opposed to the idea of making peace with Israel, does oppose the conditions under which Palestinians agreed to come to the negotiating table this time. These Palestinians represent a principled school of thinking that supports the objective laid out in the 1988 initiative but not the tactics currently being followed, on the grounds that the negotiations as now configured are humiliating to Palestinians. They are more or less aligned behind the Popular Front for the Liberation of Palestine and the Democratic Front, which formally oppose Palestinian participation in negotiations under the conditions laid down—that is, without PLO representation and without representation by Palestinians outside the occupied territories. The principled school stands in opposition to the pragmatic school, constituting a majority of Palestinians, who believe that Palestinians have said "no" to any prospect of compromise for too long, have missed opportunities, and now have no choice, if they are not to be left behind altogether, but to enter negotiations under the restrictions imposed.

Fouad Moughrabi, a leading Palestinian scholar in the United States and professor of Middle East affairs at the University of Tennessee in Chattanooga who has studied and compiled the results of an extensive survey of Palestinian attitudes in the West Bank and Gaza conducted in the summer of 1991, describes the split between the principled and the pragmatic schools as a generational difference, not wholly confined to age differences but defined by differences in political thinking as shaped by the events and realities of different eras. The old Palestinian discourse, Moughrabi says, was formed out of national dismemberment and exile and gave rise to the Palestinian resistance movement in the 1960s. The new discourse has been shaped by the experience of living under Israeli occupation, and the new generation thus formed is better able to accommodate itself to present realities. The "new brand of activists" is better educated, more articulate, more pragmatic. They are less ideological and tend to reject rhetoric in favor of defining realizable objectives. The new generation, Moughrabi concludes, now sets the tone for the whole Palestinian movement and is more inclined to rely on the "logic of accommodation and caution" rather than of confrontation.[12]

Some Palestinians see in the debate between the principled and the pragmatic schools over the wisdom of entering negotiations at this time a serious and potentially destructive split in Palestinian ranks. Ghada Talhami, a political science professor at Lake Forest College in Illinois, believes the Palestinian community has never been so divided over any issue and fears that if progress is not made—if the decision of the pragmatists, among whom she counts herself, to proceed with negotiations is not vindicated—"the letdown is going to be a tremendous loss for the PLO and for the Palestinians in general." Although she personally sees the negotiations as "a tantalizing event" with "a lot of promise," she fears that proceeding with them for too long without tangible progress will produce more violence in the occupied territories and a move by a radicalized *intifada* leadership to break with the PLO.

Most other Palestinians do not view the debate as this serious. Najat Arafat Khelil, the Washington physicist, says there has always been some disagreement over tactics within the Palestinian community. "We are all in agreement that we want a country back," she notes, but "we are not all in agreement on what the borders of that country should be. We are not all in agreement how we're gong to get there. I don't take this as division." Addressing particularly those outside the Palestinian community who exaggerate the degree of division within, she says heatedly, "I don't know why when there are different points of view on the Palestinian side everybody thinks, Boy, there is fracture and this is something terrible. When it happens everywhere else, it is a sign of democracy!"

Samir Abed-Rabbo reflects the view of those Palestinians who stand on principle against the current negotiations. Born in the Jerusalem refugee camp of Qalandiya to parents who fled a village near Ashdod in 1948, he is an angry young man who focuses his energies on the injustice done to Palestinians and, because that injustice is so personally reflected in the dispossession his parents experienced, finds compromise with Israel impossible, on principle, unless Israel makes compromises of equal magnitude.

He believes the concessions the PLO had to make to secure a place at the negotiating table for Palestinians were "too much" because he is certain the Israeli government is not serious about achieving peace and will not make compromises. The Palestinians, he feels, are too weak to be able to negotiate. "One does not go to a negotiation table almost naked," he says forcefully. "Once you go from a position of weakness, then you have to understand that you are the party that is asked to give. I do not have to engage in a negotiation process if my rights are not guaranteed. Why would I get involved in a process that is only created to legitimize the robbing of my rights?"

Asked if he thinks the Palestinians had any choice but to attend under the circumstances, Abed-Rabbo responds that "the Palestinians always have a choice. The Palestinians are the only ones who could give legitimacy to the state of Israel from a legal point of view. From a military point of view, of course, the powerful is the one who creates the facts, but from a legal point of view it is only the Palestinians who could legitimize the existence of the state of Israel."

But, he is asked, in practical terms does this distinction make any difference? Is there not a danger that Israel will consolidate the occupation, continue land confiscations, and blanket the West Bank and Gaza with Israeli settlements while Palestinians argue Israel's legitimacy from a legal point of view? He resorts at this point to the long-range view that the Palestinian left and the principled school have often adopted: something better will come along. "See, you are talking from the angle of brute force," he responds. "Brute force is ever changing; it's not a static quality. Today the Israelis are powerful, today the United States is the leader of the world. But even in our short lifetime, we have seen superpowers come and go. So I do not, as a Palestinian or as a human being, base my thinking on brute force."

Abed-Rabbo is quite frank in saying that Palestinians need a new leadership for the challenges ahead. "I would like to see a new, a fresh way of thinking, a fresh leadership for the Palestinians," he says. He is careful to give the leadership credit for bringing the Palestinian movement as far as it has, but on the whole, he says, "The older school has led the Palestinians from one disaster to another, and I think it's about time that a new thinking emerges within Palestinian circles."

The conversation comes around again to what Palestinians should or should not expect from negotiations. Reflecting his focus on the injustices Palestinians have endured, Abed-Rabbo says Palestinians have been given "a raw deal" by Israel and the United States since 1948, and the current negotiations are merely a continuation of that process. "Analyzing the facts," he says, "you will find out that the United States and Israel will only come to a conference that is guaranteed from the outset to benefit Israel. The present regional and international balance of power is only going to guarantee that Israel is going to benefit from it and not the Palestinians, not the Arabs."

Does he believe that the United States is deliberately arranging the peace talks so that Israel benefits? "I would be stupid to say otherwise," he answers bluntly. "Given the facts on the ground, I would be stupid to say otherwise." He dismisses Bush administration pressures on Israel and its rejection of Israel's request for $10 billion in loan guarantees to build housing for Soviet Jewish immigrants as not enough. This kind of pressure is employed because the American people want it, not because it is good for Palestinians or the right thing to do. Only a move to end the automatic annual $3 billion to $4 billion U.S. subsidy to Israel would prove to Abed-Rabbo's satisfaction that the United States was "resolute" on the key issues involving Israel and the Palestinians.

He is not so ideological, Abed-Rabbo notes, that he would oppose a negotiated autonomy plan for the West Bank and Gaza, so long as it were properly structured. "If you are talking about an autonomy that will only guarantee the Palestinians the right to collect garbage, then I would say, What's the use?" If, on the other hand, it guaranteed the Palestinians "complete control over their resources, complete control over freedom of expression, movement, etcetera, etcetera, I would not oppose that. I think it is a hundred percent better than what exists today."

But even this kind of autonomy would have to be accompanied by some arrangement such as the right of return for Palestinians dispossessed in 1948 or compensation for lost property that would "redress the wrongs done to me"—he brings home the personal nature of this issue for him, as for many other Palestinians—and this is where Abed-Rabbo's deep misgivings about the Palestinians' decision to enter the current negotiating process emerge again. "How are you going to negotiate, how are you going to put this issue on the agenda if you are the weakest party?" he asks.

The conversation begins to repeat itself. He is asked if the Palestinians won't always be the weakest party. He says yes, in military terms, but that's not the point. With a new leadership, he believes, the Palestinians would be capable of devising a new strategy that would be "different and effective." He will not say what he thinks that strategy ought to be, but the important thing is to strengthen the Palestinians—because, he repeated, "if from the beginning you are limping, you are the one who is going to receive the hits."

The inability or refusal of Palestinians like Abed-Rabbo and the principled school to say what they would do differently irritates those in the pragmatic school who feel that in fact Palestinians don't have any choice but to pursue negotiations now, despite their weakness, and who feel that something better won't come along, that Palestinians have been losing ground for four decades waiting for some ill-defined promise of better days. "When people present this point of view," says one woman impatiently, "I ask them what's the alternative, do they have a better idea how to do it? If they have, well speak up. But nobody's presenting a new point of view."

Another woman believes that most Palestinians have come to realize that saying "no" never achieved anything. "For a long time," she says, "we rejected peace and we put forth our own rules, and we hated [Egyptian President Anwar] Sadat because he talked about peace, and we rejected Resolution 242, and we rejected and we rejected and we rejected. I think that this is the time we should not reject peace."

The vast majority of Palestinians take this same pragmatic view. No one is happy about the conditions under which Palestinians entered the peace talks, and most are pessimistic about the prospects for the peace process, but the general view is that specifically because the Palestinians are weak they must take advantage of this opportunity or be ignored completely. The decks are stacked against the Palestinians, says AbdulSalam Massarueh, a Washington, D.C., journalist, "and they have no choice if they don't want to be singled out as the spoilers of the peace process." The refrain that they "had no choice" is heard from most Palestinians. Khalil Barhoum points out that so much has changed on the world scene that Palestinians had no other options. With the demise of the Soviet Union, they no longer have a superpower champion, Arab support can no longer be taken for granted because "provincial Arab concerns after the Gulf war have evidently replaced the Palestinian problem as the top priority," and the need of Palestinians in the West Bank and Gaza for relief from Israel's occupation grows more urgent "by the day, if not by the hour."

For all the Palestinian mainstream's acceptance that Palestinians had to enter negotiations on the terms laid down by Israel and the United States, however, and for all the majority's tendency to dismiss the seriousness of the division in Palestinian ranks over the wisdom of surrendering to these terms, most Palestinians are profoundly pessimistic about the prospects for those negotiations and profoundly worried that what they see as a likely failure will seriously radicalize the Palestinian community. Although most Palestinians point out that there is no coherent leftist or radical alternative to the pro-peace policy now being pursued by the PLO and no movement capable of leading the Palestinian community in a different direction, the danger is great that Palestinian cohesion and the leadership's mandate to pursue a moderate course will disintegrate into inchoate radicalism if moderation is denied any gains. The longer Israel refuses to make compromises, almost all Palestinians fear, the greater the danger that frustrated Palestinians will slip away into radicalism and the greater the likelihood that the moderate Palestinian polity will lose control.

Palestinians now willing to coexist with the Israeli state as long as they receive recognition in the form of a Palestinian state in the West Bank and Gaza will not maintain their conciliatory stance if it is continually rejected. A leading Palestinian intellectual, Muhammad Hallaj, who directs the Center for Policy Analysis on Palestine, a Palestinian think tank in Washington, D.C., has noted that the PLO's 1988 acceptance of coexistence with Israel effectively transformed the Palestinian-Israeli conflict from one over all of Palestine to a more manageable one simply over the fate of the West Bank and Gaza—from "a struggle about existence to a dispute about coexistence." If Israel is allowed to perpetuate the occupation, he believes, the conflict will be returned to its starting point as a zero-sum Arab-Zionist conflict over existence in all of Palestine—a conflict whose implications he believes are "too grim to require elaboration."[13]

All Palestinians worry about the power and appeal of Islamic fundamentalism in a situation in which legitimate Palestinian aspirations are thwarted. In fact, the Palestinian fundamentalist organization Hamas, which opposes accommodation with Israel, has gained strength in the occupied territories in recent years in direct proportion to the frustration of the Palestinians' political goals. The idea that Palestinians who see no hope of ever gaining independence or relief from foreign occupation would reject conciliation with the enemy they saw as their oppressor, even if they had once offered that enemy peace and coexistence—and that they would turn to an Islamic revivalist organization as the means of venting their frustration and disappointment—is not at all far-fetched. Virtually all analysts agree that fundamentalism is the refuge of people for whom secularism and modernity do not provide the answers; one analyst, commenting on the Algerian situation, has observed that fundamentalism arose there after years of disastrous state economic, social, and cultural policies and believes that "[f]undamentalism anywhere subsists on moral and material destitution."[14]

The immediate appeal of Hamas, explains Khalil Barhoum, has to do with its perceived successes. For one thing, Palestinians who turn to Hamas in desperation feel they have nothing to lose. No tactic, whether conciliation or armed struggle or uprising, has worked with Israel. "They haven't won anything through the PLO for a long time," he says, "so the PLO has just simply proved the failure of the secular nationalist movement in Palestine." At the same time, as people grow more and more disillusioned with their own situation, "they look at southern Lebanon and see a very successful effort of the fundamentalist movement driving out the Israeli occupation army—something the PLO hasn't been able to do."

Palestinian intellectual Fouad Moughrabi explains the fundamentalist phenomenon as it reaches across the Arab world. Speaking at a Middle East forum held in Santa Fe, New Mexico, in 1991, he explains that over the last two to three decades in the Arab world there has been at the popular level "a perception of repeated failures on the part of governments which are narrowly based and unresponsive to the needs of the people." The failures are multiple, he says:

> failure to bring economic reforms; failure to invest in the welfare of their own people; failure on the part of the wealthy countries to invest in the region in general; failure to confront the challenge Israel has posed to the region, not only to the Palestinians, but attacks against other Arab countries; failure to confront the United States—and the West in general, but especially the United States—when the United States has adopted policies deemed detrimental to the people. There is a sense that none of the systems that have been suggested, whether Arab nationalism, socialism, or whatever, since the post-independence period, have actually worked.

As a result of this failure of all the systems and all the options they have been offered, Moughrabi says, people begin to feel they should look back to earlier, better systems, in this case to a pure form of Islam. "This happens all the time in societies," he notes. "You go back to a restorationist image. Societies, peoples in crisis always go back and try to restore a golden era in the past. In this particular case, it's the Islamic vision—to go back to the roots of Islam, purified of all the things that have clung to Islam over the years, in order to confront the modern world—not only the challenges of their own governments but what we call the impact of modernization, the intrusions of the West."

Moughrabi is not optimistic about the future in these circumstances. If the Arab-Israeli conflict is resolved and the region stabilized, it might be possible, he believes, to channel some of this discontent into building democratic institutions in the Arab world. If the conflict continues to fester, "I think you'll have a deep sense of alienation, deepened even further by the fallout from the destruction of Iraq—the kind of alienation that could only be mobilized by Islamic groups and that could turn the region into a very, very difficult place."

To bring the urgency of his view home to the audience, he gestures toward the Israeli sharing the podium with him, Chaim Shur, editor of the Israeli magazine *New Outlook*, which promotes Palestinian-Israeli coexistence, and observes that if peace is not achieved in the next two to three years, Hamas will be the Palestinians' spokesman and the audience will be listening not to Fouad Moughrabi and Chaim Shur discussing peace but to a hardline Palestinian from Hamas and a right-wing Israeli, each talking in maximalist terms about liberating all the land from the Jordan River to the Mediterranean.

This is the last opportunity, Moughrabi believes, to achieve peace through partitioning the land of Palestine. He does not foresee that this will be the outcome of the current negotiations, and his picture of the long-range future is dismal. "My expectation," he says, "is that roughly by the year 2020, most of the countries of the region will be Islamic republics and that we will be back to where we were in the '50s with Israel. That's what I expect."

In Madrid, wrote an Israeli political columnist after the opening of peace talks there in October 1991, "the myth of the eternal Palestinian 'refusenik' died. At the same time, another myth...that 'there is no one to talk with,' a myth that was so convenient for those [Israelis] who didn't want to talk with anyone, finally collapsed."[15]

A great many myths about Palestinians and the Palestinian-Israeli conflict have been shattered in recent years, and a great many realities have changed. But it may be the great tragedy of the Palestinians that the time has passed when demythologizing and new realities have any impact on the old entrenched realities. The *intifada* has brought the Palestinians a new and vastly improved image around the world; despite the self-inflicted damage to that image suffered during the Gulf crisis, Palestinians are now much more widely perceived with a human face, as a people bent not on the destruction of another people but simply on securing their own freedom. The Palestinians themselves have changed; their formal acceptance of coexistence with Israel was a significant break with the past and with past reluctance openly and officially to cede claim to the part of Palestine that constitutes pre-1967 Israel. Palestinians have so internalized the need for peaceful coexistence that they talk even among themselves not about retaking all of Palestine but about compromising with Israel to secure a small state in the West Bank and Gaza, and it is now much more widely recognized around the world that they have reached this point of accommodation. The dignified and conciliatory public face that the Palestinian delegation presented at the Madrid conference enhanced this impression.

Nonetheless, the shattered myths, the improved image, the changes in Palestinian thinking have made no impact where it most counts, with the

Israeli government. Yehoshafat Harkabi, a former Israeli general and leading political theorist, has noted that the Palestinian-Israeli conflict reached a kind of crossover point after Israel captured the West Bank and Gaza in 1967. Until that point, Israelis and Palestinians each had what he calls a grand design that envisioned possessing all of Palestine, but whereas Palestinians sought fulfillment of their grand design as part of their national policy, Israelis divorced grand design from policy and settled as a matter of pragmatism for possessing only a part of Palestine. After 1967, however, Palestinians began to divorce grand design from policy, just as Israelis began to employ their maximalist grand design as state policy, a trend that has reached a peak with the government of Yitzhak Shamir. "Just as the first signs of flexibility appeared in the Arab position," he notes, "the Israeli position became absolute."[16]

As a result of this Israeli shift, and a political culture in the United States that supports it, the dramatic change in the Palestinian position has gone unheeded by large segments of the very audience Palestinians most need to address. The myths and misunderstandings about Palestinian thinking, about the Palestinian view of the conflict and its roots, about the Palestinians' willingness or unwillingness to compromise, remain in place—deliberately perpetuated by a maximalist Israeli government, simply misunderstood by many Israelis and many of Israel's American supporters.

Without some better understanding of the Palestinian perspective—of why Palestinians have opposed Israel and how much their position has changed over the years—no real peace will be possible. Palestinians, Fouad Moughrabi points out, "offer a vision of peace based on coexistence,"[17] but unless that is adequately understood and unless the sacrifices Palestinians made to come to that position are understood, the opportunity will slip away. Moughrabi calls the Palestinians' 1988 acceptance of coexistence an "historic" compromise—historic because of the magnitude of the compromise, because for millions of Palestinians it meant forsaking their right to go back to their towns and villages now inside Israel. For Moughrabi it meant forsaking his own right to go back to Ayn Karim, the village outside Jerusalem where he was born and which has now been incorporated under its Hebrew name Ein Kerem into Israeli Jerusalem.

"We made this important historical compromise," he says, "because we wanted to look to the future and not toward the past. We are still committed to that, to those resolutions. This is our agenda, and we'll fight for this agenda because the alternative is what they call, in the jargon of the Pentagon, low-intensity war for years to come—which will be devastating for the Israelis, for the Palestinians, for the Jordanians, for the Syrians, for the Egyptians, for the Saudis, and perhaps for Europe and perhaps for the United States."

NOTES

[1] Judith Miller, "Nowhere to Go: The Palestinians After the War," *New York Times Magazine* (July 21, 1991): 12.

[2] Walid Khalidi, *The Gulf Crisis: Origins and Consequences* (Washington: Institute for Palestine Studies, 1991), p. 21.

[3] William B. Quandt, "The Middle East in 1990," *Foreign Affairs* 70, no. 1, America and the World 1990/91 special edition (1991): 56

[4] Miller, "Nowhere to Go," 14. Emphasis added.

[5] Khalidi, *The Gulf Crisis*, pp. 15, 20-21.

[6] Omar Kader, "Apply One Standard to Iraq and Israel," *Washington Report on Middle East Affairs* (October 1990): 35.

[7] Rami Khouri, "Who Represents the Palestinians?" *The Palestinians After the Gulf War: The Critical Questions* (Washington: Center for Policy Analysis on Palestine, 1991), p. 15.

[8] Speech by Nabil Shaath to the Seventh UN International NGO Meeting on the Question of Palestine, Geneva, August 29-31, 1990.

[9] Walid Khalidi, *The Middle East Postwar Environment* (Washington: Institute for Palestine Studies, 1991), p. 6. See also two analyses by Khalil Barhoum: "The Gulf crisis and 'a new world order,'" *Middle East International* (January 11, 1991): 21, and "The war's message needs to be addressed," *Middle East International* (March 8, 1991): 22.

[10] Khalidi, *The Gulf Crisis*, pp. 24-25. Emphasis in original.

[11] Ibid., pp. 28-29.

[12] Fouad Moughrabi, Elia Zureik, Manuel Hassassian, and Aziz Haidar, "Palestinians on the Peace Process," *Journal of Palestine Studies* 81 (Autumn 1991): 43.

[13] Muhammad Hallaj, "Policy Implications for the United States," *A Palestinian Perspective on the Peace Process* (Washington: Center for Policy Analysis on Palestine, 1991), p. 18.

[14] Alicha Lemsine, "God Guard Islam from the Islamists," *Washington Report on Middle East Affairs* (March 1992): 14.

[15] Yeshayahu Ben-Porat, "There Is Someone To Talk With," *Yediot Ahronot*, Weekly Supplement (November 8, 1991): 4, cited in Leon T. Hadar, "The 'Special Relationship': Israel Decides Its Future," Middle East Resource Program Issue Paper (Washington: Middle East Policy Council, March 1992), p. 13.

[16] Yehoshafat Harkabi, *Israel's Fateful Hour*, trans. Lenn Schramm (New York: Harper & Row, 1988), pp. 42-43.

[17] Moughrabi et al., "Palestinians on the Peace Process," 38.

2   Counternarratives
Stories of Loss and Exclusion

> *[W]e can read ourselves against an-*
> *other people's pattern, but since it is not*
> *ours—even though we are its designated*
> *enemy—we emerge as its effects, its er-*
> *rata, its counternarratives. Whenever*
> *we try to narrate ourselves, we appear*
> *as dislocations in their discourse.*
>
> Edward Said
> *After the Last Sky*[1]

Dispossession is the central reality in the Palestinians' collective consciousness. The fact of having been dispersed in 1948 and left without homes or a national locus or, as far as most of the world was concerned, a national identity, is a personal and a national catastrophe whose effects Palestinians still cannot escape. The reality of dispossession has been the major, indeed almost the only, factor in shaping Palestinian political thinking over the years, particularly the Palestinian view of Israel and of what constitutes a just peace settlement with Israel. In order to understand Palestinians, to understand what drives them and particularly how they view Israel, it is necessary to understand the events of 1948 as Palestinians view them. The following traces the developments of 1948 as remembered by several Palestinians who experienced them.

It was like the movie *Viva Zapata!*, he says. "It was just like that. All of a sudden the village knew this guy had come back. All of a sudden everybody in that neighborhood knew that the son of Asma—this is my mother's name, Asma—is in town." His voice falters and he looks away. He is totally transported from the noisy restaurant in a L'Enfant Plaza hotel in Washington, D.C., where he reminisces over lunch.

George Hishmeh is an editor at the U.S. Information Agency, a tall, gray-haired man with a long, thin face that seems to add poignancy to his recollections. He is describing his return to Nazareth in 1977. Nazareth is his family's hometown, a town he had visited every Easter and summer for the first twelve years of his life, until he and his family were forced to leave Palestine in 1948. Hishmeh actually lived in Haifa, where his father, Salim

Hishmeh, was a customs officer in the British Mandate government working at the city's oil refineries, and Haifa was the city from which the family fled. But Hishmeh's return to Nazareth after almost thirty years brought back intense memories—perhaps because Nazareth has remained an Arab town, and the narrow streets and alleyways winding through the *suqs* look the way they did decades ago.

It is a beautiful town at Easter, known for its apricot blossoms. "I was surprised. It all came back to me. I knew the streets very well, the alleys," he recalls.

> That was a very emotional experience, because all of a sudden the children came out of nowhere to see who is this new guy. The kids were so excited when I told them this was my grandparents' house and I had just come from America to see it. One of the kids was so excited, he had his bicycle and he said, "Would you like to take a ride on my bicycle?" This is a very Palestinian thing, because riding a bicycle was a great thrill. Not everybody had bicycles, and suddenly to show affection to somebody and let him ride your bicycle—I mean, I was in my forties, and this boy wants me—

His voice trails off. He is caught again in the emotion of remembering. He stops himself and says matter-of-factly, "So I said to the kid, 'No thank you.' But it just hit home."

His images are vivid, the contrasts striking: the tall American surrounded by clamorous little boys on a dusty street; a man who had traveled so far suddenly returned to another time and another life; the thought of this dignified gentleman on a bicycle. Going back was "like being in a dream, really," Hishmeh muses. "Until now it's in a dream."

Hishmeh has made his way well in the world since the horrific days of 1948—the *nakba*, the catastrophe, as Palestinians call it. He edited a newspaper in Beirut for several years in the 1960s, then came to the United States in 1968 and worked for the *Chicago Sun Times* and the *Washington Post* before joining the U.S. Information Agency in the early 1970s. He is now a chief editor with USIA. He has two young children and, like many American fathers, lives in the suburbs and coaches a soccer team.

He remembers 1948 from a child's perspective. He recalls a strike by the senior boys at his school when Palestine was partitioned into a Jewish and an Arab state in November 1947, but he can remember nothing of political significance before that. Shortly afterwards, fighting between Jews and Palestinians began, and he and his younger brother were unable to go to school since they lived on the other side of town. Salim Hishmeh was afraid to take a chance with his sons; his own mother had been killed in

1939 during an attack by a Jewish terrorist organization on a civilian bus traveling between Jerusalem and Jaffa.

There was shooting every night in Haifa in the last year of the British Mandate, and George's job was to hang blankets in the windows in the hope that bullets would slide down the blanket and not penetrate. Such was the conventional wisdom, at any rate. He laughs now at their naïvete. When Haifa fell to Jewish forces in April 1948 and the city's Arab population began to leave, Hishmeh's family packed what they could and went to the port to take a boat to Beirut. Hishmeh's father put him in charge of keeping track of the family's eleven suitcases; it is a number he has remembered, incongruously, for over forty years. Because of the fighting, the port was full of ships unable to unload their cargo, and ship owners were making extra money by loading up with frantic refugees and delivering them to Beirut or Acre just north of Haifa or Alexandria in Egypt. When the Hishmeh family arrived at the port, the captain of the ship they were to take decided against going to Beirut, and the only ship they could find with space was going to Alexandria. They did not want to go there. There was an uncle in Beirut, and they knew nothing about Alexandria, but they had no choice.

One of Hishmeh's most vivid memories is of slaughtering several of the rabbits and pigeons they raised in the backyard of their home so that they would have something to eat on board ship. He has trouble with this part of the story and pauses to gain control of his voice, apologizing for the emotions that have come over him. "So anyway," he goes on, "my mother cooked all these rabbits. We had so many of them, a big bag, because they said there would be no food." As it happened, the sea was very rough, and everyone in the family except Hishmeh got seasick and could not eat the rabbit meat.

They thought Alexandria would be a temporary stop. The British government gave Hishmeh's father, as a government employee, advance pay for three months, but "we were so naïve, our parents were so naïve. All the time they assumed that after three months, things will quiet down and we'll go back to Haifa. In fact, the unkindest cut of all is that one day after the first month in Alexandria, my family decided we better go and see Cairo before they tell us to go back home. And we rushed to Cairo, made a tour of Cairo, running from museum to square to statue to royal palace, wherever."

In fact, they had a lifetime to see Cairo. The family stayed in Alexandria for several more months, and then went to Beirut, where Hishmeh remained until 1967, his mother until 1982. His father died within a few years of a heart attack at the age of forty-seven. Had it demoralized him, the *nakba*? "I think yes," Hishmeh says. "He became an easily agitated person, very nervous, very upset by the conditions. He had to start from scratch all over again."

George Hishmeh and his family were lucky. They lived in a hotel with two other families in Alexandria. They saw Cairo. They had some resources and eleven suitcases of belongings. They lost their property, their means of livelihood, their birthright, but many others among the over 700,000 Palestinians who left along with them in the year after Palestine was partitioned[2] have worse stories to tell. Vast numbers—the majority—ended up in refugee camps in Jordan, Lebanon, Syria, and Egypt. A great many others were able to seek refuge with family or friends or had enough money to rent a room somewhere until they could find new employment or learn a new occupation. Not all of the refugees by any means went to refugee camps, but everyone, no matter what his status had been in Palestine, left behind a home, land, possessions. Fewer than 800,000 of the original refugees and their offspring remain in refugee camps now, but approximately fifty percent of today's almost five million Palestinians are dispersed throughout the world, unable to return to their homeland.

Chaim Weizmann, the Zionist leader and first president of Israel, said of the exodus of Palestinians from the area that became the state of Israel in 1948 that it was a "miraculous simplification of Israel's tasks."[3] Israel's first foreign minister, Moshe Sharett, saw the exodus as "the most spectacular event in the contemporary history of Palestine, in a way more spectacular than the creation of the Jewish state"; the opportunities opened by the absence of a sizable Arab population within the borders of Israel, he believed, were "so far-reaching as to take one's breath away."[4]

These events—which allowed Israel to grow and thrive as a Jewish state without having to worry about a large non-Jewish population, which provided Israel with tens of thousands of acres of agricultural land, which enabled Israeli authorities to resettle half a million Jewish immigrants in homes and on land vacated by Palestinians, which provided space to build new Israeli towns on the sites of the more than 350 Palestinian villages demolished[5]—were for Palestinians a catastrophe, uprooting an entire society and destroying a way of life in the space of a few months.

George Hishmeh and his family were among the approximately 200,000 refugees who fled Palestine before the British Mandate ended and the state of Israel declared its independence on May 15, 1948. The exodus from Haifa had been going on since December. Early fighting in December and January led to a general breakdown of the city's leadership and services, and by January fully one-third of Haifa's 70,000 Arabs, largely the middle and upper classes, had left. Fighting continued sporadically into April, and when early on April 21 British troops began a premature withdrawal, the Jewish army, the Haganah, attacked in force. The city's remaining Arab civilian population began to flee in fear. They were demoralized, essentially defenseless, and panicked by the killing less than two weeks earlier of 250 civilians at the village of Deir Yassin, near Jerusalem, by a force made up of Irgun and the Stern Gang, two Jewish terrorist groups. Some 15,000 Palestinians are believed to have left Haifa on April 22, the day George Hishmeh left.

On the evening of April 22, what remained of the city's Arab leadership formally surrendered and urged Arab evacuation in order not to be seen to be acquiescing in Jewish rule. But Haifans were already in headlong flight. The exodus continued for a week, as terrified residents clogged ports and roads, leaving belongings behind, homes empty, agricultural land untended. By early May, only 3,000-4,000 of Haifa's original 70,000 Arabs remained.[6]

The decision by Haifa's Arab leadership to urge evacuation of the city was a decision taken in defeat, not in expectation of victory, and it was a local decision, not one ordered from outside or linked to flight from other towns and cities. There were no broadcast orders from the Arab Higher Committee or any other Arab authority instructing the civilian population in Haifa or anywhere else to leave and, except in a few instances, there were no orders from Arab military commanders to clear areas of Palestine of civilians in order to allow the military a free hand.[7]

The fear experienced by Palestine's civilians cannot be emphasized enough as a cause of their flight. A widely known story among Palestinians, a story that has become a legend, epitomizes the fear and haste in which civilians fled. The story varies in its particulars with each telling, but the essentials remain the same: a woman in or near Haifa, in her haste to escape advancing Jewish forces, grabs her infant from his crib and flees, only to discover too late that all she is carrying are a pillow and blanket.

"This story has been told and told and told again and again," notes Osama Doumani, a Sacramento businessman who first heard it himself as a nine-year-old in Acre, a town ten miles north of Haifa, before his family left for Lebanon under Haganah attack in late April. Thousands of refugees from Haifa had walked or traveled by boat to Acre in the days after Haifa's fall, and Doumani's older sister, doing volunteer work with the Red Cross among the Haifa refugees, came home one evening with the tale. "I'm not even sure if the rest of what I remember is hearsay or not," says Doumani, but the story about the woman with the pillow "is kind of imprinted in my memory."[8]

The city of Jaffa fell to Jewish forces within days of Haifa's surrender. Unlike Haifa, Jaffa, with a population of approximately 70,000, was an all-Arab city and, also unlike Haifa, had been designated in the UN Partition Plan as part of the Arab state, a small Arab enclave to be surrounded by the Jewish state and immediately adjacent to the largest Jewish city, Tel Aviv. Fighting and major disruptions of urban services began early here too, but by the time Haifa fell and the Irgun opened a major offensive against Jaffa on April 25, the vast majority of the city's inhabitants—some 50,000-

35

60,000—were still there. Several factors soon combined, however, to induce a mass exodus of civilians similar to Haifa's: three days of heavy mortar bombardment by Irgun, the knowledge by Jaffa's inhabitants of the massacre two weeks earlier at the village of Deir Yassin, the precipitate flight of Jaffa's leaders, and soon thereafter the scattering of the city's military defenders.[9] Some of the fleeing civilians walked inland; most took flight in boats, which delivered them to Gaza or Beirut or Egypt or, in overcrowded conditions and rough seas, capsized and delivered them to an early death.

"We nearly drowned, actually," says Rajai Abu-Khadra, who left Jaffa with his mother in early May, after a week of shelling near their home. Earlier fighting had been on the edges of the city, principally the northern side where Jaffa met Tel Aviv, but now the shelling and attacks were in the center of town. Abu-Khadra and his mother boarded a boat built for fifty people that in the crush of fleeing humanity had taken on several hundred refugees and, after twelve hours of storms and heavy seas, reached Gaza, less than fifty miles away.

Abu-Khadra was sixteen. His father, who had served as mayor of Gaza in the 1920s, had been the highest ranking Arab district official in Lydda in the 1930s, and had gone into exile for a year because of his activism during the 1936 Arab Revolt against British Mandate rule, had died some years earlier. Abu-Khadra's two older brothers were out of the country studying or working. He and his mother were on their own. The family owned property in Jaffa, as well as in Tel Aviv, and had extensive orange groves south of Jaffa near the town the Israelis now call Ashdod. When they left, they had two suitcases; nothing else was salvaged.

They sought refuge with relatives, and within a year Abu-Khadra had earned a scholarship to Swarthmore College near Philadelphia. He later received a master's degree from Johns Hopkins University and a Ph.D. from Indiana University. He served as economic adviser to Kuwait's petroleum minister for several years before returning to the United States in 1987 and since then has been a resident scholar at the Center for Strategic and International Studies in Washington, D.C.

Abu-Khadra, who has been blind since 1957, is a very outgoing person, open and anxious to tell his story. When his wife, who is his principal assistant, worries about the wisdom of speaking openly, he calms her. It's important, he says; a man has no dignity if he cannot speak forthrightly. He has become more political, he notes a bit ruefully, since coming to Washington, and his volubility has begun to extend to writing, which he now does voluminously. "I'm an economist, and I think of myself as a good, solid petroleum man—I'm working on a book on the petroleum exporting countries—but you come to an atmosphere like Washington and you become a political animal."

Abu-Khadra visited his old house in Jaffa in 1978. "Our house is opposite this mosque in the Nuzha area." He speaks in the present tense, as if forty-plus years have not gone by since he lived there. "When I got to the outer door," he says, "it was just as if all these years did not pass, and I was just about to open the door without ringing the bell. Then my wife was telling me, 'It's not your home any longer, you'd better ring the bell.'" The Moroccan Jewish woman living there, in what is now a rundown suburb of Tel Aviv, welcomed them and served them coffee and sweets. Abu-Khadra asked about the belongings they had left behind—"like a picture of my father"—but nothing remained. He took a photograph of the woman, as he did later of the family's orange groves when he visited them and found them being cultivated by Israelis. Even though he is blind, the pictures served (until they were lost when his home in Lebanon was robbed and vandalized some years later) as a tangible record of his loss.

"Nobody really knows what it's like," Abu-Khadra says, "except those who passed through this experience. To others it sounds bad, but really the depth of it, the dimension of it, people cannot comprehend. I personally believe that a man without a country, a homeland, is a man without roots or self-respect."

Nahida Fadli Dajani is a petite woman, quiet and reserved, but one senses immediately the strong personality, the complete self-assurance and control. She has a deep, resonant voice, the kind that carries a natural drama in it. When she reads her poetry, the emotion is palpable.

Her mother, her husband, and a younger brother sit with her in the living room of her home in the Virginia suburbs of Washington, D.C., on a rainy afternoon in October and listen to a tape in English of Dajani retelling an incident from 1948 that affected them all profoundly. It was a beautiful spring day in Jerusalem, a time when her life was full of hope and promise and "my dreams were growing and growing." She was walking home from school, a young teenager laughing and talking with her school friends, "carrying my little notebook bearing all my poems, all full of love." Some other youngsters came up behind her, talking about the big news event of the day, the killing of Hasan Fadli, a well known figure in the neighborhood. Hasan Fadli was Dajani's father.

Her mother, sitting in the quiet living room in Virginia, begins to cry. She does not understand English well, but she knows the story, and the cadences of Dajani's voice evoke memories of that day.

"My father was a freedom fighter ever since I can remember," Dajani says when the tape ends. "I remember him coming home late at night, and most of the nights we used to sleep alone—my sister, myself, and my mother. In 1939 he was deported to Lebanon for three years. I don't remember that we lived as a family. My father was all the time outside the house, and he had things to do. He was occupied by this sense of freeing his country from the British Mandate and the Jewish immigration, which later became occupation."

Hasan Fadli was shot to death on April 24 while tending a store owned by his brother-in-law on Mamillah Road in western Jerusalem. "The night before he was killed, he was patrolling as usual—every night," Dajani notes, "but he was not killed while on a mission."

Dajani's brother, Samir Fadli, who now lives in the Maryland suburbs of Washington, was three years old when his father was killed. He has only fleeting memories of Hasan Fadli playing with him, but the day they brought him home is clearly imprinted in Samir's memory. "I remember actually when they brought him in a station wagon—when they brought him dead. There is a vivid memory, a picture of that scene."

No one ever claimed responsibility for the assassination, and in the confusion of the struggle for control of the city no effort was ever made to find the assassins. They buried Hasan Fadli in eastern Jerusalem, and wife and five children, in fear for their lives, left their home on the western side of the city and stayed briefly with an uncle before being put on a truck and sent to Lebanon for what everyone thought would be a temporary stay, a matter of days. "We didn't take anything, not even our luggage," says Dajani.

They were there for years. Dajani herself went to Cyprus in the early 1950s to work for a British broadcasting station and there met her husband, Ghanem Dajani, who had fled Jaffa in 1948. After some years in Cyprus, they returned to Lebanon and raised their own children there. Nahida Dajani came to the United States in 1984 in the wake of the turmoil following Israel's 1982 invasion of Lebanon. Three daughters already lived here, and the Dajanis had earlier sent their youngest child and only son, Karim, then an impressionable fourteen-year-old, to the United States because he was becoming too much involved in Lebanon's chaotic politics—"too vulnerable," according to his father. Ghanem Dajani continued to work in Beirut in broadcasting for several more years, commuting regularly to see his family in the United States, until finally settling here permanently in 1989.

Nahida returned to East Jerusalem once, but because West Jerusalem was under Israeli control she was not permitted in to see her home. Since 1967, when Israel took control of East Jerusalem as well, she has not visited any part of the city. West Bank and Gaza Palestinians are usually permitted to travel within Israel proper, but Palestinians from elsewhere are rarely allowed in unless they travel on an American passport. Ghanem has not seen Jaffa at all since leaving over forty years ago. Nahida still writes love poems to Jerusalem, a city obviously often in her thoughts: "I am deprived to go back to my country; at least my poems can go."

She has had a good life as an adult. Even with the disruptions of Lebanon, she has managed a successful career, and she takes pride in a fine family. "I had everything," she concludes on the tape playing in the subdued living room, "except putting a rose on my father's grave."

By April 1948, when Hasan Fadli was killed, large portions of the Arab neighborhoods of Jerusalem had already been cleared out. As early as February, David Ben-Gurion had told his political colleagues that so much of the western and southern reaches of Jerusalem had been cleared of Arabs, thanks to Haganah and Irgun operations, that "[s]ince Jerusalem's destruction in the days of the Romans—it hasn't been so Jewish as it is now. In many Arab districts in the west—one sees not one Arab. I do not assume that this will change."[10] Ben-Gurion ordered the military forces to settle Jews in the abandoned Arab districts, and many suburban villages evacuated under attack by Jewish forces were demolished.[11]

The battle for Jerusalem and its environs was the hardest fought of the war, and the months-long battle was devastating for the Palestinians. By July when a cease-fire was imposed, no Palestinian village immediately west of Jerusalem remained in existence; the villages, including Deir Yassin, had been leveled and their inhabitants dispersed.[12] In addition, no Palestinians remained in either the once predominantly Arab sections of western and southern Jerusalem or the formerly mixed neighborhoods in the center of the city. Israeli leaders quickly settled Jewish immigrants in these areas, obviating any possibility that the Palestinian natives could ever return. By the time Israel was a year old, in the summer of 1949, all formerly Arab neighborhoods of West Jerusalem, as well as the sites of depopulated Arab villages, had been repopulated by Jews.[13]

The city of Jerusalem seems to call forth uniquely intense feelings among all its inhabitants that other cities do not evoke. These are emotions experienced by Palestinians no less than by Jews. Quite apart from its religious significance for Muslims and Christians from around the world, Jerusalem has been the political and emotional capital of Arab Palestine for centuries. "It's the capital of Palestine, the heart of Palestine, the center of Palestine and the Palestinians," says Hazem Husseini, a young businessman in Albuquerque, New Mexico, who belongs to a very prominent Palestinian family from Jerusalem and who has not seen his native city since his family left in the wake of the 1967 war when he was thirteen. A majority of the most prominent Palestinian families—in politics, in commerce, in scholarship—are from Jerusalem: not only the Husseinis (or Husaynis), but the Khalidis, the Nusaybahs, the Nashashibis, the Dajanis, and others—names that have been associated with Jerusalem for a millennium. Scores of Palestinian poets have written paeans to the city. Nahida Dajani writes love poems to Jerusalem, which she sees as a "beloved, hurting" city. "Once in my life," she says, "I was in Jerusalem. Now she is in me, and she will always be my first love."[14]

Jack Mahshi's family was one of the most prominent Christian families in Jerusalem. Both of his grandfathers were at one time *mukhtars*, or chief elders, of the local Greek Orthodox community, and his maternal grandfather was an iconographer, a painter of religious icons. Each of the thirteen leading Orthodox families in Jerusalem had a distinctive banner brought out only at the Easter season every year. On Holy Saturday, the *mukhtar* would personally hand each family's banner to a member of the family, and all thirteen bearers of these banners would then march in the Patriarchal processional at the Church of the Holy Sepulchre. The banner bearers marched in the same order each year; the Mahshis were always number nine. All this was disrupted in 1948, and Jack Mahshi does not know what has become of the banners or the tradition.

Yacoub Jamil Mahshi, who goes by Jack in the United States, was twenty-eight years old when his family left Jerusalem in April 1948. Now a well known landscape architect in Berkeley, California, he is a handsome man with a great shock of wavy, perfectly white hair and black-horn-rimmed glasses. He speaks unaccented English, and his office walls are lined with mementos of his life in American business: the plan of a major landscape project he designed, business club memberships and awards, photographs of himself with business contacts. But the Palestinian side of him is also very present in that office. He brings out a hefty book, the 1948 Jerusalem Town Plan, to show a visitor where in the city he used to live, and he keeps his old British-issued Palestine passport, as well as his mother's, in a desk drawer.

Mahshi was unmarried in 1948 and still living at home with his parents and a younger brother. Two other brothers were in the United States studying, and a married sister lived nearby. Their home was in a district called the German Colony in the south central section of Jerusalem. "We'd spent the months before April living through daily bombings back and forth, mortars being fired in both directions," he recalls. "Then the massacre at Deir Yassin happened and other terrorism by the Irgun, trying to terrorize the public to make them leave. We [he and his brother] told my parents, 'You'd better get out of here.' Every day we got up and would go see whose house had been destroyed. My mother said, 'No way. I'll only leave if you all do.' But I couldn't leave. I was of military age, and I wanted to help. We weren't in uniform, but we were considered as young men who should defend their country."

Jewish loudspeaker trucks soon began touring the neighborhood urging the inhabitants to evacuate, and as a result, with rumors abroad that the Arab armies were on their way to help the Palestinians, Mahshi and his brother finally decided to take the family and leave temporarily.

We packed our summer clothes. I had a car—my first car, a Morris Minor—and I barricaded it in the garage, locked the door from the inside. And we hired a taxi and left—my mother and father, my younger brother, my sister and her husband, and myself. The idea was that in a few weeks we would be back. We drove to the Allenby Bridge and crossed to Amman. We used to go to Lebanon for vacation in the summer, so we went there to wait it out. We left everything we ever owned—furniture, jewelry, car, my first car—and we never went back.

Mahshi's father was a real estate developer in Jerusalem and owned several houses and lots in the neighborhood that were either rented out or intended for Jack and his brothers. The family also owned two plots of land in the Lydda/Ramla area between Jerusalem and Tel Aviv where one of his brothers hoped to establish a dairy. Mahshi's brother-in-law owned an orchard near Majdal, which later became the Israeli city of Ashkelon, on the coast. All this property was lost.

Mahshi's father never worked again. "He did nothing, waiting to return" Mahshi says, and he died four years later. Mahshi himself left for the United States within a year. "I couldn't take it being a refugee, not being able to work." Without Lebanese citizenship, which was difficult for Palestinians to obtain, no one could work. He attended graduate school here, and when his student visa expired and an immigration officer told him he would have to return to his "country of origin," he was able, by pointing out that it no longer existed, to obtain permanent residency.

Mahshi went back to Jerusalem with his American-born wife in 1972 and visited his old neighborhood. They found the neighborhood run down and the old family house not well kept. "We just stood outside and looked at the house," he remembers, "while the Jewish family sat in the window upstairs and stared back at us. We didn't talk to them."

Nothing seems to have inspired more fear during Jewish assaults on Palestinian towns and villages than the sound of artillery screaming in to civilian areas. "We were awakened by the loudest noise we had ever heard, shells exploding...the whole village was in panic....Most of the villagers began to flee with their pyjamas on," reads a contemporary account of the attack in July 1948 on a village in western Galilee.[15] During the artillery attack on the strategic town of Lydda in the same month, Reja-e Busailah experienced a similar terror. Now a professor of literature at Indiana University at Kokomo, Busailah was at the time an eighteen-year-old new high school graduate, blind and alone in his native town. He felt the bombardment as "a period which seemed to compress much time within itself during which

41

everything turned to deafening and infernal sound....It was a time of inexpressible fear."[16]

The twin towns of Lydda and Ramla, with a population between them of probably 50,000-70,000, swollen by refugees from Jaffa and other nearby towns, lay two miles apart on the main route between Tel Aviv and Jerusalem. Although within the territory designated by the partition plan for the Arab state, the towns were regarded by Israeli leaders as an obstacle to control of the Tel Aviv-Jerusalem corridor and as a potential staging base for Transjordan's Arab Legion and a threat to Tel Aviv. Israeli forces launched a dual attack on the towns on July 9.[17]

Reja-e Busailah's family had left Lydda a month earlier for the north central town of Tulkarm, where they stayed with friends. They were one of the few families to evacuate so early. Reja-e, however, apparently feeling the need to be independent now that he had passed his matriculation exams, returned to Lydda against his parents' wishes. He could not fight because of his blindness, "but I could do other things, I reasoned: encourage the people, help raise the morale of the young fighting men of whom I could name several."[18]

There was not much time for fighting, as it turned out. Within three days of launching the attack on Lydda and its twin town Ramla to the south, Israeli forces had captured both towns and begun to expel their inhabitants. By this time in the war, so much Palestinian real estate—agricultural land, houses, commercial property—had been left behind, so many Jewish agricultural settlements were harvesting abandoned Arab fields, so many new Jewish immigrants were entering Israel in need of housing, and the military and political advantages of a country free or almost free of Palestinian Arabs had become so obvious to Israeli leaders and military strategists that if there had earlier been no premeditated Israeli policy of expulsion, one was instituted now. Thousands of Lydda's and Ramla's inhabitants had begun to flee voluntarily under the heavy bombardment and fighting of the first few days of the attack, but on July 13 the thousands more civilians remaining in the towns were ordered out. It was the largest forced expulsion of the war.[19]

Yitzhak Rabin, who twice served as Israeli prime minister in the mid-1970s and the 1990s, was a brigade commander in 1948 involved in the assault on Lydda and Ramla. When he wrote his memoirs in 1979, he detailed the discussions held before the decision was taken to clear the towns of civilians. Israeli censors excised the pertinent passage, but it has since come to light in other publications. According to Rabin's account, David Ben-Gurion met at operational headquarters with several commanders, including Rabin, but remained silent during the discussion of how to handle the towns' civilians. When Ben-Gurion, Rabin, and Israel's senior general left the meeting, Ben-Gurion was again asked what was to be done with the civilians and in answer, according to Rabin, "waved his hand in a gesture which said: 'Drive them out!'"[20]

Reja-e Busailah was driven out with everyone else. It was Tuesday, July 13. By nine o'clock in the morning, he writes, it was already hot, and later in the day the temperature rose to 100 degrees in the shade. The long column of humanity was ordered to walk eastward, not knowing where it was headed or how long it would have to walk. "Jewish soldiers were stationed all along for the distance of two hours from the town," Busailah says. They were there apparently to make sure that the procession would keep going. Several hundred people died along the way, and it took some people days to do the fifteen miles to the town of Ramallah, north of Jerusalem. Busailah was young and made it by sundown on the first day.

"Psychologically, this was one of the most difficult actions we undertook," Yitzhak Rabin recalls, speaking of the Israeli soldiers involved. "Great suffering was inflicted upon the men taking part in the eviction action," he observes, and "[p]rolonged propaganda activities were required after the action to remove the bitterness" experienced by the Israelis. He did not mention the Palestinians.[21]

The Palestinian town of Lydda has become Lod and is the site of Israel's Ben-Gurion International Airport. The city's Arab population now is minuscule, the offspring of the few hundred who managed not to leave in 1948 as tens of thousands of their fellow townsmen filed out of town. One particularly well known Palestinian is a native of Lydda: George Habash, leader of the Popular Front for the Liberation of Palestine.

A certain number of Palestinians, estimated to total about 75,000 out of the 160,000 Arabs still living in Israel as of 1949,[22] became refugees during the fighting the previous year but never left the area that became Israel. Forced by fighting to leave their original towns and villages or expelled from these areas by Israeli forces, these "internal refugees" or "present absentees"—a term coined by Israel to indicate those still present in Israel but absent from their original lands, which became for that reason subject to confiscation by Israel—have lived since 1948 as Israeli citizens, deprived of their own land but still attached to the original land of Palestine.

Suhail Miari was one of these internal refugees. His family in fact are refugees several times over. Miari is the executive director of the United Holy Land Fund, a Palestinian charitable organization, and his Chicago office is hung with Palestinian memorabilia. A map of Palestine is behind his desk. On another wall hangs a large poster drawn in the shape of an airmail envelope. The envelope is addressed to "Palestine," but the name is crossed out and the envelope bears a postal stamp declaring, "Return to sender. No such address." Miari does not even glance at the poster as he walks in and out of his office, but it is clear from his conversation that the

43

formal non-existence of Palestine as an address or a national entity is in his mind much of the time. Although Miari has been in the United States for more than twenty years and is an American citizen, he retains his Israeli citizenship, and his parents and fourteen younger brothers and sisters still live in Israel. His cousin, Muhammad Miari, is a long-time member of the Israeli Knesset, one of the few Arab members.

Miari's father was a policeman in Haifa when that city was evacuated in April 1948, so he took Suhail, then four, and the rest of the family back to his native village of Birwa, about ten miles away. Birwa was in the area designated for the Arab state according to the partition plan. Suhail's grandfather owned quite a bit of land in the village, which he and several of his children farmed. Birwa, however, was overrun by Israeli forces and evacuated in June, and again the Miaris fled, this time the entire extended family—grandparents, parents, aunts and uncles, cousins. Those who did not leave Palestine altogether, including Suhail's immediate family, moved just a few miles away to a neighboring village and for six months camped out in an olive grove, protected only by blankets hung from the olive trees.

The villagers of Birwa put up some resistance to the initial Israeli capture of their village. Twelve days after it fell, a contingent of armed villagers returned, hoping to harvest their fields. When they surprised a group of Israelis harvesting the grain crop, the Israelis ran off without a fight. But when the villagers turned over protection of Birwa to a unit of the Arab Liberation Army, this force retreated, and the village again fell to Israeli control.[23]

In December, after living in the outdoors for six months, Suhail Miari's family moved on again, to a village where they lived for four years. But this was a Druze village and in those days relations between Palestinian Muslims and the Druze, a dissident sect of Islam, were tense because the Druze were considered to be collaborators with Israel. In 1952, a group of Druze military broke into the Miari home, looted valuables, and arrested Miari's father, grandfather, and uncles. The men were held in jail for several days, on unspecified security charges. Miari remembers quite well being left with only women and children in the house. When the Miari men were released, the family moved for a fourth time, finally settling near Acre and, ironically, within a few miles of their original home of Birwa. Miari's father purchased a house and some land, including an olive orchard, which he co-owned with two brothers.

This saga of disruption and dispossession has some interesting footnotes. On a pleasant note, in the late 1980s, the Druze who had looted the Miari house in 1952 came to the family to make a formal apology and return many of the stolen belongings. The family accepted the apology and made peace after over three decades. On a more unsettling note, in 1978, after the family had finally found some prosperity and a degree of peace, the

Israeli government confiscated one of their olive orchards. Miari is outraged recounting the story of the confiscation, and his voice rises. "In 1978, in the Israeli democracy! We bought it in the '50s, you know, and after twenty years of ownership, and we have every document to prove that we bought it and it's ours!" The orchard is now a closed military area, encircled by an electronic fence.

The Israelis tried to compensate the Miari family for their lost Birwa lands in the mid-1950s, when, according to Miari, the government was under international pressure to do something for Palestinians dispossessed in 1948. But the Israeli offer was, Miari says, "very, very symbolic, to show that the land was really paid for and wasn't confiscated and everything was under control and we have no refugee problem, and so on." His family rejected the money.

Birwa has ceased to exist except in the memories of its natives. Within two months of its capture and evacuation in 1948, Israeli authorities began construction of a kibbutz on the site, and Kibbutz Yas'ur was dedicated in January 1949.[24] The only things that remain standing from the original village, according to Miari, are the mosque and part of a church. The mosque, he says, is used as a stable for kibbutz cattle. To a Palestinian, however, it is evident from other signs that a town once existed on the site. As in many areas of what is today Israel, large prickly pear cactus plants still stand there, as well as fig and olive trees—the sure signs that this was once a Palestinian village. Every year while Israelis are celebrating independence on May 15, the day that the state of Israel was declared, the former villagers of Birwa return to the site to celebrate its memory, standing amidst the olives and the figs and the cactus.

The town of Tarshiha in upper Galilee, close to the border with Lebanon, was a wealthy town, says Ghassan Bishara, who grew up there. It lay in rich agricultural country, and its wealth came from tobacco, olives, and figs, as well as from the extensive land holdings of many of its inhabitants—lands that ran down as far as Acre and Safad, scattered throughout the whole of upper Galilee. Tarshiha was a town of about 7,000, Bishara guesses, perhaps only 5,000 according to other estimates; about seventy-five or eighty percent were Muslim, the rest Christian. Christians tended to be the merchants and small craftspeople in town, Muslims the landowners.

Tarshiha did not fall to Israeli forces until late October 1948. In response to Arab harassment of Israeli lines of communication near the Lebanon border, Israel launched a major operation on October 29 intended to clear the border area as much as possible of Arabs. Within fewer than three days, a swath of northern towns and villages was captured and vast numbers of their inhabitants expelled or otherwise induced to flee. Many of these towns were quickly resettled with Jewish immigrants. In Tarshiha, most of the Israeli air and artillery bombardment focused on the Muslim sections of town, and for this reason among others most of the eighty-five or ninety percent of the townspeople who fled were Muslim. Only an estimated 700 people remained in town at the end of the attack, 600 of them Christians. Israeli authorities made a concerted effort in succeeding months to prevent the return of residents who had left, most of whom had made their way the five or six miles into Lebanon. Officials involved with Jewish settlement, concerned that at this point Galilee's population was only twelve percent Jewish, wanted Tarshiha's abandoned houses for Jewish settlers.[25]

It is striking to listen to the story of Tarshiha and the fate of its inhabitants from the perspectives of two Palestinians for whom the events of 1948 have led to quite different lives but have essentially had the same long-term impact. Both men are coincidentally journalists, but their lives have taken very dissimilar paths. One is a member of Tarshiha's Christian minority, the other a member of its scattered Muslim majority. One lived through the 1948 attack, the other knows of it intimately but only from the stories of his parents, who endured it. Both men call Tarshiha home, but one grew up there after Israel's takeover and one has never seen it.

The first is Ghassan Bishara, who as a seven-year-old experienced the attack directly but who with his mother and four brothers and sisters remained in Tarshiha and grew up as an Israeli citizen. He has been in the United States since 1967 and is the Washington correspondent for the Jerusalem Arabic-language newspaper *al-Fajr*. The second is Osama Fawzi, who was not born until 1950, two years after his parents had fled to Lebanon and later to Jordan. He is a relatively new immigrant to the United States and spends most of his time within the Palestinian and Arab community, publishing a biweeky Arabic-language newspaper, the *Arab Houston Times*, that is circulated throughout the Arab community in the United States. The paper is a satirical tabloid specializing in political criticism and exposés of the Arab governments—the kind of material, Fawzi says, that Arab leaders censor in their own press. Because of its no-holds-barred style, however, the paper in fact has a wide underground circulation in the Arab world.

Bishara's family was prominent in Tarshiha both as merchants and as landowners; as a Christian, his father had owned perhaps the only liquor store in Galilee until his death in 1945, and the family also owned large tracts of land. Bishara remembers most clearly the Israeli air attack on Tarshiha. He and his mother and the other children were running out of the town, trying to escape the advancing Israelis, and they passed a house that had taken a direct hit. "It was still going on fire, I remember very clearly, very vividly," he says. "I remember very much a horse and a cow, dead out there in the yard of the house, their stomachs are out, and some villagers are trying to take people from under the rubble of the house. They did dig out one woman who is [still] in the village now."

Bishara has light brown curly hair and a slightly darker beard just beginning to go gray, the only noticeable sign that he is in his late forties. His eyes are light-colored and smiling, and he speaks with the ease and confidence of a journalist. He is totally relaxed as he recounts his story, sitting in his Washington office with one leg thrown casually over the arm of an easy chair.

It is clear nonetheless that the bombing raid had a lasting impact on him as a child of seven. Forty-one years later, in an ironic finale to the bombing and its traumas, Bishara met the Israeli pilot who conducted the raid. Abie Nathan, now a prominent Israeli peace activist, spoke at a conference in Washington in April 1989 of having bombed Tarshiha in 1948, and Ghassan Bishara happened to be in the audience. The two men met, and Bishara told Nathan of how he and his friends had sung a song wishing for the plane to crash and for its "bones to turn like jelly."[26]

Soon after the town was taken, Bishara recalls, Israelis began destroying many of the abandoned homes, both to prevent the return of their original owners and to make room for new homes for Jewish immigrants. Some of the houses were demolished with explosives, and Bishara remembers seeing many brought down by bulldozers. "They used to bring one of those bulldozers to put a huge big chain from one wall [to the other], and the bulldozer would pull, and you see the whole thing collapsing." A number of Rumanian Jews were settled in Tarshiha, as well as in two new Jewish towns, Ma'alot[27] and Me'una, built within one or two kilometers of Tarshiha. It is not at all uncommon, Bishara notes, to find a Palestinian merchant in Tarshiha who speaks Rumanian to his Jewish customers.

Times were hard for the Bisharas in 1948. The death of Bishara's father a few years before had led to the demise of the liquor store, and in 1948 the Israelis confiscated the Bishara land. Their house was destroyed when Israeli forces razed the vacated house next to theirs and the Bishara house, which had a common wall with the demolished one, collapsed. "We were left with very meager means of survival," he remembers. There were five children, most of them young. "My mother used to go and clean houses, scrub and mop houses, Jewish houses, and clean their dishes, etcetera— simply to provide us with a means of survival. It was minimal, but we did."

Osama Fawzi is Bishara's opposite. He speaks rapidly and bounces on the edge of his chair, often keeping the room full of people in hilarious laughter with his wry remarks about Arab leaders, a hint of the kind of satire that regularly appears in his newspaper. His energy is infectious, and he easily commands the attention not just of the American who is interviewing him but of the other Palestinians sitting with him in a Houston living room.

Fawzi's parents and five older brothers walked ten miles at night into Lebanon when the Israelis attacked Tarshiha. His family tells him that his father's sister and her husband and seven children were killed by the Israelis, but it is difficult to interrupt him to ask under what circumstances. Many civilians were killed during the air and artillery bombardment of Tarshiha and other Galilee towns, and several cases have been documented of Israeli atrocities against Palestinian civilians, including women and children, during the October 1948 offensive.[28] Although most of Tarshiha's inhabitants, including much of Fawzi's extended family, stayed in Lebanon in refugee camps, his father took the immediate family to Jordan, where he was able to get a job teaching English. Osama and seven more children were born in Jordan. His first memory of learning about the Palestinians' plight and that of his own family was when he was about five years old and his parents named a newborn daughter Alia; when he asked why they had given her that name, they told him about his aunt Alia killed by the Israelis.

Separation and dispersal are the dominant elements in Fawzi's Palestinian consciousness. Some of the extended family remains in Lebanon, some has moved to Syria, and in both countries many remain in refugee camps. Fawzi and his ten brothers and two sisters grew up in Jordan, but they have scattered now. Economic opportunity is dismal in Jordan, and there are no sentimental ties to the land there anyway. "We suffer from this," Fawzi says; for a people for whom extended family ties are all-important, being scattered all over the world is extremely difficult. "I want to tell you something," he says intensely, sitting forward in his chair, anxious to make his message clear. "I live here, one of my brothers lives in Saudi Arabia, one in Germany, one in Sweden, some of them in Jordan, and we can't meet. We have no country to go to. I can't go to Saudi Arabia, he can't come to United States. Three weeks ago, we got a call from Jordan that my sister has cancer, and she is going to die within a few weeks. If we had a country, a home and our country, I could go to my country to bury her."

Fawzi has another story to illustrate his point. He had never known his father's father, who when Tarshiha fell went to Syria, so when Osama left Jordan for Syria after high school to apply to a university there, his father gave him the address of his grandfather's family. The grandfather had died by this time, but his grandmother was still alive and the family lived in a camp near Aleppo. When he entered the camp, an old man expressed interest when Fawzi said he was from Tarshiha. "From Lebanon or from Jordan?" the man asked. "I told him from Jordan," Fawzi continues, his excitement building. "He asked me, 'Do you know Abu Munir?' I said, 'Yes, he is my father.' He told me, 'He's my brother!' The old man is my uncle!" Fawzi concludes almost triumphantly.

His emotion is evident and has affected the others around him. "This is the dilemma of the Palestinians," says one man. "I mean, my hair is standing up when I hear this. That will give you a picture of what the Israelis have done to us." They all blame the Israelis. "Not only do they take the land," says Fawzi, "they have taken many things from our lives."

The Palestinians' dispossession has meant refugees and refugee camps and a permanent image of pitiable squalor that has followed Palestinians for four decades. Novelist Leon Uris, far more than any other single image-maker, has fashioned a picture of the Palestinian refugee as a repugnant individual, someone who is stupid and doltish, usually illiterate, totally un-motivated, content to live in filth—altogether a thoroughly ignoble person. This is the portrait of the Palestinian painted in Uris's two most prominent novels, *Exodus* and *The Haj*, and this is the stereotype of Palestinians held by those Americans whose main education in the Arab-Israeli conflict has come from reading Uris's novels. Uris is even more blunt in his non-fiction writings. The Palestinians, he says, are a "people who don't have the dig-nity to get up and better their own living conditions but are satisfied to live off the scrapings of charity and whose main thrust is the perpetuation of hatred."[29]

In fact, only fifteen percent of the approximately five million Palestini-ans today still live in refugee camps.[30] The vast majority of the original over 700,000 refugees—who immediately after their dispersal constituted almost sixty percent of all Palestinians—and particularly the second and third generations, have moved on, to education and gainful employment outside the camps. Those still in the camps live in part on UN charity and in part on their own earnings. Men work in the camps or in the economy of the host country, or travel to other Arab countries to work, sending money back to their families; women produce embroidery and other crafts to per-petuate the Palestinian culture; since the *intifada* in the West Bank and Gaza, everyone in camps there has worked to become self-sufficient in food production to make up for shortages caused by the uprising and Palestinian commercial strikes.

Life in refugee camps is not pleasant. The refugees are poor, the camps are squalid, the existence is hard. But Palestinians inside and outside the camps see them as centers of Palestinian national solidarity, a means of keeping the Palestinian plight before the world and before Palestinians themselves and of fostering a national Palestinian consciousness. Palestini-ans take pride in the role the camps have played and indeed see them as a means of retaining their dignity, not an indication of dignity lost.

Samir Abed-Rabbo was born in a refugee camp, but when you ask him where he is from, he names the Palestinian town where his parents and grandparents and generations before them were born, which now no longer exists. This is the way he grew up, knowing he was from a village called Yasour, just inland from the coastal town that became the Israeli city of

Ashdod, and this is the way he first knew something was different about Palestinians. "Clearly, to live in a refugee camp means you are living in a microcosm of Palestine," he explains in the Vermont office of the small publishing house he heads. "Every town is represented in that refugee camp. So the first questions you learn when you are little are that you are from Yasour, Fuad is from Saris, people are from different towns. So, since they are from different towns, you automatically start to realize that none of us in reality belongs here [in the camp]. You don't really have to be a genius to figure these things out."

Abed-Rabbo is a young man, born in the mid-1950s, long after his parents had fled Yasour. He is tall with curly brown hair and a beard to match that give him a kind of rough-hewn look. He has a wry sense of humor and wears a slightly ironic smile throughout his description of growing up in Qalandiya, a refugee camp north of Jerusalem. Publisher of Amana Books, which handles primarily books on the Middle East, Abed-Rabbo works out of a five-room office in an old building in Brattleboro. The ceilings are high and the rooms cavernous; books spill off shelves onto desktops and counters. The snowless winter landscape outside is bleak and industrial looking, but the atmosphere inside is comfortable. Abed-Rabbo allows his employees occasionally to bring their children to the office, and on this day his own four-month-old son sleeps on a blanket on the floor of his office.

The whole of Qalandiya camp is divided into neighborhoods according to the residents' towns of origin, he continues. Whenever the kids play soccer or volleyball or a game modeled after baseball called "ready" in English, the teams are formed by hometown. "So it doesn't take a genius," he repeats the point for emphasis, "to figure out that there's a problem. The people of Yasour are not playing in the fields of their town, nor the people of Saris either. Instead, they're crammed into a refugee camp that has narrow alleys and no playgrounds and is often violated by the Israeli army and agents."

The demeanor of the older people also signals to the children that there is something wrong, something unusual about their living conditions. "You look at your grandfather's face and you assume that he should be smiling. You are a little boy, and he should be playing and smiling with you, and here you look at him and you see the map of Palestine, all the misery of the camps on his face. So sooner or later, you can understand, and you start asking questions."

Abed-Rabbo's family—parents, grandparents, aunts and uncles—were among the last people to leave Yasour in June 1948 when it was surrounded on three sides. Some of the family went to Gaza, but most walked as far as the area north of Jericho, a trek of about fifty miles, before returning to Jerusalem, where the Qalandiya camp was established.

Abed-Rabbo's grandfather did not see one of his sisters or other close relatives who had gone to Gaza until after 1967, when Israel captured the West Bank and Gaza. Samir accompanied the old man on the trip through Israel to Gaza to see his sister. When they stopped on the way to find the remains of Yasour, they found only one house still standing. The rest had been destroyed and much of the former town covered over by an Israeli air-base. But Abed-Rabbo's grandfather could remember where everything once stood. He knew which piece of land belonged to what family, which had had a home on it, which did not. "It's like he's living it all over again in his head," Abed-Rabbo recalls. "He had a map of the town in his memory." After a while they told the taxi they had hired to drive them back to Qalandiya. "He couldn't take it anymore," Abed-Rabbo says. "You could see the tears coming down, he just couldn't."

Samir feels that life in the refugee camps must be looked at from three different perspectives. For the oldest generation it is hardest: "You really see what a refugee life is all about. People that never smile, they're always living in the past, hoping that life in exile ends. Their present is only temporary to them, but yet the years are piling."

For the next generation, the concerns are for the present, for making a living for their families, which is often difficult and often involves long family separations when work can be found only in the Persian Gulf countries or Latin America or the United States. Abed-Rabbo's own father went to Venezuela when Samir was only a year old. He worked as a peddler and sent money home but never made enough to return to visit the family himself, and they did not see him again for twenty-five years.

For the children born in the camp, the third generation, life in the camp teaches sacrifice and humility, inventiveness and flexibility, Abed-Rabbo believes. "There is very little for you in terms of material things. There are no balls to play with, so you have to be innovative, go around and collect all the rags and put them together to make a ball. You have to make do with very little food, and that's what I think teaches the refugee to be resilient."

He has himself shown resilience. Born into a farming family, many of whose members were illiterate, and raised without minimal advantages, Abed-Rabbo came to the United States at the age of eighteen to attend a university and now has a doctorate in international law and a successful career. In fact, his own success provides an interesting footnote to the story of his father's long separation from the family. When he could afford it, Abed-Rabbo went to Venezuela to meet his father after a twenty-five-year separation, and then he brought both his parents to the United States to re-unite them. After a year together in Venezuela, both parents returned to Qalandiya. Because his father was out of the West Bank when Israel cap-tured it, he did not have an identity card and for several years had to live there as a visitor, on a permit that had to be renewed regularly. He finally obtained a residency permit in 1989.

For Fuad Ateyeh, who also grew up in Qalandiya, life in the camps has the effect of unifying the Palestinians. "It gives us a sense of unity, that we all suffered from the same thing," he notes. Ateyeh was born a year after his parents fled the village of Saris west of Jerusalem. The village was strategically located in the corridor between Tel Aviv and Jerusalem and was a prime target for Jewish forces attempting to clear the corridor. Villagers and irregulars put up some resistance—Ateyeh's father was wounded in the fighting—but the fight was unequal and the village soon fell.

Although Ateyeh is older than Samir Abed-Rabbo, they knew each other as youngsters; they lived two doors apart in Qalandiya, but each thought of the other in terms of his original hometown. Like Abed-Rabbo, Ateyeh left the camp at age eighteen to come to the United States to study. He is now a successful businessman in San Francisco, owner of several grocery stores and a food distributorship. He has brought his parents to live with him in the United States, but two sisters and a brother still live in Qalandiya. His wife, whose family is also originally from Saris, grew up in Qalandiya as well and still has family there.

Life in the camps is hard enough, Ateyeh says, that people are constantly reminded that they are refugees, that their life there is temporary. "It also," he believes, "puts something inside you that the only way to get rid of these things is to fight, especially that the United Nations does not do anything, your enemies are not interested in doing anything, so nobody else is left to do anything but yourself. That is my feeling when I see the kids throwing stones." He is referring to the *intifada*, ignited and spurred on by stone-throwing children and teenagers, both inside and outside the camps, who finally had enough of the Israeli occupation. Ateyeh can easily picture himself, as a camp kid, participating in the *intifada*. "I was just another kid like the ones you see on TV. That's me. It's the same life."

NOTES

[1] Said, *After the Last Sky*, p. 140.

[2] The UN Economic Survey Mission and the UN Relief and Works Agency (UNRWA) estimated the number of refugees at 726,000 in 1949 (Benny Morris, *The Birth of the Palestinian Refugee Problem, 1947-1949* [New York: Cambridge University Press, 1987], p. 297). Morris uses the loose figure of 600,000-760,000 for the number of refugees, on the basis of a 1949 British analysis, but does not explain the British methodology and

uses none of his own. Morris may be trying to accommodate the very low Israeli estimate of 520,000-530,000. See pp. 297-298. Demographer Janet Abu-Lughod uses a range of 770,000-780,000. See Janet Abu-Lughod, "The Demographic Transformation of Palestine," in Ibrahim Abu-Lughod, ed., *The Transformation of Palestine: Essays on the Origin and Development of the Arab-Israeli Conflict* (Evanston, IL: Northwestern University Press, 1987), pp. 153-161.

[3] Cited in James G. McDonald, *My Mission in Israel 1948-1951* (New York: Simon and Schuster, 1951), p. 176.

[4] Cited in Tom Segev, *1949: The First Israelis* (New York: The Free Press, 1986), p. 29.

[5] Morris, *The Birth of the Palestinian Refugee Problem*, pp. x-xviii, lists 369 "Arab settlements abandoned n 1948-49." Ian Lustick, *Arabs in the Jewish State: Israel's Control of a National Minority* (Austin: University of Texas Press, 1980), p. 48, cites a total of 429 Arab villages destroyed, according to a Jewish National Fund official.

[6] For an account of the fight for Haifa and the Palestinian exodus, see Morris, *The Birth of the Palestinian Refugee Problem*, pp. 73-95.

[7] Ibid., pp. 286-291.

[8] According to another version of the story, the woman was from the village of Kabri, just north of Haifa. See Muhammad Siddiq, *Man Is a Cause: Political Consciousness and the Fiction of Ghassan Kanafani* (Seattle: University of Washington Press, 1984), p. 105, note 2. Siddiq cites this story in the context of analyzing a novel by Ghassan Kanafani entitled *Returning to Haifa*—a story clearly borrowed from the widely circulated tale of the child left behind—in which a Palestinian husband and wife are forced to leave their infant son behind when they flee Haifa. They return a quarter of a century later to find that he has been raised as an Israeli by an immigrant Jewish family. Dan Kurzman in *Genesis 1948:The First Arab-Israeli War* (New York: New American Library, 1970), p. 193, recounts the story of a woman fleeing Haifa by boat who, when ordered in a storm to throw extra baggage overboard, inadvertently throws her infant out and is left holding a pillow.

[9] For an account of the fight for and the exodus from Jaffa, see Morris, *The Birth of the Palestinian Refugee Problem*, pp. 45-49 and 95-101.

[10] Cited in Ibid., p. 52.

[11] Ibid., pp. 52 and 112-113.

[12] Map 2, "Arab Settlements Abandoned, 1948-49," and the Key to Map 22, in Ibid., pp. x-xi and xviii, show twelve Arab villages immediately west of Jerusalem destroyed by July 1948. For an account of the massacre at Deir Yassin, see Ibid., pp. 113-115.

[13] Ibid., pp. 192-193.

[14] Poetry reading by Nahida Dajani at the American-Arab Anti-Discrimination Committee annual convention, April 14, 1989.

[15] Cited in Morris, *The Birth of the Palestinian Refugee Problem*, p. 199.

[16] Reja-e Busailah, "The Fall of Lydda, 1948: Impressions and Reminiscences," *Arab Studies Quarterly* 3, no. 2 (Spring 1981): 134.

[17] Morris, *The Birth of the Palestinian Refugee Problem*, p. 203.

[18] Busailah, "The Fall of Lydda," pp. 130-131.

[19] Morris, *The Birth of the Palestinian Refugee Problem*, p. 209.

[20] The excised portion of Rabin's memoirs appears in David Shipler, *Arab and Jew: Wounded Spirits in a Promised Land* (New York: Times Books, 1986), pp. 33-34. Morris, *The Birth of the Palestinian Refugee Problem*, recounts another version of the conversation, in which Ben-Gurion is said to have made a dismissive gesture and said explicitly, "Expel them." See p. 207.

[21] For accounts of the Lydda exodus, see Busailah, "The Fall of Lydda," pp. 140-145; Shipler, *Arab and Jew*, pp. 33-34; and Morris, *The Birth of the Palestinian Refugee Problem*, pp. 203-211.

[22] Lustick, *Arabs in the Jewish State*, p. 51.

[23] Rosemary Sayigh, *Palestinians: From Peasants to Revolutionaries* (London: Zed Books, 1979), pp. 80, 89.

[24] Morris, *The Birth of the Palestinian Refugee Problem*, pp. xv, 185, and 187.

[25] Most of this paragraph is taken from Morris, *The Birth of the Palestinian Refugee Problem*, pp. 217-218, 228, and 239. The information that the Israeli attack concentrated on Muslim sections of town is from an interview with Ghassan Bishara.

[26] Bishara, "Yesterday's fighters are today's peaceseekers," *al-Fajr* (Weekly English-language edition, May 8, 1989): 4.

[27] Ma'alot became well known when Palestinian infiltrators took control of a school there in 1974, demanding the release of Palestinian prisoners. In the ensuing Israeli attack, sixteen Israeli children were killed and sixty-eight wounded.

[28] See Morris, *The Birth of the Palestinian Refugee Problem*, pp. 228-230.

[29] Jill and Leon Uris, *Jerusalem, Song of Songs* (New York: Bantam Books, 1985), p. 321.

[30] UN statistics cited in Rashid Khalidi, "Revisionist Views of the Modern History of Palestine: 1948," *Arab Studies Quarterly* 10, no. 4 (Fall 1988): 425.

3 Otherness
The Condition of Exile

> *You have worn your sense of otherness*
> *all these years as a consciousness more*
> *intimately enfolding than your own skin.*
> *Statelessness is your only state, and you*
> *have long since developed an aboriginal*
> *sense of how to live there.*
>
> Fawaz Turki
> *Soul in Exile[1]*

Jamal and Husnieh Anabtawi and their five children live now in the suburbs of Los Angeles, but they say they would rather be back home in the West Bank. Because they were working in Kuwait when Israel captured the West Bank in 1967, they cannot return home under present Israeli regulations. Jamal says that sometimes at family gatherings when his daughter Aseel plays the lute-like *oudh* and sings Palestinian songs "we cry all together, because you need so badly something very dear to you and you cannot reach it."

Only the two oldest children, now in their early twenties, have ever been to Jamal's hometown of Zeita or Husnieh's home in Tulkarm, and that only as very young children. They boast that the third child, Aseel, is the most nationalistic of them all, even though she has never seen her parents' birthplace. When the family moved to the United States in 1987, they left much of their furniture and their Palestinian memorabilia in storage in Jordan, but Aseel insisted on bringing her Palestinian artifacts. The family is anxious to show off her room, its walls hung with these symbols of Aseel's, and indeed of the entire family's, national pride and identity. The room looks like that of any American college student, until one looks closely at the adornments on the walls. The largest poster is not of a rock singer but reproduces a drawing by Palestinian artist and novelist Ghassan Kanafani of the stylized word *Falastin*, Palestine, in Arabic. Other walls are covered with blow-ups, front and back, of pieces of Palestinian currency from British Mandate days, as well as drawings and embroidered pieces from Palestine. A large stuffed bear sits on her bed wearing a T-shirt that proclaims "Palestine Forever."

The family home is large and comfortable, very American, but it is a substitute for the real thing. The Anabtawis like the United States, they mix easily in its society, they appreciate its freedoms and its opportunities. Jamal Anabtawi and his brother Yousef run two businesses, a grocery store and a real estate business, as a joint enterprise. Because their two families are here, they enjoy the extended family ties that are so important to Palestinians. But it is clear that there is still a void for them. "I think you feel attached to your homeland when you are forced not to be there much more than when you are there," Yousef says. "I believe one can forget his wife, can forget his wealth, can forget all good memories. The only place and thing he never forgets is his birthplace."

Exile and dispossession are not often thought of in connection with the West Bank and Gaza, where the principal Palestinian problem involves the lack of freedom and other frustrations of living under foreign occupation. But large numbers of West Bankers and Gazans are as much exiles as the 1948 refugees, deprived of any right to return to their homes.

Through a system of residency permits or identity cards used by Israel to control the Palestinian population, large numbers of West Bank and Gaza natives have been forced into the same kind of involuntary exile faced by their 1948 compatriots. Any Palestinian physically present in the West Bank or Gaza when Israel conducted a census shortly after it occupied the territories in 1967 received an identity card. Those born since the occupation who continue to reside in the territories also receive cards. Anyone, however, who happened to be outside the territories for any reason—work, school, vacation—when the cards were issued did not receive one, and anyone who leaves the territories to work or study and does not return regularly to renew the permit loses it.[2] The length of time between required renewals varies according to whether a Palestinian leaves via Ben-Gurion Airport in Tel Aviv or via the Allenby Bridge into Jordan, and often according to the whim of the particular Israeli official handling a case, but generally the identity card must be renewed every three years.

Thus, families who happened to be working overseas, like the Anabtawis, or students out of the country studying in that critical period when Israel conducted its census were considered automatically to have forfeited their right to live in their homeland. Thus also, young people who leave to study abroad and are unable to return before the period of study is completed are often denied their right of permanent return. Appeals are occasionally successful, usually on the basis of family reunification, but these are the exception. Those lacking a residency permit return to their homeland, if they are allowed to return at all, only as temporary visitors.

Samir Ahsrawi finds himself in this situation; he may visit but is not allowed to live in his home. A chemist in Austin, Texas, and the brother-in-law of Hanan Ashrawi, spokesperson for the Palestinian delegation to the peace talks, Ashrawi came to the United States from East Jerusalem in 1973 to study at the University of Texas. Because he was a student and found travel difficult, his family was twice able to renew his identity card without his physical presence, but on the third attempt the renewal was denied. The son of people who had to abandon their home in western Jerusalem in 1948, Ashrawi permanently lost his own right to live anywhere in Jerusalem.

When his brother applied for Ashrawi to visit in 1985, an Israeli official asked him to sign a document in Hebrew saying essentially that Ashrawi forfeited his birthright to Jerusalem. His brother, noting to the Israeli official that this effectively constituted deportation, asked for the ruling in writing, but this was refused. Ashrawi likens these tactics to "someone who abuses his wife or children and has learned how to do it without leaving scars." His brother would not sign the document but as a tactic hired a lawyer to petition for the reinstatement of Ashrawi's identity card. Although the family knew this would be denied, as it ultimately was, they also calculated that the Israelis would allow Ashrawi to come as a visitor while the administrative process went forward, which is what occurred. Ashrawi has never been charged with any offense, civil or political.

Like Ashrawi, Muhammad Hallaj, director of the Center for Policy Analysis on Palestine in Washington, D.C., and a member of the Palestine National Council, considers his exclusion from the West Bank a kind of deportation. He was born and raised in Qalqiliya, a West Bank town so close to the border with Israel that its extensive citrus lands ended up in Israel when armistice lines were drawn in 1949. Hallaj was teaching at the University of Jordan in Amman when Israel took the West Bank. In the mid-1970s he was able to obtain visitor's and work permits to teach at Bir Zeit University on the West Bank, but he was classified as what the Israelis call an "absent present." His application for family reunification, which if granted would have entitled him to an identity card and residency, was denied without explanation.

Legally, as an absent present, Hallaj says, "you don't exist. Physically you're there, but legally you don't exist." When his father died in Qalqiliya, Hallaj was not able to inherit the family house, which became "absentee property" and came under Israeli control. He could not purchase real estate. His children could not attend public schools, and he could not obtain a driver's license or a telephone in his home. Because he was on a visitor's permit, he had to leave the country every three months, usually involving an overnight stay in Jordan, in order to renew the permit.

Hallaj endured this for six years because he liked being able to live and work in his native land. But in 1981 he took a sabbatical year at Harvard, intending to return to Bir Zeit to teach, and at the end of the year Israeli authorities denied the university's application for a work permit for him. They gave no explanation.

Mahmoud H. is another West Banker who is caught outside. Now an engineer in Berkeley, California, he was working in Beirut at the time of the occupation, and the rest of his immediate family was away from their hometown in Nablus as well. Mahmoud was himself working for a Saudi Arabian company in Lebanon, an older brother and sister were teaching in Saudi Arabia and Kuwait, and his father, a local judge in Nablus, had been sent by the Jordanian government on temporary assignment to the small Persian Gulf sheikhdom of Abu Dhabi. "1967 hit me very hard," Mahmoud remembers, "because I didn't know what it was to be a refugee until then."

When his father's tour was over, his parents had no place to go but Amman, where his father again served as a judge until his death in 1976. The family did not own land or a home in Nablus, but Mahmoud's father had bought a ten-acre plot of farmland in the Jordan Valley in the 1950s that he enjoyed working on during weekends and vacations and to which he had intended to retire. Because he was not in the West Bank in 1967, Israel classified the land as absentee property and now leases it to Israeli settlers. Mahmoud's father had built a house on the land and ringed the property with trees. When Mahmoud drove through the area in 1972 during a visit to his mother's family, he found nothing standing. The trees had been removed to aid in detection of infiltrees from across the Jordan River, and all unoccupied houses had been demolished. Only a concrete bridge that his father had built over an irrigation canal remained standing to identify the property.

"So they built these fancy farms with drip irrigation systems. Very efficient," Mahmoud muses. "Certainly they do a much better job than we did. But of course they spent a lot of money." His father, without benefit of modern irrigation systems but with the help of a tenant farmer to whom he leased a fifty-percent interest in the land, had made this very dry, salty area of the low desert bloom with tomatoes, eggplant, sweet potatoes, bananas.

Mahmoud's mother applied for a residency permit for the West Bank after her husband's death, but she was turned down repeatedly, usually for no stated reason. In 1987, after years of trying, she was finally granted a permit. But his mother is a "lost soul," Mahmoud says, not happy in the United States or in Jordan, where the family's circle of friends consisted primarily of her late husband's business contacts, or even on the West Bank, where because of the family's dispersal she no longer has close ties.

Mahmoud himself is a bit lost. He feels no sense of fulfillment in the United States. "It's probably easier to be an immigrant in the U.S. than anywhere else in the world," he acknowledges, but the feeling of being without a home is still acute for him. "This is a loss that a lot of us feel," he says. "Somehow an aim is frustrated. The interesting thing is the Israelis talk about their fulfillment of these very things in Israel, but they don't stop to think for a minute how they have denied us that." The feeling of loss has less to do with whether he feels he belongs in America than with what he is missing by not being in his native land. "I feel that I'm in a position to contribute in some way" in the West Bank, he explains. "What made things worse for me is I was studying engineering, and an engineer is trained to build things, but what has happened is that all these Palestinians who studied engineering went and built buildings and roads and bridges in Kuwait, Saudi Arabia, and Iraq. But not in their own homeland."

The intensity of the Palestinians' feeling of deprivation and distress in exile, whether exile since 1948 from the lands that became Israel or more recently from the West Bank and Gaza, is often difficult for others to understand. Much of the anguish is linked to the tragic circumstances in which Palestinians feel they were removed from their homes and land, excluded from something they believed to be uniquely theirs in order to give it to another people. Many Palestinians readily acknowledge that they would not be so conscious of their attachment to Palestine if they had not been forcibly excluded from it. But there also exists among most Palestinians a real and tangible sense of oneness with the land—the particular land of Palestine and only that land—that cannot be satisfied anywhere else. This is not simply a traditional peasant society's feeling of attachment to a land it has come to know intimately through working the soil, although this physical intimacy has much to do with the Palestinians' feeling of loss. There is also for all Palestinians, the urbane and well educated as well as peasants, a sense that the land represents a cultural identity that is uniquely Palestinian.

Israeli journalist Danny Rubinstein has described the Palestinian attachment to the land in a sensitive book, *The People of Nowhere: The Palestinian Vision of Home*. Noting that before 1948 the primary Palestinian loyalty was focused on the native village, and on specific neighborhoods and houses within that village, more than on the Palestinian nation, Rubinstein points out that banishment from the village, even if only a few miles away to a refugee camp on the West Bank or in Gaza, was thus a searing experience. The individual villages and houses left behind, he says, "were, and to some degree still are, the dominant component of the Palestinian identity." Rubinstein observes that, because of the circumstances of their own exile and their move to Palestine, Israelis have been unable to empathize with the Palestinians. In contrast to the Palestinian experience, Jews moved to Palestine and consciously shed their exile identity because they wanted to integrate into an Israeli Jewish society. Israelis thus find it difficult, Rubinstein says, to fathom why Palestinians do not feel at home in Jordan or Syria or Lebanon, where they live under Arab sovereignty, speak the Arabic language, and practice their religion among co-religionists.[3]

But it is not so easy for Palestinians. The emotions aroused in Palestinians by exile are often inchoate—intense but hard to define, hard to articulate, sometimes impossible to convey to those who do not share the exile experience. Exile, and particularly the uniquely stateless exile of Palestinians, arouses a range of emotions: anger and frustration, jealousy, grief, a kind of uncertainty and insecurity, an inability to determine whether homelessness makes one belong nowhere or everywhere, even in some cases guilt.

The peculiar pain of exile has formed the basis for a rich tradition of passionate literature and poetry by Palestinians for forty years. Edward Said, the Columbia University professor, who was born in western Jerusalem in a home that he has not seen since late 1947, describes exile as a "sense of distance...from what was familiar and pleasant." He draws an analogy to a childhood experience in which, after leaving a performance he was attending with his mother to go to the toilet, he was prevented from reentering the auditorium. "All at once," he writes, "the rift introduced into the cozy life I led taught me the meaning of separation, of solitude, and of anguished boredom."[4]

This sense of the aloneness of exile and of the pain of exclusion from the familiar recurs in Said's writings ("how *abstract*, how very solitary and unique, we tend to feel"[5]), as well as in those of Fawaz Turki, another prominent Palestinian writer in the United States—born in Haifa, product of a refugee camp in Lebanon, who has been in the United States since the 1970s. Turki speaks repeatedly of exile as a "sense of otherness thrust upon us."[6] It seems to be a condition about which he is at once supremely defiant and deeply uncertain. "It seems like I have been able," he asserts, "to pick up and go 'elsewhere' with impressive ease all my life....It is as if being homeless has been my homeland, a kind of transnational place where I, along with other Palestinians of my generation, have felt the same sense of at-homeness that other folk, with a state of their own, have had." Yet his confidence is belied by his reference only a few lines later to trying to escape from "the noise of pain...the sounds of my Palestinian past rattling in my head."[7] The pain of "otherness," of "abstraction" and belonging nowhere seems to be the other side of the coin of trying to belong everywhere.

Palestinian exile poetry covers the range of emotions. The poet Fouzi El-Asmar is a Palestinian citizen of Israel jailed by Israeli authorities in the late 1960s and then kept under house arrest for over two years without ever being charged. El-Asmar, who moved to the United States in 1977, writes with a deep bitterness and sadness, as much at the Palestinians' own ineffectual answer to exile as at the condition of exile. Because he left Israel voluntarily and retains an Israeli passport and the right to return to Israel, El-Asmar does not consider himself an exile, but he writes on behalf of his fellow Palestinians who are in exile. In "The Wandering Reed" he asks:

Of what benefit is it, if man were to gain the whole world

But lose the green almond in his father's orchard?
Of what benefit is it, if man
Were to drink coffee in Paris
But none in his mother's house?
Of what benefit is it, if man were to tour the whole world
But lose the flowers on the hills of his native land?
He gains nothing but deadly silence
Within the hearts of the living.

You look through the mirror of lands not your own
And see your exiled face;
You recognize your face
Despite the deadly dust of travel
From Jaffa, to Lydda, to Haifa,
Through the Mediterranean to exile;
You recognize your face
And try to deny that face!
You worship your own face
Even though exile has obliterated its features;
The hangman of the twentieth century assumes the countenance
Of the eternal face!
You close your eyes
To worship your face in the darkness of this century.
You deny...you worship,
You deny...you worship,
And the god of truth cries to your face:
"He who denies his face
Is renounced by all the birds of paradise in this universe,
And those whom silence has turned mute
Will never be heard by the roses of the field.
He who kills the nightingale of his dreams
Will be buried in the forgotten graveyard of the living."
You open your eyes
And see the face of your country in the mirror of exile.

The deadly silence in the hearts of the living
Strips away the skin of your face;
It cuts and dries your flesh,
Then hangs what remains on poles
Under the forgotten sun of the West.[8]

Poets make up words to describe exile, like Fawaz Turki's "otherness."
Khalil Barhoum is a lecturer in linguistics, but he stumbles for words when

asked to define what being an exile means to him. "The feeling I have about Palestine is one of deprivation," he begins. He is a good-looking man in his mid-thirties with dark curly hair and intense dark brown eyes that seem to grow deeper with the effort to explain his feelings. "I don't think I will ever feel normal about it," he continues.

> I will never be the same. I don't know what "the same" means to me. All I know is when people ask me, for instance, "Why are you so active?" or "How come you know so much about the issue?" my answer is it's not by choice. I have lived through it. Nobody coached me to tell you what I have told you. I was there. It happened to me. I was the subject, so to speak; I was the victim. So, I simply cannot turn around and say, "No, I think my feelings are all misplaced. They are wrong. I'm not feeling this way. I'm feeling really chipper and happy. Maybe I should just try to forget it." You just can't.

Barhoum lives the typical American life, and he is happy and successful in it. He has been in the United States since 1975 and is an American citizen, married to a non-Palestinian American and essentially totally adjusted to U.S. society. He teaches linguistics at Stanford University and lives in a rambler-style house on a quiet, almost rural street nearby. Honeysuckle blooms outside. His two young daughters, beautiful products of their blonde mother and their dark-haired father, are growing up speaking a mixture of English and Arabic, completely at ease in both but preferring English.

But Barhoum is obviously still discontented. He is a double exile, born after the 1948 exodus but still a part of it and exiled again from the West Bank in 1967. His parents grew up in the small village of al-Malha just west of Jerusalem, which is now the Manahat section of municipal Jerusalem.[9] The village was partially abandoned in April 1948 in the aftermath of the nearby Deir Yassin massacre, and in July Israeli units overran the village and chased off its defenders.[10] Barhoum's parents lived in caves above the village for six or seven months hoping to be able to return, but when this became a forlorn hope, they walked to Bethlehem, where they were able to rent a one-bedroom house.

Barhoum, the youngest of seven children, was born in this house, and this is where the family lived until three months after Israel's capture of the West Bank in 1967. They had intended to stay, but because of the occupation and a family tragedy, they lost their means of livelihood and were forced to leave for Jordan. Three sons were working or studying in Amman, Jordan, at the time of the occupation, and when communications were cut off, the oldest son smuggled himself from the West Bank across the Jordan River, a common practice in the confusion of the early days of the occupation, to determine if his brothers were all right. On the return trip, he drowned. Because, as is still customary in Arab families, this oldest brother was supporting his elderly parents and the youngest children, including Khalil, the family was left without any means of support, and they left for a further exile in Amman.

There is for Palestinian exiles, Fawaz Turki has written, an "incessant logic showing you how, with your history deflected from its preordained course, there is no rest for you until you have regained that intangible and exquisite tool which men and women use to identify themselves as spiritual beings and of which you have been robbed."[11] This is what drives Khalil Barhoum, a kind of metaphysical imperative that leaves him unable not to pursue his identity. Despite his relative comfort in America, Barhoum would rather be in his own homeland. He returned for a visit in 1986 and found that "the minute I crossed [the bridge from Jordan], my feelings started kind of gushing out and I cried because I knew that is where I wanted to be."

Mujid Kazimi feels this same strong drive to find and assert his identity. Born in Jerusalem in November 1947 and raised in Jordan and Kuwait after his parents fled the Jerusalem fighting in 1948, Kazimi is now a professor of nuclear engineering at the Massachusetts Institute of Technology. He likes his life in the United States, and he would like to devote all his energies to his profession, but he finds himself driven by the fact of his exile to work for the Palestinian cause. Exile, he says,

> puts you in this situation where you are always trying to do too much. By that I mean that if there is, for example, a radio program or a TV program that was not giving the whole story about Palestine, then you would like to take the time to call the station, talk to them so that the other side will also be shown, or whatever is wrong will be corrected. It seems to me if I wasn't a Palestinian I wouldn't be having to watch out for that other side of me as much.

A deep sadness and feeling of frustration often hover over those who feel the pain of exile, sometimes constant, sometimes not. "I fight depression all the time, and it comes out of the Palestinian situation," says Samira F., the San Francisco librarian, whose family left Jerusalem in 1948. "I get angry when I hear a newscast and I can't talk back. I get depressed and I feel isolated. I think there is such a thing as an exile mentality." Because of her own strong feelings, Samira does not push her two American-born sons to identify with their Palestinian heritage. "I want them to be successful," she says, "and you can expend so much energy in this thing."

For others the pain is fleeting, experienced in moments when something triggers a poignant memory of home. "Wherever we go," says Nahida Fadli

Dajani, the poet from Jerusalem whose father was killed in 1948, "we are carrying Palestine in us, and we dream of it. We live these beautiful moments of going with grandma to the mosque, or the Old City, or my friends, the school, the streets that we walked in, the hills—we carry it in ourselves." Her brother Samir Fadli likens the emotion to what a child feels when a schoolyard bully takes a toy from him. "I feel like that child sometimes. It's so vivid to the child, it's so real, it's so simple. So innocent."

Fadli's use of analogy is something almost all Palestinians engage in to explain their feelings. The analogy most often used is of Palestine as a home entered by intruders who take it over. Adli Shafi, a Houston businessman from Gaza and a nephew of Dr. Haidar Abdul-Shafi, the head of the Palestinian negotiating delegation, explains his vision of what happened in Palestine. Say you leave your home briefly, he says, and someone else moves in, saying he had owned it years before. You come home and try to get him out, but he will not move. Your neighbors say they will help you, but they don't. A neighbor across the street allows you to pitch a tent in his yard, and you take refuge there, thinking "it will be only days, maybe hours" before the intruder is removed. But it goes on and on. Occasionally you throw a rock at the house, but it does no good and you are labeled a neighborhood nuisance. Finally, the neighbor in whose yard you are living says he wants to do some landscaping and asks you to move on. You must look for another place to put your tent.

Sheer frustration is often evident as Palestinians attempt to explain their feelings—frustration at the difficulty of making their pain clear to others, at the realization that after all no one but another exile can truly understand. "Can you imagine having no passport?" Karim Dajani asks, addressing Americans in general. Dajani, son of Nahida and Ghanem Dajani, was born in Lebanon, has never seen the land of his parents' birth, and came to this country as a young teenager in the midst of the turmoil of Israel's 1982 invasion of Lebanon. He has lived through the kind of experiences that few Americans can even fathom, and he can only explain the Palestinians' situation in juxtaposition to American complacency. "For you as an American to be kicked out of this country and be welcomed nowhere, acknowledged by nobody, and told you will never be able to see America from sea to shining sea—how would you feel?"

Probably hardest to take and most frustrating for Palestinian exiles is the realization that while they are not allowed to live in the land where they or their parents were born, any Jew anywhere in the world has that right, according to Israel's Law of Return. Mohammad Rajab, now the owner of a video rental store in Houston, returned to his home in Gaza in 1987 after he had been shot and almost killed by an armed robber at a store he owned in Florida. He grew up in Gaza after leaving Haifa in 1948, and his wife and children live there now. But he could not obtain an identity card from Israeli authorities, and the need to leave the country every few months to renew his visitor's permit became too odious, so he came back to the United States. He cannot really understand why he must go through this when any Jew is entitled to live in his homeland. "Why can the Jews from South Africa, from Ethiopia, come and stay and they are welcome, when they have no background [there]? What's going on? Even Russian Jews."

Some Palestinians focus their irritation on specific American Jews who have gone to Israel to live or would have the right to live there if they chose to exercise it. One man is particularly irked that entertainers Sammy Davis, Jr., and Elizabeth Taylor, both converts to Judaism with no roots in Israel, have a right denied him to live in the land where he was born.

For Wafa Darwazeh, a San Francisco businessman originally from the West Bank town of Nablus, the person who raises his ire is Meir Kahane, an American rabbi assassinated in 1990 who founded the radical Jewish Defense League and after his move to Israel in the 1970s headed Kach, an extremist organization that advocates the forcible expulsion of all Palestinians from "Greater Israel"—that is, Israel proper, the West Bank, and Gaza. "Which is more natural," Darwazeh asks, "for me to live in the United States, or Meir Kahane to come and live in the United States where he was born? But he's over there saying, 'The Palestinians are dogs. Kill the Palestinians,' and I'm sitting in the United States saying I want to go home. Naturally and automatically, a person is a citizen of the country where he is born. It's the law of all nations of the world. Meir Kahane was born in the U.S.A., and I was born in Palestine. Why should I and other Palestinians be deprived of our Palestinian citizenship to make room for him or Shamir and Begin of Poland or American, Soviet, and European Jews?"

For Nuha Abudabbeh, exile has produced a kind of alienation that she believes can never be overcome, even were she now to live in her Palestinian birthplace. Living there after so many years of living elsewhere, she says, "would be a whole new experience again" and would not be comfortable. "We've been robbed of something. I feel we have really been robbed of something forever." What she misses is a sense of belonging somewhere.

Part of Abudabbeh's feeling of not belonging has to do with the fact that her parents took her as an infant from Jaffa, where she was born, to Turkey, where her father worked as a horticulturist for the Turkish government and, although she grew up identifying strongly as a Palestinian, she did not know her hometown or her homeland and did not speak Arabic fluently. She was looked on in Turkey as an Arab. "It was the beginning," she says, "of learning that being an Arab was not very highly looked at. I remember the terminology in Turkish was *pis Arab*, which means dirty Arab." Then when she attended boarding school in Jerusalem as a young girl in the 1947-48 school year, she was regarded as "the Turkish girl" because her

Arabic was weak. The events of 1948 left Abudabbeh without even a reference point, and she has spent her adult life looking for a place to belong—in Lebanon, where she says the Lebanese "made sure I knew I was not one of them," in Libya, in Morocco, and in the United States, where she also feels like an outsider despite over twenty years here. Life as a Palestinian, she says, has been "a fragmented experience for me, very fragmented." This is a word, like Fawaz Turki's "otherness," that crops up frequently when Palestinians talk about exile.

Abudabbeh is now a clinical psychologist in Washington, D.C. She has a private practice and also treats forensic patients at St. Elizabeth's mental hospital. Because of her background, she tends to be very analytical about her own emotions on the subject of exile. Her feelings, she says, are different from those of most Palestinians. Having virtually no real memories of Palestine, she has no attachment to the soil, whereas she believes most Palestinians actually feel a part of Palestine. Nor does she share Edward Said's feeling of exclusion because "I never lived there, in a way. I have never made roots there." She also does not feel she has a strong cultural attachment to things Palestinian except as these form the basis for her identity. Her identification as a Palestinian is purely "an emotional state of being, a pure identity thing," she says, but it is no less strong for that. "There is a very strong basic identity. I don't even question that, I never have. I've always said I'm a Palestinian. There was the Arab and the Palestinian identity without whatever tangible goes with it."

Tangible things do, however, matter to Abudabbeh, at least as symbols. She grows quite angry when she talks about how Palestinian foods and costumes are often appropriated as Israeli. "Oh, oh, oh," she fumes, "I am incensed about that. That's like the hijacking of all our culture into theirs." Her own attachment to these things may not be particularly strong, but when Israel takes over these visible aspects of her identity it is like taking over her identity. Always, she says, at cultural exhibits "there's no Palestine and there's always an Israel."

For similar reasons, the objective, concrete signs of Israel's presence unnerve Abudabbeh. She describes the first time she ever saw an Israeli as physically upsetting. She was on a train traveling between Spain and France in 1963, and when passengers had to take their passports out at the border, she saw that the man sitting next to her had an Israeli passport. "I got sick in the stomach," she says. "I had never gotten used to the idea of an Israeli, period. It was something out there, the enemy, the people who took everything, possessed everything, but they never became real. I never had to encounter them." She spoke to the man and discovered that he was from Jaffa. When she said that was where she had been born, he said, "'Oh, me too'—like, you know, he was non-caring, so what." She saw the incident and the Israeli's nonchalance as another denial of her identity.

Similarly, when she went to the West Bank for the first time in 1986 and visited her mother's hometown of Tulkarm, she found it hard to deal with the fact that signs were in Hebrew and that Palestinians had in their kitchens items like butter produced in Israel and wrapped in Hebrew-lettered packages. The pervasiveness of Hebrew appeared to her as another indication that the Israelis were "the people who took everything, possessed everything."

What bothers Abudabbeh is less that Israel is there than that Israel's creation meant the negation of the Palestinians' and of her own identity, which is clearly all-important to her. Her concern is not to seek revenge against Israel but to recover her lost sense of self. Asked if the PLO's recognition in late 1988 of Israel's right to exist in her former homeland upset her, she answers, "No, no, no. I mean, that would be a very provincial way for me to think. No. I simply want to see justice for most Palestinians."

Abudabbeh has become reconciled to the sense of alienation that exile and the particular circumstances of her early life have imposed on her, and she says she has created her own "things to belong to." She identifies with women, with the poor; "if I am with other people who are alienated, I feel very much like I belong with them."

Much of the pain of exile involves not philosophical questions of existence and identity but some of the more mundane issues that incense Abudabbeh. However mundane, they are to Palestinians the signs of the loss of their distinctiveness—the "hijacking" of their culture, as Abudabbeh puts it. The standard Hebrew system of transliteration is now commonly, but incorrectly, used in the U.S. press for Arabic words.[12] Embroidered Palestinian dresses and the Arab folk dance, the *dabkha*, are often appropriated as Israeli at cultural fairs in this country. Falafel, an Arab concoction of deep-fried spiced chickpea balls often served in a pita round, is thought of in the United States as Israeli. The salad made of bulgar wheat called tabouleh is often advertised as "kibbutz salad."

These are small matters in the scheme of things, but small things are often enough to enrage. "If you see someone eating falafel," says San Francisco English teacher Amal T. in frustration, "and he thinks it's Israeli, you have to go into books and books of history to explain why falafel isn't Israeli. You go away frustrated, and he doesn't get the point. He thinks you're an agitator and gets nervous. 'Oh, gee'"—she imitates the horrified reaction—"'a terrorist!'"

Palestinians who cannot verbalize their emotions about exile express them in other ways, through the kinds of tangible symbols that do not need words—by keeping the keys to their old homes, for instance, or preserving the deeds of ownership or keeping other mementos. Some who have been able to visit their own or their parents' old village have taken a stone or some soil away with them. The Israeli journalist Danny Rubinstein describes Palestinians returning late every summer from refugee camps to harvest the olive trees that are the only remnants of their old villages along the Jerusalem-Tel Aviv highway, because these are their olives and are better than any others.[13]

Rajai Abu-Khadra, the Washington petroleum analyst, took pictures of his old home even though he is blind. Soon after the 1948 exodus, West Bank craftsmen who normally carved olive wood camels and crosses for tourists began carving an olive-wood map of Palestine for sale to refugees. The map had the expression "We shall return" written on it in Arabic. One Palestinian who left Haifa as a child and grew up in Beirut says he remembers these maps, which hung like *objets d'art* in Palestinian homes, as the first political expression among the refugees. Today, maps fashioned in a variety of materials hang in a great many Palestinian homes, and it has become a popular political statement to wear a small gold pendant showing a map of Palestine. (An almost identical pendant map, this one with the addition of the Golan Heights, is sold in Israel as a map of Israel.)

Adeeb Abed receives a regular supply of symbols from his homeland. Now the head of an Arab cultural center in Brooklyn, who came to the United States with his family as a fourteen-year-old in the wake of the 1967 war, Abed remembers as a young boy planting a lemon tree in the front yard of his home in the West Bank town of Bir Nabala; when he left, the tree was only as tall as he, but now it has grown and produces lemons every year. Whenever a friend or relative travels from Bir Nabala to the States, Abed's parents, who returned to the West Bank in the late 1970s, send several lemons back to Abed.

"All that is very real to us," he muses. "The attachment is real. It's only twenty years since the occupation; it's not 2,000 years ago. It's not something you read about in history books. [Exile is] something you're living every day." Abed is a very deliberate speaker, and none of the emotion of what he is saying comes through in his voice. He wears a black suit that complements his jet black hair and black, neatly trimmed goatee. He fingers a string of worry beads as he talks. "You know, my kids talk [on the phone] to their grandmother, and they have never seen her. Now, that's something that's not natural, and why should it be? When the Israelis talk about the Palestinians going and settling somewhere else, and the U.S. talks about less than national rights, why? Why should these things that are so unnatural for other people be accepted as normal for the Palestinians?"

Palestine has become to some Palestinians a symbol, a romantic image, while to others in exile it is still a living presence. But whether Palestine is symbol or reality, exile has created a solidarity among Palestinians that in turn gives them a conviction that Palestinians will always survive as a people. A Palestinian is "more than just the word Palestinian," observes Wafa

Darwazeh. "A whole host of other things go with Palestine: the traditions of Palestine, the culture of Palestine, the folklore of Palestine, the stories abut Palestine, the poetry about Palestine, the history of Palestine that we have in our hearts, the food of Palestine, everything. Who's going to erase that?"

NOTES

[1] Fawaz Turki, *Soul in Exile: Lives of a Palestinian Revolutionary* (New York: Monthly Review Press, 1988), p. 6.

[2] Israel does occasionally grant requests for residency permits on the basis of family reunification, although this is fairly rare. Israeli officials say that 13,500 applications were approved out of 88,400 requests between 1967 and 1987. See Frank Collins, "How Palestinians View Soviet Jewish Immigration to Israel," *Washington Report on Middle East Affairs* (June 1990): 14. Red Cross figures for the same period put the number of approved applications lower, at 9,000 out of 140,000 requests. See Jackson Diehl, "A Quiet Policy to Transfer Population," *Washington Post National Weekly Edition* (February 5-11, 1990): 17.

[3] Danny Rubinstein, *The People of Nowhere: The Palestinian Vision of Home* (New York: Times Books, 1991), pp. 16 and 43-44.

[4] Said, *After the Last Sky*, p. 48.

[5] Ibid., p. 35. Emphasis in original.

[6] Turki, *Soul in Exile*, pp. 6 and 25.

[7] Ibid., pp. 129-130.

[8] Fouzi El-Asmar, "The Wandering Reed," in A. M. Elmissiri, ed., *The Palestinian Wedding: A Bilingual Anthology of Contemporary Palestinian Resistance Poetry* (Washington: Three Continents Press, 1982), pp. 107-109.

[9] Morris, *The Birth of the Palestinian Refugee Problem*, p. 192.

[10] Ibid., p. 212.

[11] Fawaz Turki, *The Disinherited: Journal of a Palestinian Exile* (New York: Monthly Review Press, 1972), p. 166.

[12] Said, *After the Last Sky*, p. 135.

[13] Rubinstein, *The People of Nowhere*, p. 26.

4 The American Experience
Maintaining a Balance

> *To be true to their background, I have a duty not to allow my children to become so assimilated that they will not remember where they came from. Because we have a saying, "If you do not know your background, you do not know your future."*
>
> Samir Fadli
> Maryland businessman

> *There's a lot of discomfort in knowing that we are in a country that's somehow responsible for the continuation of the plight of our people. It doesn't help to be on both sides of the issue, so to speak.*
>
> Adeeb Abed
> New York political organizer

Israel has outlawed the very color combination. Red, black, white, and green are the colors of the Palestinian flag, and for that reason they cannot be worn or displayed by Palestinians in Israel or the occupied West Bank and Gaza. But this is San Francisco, and a large Palestinian flag hangs from the speaker's podium at this meeting of the local Palestinian Women's Association.

The meeting is held in the basement of an Antiochian Orthodox church, but the several hundred people gathered are a mixture of Christian and Muslim. Men are as numerous as women, and as active in setting up microphones, cameras, stage props. As at all Palestinian gatherings, it seems, children are everywhere. They all seem dressed in their best holiday finery, as are their parents. No jeans here; the men almost all wear ties, the women suits and dresses. A few women wear long embroidered Palestinian dresses.

The meeting is an hour late starting—there is much socializing to do first—and there are the inevitable jokes about Arab lack of punctuality, the kind of mildly self-deprecating ethnic humor so common in the United States. Although men have been active behind the scenes and are prominent in the audience, all the speakers are women. The first speaks in Arabic, but a non-Arabic speaker can pick up key words: *Falastin* (Palestine), *hurriyah* (freedom), *intifada*. She speaks in a cadence that suggests poetry, and it is obvious that she is savoring her words, luxuriating in the sound of them. Arabs revel in the beauty of their language, and poetry is often a mode of everyday speech. Poetry, the Palestinian writer Fawaz Turki says, is "a vital starting point to meaning...every Palestinian's idiom."[1]

A Black woman speaks next, in English. Her slogans are a bit too pat, her criticisms of Zionism too glib, her talk too much a campaign speech for Jesse Jackson. This is 1988, an election year, a year in which Jackson's support for Palestinian statehood has sparked widespread interest in his candidacy among the Palestinian community, but probably everyone in the room is aware that Jackson has just turned politician during the New York primary and repudiated the PLO. Palestinians are disappointed, although not turned off completely, and they give the speaker polite but restrained applause. A few minutes later, however, she is sent off with cheers and whistles when she closes by referring to the audience as "my brothers and sisters from Palestine."

The featured speaker returns to Arabic. She is a tall, utterly self-possessed woman who chain smokes offstage and speaks without notes. She has just returned from the West Bank and Gaza and recounts the stories of people in rebellion, being arrested, beaten, teargassed. She was herself grazed by a rubber bullet. Her speech obviously arouses emotions in the audience: collective sighs and tongue clucking greet her description of a visit to a hospital; one woman rubs goose flesh on her arm. Again, key words like *shibab* (youth) and *sumud* (steadfast) stand out.

Someone has collected television news clips of the *intifada* on videotape, and these are shown next. There are more sighs and moans for pictures of Israeli soldiers beating Palestinian teenagers. Shots of Palestinian flags and Palestinian defiance are cheered. The loudest cheers and foot stamping are reserved for a picture of a boy of about eight cranking up to hurl a stone at Israeli soldiers. These kids are called "the children of stones."

The last part of the program is lighter. A group of about fifteen children sings Palestinian songs. As the children arrange themselves on stage, a mother in the audience shouts to her daughter—first in Arabic and then, for good measure, in English—to step forward so everyone can see her embroidered dress. The singers are all of an age, cute six- and seven-year-olds who miss their cues, sing too loudly and off key, and giggle uproariously. They all seem to be lacking their front teeth. A group of older children who dance a *dabkha* try to be more mature, but there is giggling here too. The

71

girls among them all wear traditional Palestinian dresses, but the shoes are very American—beat-up sneakers, black high-tops, black patent slip-ons.

Palestinian Americans are like any other ordinary Americans. They have mortgages, they watch TV, they root for baseball teams, they go to Rotary meetings, and after a Friday night outing like this one they have to go home and put the kids to bed just like every other American. But there is a difference. Because of the bond formed by the common experience of dispossession and statelessness, Palestinian communities in the United States, and throughout the world, tend to have a high level of political consciousness and a high resistance to integration in the host society. This is particularly true here because of the strong Israeli-U.S. relationship; precisely because Israel enjoys such powerful influence and popularity in the United States, Palestinians here feel challenged to maintain and assert their identity. To a degree perhaps unusual among ethnic communities in this country, Palestinian Americans, even the American-born, remain highly conscious of and deeply involved in the politics of their native land.

Assimilation was once thought to necessitate shucking off the traces of one's native heritage. Alixa Naff, a scholar of the Arab-American community, has observed in early Syrian, Lebanese, and Palestinian immigrants—those who came to the United States before World War II—a "relatively high degree of Americanization among first generation [immigrants] and [a] relatively low degree of ethnic consciousness in the second generation."[2] That this is not true of Palestinians today is as much a function of Palestinian political consciousness as it is of changes in American society that have made preservation of a native culture and an original ethnic identity possible even while becoming integrated in the American culture.

Being Palestinian is a profoundly political thing in this country. Attachment to a foreign or parental birthplace rarely translates in the United States into political nationalism, but this is decidedly not the case for Palestinians. For the very reason that there is no Palestine, Palestinian Americans tend to be acutely conscious of the Palestinian problem in all its aspects, and it is virtually impossible in this day and age to be a Palestinian in America without also being political about it.

This political consciousness inevitably affects the degree of political acculturation that Palestinians achieve in the United States. America often demands more of its immigrants than it does of its native-born sons and daughters. The idealized image of the immigrant to America is of a person economically and politically oppressed in his own country who comes here already filled with patriotism for America's economic benefits and its freedoms, who may have cultural adjustment problems but basically comes with no lasting attachment to his original homeland, and who is so grateful for America's munificence that he ultimately gives up his language, his customs, his separate identity and hands over his children to be full-fledged

Americans. Unlike native-born Americans, immigrants must eschew criticism of any aspect of the American system or risk being thought ungrateful, and they must submerge all interest in foreign causes or risk being regarded as of questionable loyalty.

Although many immigrants have achieved this so-called ideal, for a great many Palestinians, the submergence of their political identity required to become "American" in this sense has been impossible. Large numbers of Palestinians tend to be here not by political choice but simply because there is nowhere else to go. For them, becoming American is not a choice made enthusiastically but a passive act, taken because there is no other or no better alternative. Because as far as Palestinians are concerned there has been no clear resolution of the issue of who owns land the Palestinians consider theirs, because Palestinians have no country that bears their name, there is for a great many of them a sense of incompleteness in the adoption of any other homeland, a sense of something still to come that maintains before them the vision of a foreign homeland and thus differentiates them from many other immigrant Americans.

That being said, however, it is important to emphasize that generalization about the "Americanness" of Palestinian Americans is impossible. On this as on no other issue affecting Palestinian Americans, there is great ambivalence and wide variation—in the level of adjustment to American society, in the extent to which Palestinians feel they belong to and are comfortable in the United States, in the degree to which Palestinians allow American ethnic and political prejudice to affect them. Assimilation is such an internal, individual thing that each Palestinian reacts differently to evidences of personal prejudice against him, to media misrepresentations of the Palestinian cause, and to official U.S. antagonism.

Some can separate their policy differences with the U.S. government from other aspects of their Americanness; others cannot. Some are sensitive to political discrimination, to being automatically associated, for instance, with terrorism simply because they are Palestinians; others can shrug it off as of little consequence to their integration in American society. Some are so culturally conservative that they reject most American customs and shun social contact with Americans, yet they are here by choice, as part of a chain migration that has brought their fathers and grandfathers and other members of their village here for generations. Others are wholly adapted socially, to the point of marrying non-Arab spouses and speaking no Arabic in the home (of eighty-five currently married interview subjects in this sample, twenty-eight do not have Palestinian or Arab spouses), but feel that they are here only because they cannot be in Palestine.

If the degree of "Americanness" that Palestinians feel varies widely, there is one constant: no matter how American any Palestinian may feel, being Palestinian remains a vital part of his or her life in this country. "Being Palestinian changes your whole life," explains Norma Sayage, a San Francisco real estate agent born in the United States of parents who fled Jaffa in 1948.

> It means that your whole life is circled around this cause. It is circled around gaining an identity. It's circled around becoming a person to everybody else, becoming a Palestinian and creating a Palestinian state. It really changes your whole life. It changes what you want to study, what your daily schedule is. You wake up in the morning and you think, "What can I do today?" In the end, what I'm trying to say is that being Palestinian is first and foremost with most Palestinians.

Palestinians are a very small minority in the United States, numbering probably around 200,000. No adequate census records exist, and immigration statistics have also been lacking, but informed guesswork, based on a Census Bureau extrapolation,[3] on various other population estimates from the 1980s,[4] and on the fact that as many as 100,000 Palestinians may have immigrated since 1967,[5] would place the current number of Palestinian Americans in the neighborhood of 200,000. Whatever the size of the community, it is small by comparison with other ethnic minorities in this country. At 200,000, it constitutes no more than ten percent of the two- to three-million-strong Arab-American community and equals a mere three percent of the American Jewish community.

The first Palestinians probably came to this country just over a century ago, their merchant instincts piqued by the commercial possibilities at the Philadelphia Centennial Exposition of 1876. One early historian reports that most of the Arabs at the exposition were traders from Jerusalem, who returned home with tales of "fabulous profits" to be made in America.[6] Lebanese and Syrian immigration began in this period, largely because of the promise of greater economic opportunity in the United States and probably in part specifically because of the vistas opened by the Philadelphia Exposition, but Palestinians, more economically and politically comfortable at home than their Lebanese and Syrian neighbors, were slower to begin immigrating. The Chicago Exposition of 1893 probably had a greater influence on Palestinians. Many traders from Jerusalem and the town of Ramallah on the West Bank came to Chicago to sell olive wood carvings and other crafts,[7] and it was not long after this that the first immigrants from Ramallah began to arrive in the United States.

Ramallites were the pioneers among Palestinians, beginning to come here in the early years of the twentieth century. They were Christians and could fit in more easily with the Christian society in the United States, as well as with the largely Christian immigrant community from Lebanon and

Syria. Within twenty years, no doubt attracted by the success of the Ramallites, villagers from small Muslim towns near Ramallah—towns like Deir Dibwan, Beit Hanina, al-Birah, and Beitunia, all on the West Bank—began sending their native sons to the land of opportunity. Thus began what is often called a chain migration—a "chain" that has brought generation after generation of people from the same town to the United States.

A frequent practice of these early Palestinian immigrants was to work in the United States as peddlers or as auto workers or factory workers for a few years, then to return home for a brief time and continue alternating periods at home with periods working in the United States until time for retirement. Most came initially as young, unattached men and either sent money home to parents or saved to be able to afford a bride. The bride was almost always a hometown girl and very often remained at home when the husband returned to the United States to continue working. Wide age differences among the children were quite common, the result of father's being away for long periods. This was true particularly in the 1930s and 1940s, when the Depression and World War II served to lengthen the separation. Many a Palestinian immigrant served in the U.S. military throughout the war, unable to return home.

Fuad Mogannam's father and uncle came to the United States from Ramallah as young men in 1906, and his father spent most of the next thirty-plus years here. The younger Mogannam, now a businessman in San Francisco who has himself lived in the United States for over forty years, never knew his father because he spent so much time here while Fuad was growing up in Ramallah. Mogannam's father started out peddling oriental carpets and laces in Pennsylvania. It was a long time before he could earn enough money to go back home for a bride, and World War I intervened to prevent travel for several years. Finally in 1919 he went back to Ramallah and married a local girl. Within a year they had a son, Fuad's older brother, but the father returned to the States, and so the family was separated for another long period.

Fuad was not born until 1933, the next time his father made it back to Ramallah. When Fuad's older brother turned seventeen in 1937, his father brought him to the States, but the father died here two years later, and the care of Fuad and his mother fell to the older brother. Finally, after a long separation caused in large part by World War II, Fuad and his mother came to the United States in 1948 and settled in the San Francisco area, where the older brother had moved to work in the shipyards during the war. The family still owns a good bit of property in the Ramallah area, the fruits of the father's long years of labor as a peddler. Fuad and his brother also both had a good education at a Quaker-run secondary school in Ramallah, the Friends Boys' School, thanks to their father.

The money sent back by all these early Palestinian immigrants financed a larger home, kept the children well fed and clothed, assisted elderly parents and younger brothers and sisters, and built a nest egg for later retirement. Often, as in the Mogannam case, there was enough to buy real estate at home or elsewhere in Palestine. Although many settled in the United States, ultimately bringing their wives and families here, and almost all became U.S. citizens, most retained strong ties to Palestine. Retirement was most often in Palestine rather than in America.

Political turmoil in Palestine and the creation of Israel changed many of the immigration patterns of these chain immigrants. Many who had continued to commute between the United States and Palestine before 1948 settled here permanently thereafter; although West Bank inhabitants were not displaced by the 1948 war, the economic dislocation and generally unsettled political situation caused by the war induced a great many people who already had some ties with the United States to relocate. Those West Bankers who continued the overseas commute beyond 1948 were disrupted in 1967, when Israel captured the West Bank. Many caught outside without the Israeli-issued identity cards that are a requirement for residency were forced to make the United States their permanent home; large numbers of others, even though in possession of these residency permits, chose to emigrate voluntarily rather than live under Israeli occupation.

So many of Ramallah's original inhabitants—said by legend to be the descendants of seven brothers who founded Ramallah 400 years ago—have come to the United States that only about 1,000-2,000 of the original dynasty still live in the West Bank town. The dynasty has grown today to over 25,000 people, who almost all live in the United States.

Some few natives of the smaller, Muslim towns such as Deir Dibwan continue to this day to live part time in the United States and part time at home, but the difficulties imposed by Israeli controls make this increasingly rare. It is estimated that about 7,000 American citizens of Palestinian origin now live on the West Bank,[8] many of whom have retired after careers in the United States and others of whom are on the home cycle of a regular home-United States commute.

The events of 1948 also brought a marked change in the type of Palestinian immigrant to this country. Whereas immigrants to this point had been overwhelmingly Christian, were generally uneducated, and were part of a chain migration without political motivation, those who came after 1948 tended to be Muslim in greater proportion, to be better educated, to have come singly and, very often, to have come to the United States because, unable to be in Palestine, they found nowhere else preferable to go.[9]

The 1967 war and the more than two decades of Israeli occupation since then have brought a new and much more sizable wave of Palestinian immigration. As many as half the Palestinians in this country are believed to have immigrated since 1967, either directly as a result of the Israeli occupation or because of political upheaval or economic dislocation in the Arab countries where large numbers of Palestinians live.

With the post-1967 immigrants to the United States has come an increased Palestinian political consciousness. The Arabs' abysmal defeat in 1967 brought Palestinians everywhere—the then largely apolitical in the United States almost equally with those in the West Bank and Gaza who felt the defeat and its implications directly—to the realization that no Arab state could or would help the Palestinians. The almost simultaneous rise of the PLO as the Palestinians' first organized native leadership galvanized political sentiment and gave Palestinians a greater sense of their own capabilities. The immigrants who came to the United States in the aftermath of the war and the occupation have heightened this political consciousness by bringing with them a keen sense of the urgency of the Palestinian problem, an acute awareness of the hardships Palestinians under occupation endure, and a sharp perception of how little the other Arab states are willing to do on behalf of the Palestinians.

The American reaction to the 1967 war also raised Palestinian political consciousness by demonstrating the depth of U.S. support for Israel and opening a gulf between Palestinian Americans and their adopted home. Raja S. of Washington, D.C.—a well known member of the Palestinian-American community who asked that his real name not be used—recalls his utter shock and feeling of isolation at the American reaction to Israel's victory in June 1967. "In terms of official America, the United States government, in terms of the media, and in terms of the people you meet on an individual level—what was shocking was the partisanship that appeared to me," he remembers bitterly. "It was a we-Americans-beat-out-these-Arabs sort of thing, via Israel. It's not merely pro-Israeli for whatever reason, but it was as if it was a personal victory for America. I recall that very vividly because I was really startled by it. Why do they feel that we Palestinians and Arabs are their enemies?"

The widespread sense among Palestinians that Americans not only do not support the Palestinian cause but actively oppose it—the feeling that their loyalty is questioned, that they are automatically associated with terrorism, that they are considered somehow less worthy than Israelis and American Jews—constitutes a real political problem for many Palestinians in this country. They often feel that no matter how much they might wish to become integrated in American society, they will never truly be welcome, that their politics, their very ethnic heritage will always keep them on the outside in the eyes of most Americans.

Fouad Moughrabi, the University of Tennessee intellectual, feels that living in the United States has been a bit like living in what he calls "enemy territory." Moughrabi is a student of public opinion on the Palestinian issue and is aware that the mood in the United States as reflected in polls began to change in the late 1970s—"there's more awareness now, much more support at the level of public opinion," he believes—but the feeling of hostility from Americans still crops up occasionally, as occurred during Israel's 1982 invasion of Lebanon and again during the Gulf war.

Palestinians often find that they are accepted as individuals but that the tendency always to judge them in relation to Israel imposes a barrier—in American eyes rather than in their own—that they can never overcome. Samir Ashrawi, the Austin chemist, says he finds this even among Americans who are his friends. "When it comes to who you are—and they like you as a person, they really do—but because of all they hear from their government, from all they hear in the papers, they have this one barrier," he says. "I've had it said to me, 'We like you, but we don't like your people.' My reaction to that is, what am I without my people? What I'm looking for is not just personal acceptance, because my person is to a great extent determined by where I came from."

This imposed distance and refusal to accept Palestinians for what they are have the effect of heightening Palestinian identification with their heritage and their political cause. Many Palestinians are acutely uncomfortable socially with the frequent American effort to categorize ethnic types, because it fosters a sense of being made to feel foreign. Mohammad Busailah, a retired Reynolds Tobacco executive in Los Angeles and the brother of Reja-e Busailah, who described his flight from the town of Lydda in 1948, feels this as a kind of subtle, unspoken barrier. He has been in the United States since 1957 but still feels that "I don't fit 100 percent with this society." When he came here, he says, "I came to be an American. But [they say], 'No, you are Arab.' No, I'm not, I'm an American. I'm a veteran, I have the right to vote, I served on juries, but yet I'm not accepted by the society. I want to assimilate, but I can't. I don't like to see it that way. When you are an American, you should be an American. You should maintain your heritage, but you should have a common goal as an American."

Others feel this as a kind of political categorization. "The nature of being Palestinian means you are political," says Fuad Mogannam, the San Franciscan from Ramallah. He believes that American society is structured to perpetuate ethnic differences and that the tendency to label all Arabs, and particularly Palestinians, as terrorists puts a uniquely political cast on Palestinian ethnicity. "I taught my children always," he says, "remember you're an American, you're born in this country, but also remember you're an Arab and no one's going to allow you not to be, so be proud of it and accept it. Live with it." Because of this American tendency to define ethnicity, there is no escaping the political issue for Palestinians here, Mogannam feels. If a Palestinian tries to deny being political, "nobody's going to allow it, nobody's going to hear you. The fact that you *are* makes you political."

Samir Ashrawi, the Austin chemist, agrees. "I would like to wear my ethnicity on my sleeve," he says. But for Palestinian Americans, ethnicity is a political thing, and like most Palestinians, he feels a constant need to compete with Israel for the respect and affections of the United States. For this reason he cannot comfortably admit to still feeling Palestinian without having his loyalty questioned. "Your word is suspect, it's labeled. The government, the movies, the papers, the lobbyists, the [Christian] fundamentalist groups, all those put together, [create] a kind of conspiracy of sentiment more than anything else that puts you in your place, so to speak."

The issue, in Ashrawi's view, is not in fact how loyal a Palestinian is to the United States but how well he measures up on America's pro-Israeli yardstick. "I don't think we have a loyalty problem," he asserts. "It's thrust upon us as a litmus test. It's not an American litmus test; it's not a question of whether we know the Constitution or can recite the Pledge of Allegiance with comfort. I'm sure we could all do that. It's a foreign policy test." Ashrawi deeply resents having his loyalty questioned. "Palestinians here have both gained and given," he points out. "Whatever they have taken in terms of opportunity, in terms of education, I venture to say they are very productive citizens."

Being a Palestinian American in these circumstances produces a pervasive ambivalence, a kind of love-hate relationship that is unusual among immigrant communities in the United States. Even the most alienated Palestinians appreciate American freedoms and are grateful that the system here gives them the right to speak out against U.S. policy on the Palestinian issue. They recognize and openly acknowledge that no Arab country has ever allowed Palestinians such freedom to speak, to politick, to demonstrate, to organize, simply to be Palestinian. But at the same time, they seriously oppose U.S. policy on the Arab-Israeli conflict, and they resent having their tax dollars going to the arming and succoring of their Israeli enemy.

Often this ambivalence produces anger. Nabil and Dina Khoury are more angry than most, but their feelings do reflect the extreme reaction of some Palestinians. This brother and sister have the intensity and inflexibility of youth. There are no nuances in their political register, no ambiguities, and because they are Palestinian and feel their Palestinianness acutely, they are not able to see much good about the United States. One has the sense that a few years hence, when life will have appeared to them in less black-and-white terms, some of the sharp edges of their political views may soften.

Nabil Khoury is passionate about his beliefs, friendly but disdainful of those who disagree with him and tightly sprung just beneath the surface.

When he invites a visitor to his parents' Detroit house, he is on the point of graduating from the University of Michigan medical school, but it is clear that the study of his roots and his people's problem is as important to him as his medical career. His sister Dina, a University of Michigan undergraduate, is no less passionate, no less intolerant of opposition, but she is somewhat less outspoken.

Nabil and Dina are the children of Elie Khoury, a physician who fled Jerusalem in 1948 as a boy, and Farideh Khoury, a pharmacist from Syria. The parents have been in the United States since the early 1960s, and Nabil and Dina were born here. Although they are only one-quarter Palestinian—their father is half Palestinian, half Syrian—they identify equally with their Palestinian and their Syrian roots. The fact that they are American-born seems to leave them completely cold.

Both say they will consider marrying only other Arabs because preservation of the Arab culture is so important to them. Neither wants to live in the United States. "I value it so highly I don't want to lose that," Nabil says of his Arab cultural background. He considers that he is "in the United States but I am not of it." Dina affirms that she too will leave the United States. She is not sure she could live under the political system in the Arab countries but might live in Europe

After listening to them for a while, their mother observes that she thinks she, the immigrant, is much more comfortable in the United States than her American-born children. She is not so critical, she says with some resignation. Nabil and Dina have learned their strong Palestinian nationalism and their love for the Arab culture from their parents, but their particular disdain for the United States is their own extrapolation.

Is there nothing about the U.S. system, about American culture that they value at all? "No, not really," says Dina without hesitation. "No," is Nabil's curt answer.

Nothing, really? Nothing at all? Well, maybe some things; they begin to think about it. Dina speaks first: "Some things, liberal thoughts, such as, you know, no sexism, equality for all, things like that—basic things that I think are more and more accepted in our generation. You know, the fight against sexism, the fight against racism, things like that that they really don't think about in the Middle East. It would be a big fight, especially for me as a woman, to go back [to the Arab world] against such a sexist society. I would fight against that." She thinks for a moment and concludes, "But other than that, there's really not too much in the American culture that I value very highly."

Nabil adds that he values the American organizational ability and believes that the Arabs could benefit from some better organizational skills. "What about freedom of speech?" their mother asks. Well sure, Nabil says, "those are all the liberal thoughts, the rights and freedoms" that Dina mentioned.

At which point, apparently realizing that these "liberal thoughts" are quintessentially American, the best things about the U.S. system, Nabil acknowledges that there is more that is good about what he calls Americanisms than they sometimes like to concede. "We try to reject everything, or I do," he admits.

Dina says she knows that the United States was founded on noble ideas but believes Americans have not been true to those principles. The United States, she believes, is a land "marred by prejudices and negative stereotypes which are greatly felt throughout almost all ethnic and racial communities in this country." She focuses on American society's negative aspects—"ranging from the high crime and poverty rates to the drug problems and the simplicity of the American people as a whole"—rather than on any positive aspects. Neither Nabil nor Dina comes away from this conversation any less alienated from American society.[10]

If the Khourys are unusual in the depth of their anger, they are not unusual in perceiving a fundamental conflict between noble U.S. values and what they view as the warfare the United States is ignobly pursuing against their own people. One hears this ambivalence from Palestinian after Palestinian. Nuha Nafal is an outspoken poet living in San Francisco who has faced restrictions in Arab countries because her poetry is often critical of the Arabs. She is particularly appreciative of American freedoms because here she is able to write unrestricted. "It is a privilege that I came to the United States and it gave me the opportunity to express my feelings by talking and writing," she says. "If we compare the United States to other countries in the world, I think it is the best place to live, if you don't have a feeling for your own country." Nafal believes the Palestinians can learn much from the United States and that American democracy should be emulated by the Palestinians and particularly by the undemocratic Arab regimes.

But for all America's freedoms, Nafal feels a painful barrier. "The feeling of each Palestinian, not just myself," she says bluntly, "is that we are living with people who don't like us and who help Israel against the Palestinians. When I pay my tax money, I feel that I am paying this money to kill my people." She is referring in general to the $3 billion to $4 billion of aid given to Israel every year, but she is particularly shocked by evidence that came to light early in the *intifada* that the teargas used by Israeli soldiers against Palestinian demonstrators, many of whom died of asphyxiation when the teargas was sprayed in confined quarters or at close range, had been manufactured by Federal Laboratories in Pennsylvania in early 1988, well after the uprising began.[11]

The refrain that the United States takes tax dollars from Palestinian Americans and uses the money to send arms to Israel to kill Palestinians is a growing one from Palestinians in this country. The kind of blunt cynicism exhibited by Fatima Horeish is not unusual. Horeish grew up in Lebanon, the daughter of 1948 refugees from the town of Safad, and came to the United States in 1973 at the age of thirteen. She speaks unaccented English, complete with a pronounced Chicago twang, recalls that all of her high school friends were American, and has come to feel totally at ease living in America. But she speaks with intense bitterness of how her government regards her people. She believes Israel provides one service in particular for the United States by, she claims, testing weapons on Arabs.

> America makes a weapon, and they want to test it, see if it works. They give it to the Israelis, they kill Palestinians. When Saudi Arabia wants to buy weapons, the U.S. gives 'em hell, you know. It's like the U.S. doesn't want to give them weapons, [even though] they pay lots of money for 'em. But with the Israelis, it's, "Here." The U.S. gives them a reward, I guess for each Palestinian that is killed. They give 'em more AWACS, they give 'em weapons. It's like, "Oh, you did a good job in Lebanon. Here, here's more weapons."

Other Palestinians reconcile their ambivalence about the United States and the duality of their political identity by not fully committing themselves to the United States in any political sense. Najat Arafat Khelil, the nuclear physicist in the Washington, D.C., area, expresses the sentiments of a great many Palestinian Americans, who can adjust to American society but cannot, in the absence of a Palestinian state, make a full political commitment to the United States. Khelil first came to this country as a student in 1962 and spent several subsequent years in Algeria with her Algerian husband. As a result, she was away from her home in Nablus when Israel occupied the West Bank, so she is unable to return. She feels so strongly about the Palestinian cause, she says,

> that I feel I don't want to identify in any other way. Maybe if I was a full-blooded Jordanian, I might not feel this way, because I would have it [a national identity] and take it for granted. But when I don't have it, it's something missing in my life. I feel I cannot identify with any other part of the world until I get my full identity first as a Palestinian. Then I would say, "Okay, I'm an American." Because the other identity would be there, clear, settled within me, and I'm satisfied with it.

Khelil considers it vital for Palestinians, citizens or not, to work within the American system for the Palestinian cause. She has given up her own work in the field of nuclear physics and spends all her time as chairman of two Arab/Palestinian women's organizations. She was not active until she and her family returned to the United States in 1980. "I felt, my God, how could I not be, because of how the situation is misunderstood and misconstrued. I felt that I have a duty to be active." She worked hard for Jesse Jackson's presidential campaign in 1988 because of his support for Palestinian statehood and has been a national board member of the Rainbow Coalition. "If I cannot go home, at least I try to make people more aware," she says. "I try to kind of soften the fact that I'm here, to use my presence by doing something for the cause. Otherwise, there's no wisdom in me being here. Otherwise, it would be a double exile."

Osama Doumani feels the same ambivalence but reacts by wholly committing himself to being an American while working within the system to change American attitudes. Doumani was for over five years, from 1983 through 1988, a regional director in Berkeley, California, for the American-Arab Anti-Discrimination Committee. He often found the job to be extremely frustrating, and it did not pay well for a man with two young children, but it was the times he felt he was having an impact that induced him to stay on year after year.

Doumani seems to balance his Palestinian and his American identities with remarkable ease. He is thoroughly Palestinian; he was nine years old when his family fled the coastal Palestinian town of Acre in 1948, and he grew up in Lebanon acutely conscious of being Palestinian and being dispossessed. But he is also emphatically American. He has been in this country since 1960, when he came to Berkeley as an anthropology student. Doumani says he has never stopped to think about whether he feels more American or more Palestinian, because he cannot separate the two. But what makes you one thing or another, he says, "is the kind of network that one has," and his is entirely American. "My closest friends are not Arab or Palestinian," he notes. "I mean the ones that I have emotional connections with. When the chips are down, [his American friends] are the ones I go to to talk things over, or to tell them what's on my mind, or if I'm in pain."

Doumani is so much at ease in both the American and the Palestinian worlds that he can say, when asked if the PLO represents him as a Palestinian, that it does not because the U.S. government represents him, even as he strongly affirms that the PLO does represent the Palestinian people as a whole. He is the kind of man—an intense, dedicated, almost hyperactive person who nonetheless comes across in front of an audience as completely relaxed—who can address an American audience on its own terms and in its own language. He has a deep sense of the importance of bringing Americans around to a different viewpoint. "You get a sense of responsibility," he says, "that there is so much to do, and that the United States really is a key factor in what happens to the Palestinian situation, or to the Arabs in general. Then you realize how little the American people know. But there is more caring than people give the Americans credit for. Most people say Americans don't give a damn; they care about their pocketbooks. It's true, but there are a lot of people who do care and don't have the access to any point of view other than the Israeli."

Palestinians increasingly recognize the benefits of using the system to fight the system, of using the American freedom to speak out against American policy. Fuad Ateyeh, the San Francisco businessman who grew up in a West Bank refugee camp, says Palestinian Americans try to be "messengers to the American people," bringing the Palestinian story and point of view to American attention. "We try not to persuade them to be on our side, just please try to listen to our side. You've been listening to the TV for so many years, to the Israeli propaganda for so many years, just open your eyes for five minutes and see the other side. Maybe [Palestinians] have something to say, maybe they are right, maybe they suffered so much."

The Bay area Palestinian community is generally quite active and stages frequent demonstrations at the Israeli consulate in downtown San Francisco, but Ateyeh says the object is less to influence the Israelis inside than to sway the American people who walk by and watch. The Israelis, he says, "are not going to see us. They don't care. We are really demonstrating for the American public."

The frustrations are great. Ateyeh sometimes wants to give up. When dealing with a congressman or senator he sometimes wonders, "Is he really my senator, or the senator from Tel Aviv area?" Samira F., the San Francisco librarian, speaks frequently at local church gatherings but seldom encounters the kinds of people Osama Doumani describes who care and can be persuaded, and she despairs of ever getting her message across. "I can't bring across to people the enormity of the injustice" done to Palestinians, she says. "I've seen Americans running over to small claims court over ten dollars. I mean, this business of being sticklers for justice—what's mine and what's right, and they sue each other over little things—but yet you cannot see the injustice that a whole country was stolen."

Despite increased political participation, political organizers like Osama Doumani and Najat Arafat Khelil complain about the degree of participation among Palestinians here. Khelil often has difficulty generating active participation in her women's organizations because women will usually not be active unless their husbands or fathers are. She frequently encounters women who will not even fill out a membership application until they have shown it to their husbands. Omar Kader, former executive director of the American-Arab Anti-Discrimination Committee, finds Palestinians, and indeed all Arab Americans, more than willing to contribute money to Palestinian and Arab causes but unwilling to stand up actively for those causes. "Every one of them will give," he says, "but they don't want a receipt, and they don't want to be acknowledged. They'll give you cash. They're afraid of the FBI, of the Jewish lobby, Jewish businessmen."

Palestinian Americans do not in fact lack political interest, but they have often lacked a focus. The main factions of the PLO—Yasir Arafat's Fatah, the PLO's largest organization constituting the PLO mainstream; George Habash's Marxist Popular Front for the Liberation of Palestine; and Naif Hawatmeh's more leftist Democratic Front for the Liberation of Palestine— all have adherents among Palestinians in this country, and when the PLO factions are divided, as was the case for several years following the PLO's expulsion from Lebanon in 1982 in the wake of the Israeli invasion, Palestinians in the United States are divided as well. This was a period, lasting until 1987, when disunity within the PLO was intense; some guerrilla factions under the PLO umbrella, including parts of Arafat's own Fatah, aided by Syria and Libya, were in open rebellion against Arafat's continued pursuit of a diplomatic solution, and the PFLP and the DFLP were estranged from the PLO. The discord was reflected in the Palestinian-American community. Some Palestinians report that disunity here was so serious that fights occasionally resulted at Palestinian gatherings. Since the PLO was reunified with the reinstatement of the PFLP and the DFLP in 1987, Palestinian differences in the United States have diminished, but tension and policy disagreements remain.

Turbulence elsewhere in the Middle East is also reflected to some extent in the Arab-American community as a whole, which has the effect of undermining promotion of the Palestinian cause in the United States. Strife between Lebanese Christians and Palestinians in Lebanon, for instance, particularly during the 1970s and 1980s, led to strife here.

Palestinian political activity in this country on behalf of the cause often lacks any kind of central direction. Edward Said, the Columbia University professor and probably the best known Palestinian in the United States, criticized the PLO in an Arabic-language newspaper in late 1989 for failing to provide any political guidance to Palestinian Americans. Noting that all business between PLO headquarters in Tunis and the PLO office in Washington is conducted behind closed doors, he criticized the PLO leadership for making no effort in the United States to explain the Palestinian stand through television appearances, writings, demonstrations, or efforts to mobilize grassroots organizations friendly to the Palestinian cause. He urged the PLO to work at organizing and coordinating the several Palestinian groups and communities in this country, lest the political scene in the United States "be left to coincidences and individual efforts."[12] Other Palestinian intellectuals echoed the blunt criticism.

For all the imperfections in Palestinian and Arab organizing ability and all the frustrations of political organizers, however, Palestinians have shown a political consciousness, particularly in the last decade, that begins to match the American Jewish community's in terms of intensity if not of numbers. Palestinians themselves have been involved in numbers disproportionate to their size within the Arab-American community in founding and running the several Arab-American organizations* that have sprung up in the last fifteen to twenty years to fight anti-Arab discrimination, promote greater understanding of the Arab culture, lobby for Arab causes, and promote greater Arab participation in the U.S. political system. In addition to these organizations, there are several specifically Palestinian organizations with a charitable orientation, and since 1986 a new organization called Roots has tried to acquaint Palestinian-American youth with their heritage through summer camps, trips to the West Bank and Gaza, cultural events, and weekend workshops.

Palestinians are also increasingly participating in the American political process. A recent survey of 240 Palestinians from throughout the country showed that almost fifty-eight percent of those who are naturalized citizens vote in American elections.[13] This contrasts with a figure for the general American population of only fifty-two or fifty-three percent who have voted in recent national elections.

Palestinians are slowly learning that in the United States the way to change policy is to participate and that in some localities the way to prosper in business is to have an input in local politics. In Chicago, where ward politics are a way of life and survival is often a matter of pleasing one's local alderman, Palestinians who once thought they could get by without even becoming citizens are discovering that participation can bring real benefits. Suhail Miari, a Chicagoan for over twenty years and the national director of the Palestinian charitable organization the United Holy Land Fund, notes that whereas in some Arab countries people are paid to vote, in America—at least in Chicago—it helps to "pay for" (that is, contribute to) a candidate. Palestinians who never felt a need to take heed of local politics, he says, now realize that the best way to be heard in city hall—to obtain assistance for a Palestinian neighborhood or gain protection from racial harassment or obtain a liquor license—is to have supported a local alderman. It seems to be working. The Arab community in Chicago, a majority of which is Palestinian, is now taken more seriously by Chicago politicians. The late Mayor Harold Washington announced his candidacy in 1983 at a banquet held by the United Holy Land Fund, and every Palestinian organization supported a candidate during the 1989 Democratic mayoral primary.

It is widely believed that the majority of Arab Americans, and perhaps the majority of Palestinians as well, are Republicans, largely because the

---

* These organizations include the American-Arab Anti-Discrimination Committee, the Arab-American University Graduates, the National Association of Arab-Americans, and the Arab-American Institute.

Republican party better embodies the traditional values that are important to Arabs. Fuad Mogannam, the San Francisco businessman from Ramallah, believes that in the case of earlier Palestinian immigrants, preference for Republicans derives from the fact that Harry Truman, a Democrat, was so much involved in the creation of Israel, whereas Dwight Eisenhower, a Republican, pressured Israel to withdraw from the Sinai Peninsula after the Suez War in 1956.

The Reagan years, during which U.S. ties to Israel were vastly strengthened, were a great disillusionment to many Palestinian Republican loyalists, and Palestinians throughout the country, including many Republicans, were excited by the 1988 candidacy of Jesse Jackson because of his explicit support for an independent Palestinian state. Eight Palestinian Americans were delegates to the Democratic convention in 1988, whereas the Republican convention numbered among its delegates only one Palestinian.[14] These numbers are not necessarily indicative of a trend; disappointment with Reagan and support for Jackson did not seem to translate to widespread support for Michael Dukakis in 1988, and most Palestinians are aware that, however pro-Israeli the Reagan administration, the Democratic party has also done little to advance the Palestinian cause. But the numbers do indicate one important fact: that Palestinians of both parties increasingly understand that involvement in politics is a means of advancing their interest in the Palestinian cause.

Amneh Mustafa, who goes by the name Anna outside Chicago's Palestinian community, is one who has seen the benefits of working for the Palestinian cause from inside the American political system. Mustafa lives in two worlds as diverse as her names. She was born in the West Bank village of Beitunia and came to the United States as a child in 1962. She lives in Chicago, amidst the large Beitunia community on Chicago's south side, probably the most ingrown of any Palestinian community in this country. But she travels easily in the circles of mainstream Chicago's local politics and community service organizations.

Mustafa does not look or act much like an activist. She is soft-spoken and unassuming, a pretty woman with high cheek bones and long wavy black hair worn pulled up softly on the back of her head. As the mother of seven children, ranging in age from six to nineteen, she wouldn't seem to have the time for community activism. But she manages to fit it all in, going to a meeting here and a meeting there when the kids are at school or her husband can be at home, all the while being careful to give the children a strict, traditional Muslim upbringing. She is a very articulate person, a quiet but forceful speaker. She emphasizes the human aspects of the Palestinian struggle, the simple concept that a people deprived of their homeland must have the right to reclaim some part of it, and the sincerity of her views gives them added force. She takes some time out on a frigid Chicago evening to discuss her activities. She has just come back from a meeting; the temperature outside is near zero, but she is enough of a Chicagoan now that the cold does not faze her.

Mustafa has become a kind of one-woman lobbying group for the Palestinians on the south side. She has no organization and no set agenda. She takes issues as they come, whether it is approaching a mayoral candidate to tell him about Arab community needs, or getting a local television station out to cover a Palestinian event, or helping to organize community religious groups to oppose a Ku Klux Klan anti-Black rally. "I think the southwest side is known for its racism," she says. "We're trying to take steps to modify the racism. Being Arab, we are the target of those things right here in this neighborhood." Whatever help she gives to the Black community, she figures, will help her own community.

Mustafa believes the Palestinian community has been slow to see the benefits to themselves of community interaction. "If I'm going to live in this country and be an American," she says—

> and I'm proud of being a Palestinian also—but I feel that we should interact with the rest of the community, foster better relationships with that community at large, and try through those means to let them understand our concerns, our needs, our struggles, you know. Through this way, you're going to have more sympathetic ears, you're going to get more people to listen and at least determine who's right and what's going on down there [in the West Bank]. It's about time we start having Americans come to our events, because we get more support through those means, and they'll understand more about us. Because I think the Arab community, especially the Palestinian, is the most misunderstood community in the city of Chicago. People simply don't want to associate with us. So unless we try to reach out, nobody's going to reach out to us.

Palestinians have not expressed themselves well enough to make their case well, Mustafa believes, either with regard to local community matters or in the broader diplomatic arena where the Palestinian struggle will be won or lost. She is delighted by the Palestine National Council's explicit acceptance in November 1988 of the two-state solution because "for so long, even though underneath we actually wanted peace and to sit down and negotiate peace with Israel, on the surface we acted so much as though we wanted to liberate every inch of our land. Well, we lost so much in public world opinion in saying those things." It all has to do, Mustafa believes, with how you present yourself, whether your goal is getting a street paved in Chicago or establishing an independent state in Palestine.

Some reward for her efforts came at Christmas 1988 when the local commission organizing the annual 63rd Street Christmas parade asked her if the Arab community wanted to be part of the ethnic float. This was immediately after the Palestine National Council had formally expressed its support for coexistence with Israel and declared the formation of an independent Palestinian state, and Mustafa's daughter and nephew rode on the ethnic float carrying a Palestinian flag. "It was so emotional," she remembers. "I have been active in so many things, and to tell you the truth I haven't accomplished much, I just want to try. But if I was to summarize anything that I ever achieved in my life, it was raising the Palestinian flag on the 63rd Street parade."

Cultural alienation is perhaps more common among Palestinian Americans than deep political alienation. It is still possible to live in this country without ever becoming a part of it. Cultural alienation is more often the case with women, who because of Arab cultural strictures are often prevented from integrating in American society. Based on a study of Muslim Palestinian women in Chicago, sociologist Louise Cainkar has concluded that because women are the principal protectors and transmitters of Palestinian culture, they are often deliberately kept apart from the American mainstream. "Many Palestinian men and women fear that the entire familial foundation of the society will collapse if women focus their energies elsewhere than the family." Women are so rigidly controlled by their menfolk in America's loose society, she finds, that they remain totally unintegrated, their freedom of movement far more restricted than it would be in the Middle East.[15]

This is probably more true of the Palestinian community in Chicago than of any other community in the United States. Chicago's Palestinians tend to include far more of what Cainkar calls "new peasant immigrants," immigrants from rural areas of the West Bank who began to come to the United States only after 1967 when Israeli land confiscations and limitations on water supply made farming their small landholdings difficult or impossible.[16] Because they come from a peasant and village context, these immigrants tend to be socially very traditional, and therefore strictures on women are more rigidly enforced. In Chicago to a far greater extent than in other U.S. cities, these immigrants usually cluster in neighborhoods where their social contacts are limited almost entirely to other Palestinians and where traditions, including traditional limitations on women outside the home, are reinforced. This is not to say that Palestinian women elsewhere in the United States are all unfettered or as free as men to assimilate in American society, but cultural restrictions on women appear to be more pronounced in Chicago.

Many Palestinians have difficulty accepting American social mores. The prevalence of such things as alcohol and drugs, sexual freedom, and divorce in American society stands as a serious barrier to full integration by a traditional people, Christian as well as Muslim, for whom traditional values are all-important.

Ibrahim M., a Los Angeles physician, is a man who has virtually no affinity for American culture and society. He is here from a West Bank town, still carrying Israeli-issued residency papers, and will stay for as long as is necessary to make his fortune and return home. He has a U.S. passport, but it is a convenience rather than a statement of allegiance. Asked what it means to him to be an American, Ibrahim asks in turn, "What do you mean by this question?" and when the question is rephrased, he replies simply that it is good to be an American because with a U.S. passport "you don't feel that you are a foreigner."

Ibrahim socializes exclusively with other Palestinians, largely those from his hometown, and he tightly controls his children's friendships. He sends the children back to the West Bank for schooling during what he calls the "dangerous age" in the United States, from ages twelve to sixteen. His oldest son, who spent the last two years of high school here, has no American friends because Ibrahim believes "this is what is going to change his mentality and make him do whatever he wants and go against his father."

Ibrahim's close control of his children is not unusual among Palestinians in the United States, particularly those who came here from small West Bank villages, but a great many parents, both Christian and Muslim, have succeeded in imposing strict controls on, and instilling their values in, their children without either causing estrangement in the young people or diluting their Americanness. The degree to which parents control their children, their ability to separate their own general attitude toward the United States from their distaste for some American mores, and the impact on the children of a conservative upbringing in an increasingly liberal society are all, like the question of assimilation itself, areas in which generalizations are impossible and individual personalities and preferences are wholly determinative.

Nawal Hamad, an Arlington, Virginia, bank vice president, has been able to maintain a traditional household without preventing her children from fitting in. Although she is divorced, in many ways she is a typical conservative Muslim woman. She has refused to remarry largely because bringing a man into the house who is not the natural father of her three daughters would prevent any kind of comfortable living; "what if he comes down in his shorts?" she asks as she and three of her five children sit in the kitchen of her suburban Washington home and discuss being Palestinians in America. She will not date, nor will she go out to evening social events unless escorted by one of her sons.

Yet in many other ways Hamad is quite atypical. When she was divorced, her father urged her to return to the West Bank, which she had left as a bride, and give custody of her five children to her ex-husband so that she could remarry, but she has insisted on making her own living and raising the children herself. She did attempt to return to the West Bank to live, but the Israelis refused her an identity card. So she stayed in the United States and has worked outside the home since the divorce, rising to bank vice president. She is obtaining a degree belatedly at night at a local community college. Although she socializes primarily with Palestinians, she goes out to lunch with her American co-workers, and she likes to gossip with them.

She is a woman of incredible energy. Although two of her daughters are married, three of the children still live at home, and she seems always to be cooking for them. On an overcast autumn Saturday she invites a visitor to her house to talk while she cooks an elaborate lunch. She has made sure that the two boys, Nader, who is nineteen, and Nael, sixteen, are at home, and one of the married daughters, twenty-year-old Fadwa, drops in before going to work. The other two children, both older daughters, are at work.

Hamad talks a blue streak while she kneads dough, spreads cheese, cooks ground lamb, rolls out pastry dough, and pours endless rounds of coffee. She tells a story that had a profound effect on her family. After sixteen years in the States, during which she was unable to afford a trip to her West Bank hometown of al-Birah for herself and the children, she and all but one daughter boarded a Pan Am jet in June 1987 for the long-awaited reunion with her parents and other relatives she had not seen for years. When they arrived at Tel Aviv's Ben-Gurion Airport, however, Israeli airport authorities would not let them in the country. They were held at the airport for twelve hours before being put on a plane back to the United States. The American-Arab Anti-Discrimination Committee took up the case, as one among several examples of such Israeli treatment of Palestinian Americans, and the case received considerable publicity. Israel allowed the family entry a month later, but Hamad is out a lot of money, having paid for five round trips twice over.

The conversation in Hamad's aromatic kitchen turns to bringing up children according to strict rules in America's loose environment. None of her three daughters has ever been allowed to date, go to parties, or wear short skirts or sleeveless dresses. Two of her girls are now married to men from Hamad's hometown whom she and the girls jointly selected. The boys, over whom Hamad cannot exercise as close control, are not allowed to bring girls into the house.

"We were different from everybody," her daughter Fadwa Hasan, who uses her father's surname, acknowledges without rancor. She is a beautiful young lady. Dark wavy hair falls to her shoulders and, despite very light skin, her eyes are large and dark. She had American friends growing up, but even now that she is married and working, she encounters people who "can't believe I was born and raised here because I really follow my religion."

The older son, Nader, a college student, says he had a "rebellious period" a few years before when he chafed under the restrictions. But he accepts them now with only mild, teasing protest to his mother. They seem to have a constant affectionate tug of war on this. Nader is very good looking and apparently does not lack for girlfriends, but Hamad disapproves. "She's real old-fashioned, you know," Nader says in front of his mother. "I mean, I'm not a big dater or anything, but—"

"Oh, yeah," says Fadwa ironically.

"I mean I don't bring girls here," Nader clarifies. "She doesn't meet any girls, anything like that. Girl calls me, she's kind of nasty." The whole kitchen, including Hamad, breaks up in laughter

"They're gonna get this picture of me being this Palestinian loose guy," Nader says to more laughter.

"I never said that," Hamad claims. There is more kidding; Hamad gives as good as she gets, and Nader seems to hide nothing. They all tell the story of how Hamad threw Nader out of the house and sent him to stay with relatives for three days a few years before when, as part of a high school victory celebration, he got a mohawk haircut and pierced his ear.

After a while Hamad, still making countless lamb pastries, begins to talk in a serious vein about being on her own and raising five children alone. "I never had a job before, I never worked, I never did anything," she says, remembering her first job-hunting effort when her youngest, Nael, was three.

I started looking for a job. "Did you have any experience?" "No." "Are you an American citizen?" "Yes." "Do you have proof?" At one point, I went to the employment agency, they asked to see my citizenship, and I think it was the last straw I want to take, so I said, "You carry yours with you?" She said, "Well, of course not." I said, "Well, why not?" She said, "Well, because." I said, "It's because you don't have an accent and I have an accent." But once I start working, I never had a problem with the people I work with. I start from the worst job in the bank, which is called lock box. I can read and write better English than I speak.

The kids affirm this. They often correct her spoken English.

This is obviously a very close and loving family. Hamad is proud of her children and doesn't mind indicating a little pride in herself. "I tried even harder than I would have if I had a husband," she remarks. "I always felt very proud of the kids. They were like my jewels, like when I take them with me—" She cannot finish because she is crying. She rolls out dough more industriously for a moment, and then Fadwa says, "You don't have to get emotional, Mom." Everyone laughs, and the moment passes.

The kids begin to drift away, off with friends or to jobs, and the kitchen is quieter, although Hamad still talks on. She is one of those very warm people who make a stranger feel they have known each other for years, a very down-to-earth person who speaks freely and never hesitates to tell you what's on her mind. She talks about the Israelis, about the occupation, about trying to be an American, about wanting to go home, and always about her kids, her jewels. She is not a political sophisticate, but she is a wise woman.

When lunch is finally ready, she sits down for the first time in hours. It is delicious; the *safiha*, a spicy ground lamb rolled in pastry, is better even than it looked and smelled in preparation, and served with yogurt and a salad it makes a hearty meal. For dessert there is a cheese-filled pastry called *warbad*. Hamad spent much of the morning making that. It turns out she made the cheese herself the night before. And the yogurt too, from scratch.

As the afternoon winds down, the phone rings. It is a girl calling for Nader. Hamad is curt: "No, sorry, he's out, and he won't be back until late." Will Hamad have him return the call? "If I'm up when he gets back." Click.

The alienation from American society expressed by the young American-born Palestinians Nabil and Dina Khoury is not typical of second-generation Palestinians in the United States, but the affinity they feel for the Palestinian cause clearly is. Until recently, the conventional wisdom about the American-born children of immigrants held that they rejected their parents' ethnicity in an effort to appear wholly American. But the political bonds felt by most Palestinians are so strong that only a small number of second-generation Palestinian Americans have taken this route.

Most are able to handle their dual identities comfortably, for two principal reasons: the increasing ethnic consciousness in American society as a result of growing ethnic diversity throughout the country has overturned the old conventional wisdom about the second generation, and the heightened visibility of the Palestinian struggle as a political issue has tended to make Palestinians more assertive about their Palestinianness.

The very tendency in America to categorize by ethnic background that Mohammad Busailah, the retired tobacco executive, complained kept him from truly integrating in American society has also tended to ease the burden of ethnicity for American-born Palestinians. Nader Hasan, the son of Nawal Hamad, says that among his friends "everybody's sort of looking to where their heritage is." Roots have become important to young people now and, according to Hasan, "it's sort of prestigious" to be able to speak a language other than English.

The younger generation's ability to balance two identities seems to depend heavily on their parents and on whether parents force feed Palestinian culture to the children. It seems often to be the case that when parents impose a strictly Palestinian culture on children, they produce children who are severely alienated from American society and often cannot quite fit in with Palestinian society either. This seems to be a problem more in Chicago, and perhaps in Detroit, where Palestinians tend more frequently to cluster in neighborhoods, than elsewhere in the country, where such ghettoization of Palestinians is unusual. Sociologist Louise Cainkar has found that Muslim Palestinian girls born and raised in Chicago "face many challenges mediating the American culture they identify with and the Palestinian culture to which their compliance is expected. By adulthood, they find themselves marginal members of both American and Palestinian societies." Their enforced isolation from American society as a result of their traditional upbringing keeps them outside the American mainstream, while at the same time members of the immigrant community see them as "culturally deficient."[17]

Most Palestinian parents in this country seem to make an effort not to force their culture and identity on their children but to allow them to make their own choices. This is particularly true with the large numbers of Palestinians married to Americans of non-Arab ancestry. But even where both parents are Palestinian, there usually seems to be an awareness that the children are growing up in a non-Palestinian culture and must adjust to it even if they maintain a Palestinian consciousness. The result seems to be a generation of Palestinian youngsters who can identify with America without losing their pride in their heritage or their interest in the Palestinian cause.

"I was raised to be in the middle," says Hanan T., the teenaged San Francisco-born daughter of parents from Nablus and Bethlehem, "between those who totally reject the fact that they're Palestinian and those who are so totally involved that they don't fit in here." Hanan is the daughter of Rafiq and Amal T., a grocer and a teacher who both found themselves exiled from their West Bank homes when Israel refused to renew their identity cards during studies in the United States in the early 1970s. Both parents feel they are here not by choice but because they have to be, and Hanan has been raised with an acute consciousness of being Palestinian and being dispossessed. Reflecting her parents' sentiments, she identifies as a Palestinian first. She knows Palestinian young people who deny being Palestinian but says, "That's insane to me. That's the last thing I'd do."

But Hanan is also totally an American. Her best friends at school are non-Arab, and she takes part in extracurricular activities at school. She is as comfortable in a school performance of an American musical as she is performing a *dabkha*, a Palestinian folk dance, at the local Arab Cultural Center. When asked if she would like to live in Palestine if there is an independent state, she is surprised at first because she has never thought about it. Her personal horizons are American.

Susan Ziadeh, who is a project director at AMIDEAST in Washington, D.C., working on a program to help strengthen political institutions in the Arab world, believes that for Palestinian Americans, because of their dispossession, the "sense of ethnicity is so important to them that their need to pass it on to their children is probably a little bit more heightened than with other peoples." But it is equally important, Ziadeh believes, not to force it on the children. Her parents, both Christians from Ramallah—her father is the noted Islamic scholar Farhat Ziadeh—"didn't impose things on us, they just taught us to enjoy those aspects of our culture that were important. The identity came to grow on us because we liked Arabic music, we liked Arabic food, we liked dressing up in Arabic costumes when there was something at school."

The children were also encouraged to participate with other non-Arab Americans in various youth activities. Ziadeh was not allowed to date in high school—a stricture that she considered at the time "just devastating, embarrassment upon embarrassment"—but she was allowed the freedom to attend parties at which boys were present, a kind of happy middle ground between America's total freedom and the restrictions of traditional Palestinians. It is foolish, Ziadeh believes, to "raise a child totally alienated from his own environment, because eventually he has to interact with that environment."

Nawal Hamad's experience with her five children gives a striking picture of how, at least superficially, differences in upbringing can produce differences in outlook. When Hamad was divorced and forced to go to work, her youngest child, Nael, was placed in nursery school at age three. The other children had spent their preschool years at home with Hamad. As a result, Nael likes peanut butter and jelly and drinks milk, while the other children have never become accustomed to either. The other children understand Arabic, but to Nael "it's noise." In addition, Hamad never had as much chance to familiarize Nael with his Palestinian heritage. Because they had stayed home with her before starting school, she says, the other children "had a feeling of being Palestinian."

Ironically, the Israelis succeeded in raising Nael's Palestinian consciousness. He has been acutely aware of being a Palestinian since Israel turned the family away at Ben-Gurion Airport on a trip to Hamad's hometown in 1987. The others were also reminded that no Palestinian can lose that identity altogether. "When I'd say I'm an American," Nael's brother Nader says, "I used to think big." But, despite being born and raised in the United States, in Israel because "my name is different, I have a different background, they spit on my passport." The Israeli soldier who detained and interrogated them, Nader says, referred to them repeatedly as "you Americans," but "here we were getting in trouble for being Palestinians."

The *intifada* in the West Bank and Gaza has also had a marked consciousness-raising effect among Palestinian youngsters in this country. At the height of television coverage of the uprising, countless parents found teenaged children who usually never watched anything but MTV wandering in during news broadcasts to observe their West Bank-Gaza peers fighting Israeli soldiers. Fuad Mogannam, who has been in San Francisco for over forty years, believes that because of the prominence of the Palestinian issue in the news, both before and since the *intifada*, his five children, now grown, are "more Palestinian than I am."

Ghassan Bishara, Washington correspondent for the Jerusalem Arabic-language newspaper *al-Fajr*, finds that the Palestinians' diminished use of terrorism has made it easier for Palestinian-American youngsters to identify with their Palestinian heritage. Now, he says, for the past few years and particularly since the *intifada*, Palestinians are more often portrayed in the American press as guerrillas than as terrorists, not desirous of throwing Israelis into the sea but merely of having a state of their own, and young Americans can identify with that goal. The effect has been obvious on Bishara's own young daughter. Born of a Swedish-American mother, his daughter is very much interested in politics, even as a pre-teen, and her interest encompasses the Palestinian issue, with which she can comfortably identify. Nowadays, Bishara says, "there isn't that reason for my daughter or for other Palestinian daughters to shy away from the fact that they are Palestinians. My daughter doesn't mind it at all. She brags about it."

Omar Kader is about as American as they come, with the kind of easy-going openness and self-confidence, an indefinable style, that is unmistakably American. He is an imposing man physically, quite tall and broad although not overweight, with an expansive personality to match. He is warm and engaging, always smiling. The most noticeable things about him are his enthusiasm—about being an American, about being a Palestinian, about life in general—and his sense of humor. Kader runs a successful company that designs security systems for large installations, systems designed chiefly to thwart terrorist attacks, and he is not unaware of the nice irony of a Palestinian specializing in counterterrorist techniques. He did his doctoral dissertation on terrorism and is often called on for television commentary on the issue. Before establishing his own business, Kader served as executive director of the American-Arab Anti-Discrimination Committee from 1984 to 1985.

Born and raised in Provo, Utah, Kader grew up being called "nigger," because of his name rather than his coloring. His was the only Palestinian family in the area, and they were a novelty. His family is from the small village of Shufat, originally just outside Jerusalem but incorporated by Israel into the Jerusalem city limits after 1967. Kader's father first came to this country in about 1910 as a very young man and worked as a peddler, then a factory worker before making his way to Utah and buying a small farm. Eventually, he went back to Shufat to marry, and after bringing his wife to the United States, they raised eight children on the farm. Omar was number five.

They gave the children a strict Muslim upbringing, although it did not take entirely on Omar. When Kader's father took him back to Shufat at age eighteen and arranged a marriage for Omar with his first cousin, he backed out and returned to the States. Later he converted to the Mormon religion. But the important things about growing up Palestinian in the United States definitely rubbed off. "I've inherited a wonderful tradition of Utah Palestinian," he says. "It's a wonderful tradition out there of simplicity and responsibility and discipline, and I took it seriously—that if you work hard, you get rewards."

His Palestinian father's contribution to the "tradition of Utah Palestinian" made him a good American. "He was really a very generous, very patriotic man," Kader recalls.

> We grew up always giving, locally. Every time there was a crop—say I'd load up the cherries to take them down to the rail station to sell them—we always had to go by the fire station, the police station, and the state mental hospital and do drops. Every day, all summer. When I got ready to do my dad's will for him, I said, "Say you should pass on and you don't have a will, then the government taxes us higher." He said, "Who's going to pay for defense, who's going to pave the roads, and who's going to pay for the police? You got to pay taxes." When I got drafted, he had tears in his eyes for joy, that America thought enough of Moses Kader's son to take him.

Being a good American was no different from being a good Palestinian in his father's eyes. They were all raised to be proud of their heritage. "I mean, we were Palestinian Muslims. Don't you wish you could be one?" Kader says, laughing. "That's the attitude we grew up with." This is where his enthusiasm for his roots shows through. He is so enthusiastic in fact that he believes American hearts and minds could be won if every Palestinian American just invited a friend in for Palestinian food. "Really. Palestinian cuisine, and the culture, are the most charming, gracious, wonderfully explanatory—" he doesn't finish because he has remembered something else—"the needlework! My mother makes beautiful embroidery. If people could see that kind of culture!"

Kader has an interesting faith in American sophistication and in the power of ideas in this materialistic, image-conscious society. "This is a country of ideas. Ideas rule. Even unpopular people with good ideas rule." He mentions an American politician who he says is "an SOB in everybody's book. But he's bright, he's bright. His ideas carry the day." The same could apply to the Palestinians. Many Palestinian Americans believe that Yasir Arafat presents a poor image for Palestinians in the American media because of his appearance, but Kader dismisses the notion that Americans will listen only if the speaker is personally attractive. Edward Said, the leading American spokesmen for the Palestinians and a very good looking man, could look like Arafat, Kader says, and lose none of his popularity and persuasiveness, "because he's a brilliant theoretical, descriptive writer."

Kader knows how it is to get ideas across. He has run political campaigns and believes the clash of ideas is what democracy is all about. "This democracy works!" he says with renewed enthusiasm. "But you've got to know how to make it work. I just know that the Harry Truman, Barry Goldwater, seat-of-the-pants, American, tell-it-like-it-is is admired in this country. You've just got to jump in and be willing to compete." Palestinians, he believes, have not been successful at competing in the American arena.

Kader has a keen political and public relations sense, and he has a better understanding than most Palestinians of what works with Americans and—particularly rare among Palestinians—of the fears and psychoses that motivate Jews and Israelis. There is a logical progression to his ideas. "I'm convinced that the clash of ideas is the arena that we [Palestinians] belong in," he begins, "because we never lose an argument when it comes to morality, justice, human rights." Palestinians, he feels, stand on the high ground when the discussion is about the justice of Palestinian dispossession, the morality of the Palestinian struggle for independence and their fight for human rights. "That's why eventually this helium balloon's going to come down to earth," he continues. "The Israelis are going to have to deal with us. Their fear is that when they come down to reality, they'll have to go away. They don't have to go away! We'll deal with them, we recognize them. Just define your boundaries and work with us. Just learn to live with us. We're your equals." He pauses for a long moment. "And that's the saddest part about it all, that Jews do not accept us as equals."

Does he think Jews are racist or are they fearful, are they so insecure after centuries of persecution that they cannot recognize Israel's strength? "Fear is the underlying motive," he answers unhesitatingly. "But the manifestation of that fear is racism and bigotry. And this is where I fault Palestinians. Palestinians don't understand that Israelis and Jews are afraid of Palestinians. They don't hate us, they *fear* us." All of his points are made emphatically, and the word fear is heavily emphasized. What should Palestinians do about that? Again without hesitation: "Sympathize with them. Sit down with Holocaust victims and say, 'Tell us the story of the destruction of your family. Tell me everything about being Jewish. Tell me about it! Educate me! And then let me tell you about my little village of Shufat.' Every discussion I've ever had that started out like that ended up talking about Palestinian refugees and sympathy."

The problem for Palestinians, Kader realizes—speaking with both a Palestinian's profound understanding and an American's distance and perspective—is that they are "so persecuted. It's hard to take a victim and say, 'This other person's more of a victim than you.' Pain is hard to measure." This leads him into a discussion of victimhood and the language of losers, leading full circle to why Palestinians have not won the battle of ideas in which he thinks they have a natural advantage. Throughout, he speaks alternately of Palestinians as "we" and as "they," unconsciously highlighting the duality of his Palestinian-American identity.

> Palestinians have been victims for so long that they have come to acculturate the attributes of victimhood. We get together and see who can tell the worst story of discrimination, of rejection. The person who comes in with the good news is some kind of a Pollyanna with his head in the clouds. And [the response is that] this Pollyanna just hasn't been to the refugee camps, you haven't seen the sadness going on. Well, for those of us who are eternal optimists, I see that, and there's hope. We can bring them out of it. All we have to do is organize. All we have to do is organize and we'll win. Americans don't like losers. They love underdogs, but not loser underdogs. You've got to be a winner underdog and have a positive outlook. We glory in suffering, we glory in persecution, and I think that's wrong.

He has the optimistic, can-do approach of an American, but like most Palestinian Americans, Kader realizes that the battle for Palestinian rights, for Palestinian independence and statehood, will be won in the United States if it is won at all. And it will only be won, he believes, by talking to Americans in a language they understand.

About that duality—can he separate being an American from being a Palestinian? Very definitely, he says, but they are still interlinked. The struggle for Palestinian statehood, Kader says, "is an intellectual commitment to me. It's a matter of fairness and justice. It's based on American values, getting a Palestinian state. It's in the American national interest, and it's justice. It's just an American, Jeffersonian, constitutional, Bill of Rights issue." Would he live in a Palestinian state? "Hell no. There isn't any greater country in the world than America. Why would I give that up?" But how does he feel about being Palestinian, how does he feel when he is on Palestinian soil? "It's just wonderful because there's just something about breathing in from every pore the history, the feeling that this is where you belong because your roots are here."

How will he reconcile his twin identities when—Kader himself, the eternal optimist, would say "when" rather than "if"—there is a Palestinian state in the West Bank and Gaza? "If somebody said 'I want to go back,' I'd contribute to buy him a ticket. I'll even contribute to build nice settlements and things like that, and I'll go visit them. And I'll make damn sure the Israelis never take it away, by influencing American public policy, and I'll go lobby Congress for foreign aid as an American. You know, we have an obligation as Americans to the Palestinians because we as Americans"— he begins to tap a finger on the table, hard, in rhythm with his last few words—"have caused the demise of the Palestinians to fester."

NOTES

[1] Turki, *Soul in Exile*, p. 45.

[2] Alixa Naff, *Becoming American: The Early Arab Immigrant Experience* (Carbondale, IL: Southern Illinois University Press, 1985), p. 13.

[3] Cainkar, *Palestinian Women*, p. 58, extrapolates a 1988 figure from an unofficial 1984 Census Bureau estimate by adding a specific number of Palestinians every year for four years. Adding 6,997 Palestinians a year to the Census Bureau's 1984 estimate of 87,700, Cainkar arrives at a rounded figure of 115,000 in 1988. If one adds 6,997 Palestinians every year for eight more years (1985-1992), the 1992 total would be 144,000. These figures are probably low, however; the Census Bureau report, for instance, does not take account of Palestinians who immigrated before 1940 or their descendants. Extrapolating from census figures for Palestinian Americans cited in Naff, *Becoming American*, p. 117, would yield a total of 40,000-45,000 pre-1940 immigrants and descendants. These additional numbers could raise the total Palestinian-American population in 1992 to as high as 189,000. Immigration statistics are also lacking. Early in the twentieth century, Palestinians were counted together with Syrians and Lebanese under a catchall category called "Turks" or "Syrians." The Immigration and Naturalization Service did carry a "Palestinian" category based on country of birth for many years, but this was dropped after 1967, the year Israel occupied the West Bank and Gaza. This was also the year in which relatively large-scale Palestinian immigration to this country began. Figures for Palestinian immigration are now buried in statistics for other Arab countries.

[4] Elias H. Tuma in "The Palestinians in America," *The Link* 14, no. 3 (July-August 1981): 1-14, cited in Gregory Orfalea, *Before the Flames: A*

Quest for the History of Arab Americans (Austin: University of Texas Press, 1988), p. 325, note 2, uses a figure of 110,200 in 1981. Janet Abu-Lughod, "The Demographic War for Palestine," *The Link* (1986), cited in Cainkar, *Palestinian Women*, p. 58, gives a figure of 108,000 in 1983. *The Palestinian Statistical Abstract for 1983* (Damascus: Palestinian Central Bureau of Statistics, 1984), cited in Laurie A. Brand, *Palestinians in the Arab World: Institution Building and the Search for a State* (New York: Columbia University Press, 1988), p. 9, gives a figure of 130,000 in 1986. This last figure does not include Palestinians who immigrated before 1948 or their descendants. Each of these figures, extrapolated to 1992, would yield a total between 175,000 and 200,000.

[5] Orfalea, *Before the Flames*, p. 325, note 2, estimates that two-thirds of the immigrants from Jordan since 1967 and half those from Lebanon, Syria, Iraq, and the Persian Gulf states in the same period have been Palestinians. Using these assumptions, the number of Palestinian immigrants from 1968 through 1985 (the last year for which Orfalea gives immigration figures) would be 96,600.

[6] Cited in Naff, *Becoming American*, p. 77.

[7] Philip K. Hitti, *The Syrians in America* (New York: George H. Doran Company, 1924), p. 48.

[8] Jackson Diehl, "7,000 Palestinians With U.S. Passports Caught in Uprising," *Washington Post* (September 16, 1989).

[9] Orfalea, *Before the Flames*, pp. 141-142.

[10] The preceding paragraphs are based on an interview with Nabil and Dina Khoury, as well as on a letter to the author from Dina Khoury, January 16, 1990.

[11] *International Human Rights Law and Israel's Efforts to Suppress the Palestinian Uprising: 1988 Report of the National Lawyers Guild* (New York: National Lawyers Guild, 1989), pp. 32-33.

[12] Hisham Milhim, "Edward Said on PLO Dealings With United States," Kuwait *Al-Qabas* (October 7, 1989), in FBIS-NES-89-201 (October 19, 1989): 1-6.

[13] Fouad Moughrabi and Pat El-Nazer, "What Do Palestinian Americans Think? Results of a Public Opinion Survey," *Journal of Palestine Studies* 72 (Summer 1989): 93.

[14] Information from Arab-American Institute, Washington, D.C., by phone, July 29, 1988.

[15] Cainkar, *Palestinian Women in the United States*, pp. pp. 135-136.

[16] Ibid., p. 184

[17] Ibid., pp. 168-169.

5   West Bank U.S.A.

It is in our blood to come here. We say that when a baby is born from Ramallah or from Deir Dibwan, the first word he says is "America."

Fuad Mogannam
San Francisco businessman

We have made a study, and we came up with a population of 7,700 or very close to it. Half are in Deir Dibwan and half are outside of Deir Dibwan, the majority in the U.S.A.

Hazem Monsour
Albuquerque jeweler

George Salem has been interested in politics since he was in school running for student council president—against the wishes of his non-political parents. Now a Washington, D.C., attorney and Republican activist who served as Solicitor of Labor during the administration of President Ronald Reagan, Salem was a young teenager when the founding of the PLO and the Israeli occupation brought some focus to the Palestinian struggle, and so he never personally experienced the dilemma that an older generation of Palestinian immigrants from Ramallah faced about whether to identify as a political Palestinian or a cultural Ramallite.

The Ramallah community in this country is amazingly close knit. A federation representing the entire community, the American Federation of Ramallah Palestine, was formed in 1958, and every American city with a sizable Ramallah population has a Ramallah club, a community center where social and cultural events are held. Often Ramallites live together in neighborhood clusters. The federation has an annual convention that is both a major social event and a business/political meeting. Begun originally with the intent of bringing young Ramallites to a setting where they could meet and eventually marry other Ramallites—in the words of George Salem, to "continue the lineage"—the annual convention is considered essentially a family reunion. Salem and others believe a majority of young

Ramallites still do marry others from Ramallah families; most of the remainder tend still to marry other Palestinians or other Arabs. For Ramallites and chain immigrants from other towns, intermarriage with non-Arabs is much less common than is true among Palestinian Americans in general.

The Ramallah federation has helped to preserve Palestinian identity in both a cultural and a political sense, although politicization has been a gradual process over the years. According to George Salem, who grew up in Jacksonville, Florida, with thirteen Ramallah families living within a three-block radius of his house, Ramallah people did not have a broad Palestinian identity in the 1950s and early '60s. "It was more of a village consciousness," he says. "We knew we were from Ramallah; we didn't really know whether it was Jordan or Palestine or what."

At first, the major focus of the Ramallah federation was on Ramallites in the United States rather than on the Palestinian problem as a whole. Originally, says Susan Ziadeh, the daughter of a Ramallah family, the federation was "a way of socially keeping the Ramallah families together, providing a place where once a year they meet, they see classmates, they see family, they see friends, the young people have a chance to interact. And it was seen as a way of providing some sort of organizational instrument whereby the Ramallah people here in America could have a society that looked out for their needs. Their focus was here."

The awareness of being Palestinian rather than Ramallite and of the Palestinian issue as something broader than the Ramallah community in America did not come until the mid-1960s with the formation of the PLO and the Israeli occupation. Even then, Ziadeh says, although Ramallites began to conclude that they "could no longer afford the luxury of not being political," the shift was gradual and did not translate into political activism until the late 1970s. In the last decade, however, she believes, there has been a "tremendous" shift within the federation toward greater politicization and a greater community awareness—a heightened sense of the need to work not merely for Ramallites in the United States but for Palestinians everywhere.

There is still some argument over how explicitly political the federation should be. George Salem's own immigrant parents and most of their peers made a deliberate effort to steer away from political issues in the 1950s "because of the volatile politics of the region for centuries and the fact that occupiers had just taken over Palestine." Many members of this old guard still try to insist that the federation be a primarily social body.

But inevitably, politics have intervened. The word "Palestine" was added to the federation's name in the 1970s, an unmistakable political statement. Salameh Zanayed, who immigrated to the United States in 1961 and owns a travel agency in Chicago, was involved in politicizing the organization when he was federation president in 1975. It was a period, he says, that was the turning point of the federation's existence. He delivered a speech, he recalls, saying that the federation had "two obligations, an internal obligation and an external obligation. The internal obligation is to keep our youth together, keep our heritage, our culture. And we have an external obligation, to be Palestinian and stand up with other Palestinian groups."

The federation has formally expressed its support for the PLO, and two of its members serve on the PLO's legislative arm, the Palestine National Council. Samir Totah, a Berkeley pharmacist, was selected by the PLO leadership in 1985 when he was federation president, and Jawad George, a Washington, D.C., attorney, also represents Ramallah. In 1988 the federation elected two others, Salameh Zanayed and Hanna Ajluni, a leader of Detroit's Ramallah community and executive editor of *Hathihe Ramallah* magazine, to serve in the next Council session.[1]

Despite its support for the PLO, the federation tries to avoid becoming involved in intra-PLO politics by not supporting one PLO faction or another. Although many individuals are supporters of Fatah or other factions, they know enough, according to Karim Ajluni, who was also involved in formalizing the federation's turn to a more political outlook in the 1970s, to mute their views when attending a federation function. Ajluni likens the federation's political neutrality to Ramallah's position in the past as a Christian town surrounded by Muslim villages; although there have rarely been sectarian divisions between Palestinian Christians and Muslims, it was always thought best for Ramallah to avoid favoring any particular Muslim town. So with the federation and PLO politics.

George Salem's family has a long history in this country. His grandfather first came before World War I as a teenager and enlisted in the U.S. Army during that war. Working as a peddler before and for several years after the war, he was able to save enough money to buy real estate throughout Palestine. He became quite prosperous, and by 1948, having returned home and become *mukhtar* of Ramallah, he owned considerable property on the main street in Haifa, the building that housed the electric authority in Jerusalem, and thousands of dunams* of agricultural and citrus land near Jaffa and Jericho, as well as several businesses in Ramallah. All the property in areas of Palestine that came under Israeli control in 1948, constituting the bulk of his holdings, was lost, and in his fifties he returned to the United States to begin peddling again with nothing but the cash from a $10,000 life insurance policy in his pocket. He had been a multimillionaire.

His sons, one of them George Salem's father, came with him on student visas and settled in Florida. Salem's father married a young woman from Ramallah whose family immigrated in 1950, and George was born in 1953.

---

* A dunam equals 1,000 square meters.

He is himself married to a Ramallite whom he met at a Ramallah federation convention. Their three young children are not growing up in quite the insular setting in which Salem himself was raised, but he and his wife speak Arabic to the children and socialize with other Arab families so that the youngsters will absorb Arab and Palestinian values and culture.

Although many and by some accounts a majority of Palestinians in the United States are Republican, Salem was unique in his close association with the Reagan administration, which had a strong pro-Israeli bent. Salem himself does not see this as unusual. He acknowledges disappointment with Reagan policy on Israel and the Palestinians, but he does not think it was much different from the policy of past administrations. He blames the increase in aid to Israel on Congress and believes Congress would have had a much freer hand to bestow massive amounts of aid on Israel and restrict arms sales to Arab countries under a Democratic president.

Salem openly expresses his support for the PLO as the legitimate representative of the Palestinian people, and he advocates establishment of an independent Palestinian state in the West Bank and Gaza—in opposition to the policies of both the Reagan and the Bush administrations. But he feels that by working on the inside he was able to advance the Palestinian cause in small ways. He assisted, for instance, in arranging the meeting in March 1988 between Secretary of State George Shultz and Palestinian Americans Edward Said and Ibrahim Abu-Lughod, Shultz's only official meeting with Palestinians during his six years in office. Most important, Salem believes that, as the first Palestinian American to win a presidential appointment requiring Senate confirmation, he was able both to help improve the Palestinian image and to encourage other Palestinians to strive for public service.

The Ramallah community's tight bonds and its sheer size have inevitably aroused some antagonism among other Palestinians. Immigrants from other West Bank towns sometimes criticize the Ramallites' supposed lack of political interest in the Palestinian cause. They have become too comfortable in the United States, is the charge, have forgotten their people's problem, and only maintain their ties in order to find a spouse. Ramallites dismiss the criticism as mere jealousy by other immigrants who have only in recent years been able to emulate the Ramallah community with town associations of their own.

Others criticize all the chain immigrants, those from the smaller West Bank villages as well as Ramallites, for a clannishness that is seen as excessive and damaging to Palestinian unity. The belief is that because their solidarity is town- rather than nation-centered, or because they came here originally for economic rather than political reasons, or because they have comfortably assimilated in American society, the chain immigrants are not properly dedicated to the cause or at best have had no experience of the suffering that other Palestinians, living either in refugee camps or under Israeli occupation, endure.

Some of this criticism is disingenuous, coming from 1948 refugees or their children who suffer the emotional turmoil of exile and cannot imagine that anyone who has not endured precisely what they have, who chose to leave Palestine voluntarily for whatever reason, can possibly be suffering. Those who criticize the chain immigrants for living the easy life in the United States tend often to be living in comfort themselves. On the other hand, the criticism has elements of truth in it. Among Palestinians in this country, there is no question that the most clannish, the most inclined to live together in neighborhood clusters, the most likely to impose a strict upbringing on their children, the most likely to demand that children marry fellow townsmen or at least not marry outside the Palestinian community, are chain immigrants, whether Muslim or Christian. It is also true, in a paradoxical way, that chain immigrants, having more often come for economic reasons and having been in the United States long enough to settle in, albeit often in their own neighborhood enclaves, tend to be more content here than many other Palestinians.

Ramallites and most of the other chain immigrants openly acknowledge their clannishness. "If I married a girl from another town, say Bir Zeit, she would be considered a stranger," says Fuad Mogannam. Even though Bir Zeit is largely a Christian town? "Yes. It has nothing to do with religion," he says. "If you marry a Lebanese, in the eyes of the Ramallah people, they're a foreigner. But, for instance, there are 350 Mogannams in the San Francisco Bay area. If I was to make a calendar of events for a whole year, I would not be able to go see them all. So why do I need to go somewhere else? You can multiply the Mogannams by the Ramallah people—six, seven thousand Ramallah people [in the Bay area]. Why do I have to go to the Palestinian community or the American community?" Three of Mogannam's four sons are married to Mogannams. The fourth married into another Ramallah family.

A great many Ramallites do indeed marry non-Ramallites and even non-Palestinians. They are not ostracized, but their marriages are the topic of much gossip, for they are considered to have gone outside the fold. "The Ramallah people are so chauvinistic," complains one young Ramallite in confidence. "You get Ramallah people together, and the first thing they ask is what clan are you from?" Although a great many Christians from the towns of Ramla and Lydda, which were captured by Israel in 1948, settled in Ramallah forty years ago and now think of themselves as Ramallites, this young person notes, the original Ramallah people still regard them as not from the tribe. "I get so angry with them. I tell them, 'You're here and they're there. Who's the one who is the protector of the land? Who's the one who is maintaining everything that's going on there? It's them; it's not you.' But they have difficulty with this."

Ramallites are not alone in their insularity. Many Palestinians from the other small West Bank villages that have been involved in a chain migration to the United States are just as closed to the outside—by choice. Freddie Ahmad, for instance, a young American-born pharmacist from a Beit Hanina family, says he was so insulated growing up among other Beit Haninans in Dearborn, Michigan, that he never even experienced ethnic prejudice until he graduated from college and was applying for an internship. This is particularly remarkable in view of Dearborn's reputation for severe anti-Arab prejudice. Arabs who work in the auto manufacturing plants there are a very visible ethnic population, and almost all Palestinians who grew up there report being called "camel jockey," "sand nigger," and various other epithets throughout their childhood. Dearborn currently has a mayor who ran on an explicitly anti-Arab platform.

Freddie Ahmad avoided all of this discrimination because he lived in so closely knit a community. He has since moved away to Brooklyn, where he owns a pharmacy and in 1988 won a Pharmacist of the Year award for the New York City area from a pharmaceutical company for his work with diabetic patients. But he believes that Muslims cannot truly assimilate in American society. He never did himself, and he does not expect that his seven young children ever will. "Our culture does not allow it."

Mohamed Odetalla is another young Beit Haninan who would agree. Born in Beit Hanina and brought here at the age of seven after the 1967 war, he grew up in Dearborn and began calling himself Mike outside the Arab community to make it easier for Americans and to try to avoid discrimination. He lives in a non-Arab suburb of Detroit now, and he and his father operate a grocery and liquor store that serves a non-Arab neighborhood made up chiefly of auto workers. But he is very strong on the importance of maintaining a Palestinian culture. His wife Sana is a cousin several times removed whose family left Lifta, a village neighboring Beit Hanina, in 1948. He believes—"one hundred percent," he says—that his children should marry Palestinians.

Marriage seems to be the issue, in fact, that most decisively separates the social attitudes of chain immigrants from those of other Palestinian Americans. Among Palestinians who migrate independently, intermarriage with non-Palestinians and non-Arabs is very common, even among the most fervent Palestinian nationalists (of eighty-four currently married interview subjects in this sample, twenty-seven do not have Palestinian or Arab spouses). But intermarriage seems to be rare among chain immigrants. "I married a Palestinian," says Odetalla, "all my brothers married Palestinians, for the simple fact that it's easier to get along with somebody of your own culture, your own heritage. And I want to perpetuate the Palestinian cause until I believe it's done and over with. If my son would marry a non-Palestinian, I would really believe it would sort of dissolve."

Bahjat K., who considers himself a keen observer of the Palestinian community throughout the world, believes that the chain immigrants' clannish village mentality no longer exists among Palestinians anywhere else. He finds these West Bank immigrants—all but the most recent of them—to be politically unsophisticated, in the sense of being doctrinaire and inflexible, because they have not shared the experiences of Palestinians living under occupation or in the Arab world and therefore have not undergone the political maturation process that has occurred elsewhere in the Palestinian community. "A lot of them have not really experienced some of the things that go into making up the modern Palestinian political consciousness."

The 1948 refugees underwent a profound social transformation as a result of their expulsion and the total destruction of their societal structures, Bahjat points out. "They were uprooted from the village, the whole village society was shattered. You manage to get what you can get through education, merit, politics—which are the values that I read in modern Palestinian political culture. They're not the values of the village." Society has also changed on the West Bank as a result of the occupation, he feels, leaving the chain immigrants in this country behind, both politically and socially. "The old country has changed," he says, speaking specifically of the West Bank. "The old country has been revolutionized by the occupation and unemployment, working in Israel, and working in the Gulf, and the destruction of families, and the urbanization of Ramallah, and fifty things that have happened in the past twenty years that have bypassed these people. The only place that some of these villages exist is in the minds of these people who came out of them."

Bahjat's case is somewhat overstated. While it is true that the chain immigrants tend more often than other Palestinians in this country not to be educated and to live and work in the kind of circumstances that require no education and none of the political and social interactions that naturally serve to broaden horizons, it is inaccurate to assume that all chain immigrants are uneducated and therefore socially or politically unsophisticated. It is also incorrect to assume that political sophistication comes only with suffering. The fact that someone has not had a direct experience of expulsion, or of living in a refugee camp, or of Israeli air raids or Syrian artillery attacks or imprisonment in an Israeli jail does not make him less politically sophisticated.

There is no question, on the other hand, that segments of the chain immigrant population—particularly those who live in neighborhood clusters in Chicago or in the Detroit area—live in a culturally frozen environment, as Bahjat K. notes. Essa Sackllah, a Ramallite born and raised in Dearborn who now owns a delicatessen in Houston, finds that many Ramallah people here are "more old country than the old country" because this is for them the best way to preserve their identity. "My parents came here in 1967," says Fadi Zanayed, another Ramallite who immigrated at the age of six and is now an attorney in Chicago, "and I think for them the Palestinian culture froze." Customs may have changed at home in the intervening decades, but the customs they learned there and brought with them are "the way they knew it back then. This is the way they lived all the time, and this is the way it's going to be."

Suhail Miari, the director of the United Holy Land Fund, has observed a similar cultural inertness in most of the chain immigrant groups in Chicago. "They don't know," he says, "that the people there have adjusted to a new social fabric. Change is faster there, but they don't accept that. Society develops, but when they come here, they are a little bit reluctant because they face something completely different and they don't want to take all of it. They want to hold whatever they brought with them."

Perhaps the greatest disadvantage to Palestinians in the chain immigrants' insularity and their tendency to shun outsiders, including other Palestinians, is that it leads to disunity. Bahjat K. laments that many of these village immigrants carry on Hatfield-McCoy type feuds that, although basically family feuds, prevent unity on political issues as well. Such inter-family and inter-village feuding was a major cause of Palestinian helplessness in the face of Zionist organization in 1948 and the years before.

Hashem O., a Chicago attorney who is himself a third-generation Palestinian from Beitunia, a Muslim village that has sent large numbers of immigrants to Chicago, worries about Palestinian ineffectiveness if the chain immigrants' town-centered loyalties are maintained. He believes that the impulse behind formation of the town associations is that "it brings you closer to the soil, like being a Chicagoan versus being an American. You've narrowed down where your feet stand." But, while he can understand the impulse, Hashem disapproves of the exclusiveness of town associations. "It sets up a kind of tribal approach," he says. "What is so important about Beitunia versus Jerusalem versus Ramallah versus Qaloniya or Haifa or any other Palestinian village? The idea is that loyalty should be to a nation, not to a tribe or village." He acknowledges that in the United States he feels as much like a Chicagoan as he does an American, which is why he can understand the desire to be "closer to the soil," but only in certain circumstances. "When I'm overseas, I don't say I'm a Chicagoan, I say I'm an American." The same should apply, he thinks, when Palestinians are overseas—that is, in the United States.

On the other side of the coin, there is something to be said for clan ties as the very links that have made Palestinian survival possible these forty years in the absence of a state. One researcher who has studied the large Palestinian community in Kuwait concludes that "the informal fundamental apparatus comprising family, neighborhood, village, town, and friendship provided the basis for a new and different Palestinian superstructure. Without the family and other basic social relationships, Palestinian society would have been totally fragmented and almost non-existent after 1948."[2]

Town and village associations are not a phenomenon limited to Palestinians in the United States. Palestinian emigrants everywhere have formed village networks that preserve the structure, the cohesiveness, and the identity of villages destroyed in 1948. Many hold annual reunions in Kuwait or Amman, Jordan, that bring villagers and their descendants from throughout the world. Marriage feasts, funerals, and religious festivals are held in common. Some villages, even though non-existent in fact since 1948, still have *mukhtars*; they sit in some diaspora city such as Amman and function in a largely ceremonial capacity, but in many cases they still issue all birth and death certificates for the village.[3]

The strong village consciousness has accounted in large measure for the Palestinians' political survival. One researcher has found that because of the common experience of dispersion and dispossession and the need for a kind of "collective security" in the diaspora, extended families have looked to the village as a protector.[4] One could extend that by saying that for the same reason, because of a collective experience of destruction, the networks of villages destroyed in 1948 that have grown up over the years have tended to achieve a kind of national solidarity and to look to the nation for the preservation of identity. The same can be said for the village and town associations in the United States. Although these represent towns that still exist in the West Bank, and they lack the experience of destruction that motivates the other village networks, they share a similar sense of the need to preserve their heritage and culture.

Whatever the pros and cons of the existence of separate town organizations, the argument has in fact already largely been decided in their favor. The Ramallah federation is thriving; about five hundred families are represented in the Deir Dibwan Association, formed in 1978; the Beit Hanina Federation was organized in 1986; al-Birah has an association; a group representing Bir Zeit has recently been formed; and a Beitunia association, centered in Chicago, where virtually all immigrants from this town have settled, is in the process of organizing.

For every theory about chain immigrant clannishness there is a notable exception, and for every immigrant who acknowledges being ingrown and unassimilated there is another who is neither. Karim Ajluni, the Detroit attorney who was involved in politicizing the Ramallah federation, and his family have achieved an easy balance among the many cross currents facing Ramallites and other chain immigrants. They are able to be active Ramallites without diminishing their national Palestinian consciousness; they are at ease in the United States, fully assimilated and content, without diluting either their cultural identification with Ramallah or their political identification with the Palestinian cause.

They discuss being Palestinian and being American over dinner in their comfortable suburban Detroit home. It is clear that Karim and his wife Suheila have moved beyond the insular, neighborhood-cluster, marry-inside-the-clan existence of many chain immigrants. They are themselves both Ramallites and both Ajlunis, but they have allowed their children the freedom to be Americans as well as Palestinians, and they identify themselves as both, in equal parts.

Their older son Maher is married to an American-born Ramallah girl from San Diego, Judy Misleh, whom he met at a Ramallah federation convention, but they have no objection that their three daughters, Giselle, Marianna, and Suzanne, are married to American men of English and Irish descent. Karim and Suheila live in a well-to-do suburb but remain active in the local Ramallah club and in local Palestinian affairs. They spearheaded a fund-raising drive to furnish an Arabic cultural room in the Heritage Center at Wayne State University in Detroit, and they sponsor an annual event to raise scholarship money to send students to Bir Zeit University on the West Bank.

Maher recalls that as a teenager, he was not politically conscious at all. His parents took him to Ramallah for a few months when he was eighteen, and he remembers most how disappointed he was with the town. Conditions were more primitive than he had expected in the 1970s, he says, and the town did not live up to the romanticized image his parents had always painted. This brings laughter around the table, even from the parents. Suheila says she still has a great affection for the town where she grew up, but she acknowledges having found it much smaller than she had remembered. She had left in the late 1950s after graduating from college in Beirut and marrying Karim, who had already been in the United States for a decade.

Maher's early lack of interest in the Palestinian cause and his disappointment with Ramallah have not prevented him in recent years from taking a strong interest in the cause and in improving the Arab image in the United States. Until recently in radio broadcasting, he is still involved in producing a series of thirteen-segment radio shows on Arab culture called "Arabesque." He and Judy are also involved in organizing an American Ramallah club for young adults to promote group activities that will preserve the Middle East heritage. His interest is broadly focused on Palestinian and Arab issues rather than only on Ramallah.

The conversation at dinner turns to discrimination in the United States. They all say they have not experienced much anti-Arab prejudice. Karim believes that the best advertisement for Palestinians is that they are able to mingle easily with other Americans and show themselves to be decent, educated people who are not terrorists. Everyone at the table agrees. The youngest child, Sameer, although he says he does not keep up with the Palestinian issue now because he is still busy with high school, believes the best thing he can do for Palestinians is to have people get to know him, discover he's all right, and then learn that he is Palestinian. His best friends at the private school he attends are Jewish, who all know he is Palestinian and have no problem with it.

When Karim notes that Palestinians can better integrate in American society because most do not live together in ghettos, Sameer, offering some unusual wisdom for a teenager, comments that this in itself tends to lessen discrimination. Those on the outside, he says, do not see Palestinians as an exclusive community, and those on the inside don't feel different and thus don't feel that others look on them as unusual.

Consuelo Saah Baehr was already an established novelist when she decided to tell the Palestinian story with her 1988 novel *Daughters*, but she had never written about Palestinians before. Set in a fictionalized Ramallah, *Daughters* is a family saga that traces the lives of three generations of Palestinian women from the late nineteenth century through the 1950s. There are no explicit politics here, just a story of Palestinians as decent people, which is politics enough nowadays.

"I think on the whole I did a marvelous thing for the understanding of Palestinians," Baehr says, relaxing in a suburban Washington, D.C., hotel room during the annual convention of the American-Arab Anti-Discrimination Committee, which she has been asked to address. She doesn't like public speaking, but she likes to write, and she likes especially to talk about writing. "Just to disseminate the idea that Palestinians can be lovers, businessmen, neurotic, cranky, whatever—handsome or not handsome, mean-spirited or generous, complicated or simple. And they *adore* the land. They name every little bend in the road, like the Bosom of Pleasure. That's how intimate they feel to the land." She is pleased that reviewers have commented that the book puts a new light on the Palestinian people; much of the comment has come from Jewish critics who say the book fills a need for more knowledge about Palestinians.

Baehr is a short, energetic woman with a down-to-earth manner and an engaging lack of pretense. She thinks she must be a lazy person because it took four years to write and do the research for *Daughters*, but not many would agree that writing four novels while raising three children and running a household was particularly lazy.

She is definitely not cast in the usual chain immigrant mold, and identifying strongly with the Palestinian cause is a relatively new thing for her. Born in El Salvador of a Spanish-French mother and a Palestinian father from Ramallah and sent to American boarding schools from an early age

112

after her parents divorced, she grew up knowing little about her Palestinian heritage. Her father did not talk much about it, and she did not see her Ramallah aunts and uncles enough while in boarding school to learn much from them. Because of the political stigma and her own ignorance of her heritage, Baehr found that she was nervous about acknowledging her Palestinian identity. "I never denied being Palestinian," she says, "but I found that I always hedged by saying my mother is French and Spanish and my father is Palestinian. I know that I hedged, and I know that I felt a flutter inside whenever I would admit [being Palestinian], although I always admitted it. There was no rational fear behind it; it was just that admitting to being an Arab, or pointing out that you're an Arab, involved explanations which I didn't have because I didn't know enough about my background."

Ironically, Baehr's Palestinian consciousness was raised by her husband, a non-Arab American who just happened, "serendipitously," to have been pro-Palestinian and well informed on the Palestinian problem even before they met. "For the first time in my life, I found myself having a dialogue about it with someone who was very sympathetic, and it sort of made me an activist." Her children, now in high school and college, are only one-quarter Palestinian but when asked their heritage they say Palestinian, and "they seem to enjoy the idea that they have a cause." Baehr considers them quite "courageous"; they have all attended a Long Island high school where Leon Uris's novel *Exodus* is required reading for a course on the Middle East and where other students are so free with unthinking racial epithets that they call anyone with a tan a "nigger."

Baehr is now acutely conscious of and assertive about her Palestinian identity and about the importance of getting across to the American public an idea of Palestinians as human beings with values and concerns like anyone else. "I'm just a very plain person who just happens to be Palestinian and who writes books, and somehow the two things melded at this point, and this book came out, which I believe will bring the Palestinian image to a lot of people who wouldn't otherwise have known about it, and perhaps dispel some of the myths."

Sibyl Belmont is another Ramallite with an exotic background, an active non-Arab husband, a late-blooming political consciousness, and a drive to set the record straight about Palestinians as ordinary, decent people. She seems to be a woman who is always busy—teaching piano, conducting dialogue between Arabs and Jews, demonstrating for Palestinian rights, or talking to church groups and schools. She is an articulate woman with very short, graying hair and a ready smile. Never too busy to talk about Palestinians, she invites a visitor to her Lexington, Massachusetts, home and shows off her Palestinian-decorated music room, the embroidered pillows in the living room, the black-and-white checked *khaffiyahs* hanging in the entry hall. Her husband Peter is Jewish, but he is as much interested in the Palestinian question as she is and throughout the conversation brings out mementos of Sibyl's father and her Ramallah background as if they were his own.

Belmont's father was Khalil Totah, a prominent Ramallah educator, her mother an American Quaker from South Dakota who went to Ramallah in the late 1920s to teach at a Quaker-run school there. In the 1860s two Quakers from Maine, Eli and Sibyl Jones, opened a school for girls in Ramallah. Early in the twentieth century a companion school for boys was opened, and since those early days generations of children, Muslim as well as Christian and Quaker and coming from throughout Palestine, have been educated at the Friends Girls' and the Friends Boys' Schools.

Khalil Totah, who had attended the girls' school before there was a boys' school, became principal of the boys' school in the 1920s and later married the young South Dakotan woman who taught at the girls' school. The young woman's parents were apprehensive about her marrying an Arab, according to Belmont, but he visited them in South Dakota "in the middle of the worst blizzard, and he really bowled them over. My father was very charming. He had a wonderful command of English and liked to tell a lot of jokes, but he also liked to recite poetry. He was just a showoff. He genuinely loved this stuff, and it meant a lot to him to learn this poetry in another language. So they calmed down, and he was able to convince them that this marriage was fine."

Sibyl, who was named for Sibyl Jones, was born in Whittier, California, while her parents were on a fund-raising tour of the United States, but she lived in Ramallah until she was twelve. Belmont can remember that during World War II Australian and New Zealand Quakers from a non-combatant medical group, the Friends Ambulance Unit, frequently visited the family home in Ramallah; Sibyl played the piano for them and her brother the violin while her parents served afternoon tea. Her father resigned from the school and moved the family to America toward the end of the war, a trip that had to be made by ship in convoy through the Mediterranean and across the Atlantic.

Belmont grew up in the United States aware of being a Palestinian culturally but uninterested in the political issue. She was so non-political in fact that when she married a Jewish man, who was himself uninterested in the issue, in June 1967 both were basically unaware of the irony of a Palestinian and a Jew marrying in the period when Israel captured the West Bank and several other Arab lands. Sibyl did ask a cousin not to discuss politics at the wedding, but Peter Belmont claims that that admonition was the only politics he heard until 1980.

Sibyl's politicization began in 1980 after she had heard several speakers, both Arab and Israeli, talk about human rights and the conditions under which the Palestinians were living. Then she began on the politicization of Peter. "I left things around on coffee tables for Peter to read," she says—translations from the Israeli press on the treatment of Palestinians, human rights magazines with "descriptions of prisons, torture and roundups and deportations and the whole works."

She did not know how he would react. "She didn't know if I was a Zionist, we never discussed politics," Peter says. At first he ignored the material, telling her he didn't have the stomach for it. But something induced him to write a letter to the editor, and it was published immediately. That led to more reading, more writing of letters, more published letters, and a sort of crusading zeal. "He started writing regularly," Sibyl remembers. "He got published in the [*Boston*] *Globe* about three times a year, and the *New York Times*. So little by little, the more he wrote, the more he needed to look up things and read, so we started building a library." Peter is proud to show off a sheaf of published letters to the editor appearing in major U.S. newspapers. "What happened was that I became a fighter, through words, in this struggle," he grins.

Sibyl still doesn't like to talk politics—not explicitly at any rate. Her crusade is to improve the Palestinian image, and she has been very active in two Arab-Jewish dialogue groups in the Boston area for years. "I'd really like to break the stereotype of Palestinians," she says.

> There are so many people who just have a shocked reaction when they find out you're Palestinian. I've just felt that people can't really deal with it. Some Jewish people, very educated, very liberal in every other way, but if you are Palestinian, there's something about you that is not to be trusted. That comes through to me with people I know very well, it comes through much more with people whom I've just met, when they find out. I tell people about my experience in this country, a feeling of alienation, even as an American—I'm part American, I'm not totally Palestinian—but my politics are Palestinian enough for them for me to be a threat to them.

She has had mixed success with her two dialogue groups, but they are still meeting, and that is what's important to Sibyl. And they have led to other things, to other opportunities, through schools and churches, to get the Palestinian point of view across. She has relatives in the United States who work in Arab-American organizations but who "don't want to think about Palestine all the time." Belmont cannot understand that; "I feel guilty if I don't do something for Palestine."

115

They call it "West Bank U.S.A."[5] or "Little America" or any of a number of other cute labels to characterize the strength of its ties to the United States. The town is Deir Dibwan, a Muslim village of 7,500 or 8,000 people about five miles east of Ramallah. Its people have had such a wanderlust that at any one time in the last few decades fully half its inhabitants have been outside earning a living in Central or South America or the United States. The vast majority come to the United States. The tradition of emigration has made Deir Dibwan a wealthy town, at least in relative terms. American earnings are sent back home to build large houses and buy property, and the decade-old Deir Dibwan Association in the United States regularly sends money home to help with the town's social needs. More than Ramallah, Deir Dibwan still tends to attract its emigrants back home, either in the kind of long-distance commute that most Ramallah people abandoned long ago, or permanently to retire.

Immigration here began in the 1920s, when a few young men began coming to the United States to peddle goods. In those early days, according to Hisham Muhyeldin, a physician from Deir Dibwan who has been studying and practicing in the Los Angeles area since 1979, immigration was still a rare thing, involving only seven or eight families. The arrival back home of a young man who had spent several years in the United States was a big event in the village. "If you are five, six years in United States, and you go back," Muhyeldin says, "they know this man is coming, they were counting the days 'til he arrives, and they celebrate his arrival."

Emigration to the United States did not begin on a large scale until the late 1950s and '60s and has now become so common and the commute so frequent that the return of a native son is hardly noticed. The principal problem these days is that many Deir Dibwanians who stay away too long lose their Israeli identity cards and are allowed to remain there only on visitor's permits. Many have successfully applied for residency on the basis of family reunion, but more have been denied.[6] The parents of San Franciscan Asad Salameh returned to Deir Dibwan in 1980 after being in the United States for fourteen years and have been living since then without identity cards. They have had to leave briefly every few months in order to renew their visitor's permits, a hassle they are willing to endure just to be home.

Hisham Muhyeldin's own grandfather was one of the early travelers to the United States, coming first in the mid-1920s. He brought his son, Hisham's father, briefly in 1950, but the younger man had other things in mind for himself and ended up serving in the Jordanian government as a cabinet minister and in Jordan's parliament as a West Bank representative in the 1960s. Hisham himself retains very strong ties with Deir Dibwan and has no intention of staying in the United States permanently. Although a U.S. citizen, he has deliberately avoided becoming assimilated in American society, which he generally disapproves of, and most of his American contacts are relatives and friends from Deir Dibwan. He has thus far been able to retain his identity card by traveling back home every three years, and he fully intends to return to Deir Dibwan some day. He believes most Deir Dibwanians are like him. Asked if his prospective son-in-law, a Deir Dibwan native in the United States studying dentistry, will stay here after his studies, Muhyeldin grows a little irritated with the questioner's obtuseness. "I don't know what you mean, will somebody stay here or go back, because from Deir Dibwan, I assure you, ninety-nine percent of the Deir Dibwan people are back and forth. Not more than one percent from Deir Dibwan stay here for good."

Mike Hazem Monsour is among the one percent. He has managed to feel more at home in the United States than many of his fellow townsmen—to the point that he cannot really distinguish where being Palestinian leaves off and being American begins. His father began coming to the United States in the 1920s. He peddled bedspreads and linens in the poor sections of San Francisco and earned enough to send money home to his wife, raise five children, and buy property around Deir Dibwan. He became an American citizen and typically spent two years here and two years at home. When Hazem, the only son, was born in 1939, his father registered him at the U.S. consulate in Jerusalem as a U.S. citizen, but Monsour did not come to the United States until 1956, when his father brought him here to attend school.

A tall, slim man with light, sandy blond hair and aquiline features, Monsour is often mistaken for a German. He is a fastidious dresser and even in a sports shirt looks neat and pressed. He greets a visitor in the office of his Albuquerque, New Mexico, jewelry store in a finely tailored suit. He has set aside the afternoon for this talk, he says, and is anxious to discuss the Palestinian situation. He loves to talk, and he has quite a story to tell, a story that epitomizes the Palestinian problem and that serves to define the boundaries of a Palestinian American's twin identities.

Monsour's mother never came to the United States when her husband and only son came, and she continues to live, now an elderly widow, in Deir Dibwan. In 1984 she became ill, and Monsour went to the West Bank to visit her. It was his first visit in over twenty years. Israel captured the West Bank shortly after he had come home to marry a Deir Dibwan girl in the early 1960s, and so he had never gone back until his mother needed him. He had also begun to think it might be nice to build a home there and perhaps spend a few months or even a few years at a time in his old hometown.

One evening while having dinner with his in-laws, Monsour was arrested by Israeli authorities. No charges were specified, but repeatedly over the next three weeks, Israeli interrogators attempted to get him to admit that he supported the PLO or the PFLP or Fatah, that he knew Yasir Arafat or George Habash, that he had been "trained for the PLO" on a previous trip to

Lebanon. He says that he was made to stand throughout the first night handcuffed and with a bag over his head. When he passed out, he was kicked and made to get up. The next morning he was repeatedly beaten. He says he admitted nothing, but that finally he twice signed Hebrew-language confessions that he could not read and of whose contents he was not informed. Monsour was finally released three weeks later—thanks, he believes, entirely to the efforts of New Mexico Senator Pete Domenici, then-Congressman Manuel Lujan, and then-Governor Toney Anaya, who pressed for State Department intervention. No charges were ever brought.[7]

Monsour's reaction to his ordeal provides a striking example of the duality so many Palestinians feel about their American and their Palestinian identities. Monsour approached his trip to the West Bank as an American, with an American mentality. "I forgot that I was born there," he explains, sitting in his jewelry store several years later, "and for a moment when I went back I thought of the American due process of law, but when you go there, there is no such thing. I never in my life thought that they will do what they did to me, on the ground that I was innocent. I never done a doggone thing other than shoot my mouth off here and there and articulate my thought as an American citizen, just using the First Amendment and my rights as an American."

But he reacted as a Palestinian. "I felt the nationalism more so than any other time in my life," he says. "I think I would be lying if I told you that I did not get involved emotionally to the point where I felt like I'm more of a Palestinian than an American when I was in prison." That renewed Palestinian consciousness has not left him. He has spent considerable time since his release traveling throughout the United States speaking about his prison experience for the American-Arab Anti-Discrimination Committee, and he has become very much wrapped up in the Palestinian cause.

At the same time, Monsour again thinks of himself primarily as an American. "We're pretty much like the American Jews in a way," he explains when asked how he balances his Palestinian consciousness with his feelings for the United States. "You're a loyal American but you always feel like you're obligated to help somehow." There is no contradiction in his mind. No matter how strongly he feels for the Palestinian cause, he says he chose "from the very early stages of my life to be identified as an American Arab. I hold an American passport, I work here, I live here, this is my home, this is my country. I am an American by choice." He is active in the community. Several pictures of himself with national and local political figures, including Senator Robert Dole, adorn the walls of his office. He is a deputy on the local reserve sheriff's force.

Monsour shows remarkably little bitterness over his experience in an Israeli jail. There is no anger in his tone as he talks about it, and his demeanor is relaxed and matter-of-fact. The ordeal did change his perception of Israelis: "I always thought that the Israelis were a little bit more civilized than what I saw. What I saw made me respect them less." But it did not radicalize him. "I want some harmony between the Arabs and the Jews. I'm tired of what's going on—the killings, the refugees, the manipulations of the Palestinians." Harmony has to be between equals, he says; it cannot be achieved by Israelis imprisoning Palestinians. "When I am asked," Monsour says as the afternoon winds down, "do I have any animosity, would I kill them—I do not have anything in my heart like that. I would punch them in the mouth, but not kill."

Norman Assed has been in this country since he was seven years old and, although he grew up in the Beit Hanina community in Dearborn, Michigan, where many others never assimilated, he is so thoroughly American by now that being Palestinian is an integral part of his American identity.

Like the immigrants from other West Bank towns involved in a chain migration to this country, Beit Haninans, who Assed estimates number about 5,000, tended until relatively recently to be clannish and non-political and to avoid identification with the wider Palestinian cause. "The reason for that," Assed explains

> is the success that they've had economically speaking, business-wise. They've gone from peddlers to store owners. We've probably got over 350 supermarkets in Brooklyn owned by people from Beit Hanina, no exaggeration. Very successful people. And what they've done with their children is taken them into the business rather than send them to school. I mean, Beit Hanina is very successful financially, the whole village has done extremely well, and they've helped each other out. So in Cleveland, San Francisco, Detroit, and New York, where our concentration is, there has been a trend toward let's make more money, and Palestine is in the back of their minds but not as much as making the buck.

This is now changing, Assed believes, because of education. The younger brothers and sisters—the ones not taken into the stores—are going to school instead, and their children in turn are getting a college education. "So as they get educated, they become aware," Assed says. "They become involved politically."

Assed himself, who is still better known among Palestinians by his Arab name Naim, has been politically active since he joined an organization to help Palestinian refugees at the age of eighteen. He became political well before most others of his generation, but his story is otherwise typical of Beit Haninans. His father was the pioneer of the family, coming to the United States in 1914. He served in the U.S. Navy during the two world wars, working as a translator in Portland, Oregon, but he always kept his ties to home and traveled back regularly. He married a woman from Beit Hanina and, as with so many other families, when the children came, mother and kids stayed in Beit Hanina while father worked here.

When Assed was seven, however, his mother developed cancer and brought the family to Dearborn to join her husband. She died three months after arriving here in 1954. Assed's father maintained the village traditions and, when Naim was only fourteen, sent him back home to marry a local girl. Naim returned to Dearborn with his bride, by now expecting the first of their five children, when they were both fifteen, and he has been working ever since. He owns two jewelry stores in Albuquerque, and his son owns one in Santa Fe.

Sitting in the back of one of his stores talking about his experiences, one gets the impression that Assed would be comfortable anywhere. He has short, very curly black hair and dark eyes and wears a mustache. His voice is husky, and he talks rapidly, sometimes tending to leave sentences unfinished in his haste to move on. Pictures of his family are all over the office, and behind his deak hang a bronze map of Palestine and a framed poster declaring "Palestine: Statehood Now!"

Although Assed maintains ties to Beit Haninans elsewhere in the country, he is completely at ease in Albuquerque, where there are few. He mixes easily in local business, as well as local politics. His manner is open and friendly, and he comes across as the consummate extroverted American politician. Throughout the meeting in his office, he is constantly interrupted by phone calls, including one from the mayor, with whom he is on a first-name basis. He is also personally acquainted with several other powers in local Democratic politics.

Much of Assed's involvement in politics is directed at promoting the Palestinian cause. He was urged to run for the position of local county Democratic party chairman a few years ago but refused because he knew his primary interest was the Palestinian issue and thought it unfair to represent a general electorate. But he is proud as a Palestinian to have been asked and believes it is important for the cause to keep up his contacts in local politics. He is convinced that working within the U.S. political system is one of the best ways of advancing the Palestinian cause. "I know it's hard," he acknowledges, "like a drop in a big ocean right now, but honestly, it can be done. I believe in the system." He directs most of his own work through the American-Arab Anti-Discrimination Committee. He was an organizer of the local ADC chapter in Albuquerque and served as chapter president in 1988, before joining the ADC's national executive committee.

Assed served as one of the eight Palestinian-American delegates for Jesse Jackson at the 1988 Democratic national convention, and he found that just his presence there, as a well dressed, respectable businessman with a legitimate political interest, had an impact on the pro-Israeli members of the New Mexico delegation. "Every morning [during the convention] I'd get up, say good morning to them, have doughnuts with them, coffee, sit with them, chat, laugh, and in less than a week's time at the convention, with the delegation staying together at the hotel, it made sense to them that there are people who want to live genuinely in peace."

Two women, both delegates who Assed says met every morning with representatives of the main pro-Israel lobbying organization, the American Israel Public Affairs Committee (AIPAC), approached him at the end of the convention and told him they admired his actions. "She says, 'I know what you're trying to do for your people. It's just that we've been hurting so much.' And I saw a crack! I said, I can't believe it, just by being nice to them!"

Assed can understand the unique fears of Jews and the fact that these fears are transferred to Palestinians, and he believes Palestinians could respond better than they do to Jewish concerns. "[Jews] need to deal on a one-on-one basis. It doesn't serve us any purpose, terrorism. I'm sorry, honestly, I hate to—" This is where he begins to swallow the ends of his sentences. "A lot of Palestinians probably disagree and feel that some terrorism, especially within the occupied territories, is justified; that's the way to liberate Palestine. But it isn't. All it does is promote and foster this belief in [Jewish] minds that we've got to defend ourselves because the Palestinians want to destroy us."

Assed has probably more readily internalized his Americanness than most Palestinian immigrants, including many who have come here as children. He does not hesitate to identify himself as an American first without fear of being accused by other Palestinians of lacking dedication to the cause, because he knows—and he knows everyone else knows—that his dedication cannot be questioned. What he most likes about the United States is precisely that he can openly support the Palestinian cause without fear of repression. He calls his children "very American," but he has tried to help them achieve the same kind of easy commerce in both worlds that he has achieved. They have visited Beit Hanina frequently and attended school there for brief periods, and they all speak and read Arabic. Assed will never forget Beit Hanina. He owns a house and land there—including fifty-one dunams confiscated by Israel—and he talks about possibly retiring there some day. The Assed property is "not land that I bought. It's land that's been given to me, handed down to me through centuries. I date my ancestors back to 700 years. It's hard to give that up."

The Israeli occupation has been the great leveler for the clans of Palestine. When Palestinian Americans visit the West Bank or Gaza, they find they are not treated specially because they are members of a clan or even because they are Americans. They are treated like every other Palestinian, and they learn that clannishness in Palestine is meaningless today. Khalil D., a liquor store owner in Los Angeles from Deir Dibwan, puts it this way: "That individual from Deir Dibwan, he is not especially treated because he is rich or because he is an American citizen or because he is from Deir Dibwan. He is treated as bad as any other Palestinian is. So that's why you can't say we are different about anybody from Deir Dibwan or from Ramallah or from the West Bank."

Strong clannishness is no longer really possible for Palestinians. If it was once widely true that Ramallites in the United States did not look beyond the concerns of Ramallah, that Beit Haninans cared only for their grocery stores, that Deir Dibwanians did little for the broader Palestinian cause, this is decidedly no longer the case.

NOTES

[1] Interview with Hanna Ajluni, Detroit, Michigan, March 24, 1989, and letter from Ajluni, January 19, 1990.

[2] Shafeeq N. Ghabra, *Palestinians in Kuwait: The Family and the Politics of Survival* (Boulder, CO: Westview Press, 1987), p. 169.

[3] Ibid., p. 147.

[4] Ibid., p. 133.

[5] The term "West Bank U.S.A." comes from an article with that headline by Joel Greenberg in *The Jerusalem Post International Edition* (Week ending April 18, 1987): 13.

[6] Ibid.

[7] Details of Monsour's imprisonment are cited in John P. Egan, "An American Testimony from an Israeli Prison: The Case of Mike Monsour," *Journal of Palestine Studies* 53 (Fall 1984): 118-125.

6   Palestinians and the Zionist Ideology

When Herzl came up with Zionism in 1897, his idea was, as far as I was concerned, a beautiful idea. The idea went wrong when they decided Palestinians were grasshoppers.

Karim Dajani
Student

An understanding of how Palestinians view the ideology of Zionism and how they relate this ideology to what they see as Palestinian victimization by Israelis is critical to an understanding of how Palestinians view the process of making peace with Israel. Unlike Jews and most Americans, Palestinians consider Zionism not as a benign ideology whose principal aim is to provide a haven from suffering for Jews, but as an elitist philosophy that is by definition racially and theologically exclusivist and has proved in practice to be aggressively expansionist. Palestinians perceive themselves to be the victims of, not the aggressors against, Zionism and for this reason have found compromise particularly difficult.

Raif Hijab doesn't smoke, but he has an addiction to coffee and, almost as strong, to sitting in coffee shops talking politics. He has been pursuing a doctorate in electrical engineering at the University of California, Berkeley, for too many years, by his own admission. But he has involved himself so deeply in politics so many times—whether it is working on national political campaigns or canvassing for local referenda—that he has repeatedly put off writing his dissertation. By early 1988, he has decided to swear off politics until he has his doctorate, but in the middle of both the Jesse Jackson presidential campaign and the battle over a Berkeley city council vote on whether to adopt the Gaza refugee camp of Jabalya as a sister city, it is obvious that he is having severe withdrawal pangs. He consoles himself with more coffee and some informal political discussion.

Hijab is a man in his early forties, although he doesn't look it. He knows that's older than the norm, even for graduate students, but he had a career in electrical engineering, working in the Middle East, Europe, and the United States, before pursuing doctoral work. He has been a U.S. citizen for many years, but it is the Palestinian issue that most animates him and to which he devotes his political energies.

In a noisy coffee shop on the Berkeley campus, Hijab grapples with the question of Jews and their self-perception and how this perception affects Palestinians. He says first of all that, as far as he is concerned, there is no question that Israel is in no danger from the Palestinians. "I think the PLO and many in the Palestinian political scene have long recognized that they cannot close their eyes and open them and see a Palestine with no Jews." Many months before the PLO explicitly accepts a Palestinian state limited to the West Bank and Gaza, he says he believes this is the only realistic solution, even though it is unfair because it would leave the Palestinians in control of only twenty-three percent of their original homeland. The critical issue for Hijab is less the kind of peace settlement that might emerge than how Israel is likely to behave in its aftermath. The real issue, he says, is not that Israel's security might be endangered by an independent Palestinian state, but whether a Palestinian state might be threatened by Israel.

He treads carefully as he discusses this issue, thinking his thesis through as he goes along and choosing his words carefully. "I'm scared that the Israelis will not deal from a position of equality. For one thing, they have been using large numbers of West Bank labor. That's a relationship that would have to be changed somehow. Israelis have, I'm sure, more than one lever to blackmail a West Bank state in many ways economically. It's something I feel uneasy about."

He seems to feel that because of the Israelis' psychological makeup, they are incapable of dealing with any Arabs on the basis of equality. "There is a dangerous side to Israel," he says frankly. He has felt it in interactions with Israelis at Berkeley. He mentions particularly a visiting Israeli history professor with whom he had lengthy discussions. "What struck me—I don't remember the exact words—was the paternalistic, contemptuous attitude he had toward Arabs and Palestinians, and this you can see again and again and again among Israelis. They think that they are better. For one thing, they built up the land; that is why they are entitled to it. They are more capable; that is why they are entitled to it. You can go on and on. They really have no respect for the Arab."

There is no anger in his voice as he explains his conclusions. He speaks softly and without urgency, despite the din of the coffee shop. "I think there are a lot of Israelis who think they are inherently superior to their neighbors," he continues.

> If you address this element, it is a problem with Israel that has nothing to do with the Arabs or the Palestinians. It is a problem with the makeup of that society. The very idea, for one, that Jews are only safe there, in a Jewish state, with Jews having the absolute superior-

ity in arms. I know that they have their own reasons, the Holocaust experience and all that, for all this paranoia—and that's all it is—but what I am trying to say is that as Palestinians in a Palestinian state next to this neighbor, we have to be on the receiving end of this attitude. I don't know how it would play out. It's one of the things that one has to think of further down the line.

The Jewish feeling of superiority, which Hijab perceives in common with countless other Palestinians, is the reverse side of Jewish insecurity, both produced by the same experience of suffering, the same attitude that Jews are unique in the world—unique in their accomplishments, as they are unique in their suffering. As the perceived victims of Jewish superiority and, in their firm view, not the cause of Jewish suffering, Palestinians usually find it difficult to empathize with, and often even to recognize, Jewish and Israeli insecurity. Hijab recognizes it but has little sympathy for it. "I can understand their insecurity," he begins, "but, you see, you don't have to accommodate everybody's paranoia. If you have somebody working with you in the same office who has some weird attitudes, you might accommodate them, but only so much. You see," he continues,

I don't as yet understand the Jews. I think there is a lot more to it than anti-Semitism. I have some difficulties with anti-Semitism. It's difficult for me to believe that it is some kind of God's curse or whatever it is that made people react to them in certain ways everywhere they went. It is difficult for me to believe that anti-Semitism is like they like to believe, intrinsic to the Gentile or something like that. It's ridiculous. I look around me. First, there is racism I think in everybody. No matter where you go. The one thing that made me realize it was something very simple. In my stay in Norway once in a small town, walking down the street, a five-year-old child turned to his mother and said [about Hijab], "Mother, look how black he is." This child had never seen anybody that dark. You know how blond the Norwegians are, most of them anyway. What I am trying to say is the origins of racism or prejudice can be very innocent. But how does it get to the intensity of, say, the Nazi attitude toward Jews? The Jews try to reduce it to too simplistic terms by saying, "We are not safe among Gentiles, and the solution is to barricade ourselves in another Masada." I just don't accept that, I don't buy that.

Does Hijab accept that there was a Holocaust? "Yes," he says without hesitation. Is he saying that Jews brought it on themselves? "No, no," he responds emphatically. He is even a little irritated at the automatic assumption that he might be showing anti-Semitism himself. He is seriously attempting to delve into the issue, to get past the pat answers and the uninformed assumptions and fathom the causes for a phenomenon that affects Jews directly but has an indirect spinoff effect on Palestinians.

"I've been interested in this thing because I think as a Palestinian I cannot escape the issue of anti-Semitism and Jewish paranoia." He muses about its origins, wondering whether anti-Semitism arises because Jews never converted when Christianity began. He acknowledges being on unsure ground but thinks there is some logic to this theory. But Jews, he believes, sometimes invite the reasons for their paranoia.

> There is a cycle, a vicious cycle. By being super-protective of themselves, they alienate themselves. This doesn't justify anti-Semitism, it doesn't justify being against them. But as a practical matter, it leads to anti-Semitism. The thing about it is for some reason the Hebrews maintained their continuous attachment to this part of history. In other words, I guess when a Jewish child is born, they're immediately burdened with three thousand years of Jewish history. Perhaps the answer to it is you must look for the cause within that Jewish upbringing.

Hijab has not found many Jews in the course of his coffee shop discussion who will agree with his theories. "From my perspective I've tried to reason with them," he says. "I've tried to see it from their point of view. But they always tell you, 'But we're something special, we're different somehow. Whatever rules you apply to the world, we need these special rules, we need this special consideration.'" This is where Hijab's understanding for Jewish history and his sympathy for Jewish insecurity give out. This is where for him the coin flips over from Jewish insecurity to Jewish superiority, and where Palestinians begin to be affected.

Palestinians must, he feels, deal with Jewish fears in some way "because after all it is a major reason for our plight, I think," but he does not have any real answers. "I don't see how we could solve it. It's really the Israelis and other Jews who have to come to terms with their own—" his voice trails off. After a moment, he begins again. "I personally do not like the way the Jews define themselves. I do not like this idea about their being special. There is an attraction to it, an attraction to the idea of saying, 'I'm special.' Anybody might want to say that." In fact, precisely because of the attraction, precisely because superiority is the reverse side of insecurity, the problem is hard for Jews to recognize and very difficult to overcome. "But it is not humanistic," Hijab concludes, because the attitude of superiority prevents Jews from regarding Palestinians as human beings.

Hijab's critical analysis of the Jewish psyche has not kept him from an appreciation of Jewish accomplishments or blinded him to the negative effects of this conflict on Palestinian attitudes. Another aspect of the same paranoia that has produced a sense of superiority among Jews, he recognizes, has been a drive to achieve. "The fact that Jews have always been just outside the mainstream has caused them to struggle but has also enabled them, the great ones among them, to see things that the rest of us didn't see. I just want to acknowledge both sides," he says with a smile.

His acknowledgement reminds him of something else, which he finds painful but is not reluctant to bring up. "There is no doubt that the Palestinians hate Jews," he says bluntly. "It's natural. You wouldn't expect it to be otherwise. The problem is to get people to come to terms with it. To try to make sense of it. The Palestinians on the West Bank had a better chance than most, being forced to interact with Jews, with Israelis. As a matter of fact, in '68 and '69 the Palestinians on the West Bank had this kind of admiration that I think the defeated have for the victor. But, of course, most Palestinians have not had this exposure." And, he believes, even West Bankers soon lost their admiration under the hardships of occupation.

Hatred accomplishes nothing, Hijab believes. "I've been telling my friends that to begin to be victorious with the Israelis, you must make sure we don't hate Jews. Israel and Israelis are the enemy of the Palestinians. But that's not the same as hating Jews, because if you hate Jews, you will deal with them much in an irrational way, which will never lead you to where you want to go." Israelis, by contrast, he believes, do not hate Arabs. "They are contemptuous of Arabs—very different."

Raif Hijab doesn't have the answers, and he is not optimistic that answers will be found, or indeed that enough people on either side are even trying. Like most Palestinians, he puts the principal burden for trying on the Israelis, who may think like victims but have not actually been the victims for over forty years, or acted like victims. The answers will not come, he believes, until Palestinians stop hating, but more important, they will not come until Israelis stop treating Palestinians with contempt. The answers lie in each side's willingness to treat the other with equality.

It is in discussions of this sort where understanding between Palestinians and Jews or Israelis most fundamentally breaks down. One can seldom expect even to obtain a hearing if, like Raif Hijab, one says that Jews or Israelis have a psychological problem or act superior or are in any way to be faulted in the area of human rights. It is difficult if not impossible for most Jews to understand that criticism of Jews as Jews—that is, for the acts Jews have committed in Palestine in their drive to establish a state for Jews—is seen by Palestinians not as anti-Semitism, not as ethnic prejudice, but as simple political discourse.

The fact that Palestinians for decades referred to Israelis as Jews rather than as Israelis—and still often do—has always been taken by Jews as a clear sign of anti-Semitism. But for Palestinians, calling Israelis Jews involves nothing more complicated or sinister than the fact that Zionism itself called Jews Jews before there was an Israel. Zionism was presented to Palestinians, and to the world, from the beginning as an ideology directed at establishing a state for Jews, and since Jews throughout the world now have automatic nationality rights in that state, Palestinians have simply called its inhabitants by the broad designation given them by Zionism. Palestinians did indeed initially refuse to accept that Judaism had a right, as a religion, to establish a nation on land the Palestinians regard as their own; reference to Israelis as Jews did for many constitute a refusal to recognize that Jews had the right to a national in addition to a religious identity. But most Palestinians never felt that their designation of Israelis as Jews constituted anti-Semitism; they were, and are, well aware that in the Zionist ideology itself the distinction between Jews and Israelis has always been and remains deliberately blurred, if it exists at all.

It is important to remember where Palestinians are coming from when they talk about their perceptions of Jews. They begin at a different starting point than do Jews and most Americans. They do not accept that their own opposition to Israel and Zionism is, as it appears to Jews, a continuation of the centuries of persecution that Jews have suffered in Europe and elsewhere in the world. Few Palestinians can accept the Jewish perception that suffering is suffering, that they hurt as much whether it is inflicted at the hands of Europeans or of Arabs, and that Palestinian and Arab hostility seems to Jews to be merely part of a continuum. The reasons are secondary, the persecutors indistinguishable; the fact of suffering is what is paramount in the minds of Jews.

Almost universally, Palestinians confronted with this argument will say that their opposition to Israel and Zionism is totally unrelated to earlier European persecution of Jews. They know what they consider the facts of their own situation—that a people who claimed an ancient heritage in Palestine but did not live there in large numbers began to arrive en masse with the intention of displacing the native Palestinians and eventually, as the result of a heinous crime against them with which the Palestinians had no connection, won the world's sympathy and the world's approval to proceed with the dispossession of the Palestinians—and they cannot accept that European crimes against the Jewish people justify Jewish crimes against the Palestinian people, or that the Palestinian struggle to regain their homeland bears any resemblance to pogroms in Europe or the Holocaust.

Palestinians frequently observe in discussions on this topic that Jews who lived in the Arab world for centuries before Israel's creation were treated much better than their co-religionists in Europe, that Oriental Jews suffered no pogroms and no persecution. This is true in a strict sense but somewhat disingenuous. Even though Jews in general did not suffer as much physical persecution in the Arab world as they did in Europe and at times served important roles in the courts of Arab rulers, the fact is that generally as non-Muslims in an Islamic land these Jews were treated as second-class citizens, living under restrictions that often hindered the practice of their religion and limited their economic opportunity. Jews lived in much the same condition of social, economic, and political inferiority that Palestinians now complain of under Israeli occupation.

Nevertheless, Palestinians like to point to the fact of the Jews' greater physical safety in the Arab world to demonstrate that their hostility to Israel is politically rather than racially motivated. Palestinians contend that Jews fought for the establishment of a state not because Arabs treated them as second-class citizens but because Europeans persecuted them, and they cannot for that reason accept that the burden for making restitution for Jewish suffering should fall on the Arab world, certainly not on them.

More than that, most Palestinians do not believe that anything the Palestinians can do could possibly be enough to heal the Jewish psyche, to ease the Jewish burden of fear. "What can we do?" Muhammad Hallaj, the Washington, D.C., intellectual, wonders. "We can't be Israel's psychoanalyst. We can't cure the Israelis of their paranoia. These people have a heavy burden that they're carrying, they brought from Western Europe. We didn't give it to them, but they want us to cure them of 2,000 years worth of paranoia. It's too big for us, we're not that clever. So if we're going to wait until Palestinians are able to reassure the Israelis that a Palestinian state would be absolutely no problem for them, forget it."

Abdur-Rahim Jaouni, the geochemist in Berkeley, California, discusses the problem in similar terms. Born in Jerusalem and a resident of the United States, although not a citizen, since 1972, Jaouni is a bit brusque, and he does not suffer fools, or foolish questions, easily but there is an engaging enthusiasm about the way he puts his case. He is thin and wiry and high-strung. Even though he has come to a Chinese restaurant with two other people for a discussion of the Palestinian situation, he is so concentrated on the subject that he has decided to eat beforehand so that he can devote his full energies to politics. He talks while everyone else eats.

Jaouni is asked if he can understand that Israelis, despite their overwhelming military strength, genuinely feel insecure after the Holocaust and forty years of Arab hostility. "I would like to deal with these things separately," he says. "Let's take the Holocaust. I don't see that we, the Palestinians, are a relevant party to that. It is between the Jews and the Germans. I can see their fears, but I put it back again: how am I, a Palestinian, supposed to relate to that? I will never be able to see it. That was the Germans. I don't see the connection. If somebody hits you, you come and hit me? I am irrelevant to that."

This is what virtually every discussion of this subject with Palestinians comes around to—to the thought that Jewish fears, Jewish psychoses, Jewish insecurity are all understandable but that Jewish anguish in no way justifies the displacement and dispossession of Palestinians. Most Palestinians sincerely do not see that in the Jewish mind there could be any connection between their suffering at German hands and their later suffering at Arab hands, because to Palestinians the two are entirely unconnected issues; although Jews suffered unjustifiably at German hands, Palestinians reason, they brought Arab hostility on themselves by taking Palestinian land. And if Jews are still insecure because of what Germans did to them, no amount of Palestinian reassurance will ease their pain.

"Arab hostility and the Holocaust, they are completely two separate historical events," Jaouni repeats. "Are we going to do what the Germans did? I don't see the connection."

At this point another Palestinian, Raif Hijab, breaks in. "I think it's important that non-Jews at least realize the Palestinian perception. One thing is clear, that many Jews, survivors of the Holocaust and others, project the Holocaust on the Palestinians. We're the object of the thing, we're not the actors. We're simply being defined some way."

Although Hijab has hit on the essence of the Palestinian perception, Jaouni at first pays no attention and goes on talking. But Hijab comes back to it. "Not only is there a Jewish projection," he notes, "there is a Christian Western projection. The West—Europeans basically, or if you extend the culture to include the U.S.—collectively feels the guilt of what happened to the Jews. But they project themselves onto all of mankind. All of mankind is responsible; if we're responsible, then you're responsible."

Jaouni has begun to listen intently. "Yes, yes," he nods vigorously. "This is very profound."

"Actually," Hijab continues, "this is exactly the reasoning used by Churchill and others, who said, 'We are responsible for what happened. But not only are we responsible; everyone else is responsible. So, we've got to redress the Jews, but we don't want to pay for it, so you pay the price.' But they included non-Europeans in the group."

Jaouni cannot understand why Jews sought recompense from Palestinians rather than from Germans and Europeans. "Why don't the Jews fight that politically in Europe? Why didn't they fight the Germans politically?" The irrelevance of the Palestinians to historical Jewish suffering is so clear to him that he reiterates his views at every opportunity. "I think there is a cause for Arab hostility," he says, summarizing his feelings.

> It's not that it's out of the blue I hate the Jews, I hate Israel. It's a historical cause, what they did to the Palestinians. You cannot deny that. Now, when somebody comes and starts fighting you and kicking you around, what would you do? Are you going to sit around

and say, "Okay, I'm a Christian, hit me on the other cheek?" It's not going to happen. So there is every reason for this Arab hostility. [Jews] lump everything together. They put the Holocaust and Arab hostility together, but each of them is a different experience and has a different reason for it. The Arab hostility, I can see it because they injured me.

Palestinians differ very basically from Americans and most Jews and Israelis in their perception of Zionism and of what precisely the Zionist ideology means for both Jews and Palestinians. Americans generally perceive Zionism in its simplest and most romantic terms, as an ideology whose goal is the creation and maintenance of a haven from persecution for the Jewish people. As such, Zionism is regarded as a benign, even laudable political theory. Even most Jews and Israelis do not look beneath the surface of this definition to the implications of Zionism. Palestinians, on the other hand, focus on what Zionism's goal, the creation of a Jewish state, has meant for the non-Jews who live on the land on which Zionism set its sights.

To Palestinians, Zionism means not primarily that Jews gain a refuge from persecution, but that Palestinians lose their place in their own homeland. To Palestinians, Zionism's drive to establish a specifically Jewish state means that Jews intended from the beginning to exclude the native inhabitants of Palestine. Palestinians regard Zionism as by its very nature an exclusivist ideology based on a single religious/ethnic identity that necessarily excludes all who are not Jews. The mere presence of substantial numbers of non-Jews in a Zionist state is a threat to its Jewishness and therefore to its very essence. Palestinians believe Israel could never have fulfilled the goals of Zionism and become a Jewish state if Palestinians had remained in their homes in 1948 and continued to multiply.

Zionism has been inhospitable to non-Jews since the creation of the Israeli state. Although Palestinians who remained in Israel in 1948 or have been born there since then are citizens of Israel, the Zionist ideology does not have great tolerance for ethnic diversity. Israel distinguishes between citizenship and nationality and, while Palestinians may be citizens, they may obviously not be Jewish nationals. Many rights derive from nationality rather than from citizenship, and every organ of the state in Israel is mandated by law to work for the welfare of Jewish nationals. The Law of Return gives all Jews anywhere in the world nationality status in Israel, no matter what their citizenship in any other country and whether or not they wish to live in Israel. An Israeli court has declared, "There is no Israeli nation separate from the Jewish people. The Jewish people is composed not only of those residing in Israel, but also of Diaspora Jewry." Jews automatically gain citizenship upon entering Israel. No Palestinian not born in Israel may become a citizen, much less a Jewish national.[1]

Palestinians believe that there has never been room in Zionism's calculations for Palestinians—not today, not before Israel was created, not even before the Holocaust brought to full flowering the seeds of a deep fear in the Jewish psyche. "You should never lose sight of at least what a Palestinian perceives to be a Zionist agenda for the area," notes Samir Ashrawi, the Austin chemist, "and the Zionist agenda for the area excludes completely the presence of a Palestinian nation. At best, it has a provision for very docile inhabitants of Judea and Samaria"—that is, the West Bank. Ashrawi recalls a refrain uttered frequently by Israeli right-wing extremist Meir Kahane, who until his assassination in 1990 openly advocated expulsion of all Palestinians from Israel and the occupied territories, to the effect that his anti-Arab statements actually expressed views that every Israeli had in his heart but was reluctant to voice.

There are Palestinians who, like Omar Kader, the Utah-bred former director of the American-Arab Anti-Discrimination Committee, can empathize with Jews and who for whatever reason do not themselves feel victimized. But the Palestinian, even the Palestinian living in the comfort of the United States, who does not feel victimized is the exception rather than the rule. There are also Palestinians, and many of them, who can genuinely sympathize with past Jewish suffering. But the sympathy has an automatic disconnect that divorces Jewish experience in Europe from any relevance to Jewish and Israeli experience in the Middle East, and it is always muted by the perception that restitution was made to Jews at Palestinian expense.

Ghada Talhami can understand the impulse that led to Zionism, and she can feel for Holocaust victims. "I certainly sympathize with the Holocaust victims, I certainly do." Talhami is a professor of political science at Lake Forest College in Illinois. Originally from Nablus, she has been in this country since coming here as a student in 1958. But sympathy for Hitler's victims, even some understanding of the reasons for Zionism, do not translate to an understanding for Zionism's policies and actions in practice. "I think two wrongs don't make one right, let's put it this way," Talhami says. "Making the Palestinians pay for the Holocaust was horrendous, was a tremendous atrocity. And, worse yet, the Zionist leadership knew exactly what they were doing. The state of Israel was not built by victims of the Holocaust. It was built by political manipulators, people who knew how to lobby with Britain; they knew how to lobby at the centers of power."

This realization is what most distinguishes Palestinian perceptions of Zionism from Jewish and American perceptions. If the latter tend to focus primarily on the Holocaust as the impetus for Zionism and for Israel's creation, Palestinians remember an earlier origin. "Even the myth that Palestine was not populated," Talhami recalls—

I think [early Zionist leaders] knew exactly that Palestine had a lot of people. I have quotes by Ahad Ha'am, the famous linguist [a late nineteenth-century Zionist theorist who had reservations about Zionism's studied ignorance of Palestine's Arab population]. After he visited Palestine, he went back to Europe, and he published letters to the Zionist organization saying, "Look, there are thriving villages and towns and orange groves. It's not an empty desert." They knew exactly what they were doing. They were very cynical. It was a cynical scheme, a cynical scheme. So I think one should separate between victims of the Holocaust and the Zionist movement. They really don't belong with each other, they just don't.

For Khalil Barhoum, the Stanford linguistics lecturer, what he calls Zionism's racist nature and what Zionism has done to Palestinians serve to dilute the goodness of its mission in providing a haven for Jews. As a Palestinian, Barhoum cannot easily relate to Jewish suffering because of his own sense of victimization and, as with almost all Palestinians, one comes to an inconclusive end in discussing Zionism's perceived mission of salvation with him. Palestinians recognized from early on, he says, that Zionists did not want the Palestinians in a Jewish state.

My father tells me about Jewish friends that he had. It's not like there was fighting the whole time; fighting only occurred when the intentions of the Zionists became clear to the Palestinians. It was obvious that they wanted the land to themselves. It was a question of either-or, rather than "let's all share the land; we Jews were persecuted in Europe, so thank you very much for allowing us in, and let's see what we can do together." No. It was more like "you are a hindrance to having our nation established, so we must push you out of the way and then perhaps we can talk about what to do with you afterwards."

Can he conceive of this exclusivity as resulting from persecution, from a sense that Jews could only be safe among Jews? "No, I can't," he responds, "and I'll tell you why. The Zionist movement came long before the Holocaust and Jewish persecution at the hands of Germans in World War II." But there had been persecution for centuries before Hitler. "Yes, of course, but then again, the question to be asked is why is it that all these persecuted Jews all around the world are still living where they have been persecuted for centuries? Why don't they go and live where they have a state and a nation?" This is a common theme among Palestinians, that only a minority of world Jewry actually lives in Israel and that Palestinian displacement occurred in the name of a goal that has not been achieved.

Can he see any analogy between the Jewish situation before 1948 and the Palestinian situation today? "Absolutely, I do," Barhoum responds. "Both peoples have lived in a diaspora-type situation. Both peoples were oppressed. I see myself as a wandering Jew too, because I have no place to go." Can he therefore sympathize with the Zionist impulse? "You're asking the wrong person," he says finally. "You're asking the victim. That's like asking the chicken to acknowledge the right of its killer to put the knife to its neck. Would the chicken see the point in him killing it because he needs to eat? From his point of view, of course, the killer may think he has a perfect right to commit the act." For Barhoum, as for most Palestinians, what it finally comes down to is that whatever the merits of Zionism in the abstract, whatever the Jewish need for an exclusive refuge, nothing justifies the displacement of Palestinians.

For some Palestinians, the idea of Israel as a refuge from persecution breaks down in this day and age when Jews do not suffer persecution in most places in the world. "The people who come from the United States, they are not persecuted Jews; they moved because it's an opportunity," notes Terry Ahwal, former American-Arab Anti-Discrimination Committee coordinator for the Detroit area. In Israel, she points out, they receive a special housing subsidy and other assistance as immigrants—benefits that are not available in the United States. "See, to me, we have to take them and judge them on an individual basis," rather than in the aggregate as Jews who automatically merit special treatment. She believes people like Meir Kahane, for instance, "if they were in any other country, they would be criminals in jail. I mean you cannot just say Kahane is persecuted and therefore he deserves a state that is named Israel. They're the lowest people, who are allowed to do whatever, basically because they're Jews."

Ahwal sympathizes with Jews without reservation because of the Holocaust—"the biggest atrocity in this century is the Holocaust; I mean, I cannot in my life think of anything that would justify this horrendous crime"—and she affirms the right of any Jew born in Israel to live there. "That's all he knows is Israel, so this is the country where he lived and was born, and he has the right to stay in it." But, like many Palestinians, she regards Judaism as a religion rather than a nationality, and she cannot sympathize with the idea that Jews from anywhere in the world, simply because they practice or were born into a particular religion, have automatic immigration rights to a country where she and other natives are denied the right to live.

She believes Palestinians have the same humanitarian obligations that she expects of Jews. "If the Palestinian state is going to come to be," she says, "I hope it's not the cause of the destruction of others. I do feel sympathy for the atrocities [that is, for Jewish victims of Nazi atrocities]; however, they destroyed another community so they could have justice for their own cause, and that's where I disagree. I want the Palestinians to live in peace, to live in justice, but not to destroy somebody else's community."

Some Palestinians refuse to credit psychological fears at all as a motivating factor behind Zionism. Samir Abed-Rabbo, the Vermont publisher, believes, with many other Palestinians, that Zionism is a classic colonialist enterprise, launched at a time when colonialism was in vogue. "The nineteenth century was a century where the old colonial powers wanted to conquer everybody else, and Herzl and his Zionist movement, in alliance with these powers, wanted also to have a colony of their own," he says. "The British were out conquering a large part of the world, the French were conquering a smaller part, even the Portuguese were conquering a part of the world at that time. Germany had its own colony, and [the Zionists] looked around and said, 'Oh yes, since they are conquering and we are here—we seem to be left out—why don't we, in association with a colonial power, take our people and go establish a Zionist colony?'"

Abed-Rabbo discounts the notion that the need to end the European persecution of Jews outweighed the colonialist impulse because, he says, other peoples have been persecuted as badly. When it is observed that Jews have been persecuted in many places, he mentions the Gypsies; when it is observed that the scale of the Holocaust was more massive, he mentions the massacres in Cambodia. "I am not belittling the Holocaust," he says, but "throughout history suffering is not the monopoly of the Jews." Mankind should learn from the suffering it has inflicted on all peoples, he believes, but should not glorify the suffering of one people.

> Throughout history we have these kind of experiences, but we never learned from them. You cannot try to just segregate one holocaust and ignore the rest—or not even ignore, just put them aside for a while and concentrate on one experience and say, "But the magnitude is so big." The killing of one human being is so big to me. And [Elie] Wiesel going around and making a profession of talking about the Holocaust and forgetting the meaning of the Holocaust— when I hear that, that gives me an indication that people are engaging in show business or are motivated by political considerations, and they are not involved in studying and preventing similar things from happening.

The idea that Jewish fears have been manipulated by Zionist and Israeli leaders for cynical purposes is prevalent among Palestinians. Mohamed Odetalla, a young Detroit area grocery and liquor store owner, echoes many Palestinians when he says he believes that Israeli leaders "have a need to keep the people insecure. They like the state of siege. It justifies building

135

settlements, expropriating land, getting money, donations from the Jews in this country. I think their intention is to keep this feeling of Israel being the underdog in the eyes of the world."

Samir Ashrawi believes that so much talk of Jewish fears and Jewish complexes and Israeli insecurity diverts attention from what should be the main issue, which is Palestinian insecurity. Palestinians are the ones without a homeland; Palestinians are the ones whose right to exist is not recognized by their principal opponent; Palestinians are the ones who live in refugee camps; Palestinians are the ones who live under occupation in the West Bank and Gaza; Palestinians are the ones whose homes have been destroyed, whose land has been taken, who have been expelled from their homeland. All this is a "natural conclusion, a natural step," Ashrawi believes, arising from the Zionist agenda, from Zionism's inability to accommodate non-Jews. Focusing on the state of the Jewish psyche is merely another way to manipulate world opinion.

"I don't disagree that the perception [of Jewish suffering] exists," Ashrawi acknowledges, "and the anxiety is well founded in the experiences in Europe—Eastern Europe and Central Europe. But today, if you look at the history of the conflict between Israelis and Palestinians and at the facts on the ground, a Palestinian person should have much more a perception of lack of security because he's always on the losing end. He's always been the victim." What he is saying—he repeats it for emphasis—is that Jews may have a reason for anxiety growing out of their European experience, but they have been so dominant in the Middle East that they have little reason to extend that anxiety to their Middle East experience.

Ashrawi is an intense young man, and he has a way of commanding the attention of a roomful of people, in a quiet sort of way, just by stating his case slowly and persistently. Someone interrupts him now. A young Syrian American, Ronnie Hammad, makes the point that, although Israeli fears are manipulated by the Israeli leadership, they have for that reason become a reality for the Israeli people. "Whether it's true or not, whether it's well founded or not," Hammad asks, "do you from your experience with Jews and Israelis find that they have sincere, legitimate concerns?"

Ashrawi thinks their fears of Palestinians and Arabs are too preposterous to be entertained. He cites an example. When he lived in Jerusalem, he met a young Jewish girl from New York who asked him if it were true that the older Palestinian men who walked along the street with their hands clasped behind their backs inside the folds of their *abayas* were actually carrying knives to stab Jewish girls. Everyone in the room bursts into hilarious laughter at the absurdity of the idea. Hammad cites a similar example, but persists with his question. Ashrawi will not credit such fears. "I'm saying that the question has never been asked—and it should be asked— what are the Israelis saying to the Palestinians to secure their existence?"

136

The issue for Ashrawi is not how much fear Israelis have at this point, but what Israelis are willing to do about Palestinian fears.

> You see? That's really the point that I'm driving home. I don't doubt the sincerity of Jews, some Jews and some Israelis in Israel, that they do indeed sit at home thinking, "Look we've had '48 and we've had that," and there's certainly sufficient revision of history to make you believe that they've been always under attack. And I'm sure some of them are genuinely concerned because they have children like we do, and any person would like to live in a house and go to the beach and make money and live in peace and enjoy life. I don't have a problem seeing their humanity, you see. But I think that the Palestinians are the ones who have been the true victims. I've never really heard a Palestinian [official] position asking, "What assurances are you [Israel] giving me?" And I've never heard anybody in the world asking that question in a serious manner: what assurances is Israel giving?

The question of Jewish fears and anxieties always comes around to the matter of Israeli security, the issue on which all discussion of peace proposals and peace negotiations and peace settlements seems to hinge, and Ashrawi's question highlights the uniquely Palestinian perception of this most central issue. Because they see themselves as the primary victims, Palestinians are fundamentally unable to view Israelis as victims. Because they are unable to connect the Jewish experience in Europe to the Israeli experience with the Arab world, they cannot see themselves, as many Israelis do, as latter-day Nazis. As far as Palestinians are concerned, their own hostility toward Israel is based on legitimate grievances, not the racial hatred that drove Naziism. Most significantly, they are unable to understand Israel's concern for security because the facts on the ground point so overwhelmingly to Israeli dominance.

From the Palestinian perspective, Zionism, far from being threatened by Palestinians or any other Arabs, has only expanded its territorial dominion as time has passed. At the start of the British Mandate in 1922, Jews in Palestine owned only 2.9 percent of the land. By 1947, the year Palestine was partitioned, Jewish land ownership had more than doubled but still totaled slightly less than seven percent. [2] The UN partition plan granted the Jewish state fifty-five percent of the land, despite the limited Jewish ownership, and by the end of the 1948-49 war Israel controlled seventy-seven percent of Palestine. The 1967 war brought 100 percent of what had been Palestine under Israeli control, along with vast tracts of other Arab lands.

Zionist leaders were fairly forthright early on in stating that their goal was to take over all of Palestine in stages—which is what Israeli leaders today charge is the Palestinian strategy. David Ben-Gurion told Jewish Agency officials in the 1930s that his ultimate goal was the establishment of a Jewish state in all of Palestine and that acceptance of partition—that is, of a state in only a part of Palestine—would be merely an interim measure until Jewish forces were strong enough to take all the territory.[3] In a report to party colleagues at about the same time he described acceptance of partition as "a stage in the realization of Zionism."[4]

Almost all Palestinians, at least most of the educated, know by heart the statistics on Zionist/Israeli land control, and it is the reality of these figures, of Zionism's continual expansion, rather than the condition of the Jewish psyche, that determines Palestinian views of Israel's security. Fuad Ateyeh, the San Francisco grocer and food distributor who grew up in Qalandiya refugee camp on the West Bank, points out that because his generation, born after 1948, knows nothing of living with Jews in a more or less equal status under a common British hegemony and has no contemporary knowledge of the Holocaust, "we don't know anything about the Jews except they have the force to do anything they want, by force."

The notion that Israel should feel insecure for any objective reason seems so unlikely to Palestinians that it is difficult to get them to focus seriously on the subjective feelings that create a sense of security or insecurity. Palestinians laugh at the idea that they could possibly be a threat to Israel or to Jews. Because they do not consider themselves a threat, and because Israel's strength has finally convinced most Palestinians that they must coexist with an Israeli state, the solution to Israel's security problems seems classically simple to them: the only way to be secure, to put an end to the Arab hostility that is nowadays the only cause of Israeli insecurity, is to become a part of the neighborhood. Israelis and their American supporters like to say that Israelis are a nice group of people who live in a bad neighborhood. Palestinians respond that if Israelis treated Arabs as equals and ceased trying to dominate the neighborhood, they would find it isn't so bad after all. Obviously, nothing is truly that simple, but the Palestinian sense of their own insecurity is so very strong that this will always determine how they view the issue of Israeli security.

Samira F., the San Francisco librarian, raises the issue of Zionism as a colonialist power in the context of how Israel fits into its Middle East neighborhood. In her view, Israel is a Western implant in an Eastern society. She sees it as an outpost of Western imperialism, a colonial proxy doing the bidding of Western powers desirous of keeping the Arab world disunited and submissive. Israelis, she feels, like any colonials, look down on the "natives," who have no rights to independence or even to equality. "Don't tell us, 'You don't have any rights,'" she says. "If the West, if the Americans, if the Jews, the Israelis acknowledge that we have rights, then I think Palestinians will be willing to compromise and come to terms. It's this business of denying the Palestinians that they have rights. There's a psychological block there." Security, Samira believes, can come for Israel when it stops acting primarily in the West's interests. "The security is going to come from some kind of acceptance. They've got to get accepted. They are outsiders as long as they remain Western. I think that's the part I resent most about the creation of Israel, not just the fact that we were dispossessed, but that they have in a way interfered with progress and remained an outpost of Western imperialism in the Middle East."

The perception of Israeli arrogance, of a people with a superiority complex implementing an exclusivist ideology, is pervasive among Palestinians, as is the belief that less exclusivism, less superiority could win Israel a great deal of security. This can quickly become a circular argument—Jews claiming that they crave acceptance but that Arabs withhold it, and Arabs contending that Jews don't want acceptance from Arabs. There is a certain amount of defensiveness in the Palestinians' belief that it is all the Jews' fault and that all would be well if only Jews were more like Arabs, but the argument always for Palestinians comes down to Zionism's exclusivity and Zionism's capacity for hurting Palestinians.

For many Palestinians, Israel's professions of fear for its security appear to be a matter of guilt rather than real fear. "I'm not convinced personally that many Israelis really sincerely honestly inside think that a Palestinian state in the West Bank and Gaza would be a security menace to the state of Israel," says Muhammad Hallaj. "I think this is a guilty conscience coming out. They know that in the rest of the place, the other eighty percent [i.e., Israel proper], Palestinians still hold deeds to that land, and they're taking it, okay? And they can't believe that they could do this to somebody and he would live with them in peace. I think this is the problem Israelis have, the guilty conscience problem, not really fear of a Palestinian state."

"They know their presence there is illegal," says Yousef Anabtawi, the Los Angeles area grocer,

and they want to legitimize their existence, so [Palestinian recognition] is very important to them. Israel has the "complex of the quarter." They said to the whole world, "Give us a small piece of Palestine, a quarter piece of Palestine to establish a national home." From that quarter they took over half, and from the half they took over three-quarters, and from the three-quarters they took it all. Now, they are not willing to give one-quarter to the Palestinians because they are afraid the Palestinians would do the same thing. It is a complex they have. The moment you use a policy, you will not let anybody use it against you. Until now, Israel's borders were not identified. Until this moment. Maybe after ten years they will want to make another war, they'll take Jordan. Their strategy is, where the security of Israel, that's where its borders are. Like when they went to Baghdad to bomb the atomic reactor [in 1981]. Their security is there, so they got the right to go there.

Diana Khabbaz does not speak of Israeli guilt, but she believes that a sense of security can come only from Israelis themselves, not Palestinians. A senior manager at a large computer corporation in the Boston area, Khabbaz has been in this country since 1960 when she came as a teenager from the West Bank town of Beit Jala. "Lots of security is inside you," she says. "To what level are they going to feel secure? I'm not sure. What boundaries are they going to have to feel secure?" Her questions reflect the views of many Palestinians who feel that if Israelis do not feel secure now with the extended borders Israel holds, they will never feel secure and that the solution to their insecurity lies within themselves, not primarily with the Palestinians or their other Arab neighbors.

Although anger governs the attitudes of many Palestinians toward Israel and Zionism, a great many can see the possibilities for understanding between Israelis and Palestinians, at least from their own side. There is considerable doubt, however, that Israel itself, given its Zionist ideology, is capable of reaching an understanding with Palestinians.

Karim Dajani, the son of Nahida and Ghanem Dajani, can even ascribe beautiful motives to Zionism, but he has no faith that Zionists will ever treat Arabs as equals. Dajani is a graduate student in San Francisco, a young man with a wisdom beyond his years and a hip, with-it demeanor that initially gives the impression that he is a wise guy. Most people would not recognize him as a Palestinian; strikingly blond even down to his eyelashes, he has a full head of very curly hair, but his eyes are deep brown. He grew up in Beirut during the civil war and learned what it is like to be a Palestinian by living the reality of it. Now, having come to the United States at the age of fourteen in the middle of the 1982 Israeli invasion of Lebanon, he is trying to study about the issue from books, and it has given him a different kind of understanding—a different and somewhat more moderate perspective. He calls it sense; he feels that he has grown beyond the kind of rhetorical excess that so often substituted for action among his peers in Beirut. "A lot of the hype and flamboyance that I felt when I was fourteen, I realize at age twenty is useless," he says. "It's not about who screams louder, it's about who makes more sense."

Dajani's study has given him a different perspective on Zionism. He is one of the few Palestinians who can say that to him Zionism is a beautiful idea, a pure humanitarian idea in its original conception. What appeals to him is that Zionism was conceived as a refuge for exiled Jews—"something that I as a Palestinian, an exile so to speak, cannot but appreciate." But he

140

comes around to the view of most Palestinians on how Zionism has been implemented in practice. "The idea went wrong when they decided the Palestinians were grasshoppers and when they decided they were going to crush these grasshoppers, that they didn't want them to be part of that land." He is referring specifically to a statement made by Israeli Prime Minister Yitzhak Shamir in early 1988 that the Palestinians engaged in the uprising were nothing but grasshoppers that the Israelis should crush, but he is applying the insect analogy to Zionist treatment of Palestinians from the beginning. "When the Jews came in and took over Palestine, they didn't want any Palestinians. They wanted to erase that reality from the many pages of history. That's where the idea went wrong."

Dajani's uncle, Samir Fadli, strives to teach his son understanding but finds it difficult to pass on to someone so young his sense that Zionists committed an injustice against Palestinians because they regarded Palestinians as less than equal, as well as his feeling that those same Zionists nonetheless have equal rights as human beings. "The Palestinian believes that there's an injustice that happened, and that injustice should be corrected before anything should go on," he says.

> Now, this injustice hasn't been corrected. But I'm put in a very awkward situation at the moment. I have a son who's nine years old. What am I going to tell him about his background? What values am I going to create in this nine-year-old to be a productive human being? I can't ignore the fact that he's of a Palestinian origin. And at the same time I don't want him to be a one-track-minded human being. I want to make him realize that he is a unique human being, equal to every human being on earth. I cannot tell him that if you will go to Palestine—or Israel at this point—you will be a second-class citizen. If I do that, I will be doing the biggest injustice for this nine-year-old. And at the same time, I don't want him to be a radical. So I have first of all to start with the fact that he is a unique human being that has equal rights in the United States, in Israel, in Europe, everywhere. Yet I want him to live peacefully with the Jewish nine-year-old, and I want him to realize that the Jewish nine-year-old also has the same rights, as equals. But [take] any child who is just growing up, nine years old or ten years old, and you instill in him this arrogance that you are better than the other person, you are superior to the other person. How can this person within the next ten years sit down and talk on the same level to the other person? This disturbs me in the Israeli.

Omar Kader thinks Jews will themselves ultimately point out and correct the inequities in the Zionist system and the injustice done to Palestinians.

For one thing, he believes, "truth always, always surfaces," and some enterprising scholar will eventually unearth the truth in this situation. But more than this, Kader believes that Judaism's humanist tradition will force Jews to a critical self-examination that will throw new light on the issue. "Eventually," he says, "the truth of how the Jews have treated Palestinians will be written about by Jews, because true to their nature—true to themselves, true to their culture, true to Jewish tradition and morality, fairness, justice, mercy—they'll expose themselves on that."

Kader carries his argument to what for many Palestinians is its logical conclusion, a conclusion that is anathema to Jews today but that ultimately depends on Jews for its accomplishment: because Zionism is an exclusivist, religion-based ideology that cares nothing for the rights of non-Jews and because Jews have a long moral, humanist tradition, Jews will themselves eventually dismantle Zionism.

The Arabs will have no hand in this process, Kader says. "I think that Jews will dismantle it, not Arabs. When the Arabs let off on Zionism, the Jews will start their introspection. They'll realize what a faulty and what a weak intellectual path they've been on for all these years." This point will come after a peace settlement, he believes, after the Palestinians and other Arabs are content enough to "let off on Zionism" and after Israel feels it can afford the luxury of looking inward.

This transformation does not mean the dismantling of Israel, only of Zionism and its exclusivism, Kader says. But if Zionism ends, isn't that the end of Israel as a Jewish state? Not necessarily, he responds. He foresees a state in Israel that is

> based on the power of Jewish tradition and culture. See, that's what's crazy about this, is Zionism is an intellectually anemic ideology. Judaism is this incredibly powerful, cultural, social, political force, and they've replaced it with this weak Zionism. Can you imagine substituting the Republican party for the Bill of Rights or the Constitution and the tradition of liberties and freedoms? Can you imagine the platform of the Democratic Party substituting for the Constitution? That's essentially what the Jews have done with Zionism, is substituting it for the history, the religious, the cultural, the social traditions of the Jews. I mean, Zionism has nothing. What does it have? It has a hundred years of history? It's a frivolous political theory in the face of [several] thousand years of culture.

A state based on Jewish tradition would be humane and, because exclusivism is not humane, it would be pluralistic, Kader believes. Zionism, as opposed to Judaism, has been neither. "The only face of Zionism that we know today is the suppression of the Palestinian culture. We've seen it only as an arm of Jewish terrorism. I don't see a positive attribute to Zionism. In the twentieth and twenty-first centuries, where democracy is contagious and sweeping, Zionism is anachronistic. It's an eighteenth-century notion, at best nineteenth."

What Jews want, Kader says, is "a dominant piece of Palestine for their own people." He pauses for emphasis. "They can have it. They just can't start with population transfers. The attack on Zionism is not an attack on Israel as a state to stay there," he repeats. "Israel's not going to go out of existence." He does not believe that the destruction of Israel was ever a serious goal of the Palestinians. Any Palestinian who seriously considered this a possibility, he says, "was fooling himself, when a superpower like the United States was backing it as forcefully as it was. I don't doubt that Israelis felt that they could go out of existence and feared; I don't discount their fears. But the Palestinians who thought that or remain to think that are no longer part of the mainstream. We don't debate Israel's existence; we debate the definition."

Most Palestinians, like Kader, look at Zionism not for what it did *for* Jews but for what it did *to* Palestinians. It is difficult and at this point probably impossible for Jews to share this perspective, and particularly to entertain the notion of dismantling an ideology that gave them salvation. But it is important to remember that when Palestinians speak of Zionism coming to an end, they are speaking from the perspective of a people over whom Zionism has been consistently dominant for a century and who perceive themselves to have experienced only harm at Zionism's hand. It is also important to remember that if they speak of the end of Zionism, they no longer speak of the end of Israel.

NOTES

[1] On the situation of Palestinians living in Israel, see Lustick, *Arabs in the Jewish State*. The quotation is cited in Sheldon L. Richman, "Zionism Mandates Official Discrimination Against Non-Jews," *Washington Report on Middle East Affairs* (December 1991/January 1992): 22.

[2] Appendix I, "Population, Immigration, and Land Statistics, 1919-1940," in Walid Khalidi, ed., *From Haven to Conquest: Readings in Zionism and the Palestine Problem Until 1948* (Washington: Institute for Palestine Studies, 1987), p. 841; and Morris, *The Birth of the Palestinian Refugee Problem*, p. 170.

[3] Cited in Ibid., p. 24.

[4] Cited in Shabtai Teveth, *Ben-Gurion and the Palestinian Arabs: From Peace to War* (New York: Oxford University Press, 1985), p. 188.

7 Israel and
"The Palestine We Can Have"

*There are two Palestines: there is the
Palestine of the heart and the Palestine
we can have.*

Hanan Ashrawi[1]
Bir Zeit University

*I would settle for a state on the West
Bank and Gaza. Enough killing, enough
bloodshed, enough jailing, enough suffering, enough scattering all over the
world. At least we would have someplace where we can have our foundation. But to go and ask for the whole
thing, I think we are asking for the impossible.*

Fuad Ateyeh
San Francisco
businessman

In November 1988 by an eighty-two-percent majority, the Palestine National Council, the legislative arm of the PLO, formally declared its acceptance of what has come to be called the two-state solution—that is, an Israeli and a Palestinian state existing side by side. In a declaration of independence and an accompanying political statement—adopted by a vote of
253-46 with ten abstentions following a three-day meeting in Algiers—the
PNC declared the existence of an independent Palestinian state, recognized
Israel's existence, accepted UN Security Council Resolutions 242 and 338,
which the United States regards as the principal bases for a peace settlement, and renounced terrorism.

The recognition of Israel was implicit rather than explicit: in accepting
the UN partition resolution of 1947 as providing the basis for the international legitimacy of a Palestinian state, the PNC by implication acknowledged the legitimacy accorded to Israel by the same resolution; by limiting
its demand for an Israeli withdrawal to "all the Palestinian and Arab territories it occupied in 1967," the PNC tacitly accepted Israel's existence within

its pre-1967 borders; and the call for "arrangements for the security and peace of all states in the region" implied acceptance of an Israeli state.[2]

Neither Israel nor the United States considered the PNC's implied recognition of Israel adequate. The United States had, since 1975 when then-Secretary of State Henry Kissinger made a pledge to Israel, demanded explicit PLO recognition of Israel's "right" to exist as a condition for any U.S. dialogue with the PLO. PLO Chairman Yasir Arafat finally made the recognition explicit, on demand from the United States, at a news conference in Geneva a month after the PNC declaration, affirming that the PLO accepted "the right of all parties concerned in the Middle East conflict to exist in peace and security...including the state of Palestine, Israel and other neighbors" and that Palestinian "survival does not destroy the survival of the Israelis as their rulers claim."[3] A day earlier during a speech to a special session of the UN in Geneva, Arafat had said, "Our people...does not seek its freedom at the expense of anyone else's freedom, nor does it want a destiny which negates the destiny of another people."[4]

The PLO had essentially, although not explicitly, accepted the two-state solution in 1974, when in the wake of the October 1973 war the PNC expressed its support for establishment of a "national authority" on only a portion of Palestine. But the policy was highly ambiguous: there was little support within the PLO at that time for an expression of even implicit acceptance of Israel; the PLO described its strategy as merely a "stage," implying lingering hopes for taking back all of Palestine; and armed struggle against Israel, which had been the guiding principle since the PLO's foundation in 1964, was retained, along with diplomacy, as a pillar of the PLO strategy.

The PLO was reluctant in this period to make concessions openly and explicitly, and it was unable to gain a hearing in Israel or the United States for what concessions it had made. In the words of one Palestinian scholar, "Most PLO representatives were too inept to persuade their Western audiences that a major change had taken place, and the handful of articulate Palestinian intellectuals were no match for the scores of Israeli and American Zionist academics, analysts, and journalists who persistently questioned Palestinian intentions and opposed Palestinian aspirations."[5] With the PLO's explicit acceptance of Israel and of its right to exist in 1988, the mainstream of the Palestinian movement officially went on record as favoring an outcome—coexistence with Israel—that had for some time been accepted as inevitable by the majority of Palestinians.

Despite this majority, one finds among Palestinians a full range of opinions on the issue. A small number, reflected in the eighteen percent who voted against the PNC platform, remain unable to reconcile themselves to coexistence with the state that they feel took Palestinian land. Another proportion, also reflected among the eighteen percent, accepts a two-state solution but has deep misgivings about the wisdom of explicitly declaring for such a solution before Israel and the United States are ready to recognize the legitimacy of Palestinian nationalism.

This same school of thought tends to object on principle to the concessions Palestinians made in order to be represented in the peace talks that began in Madrid in October 1991. These Palestinians object particularly to the prohibition imposed on including in the Palestinian delegation any representative from East Jerusalem, any diaspora Palestinian, and any representative of the PLO. This group does not oppose the two-state formula and does not oppose negotiations with Israel, but feels that the Israeli-imposed restrictions on who negotiates for the Palestinians, and the U.S. acquiescence in these restrictions, clearly indicate that neither Israel nor the United States is serious about negotiating a real peace agreement. Palestinians, they feel, should not open themselves to the humiliation of making more concessions themselves when they are certain Israel will make none.

Even within the mainstream, there are shades of difference in viewpoint—what might more accurately be called differing frames of mind—about the kinds and the timing of Palestinian concessions to Israel. For all Palestinians, recognizing Israel's existence, and particularly its right to exist, has been extremely difficult because this has meant relinquishing all claim to three-quarters of what was once Palestine—that is, what is now Israel proper—without any guarantee that Palestinians will be accorded the right to live independently in the remaining one-quarter, the West Bank and Gaza.

"Don't forget that we are sacrificing a lot by accepting the West Bank" and Gaza as the limits of a Palestinian state, says Yousef Anabtawi, the Los Angeles area grocer, expressing the views of the vast majority of Palestinians. Although Anabtawi is from the town of Zeita on the West Bank, it is so close to the border with Israel that his family lost seventy acres of agricultural land lying farther west when armistice lines were drawn in 1949. "They say 'territory for peace,'" he comments—referring to the formula, supported by the United States and by most opposition elements in Israel, that calls on Israel to trade land in the West Bank and Gaza for peace from the Arabs—"but we are giving them peace and land at the same time, because Palestine 1948, it's ours." Anabtawi is expressing an almost universal feeling among Palestinians that in formally recognizing Israel and thus ceding their claim to the lands within pre-1967 Israel, the Palestinians have already given Israel land and are now also willing to give it peace if Israel will relinquish the West Bank and Gaza.

Osama Fawzi, the Houston journalist whose family fled the town of Tarshiha in 1948, is among the unreconciled. "I don't believe in the small state," he says, referring to a truncated West Bank-Gaza state, "because

146

Palestine is the whole of Palestine. The problem did not appear after the '67 war; it began before, and the PLO is before '67. You know, the Palestinian people are Muslims and Christians and Jews; there were Palestinian Jews before 1948 in Palestine. They are Palestinians—not the Jews who come to our country from Africa, [but] Jews who were born there." What about Jews who have been born in Palestine since 1948—does he accept their right to live there? "I know that in Israeli society there are citizens born there, who didn't know other countries," he answers. "But this is not my problem. This is an Israeli legal problem. They've made this problem for their kids, not me. I have the right to return to my home, to my land, my father's land, my father's home. I have the right to live in his home, not the Jew comes from Poland who lives in the same home. For me it's a simple case; for them it's complicated because they created the situation for their society, not me."

For other Palestinians, nothing about the situation is so black and white. Samir Abed-Rabbo, the Vermont publisher, has serious reservations about the two-state solution but, unlike Osama Fawzi, no expectation that things can return to the situation before 1948. His principal concern is with Zionist intentions toward Palestinians—with how a small Palestinian state would fare in the shadow of Israel and whether, in light of Israel's continued rejection of Palestinian nationalism, recognition of Israel has weakened the Palestinians.

"I don't want a state for the sake of establishing a state," he says. "The flag is always in my heart. Nobody can erase it from my memory, and I am here whether they recognize me or not." He wants a state that will not be at Israel's mercy and will not compromise basic Palestinian rights, and he does not believe that the state now envisioned can be truly independent, of Israel or of its Arab neighbors. "Even if a Palestinian state is established, I see the government of this state doing police duty on behalf of Israel. Even if a state is established, our workers will continue to be used as cheap labor by Israel. And not only for Israel, but also for Jordan, Kuwait, and Saudi Arabia. How is it going to be self-sufficient? How is it going to be independent if a ship is to unload in Gaza, and to go to the West Bank it has to go through Israel, and Israel has direct control over that corridor?"

More fundamentally, in Abed-Rabbo's view, the two-state solution does not address the core issue of the Palestinian-Israeli conflict. "To ask a Palestinian who is from Haifa or Jaffa or Yasour to recognize the legitimacy of Israel is like asking the Jews, although they have been compensated for the crimes of Hitler, to accept the legitimacy of his acts," he asserts. "The Palestinians have not been compensated. If you are trying to establish long-lasting peace, you have to address all the factors involved, and one factor—the most important one—is how you are going to rectify an injustice. You do not rectify an injustice by an injustice or by partial justice. You can't. First of all, you have to address yourself to that injustice."

The injustice, Palestinian dispersion in 1948, could be rectified, Abed-Rabbo believes, either by allowing displaced Palestinians the right of return to their former towns, if they so desire—on the understanding that they will be treated equally with Jews—or by compensation for those who choose not to return. This demand is in line with the official PLO position, but Abed-Rabbo doubts that Israel as now constituted, as an exclusive Jewish state, could ever grant Palestinians the right of return or even equality with Jews. If Israel acknowledged that Palestinians had equal rights, he believes, it would basically be abandoning Zionism. "The Zionists went to Palestine claiming that nobody was there, and all of a sudden you come and you say, 'Yeah, these Palestinians have been there all along, and we have been lying'—then you are, in a way, telling the whole world and yourself, 'We have been deceiving you and ourselves.' It takes a big, visionary people to do that, and I don't think Shamir or Arik Sharon or any of these are that kind of people. Colonists will only change if they are forced to do so."

This is where his strongest reservation about the two-state solution arises because he does not believe that, without dismantling Israel's discriminatory institutions, lasting peace can be achieved. "I am a strong believer," he says, "that in order to move forward with the [peace] process, the laws and institutions that discriminate against the Palestinians, whether they are so-called Israeli Arabs or Palestinians of the territories, like myself, have to be abolished. In saying this, I am not saying that the Jews have to be thrown into the sea, I am saying that in order for peace to have a chance, the character of the state of Israel has to be changed." He likens the situation to the race situation in the United States: only when anti-discrimination laws were passed, only when anti-racism became institutionalized, was there any progress toward racial harmony.

He believes that there can be true peace between Israelis and Palestinians only when Jews recognize and treat Palestinians as their equals and as a people against whom an injustice was committed. Until that time, he says, all efforts to deal with the Palestinian issue will be no better than giving a man suffering from a headache a remedy for his foot. "I don't believe that having two states is a viable solution when one state is as powerful as Israel and two-thirds of the other state's population is in exile. The two state-solution will provide only a short honeymoon."

Abdullah Wajeeh, who sits on the PNC and was one of the forty-six who voted against the political declarations in November 1988, has reservations as well, but he typifies those dissidents within the Palestinian movement who have bowed to the mainstream view and accepted Israel's existence as inevitable. Palestinians like Wajeeh have for some time recognized the reality of Israel but, out of a principled refusal to grant Israel legitimacy in what they consider the Palestinian homeland, have refused to accept formal coexistence with Israel. A professor of mathematics in Detroit, Wajeeh and his fellow PNC dissidents voted against accepting the two-state solution but in the end lined up behind the majority. "The decision was taken. I was opposing it," he says. "I spoke and I lost my voice speaking against it, but when the vote came out and passed, I am with it. I am for it, and I will defend it. And this is not only about myself. I'm talking about this is the attitude of the people who attended that session."

Wajeeh harbors no bitterness at having lost his fight, and he has no hesitation about speaking of Israel as a reality. "Our leadership, I think, came of age, they matured," he says. "I think we've become more realistic." Wajeeh is a tall, distinguished looking man with close-cropped graying hair. He has just given up smoking, and he plays with a string of amber beads "to keep my fingers busy." He is good natured but intense, and it is easy to picture him arguing his case vehemently at the PNC meeting.

Reality for the Palestinians now has to do, he believes, with cutting their losses and accepting what is possible rather than striving for dreams. International politics and the demise of the Soviet Union limit the Palestinians' possibilities, he realizes, "and most of all—unfortunately I say it with bitterness—that the Arab countries have not given us Palestinians a hand to do what we are supposed to have done." While the Palestinians have waited for the superpowers and the other Arabs to help them, too many of their number have suffered. "To relieve the agony and the suffering of the Palestinian people," he says, "I will accept a state on the West Bank and Gaza. I know that I cannot ask for all Palestine while living in the United States, having a steak for dinner maybe and some wine, while in the meantime a man and his family are in the refugee camp in Lebanon or he's in Yemen, his son is in Cairo, his sister is in the West Bank, his aunt or his uncle or his brother in Gaza. These people have paid enough."

The degree to which any individual Palestinian is willing to make compromises to achieve a peace settlement with Israel is often a matter of his or her temperament—of the level of cynicism or anger or optimism. The views of three well known Palestinians illustrate the point. All three are from the West Bank, although their experiences of Israel and Israelis have been wholly different. One, Salah Ta'mari, is a high-ranking Fatah military commander whose views of Israelis have been formulated under fire in Jordan and Lebanon, in internment as a prisoner of war, and through a unique friendship with an Israeli journalist and his wife; the others, Muhammad Hallaj and Emile Sahliyeh, are intellectuals and academics who have lived and taught under Israeli occupation. Despite different experiences and vastly different temperaments, all three come out in the end at the same place on a peace settlement. They can reasonably be said to reflect the range of views within the Palestinian mainstream.

Salah Ta'mari is the *nom de guerre* of As'ad Suleiman Hasan, a native of Bethlehem with a master's degree in English literature and a quarter-century career as a military commander in Fatah. As a student in Cairo in the mid-1960s, Ta'mari became an activist in the then fledgling Fatah organization and, when he had finished his studies, assumed a military command in Jordan, later moving to Lebanon. As a military commander, he always answered directly to Yasir Arafat and presumably still does, although he no longer performs a military function. In 1982 during Israel's invasion of Lebanon, he gave himself up to Israeli military forces in Sidon and remained a prisoner, one of the highest ranking military officials ever held by Israel, for a year and a half.[6]

Ta'mari came to the United States in 1986, after being expelled from Jordan when King Hussein closed the offices of Fatah and the PLO in a dispute with the PLO over peace negotiating tactics. He is on the staff of the Arab League mission to the United Nations and spends a great deal of time working with Palestinian-American young people, primarily to acquaint them with their Palestinian culture and heritage. Working with children and youth has been of particular importance to Ta'mari for some time. He headed the Fatah youth organization Ashbal in Lebanon before the Israeli invasion, familiarizing Palestinian youngsters, primarily from refugee camps, with their people's history and culture by teaching them handicrafts, music, poetry, and art and organizing summer camps. The children were also given training in the use of weapons, a program begun after the massacre of Palestinians by Christian Lebanese militiamen at the Beirut refugee camp of Tel Za'tar in 1976, during which thousands of children unable to defend themselves were murdered.[7]

Ta'mari's story has many of the elements of a Hollywood contrivance: the intellectual revolutionary who can discuss T. S. Eliot as easily as he can military tactics, who organized a Palestinian children's orchestra amidst the bloodshed and desperation that descended on Beirut in the mid-1970s, who spent his spare time reading Zionist history, who ended up in an Israeli prison camp discussing the fine points of political theory with camp commandants and Israeli journalists. The romance and uniqueness of this intriguing man do not end there. Born into relative poverty in Bethlehem, one of the ten children of a cook, he is married to a former queen of Jordan, Dina Abd el-Hamid, the first wife of King Hussein—a woman Ta'mari once cursed as an impoverished youngster and whom he married, ironically, in an underground hideout in the midst of the Jordanian-Palestinian civil war in 1970.

But there is nothing contrived or romanticized about the man himself. A tall, lanky man with an almost ascetic demeanor, he is interesting not because he is suave and dashing but precisely because he is not. His hair is disheveled, his eyes bloodshot, his khaki trousers unpressed. What stands out about him is his fervor, his single-mindedness. He has no time for social niceties or small talk. It is somehow incongruous to meet him in the northwest Washington apartment of a friend of his; his dedication and ardor for the Palestinian cause, although highly intellectual, seem better suited to the underground or to a youth camp than to the salons of a place like Washington, D.C.

Ta'mari seems to begin any interview by assuming command of it. Aharon Barnea, an Israeli journalist who interviewed Ta'mari during his Israeli captivity and later formed a close friendship with him, describes being immediately put on the defensive in his first meeting when Ta'mari began by accusing the Israelis of indiscriminate killing of civilians during bombing raids in Lebanon and angrily noted that, after the Jewish experience in the Holocaust, Israelis should be more sensitive to their prisoners of war.[8] Many years later, in a Washington apartment, Ta'mari again takes charge of an interview, launching without preliminary and without questions into a long monologue on Israel.

Palestine "is my country," he says. "It's not theirs. All of it, all of it, from Nakura to Eilat. If you want to discuss things from the standpoint of right and wrong, they have no right to be there. That right given to them by a Bible? That's not my Bible. But they are there, there are people who were born there, they have originated there. That's a different story. But on principle they have no right to be there. It's my country, it's where my father, grandfather, forefathers lived for generation after generation. So how the hell could it be their country?"

There is something powerful and mesmerizing about the way Ta'mari talks, and one is hesitant to interrupt him for fear of breaking whatever spell it is that he has cast, or perhaps of arousing his anger. The utter surety with which he speaks conveys a sense of inadequacy in the listener that is strangely enervating.

He goes on, talking now about reality rather than about principle. "We believe in the two-state solution," he says, "not because this solution is the most just. It is the least unjust solution. We accept it. When I talk about principle, it's for the record, that on principle they have no right to be there, on principle it's my country, on principle we have the right to return. But they are there. I concede to that. We can live together, we can live together, and it's inevitable. Living together, coexistence, is inevitable."

The idea of coexistence between the Jewish and the Palestinian people does not bother Ta'mari, but like many Palestinians, his acceptance of the two-state solution—of a solution that will require Palestinians to forfeit any right to sovereignty in three-quarters of what was once Palestine—is reluctant. He has difficulty primarily, like large numbers of Palestinians, with the formula that requires recognition of Israel's "right" to exist rather than simply of its existence.

Ta'mari distinguishes between the people and the state of Israel on this question. Those who demand this recognition from the Palestinians, he says, treat the state and the people as one, "so we get stuck, we get cornered." If Palestinians refuse to recognize the state's right, they are accused of wanting the extermination of the people; yet if they accept the people's right to exist, they are also accepting the state's right, with which Ta'mari and many others have problems. "The Jews, the Israelis have the right to exist," he says. "They are like other human beings who have the right to exist. As for the state, it's something else. If the state of Israel is built on justice, then maintaining justice for the Palestinians will help her flourish and survive. If maintaining justice for the Palestinians harms the state, that means there is something very wrong with the very foundations of that state."

It is for these reasons that accepting the two-state solution has been difficult for Ta'mari and other Palestinians. "If we accept, it is because we are suppressed." But there is a more positive reason as well. "If we accept, it's because we are eager to have peace, and it is well known that the oppressed are more creative in finding ways and means to achieve peace, because they have the interest in maintaining peace and justice, not the oppressor."

At about this point, Ta'mari lights a cigarette that he has been fingering unlighted since he began to speak. The action does not break his stride. "No matter how strong [the Israelis] are now, no matter how strong they may remain for the future, yet there will come a time when they will have to concede the idea of coexistence." He believes that the Palestinians have shown their creativity by accepting the two-state formula and that the burden is now on Israel to show that it is willing to accept coexistence. In Ta'mari's vocabulary, coexistence and justice, for Jews as well as for Palestinians, seem to be synonymous. Thus far, he feels, Israelis reject coexistence because of their dream of establishing an exclusively Jewish state.

But to Ta'mari's mind, this striving for exclusivity has destroyed the values of Judaism. "If you bring all the prophets, if you bring ten tribes and give them control over a people, after a while they have to use the same tactics that other occupiers use: divide and rule, the carrot and the stick, tempt people, buy people, banish people, crush people." If Israelis continue their exclusivity and refuse to work for coexistence, he says, "they will lose forever the moral force that maintained their survival for so long. And what they lose, we acquire, we take."

Ta'mari had read quite a bit about Israel and Israelis, but he never directly encountered them until the Lebanon war. "Although I know that Israelis were our bitter enemies," he says, "yet somewhere in the back of my mind, somewhere deep in me, I believed that certain things the Israelis

152

would never do, no matter how brutal they are." What changed his mind was the Israeli practice in southern Lebanon of stamping an identifying number on the backs of all inhabitants' hands. "The justification was they needed it for identification. But what came up to my mind when I saw it was the tattoo—the Nazis and the set of numbers [tattooed on concentration camp inmates]. I could have never imagined the Israelis do that. Ne-ver." He draws this word out. "Ne-ver."

This leads into a long discussion of Israeli practices in the West Bank and Gaza since the *intifada* began. His principal theme is Israel's similarity to the Nazis. "Why should they be different?" he asks. "What did the Nazis do that the Israelis are not doing? Kill children? They are. Gas chambers? Well, they are bringing gas to the people." He is referring to teargas and the numerous deaths induced from inhaling teargas at close range.

Ta'mari's Israeli friend, Aharon Barnea, found it impossible to understand how a man of Ta'mari's "intelligence and open-mindedness" could possibly equate Palestinian suffering to Jewish suffering at Nazi hands and finally put his comparison down to "pure propaganda."[9] This is indeed an area where there will probably never be understanding between Jews and Palestinians. The monstrousness of the Holocaust—and, perhaps more significant, the depth of Jewish feeling about the Holocaust—do not come through to Palestinians because of their own suffering. By the same token, the Palestinians' sense that the suffering of any people simply because of their ethnic identity is an injustice, whether inflicted on Palestinians because they are Palestinians or on Jews because they are Jews, does not come through to Jews.

Salah Ta'mari seems a bit out of place in the United States. He lives and breathes Palestinian politics and is by his own description "the core of the core of the core of the PLO." He is here chiefly because he has nowhere else to go, although he also believes that more can be done for the cause from here, that only the United States can obtain justice from Israel for the Palestinians. He loves America's natural beauty, but he identifies with the alienation of Native Americans—"they are the closest to us in the way they feel"—and he is bitter about the U.S. attitude toward the Palestinians. "What's going on now is shocking," he says. The U.S.-PLO dialogue, conducted from late 1988 when the PLO recognized Israel until June 1990, when the United States suspended contact after an abortive Palestinian terrorist attack on a Tel Aviv beach, was a sham, Ta'mari believes. The United States was engaged in dialogue, he felt, not in order to achieve peace but to try to outmaneuver the PLO, to fragment it and divert it so that Israel could crack down harder on the *intifada*.

Ta'mari ends on a poignant note, talking about his fear that Bethlehem when he sees it again will not be like his romantic memories of it. "You know, when I was young, I always thought that the buildings in Bethlehem were the highest in the world. Although I have seen the Empire State Building, I have seen the Sears Tower in Chicago, etcetera, I still believe that those buildings [in Bethlehem] are much higher. I am afraid to go back and then that building will shrink. I don't want it to shrink. Honestly, I don't want it to shrink."

When was he last in Bethlehem? "I reached the suburbs of Bethlehem as a commander in '67. It was so strange to be there after you crossed the river. I felt I belonged."

Muhammad Hallaj and Emile Sahliyeh represent opposite sides of the same coin on the question of dealing with Israel—Hallaj approaching the problem with something of the same anger and combativeness that characterize Salah Ta'mari's views, Sahliyeh with a kind of hope that looks for possibilities rather than problems. They both, however, start out from the same sense that the only justice for Palestinians lies in independence, and they both reach the same end in the conclusion that a two-state solution is the only realistic possibility.

Muhammad Hallaj is a political scientist and a political commentator, and he would rather talk about politics than about himself, but he doesn't hesitate to answer a question about his personal identification as a Palestinian because this has political implications for the Palestinian cause as a whole. "I'm always amazed," he begins over coffee in the offices of *Palestine Perspectives*, a magazine he edited for several years in the 1980s, "how in this country in particular that point [the existence of a uniquely Palestinian identity] has always been questionable." Pro-Israeli commentators have long maintained that, at least until recently, Palestinians never had a separate Palestinian identity, that they thought of themselves as Syrians or as part of the collectivity of Arabs or, during the Jordanian occupation of the West Bank from 1948 to 1967, as Jordanians. But Hallaj disputes this. Born in the 1930s during the British Mandate in Palestine, he says that he always knew he was a Palestinian and different from Jordanians, Syrians, Lebanese, and other Arabs.

He is a warm, friendly man with a wry sense of humor, and he laughs as he says this, as if the absurdity of having to affirm so essential a part of his identity is self-evident, like having to assure everyone that he has known all along that he is male. "We knew there were circumstances that led to the fact that we didn't have our own independent country, our own government, but that has nothing to do with the clarity of our identity in our minds. We were Palestinian."

Neither clarity of identity, however, nor the simple belief in the justness of their cause will win the Palestinians their independence, Hallaj believes, without a change in the balance of power. He finds a West Bank-Gaza state an adequate if not just solution because it would solve "some of the most pressing needs of the Palestinian community: a place where they can be relatively secure, where they belong as of right, not by sufferance. Right now, every Palestinian on earth today lives by sufferance and not by right. Everywhere." But the Palestinians will not attain that state without a struggle.

"I think the conditions for a fair settlement don't exist," he says. "There's no way a fair settlement in the Middle East can happen as long as the balance of power is so out of kilter." He has a political scientist's explanation for how this applies to politics as well as to military power. "Politics is different from adjudication as a process. You see, in a legal context the weak can win. You can go to court and win that case, even though you are poorer and less muscular and even less clever than the other guy. And the reason is that in the system of courts, the judicial process, there are agreed rules, and all you have to do is show that your case is compatible with the agreed rules and you win." It does not work this way in politics, he says. "Politics is warfare by other means. It's a power game," and the Palestinians do not have the power.

The major problem is that, in Hallaj's view, Israel cannot willingly make territorial concessions in the West Bank and Gaza without compromising Judaic history. "This is something a lot of people, including Palestinians, don't seem to realize: that Israel really came to being in '67, not in '48. In Jewish history and religion and Zionist ideology and mentality, the land of Israel is the West Bank, not the coastal region. It's Jerusalem and Hebron, Nablus. I'm not very optimistic about the possibility of Israel, without bitter struggle, giving up any part of the West Bank."

Redressing the imbalance of power and forcing Israel to accept territorial compromise does not necessarily mean war, Hallaj says. Political strength is as important as military strength, and he feels that the Arab states have it in their power to force a change of viewpoint on Israel and the United States without using arms at all. The trouble is, they do not use their political strength. Take U.S. policy in the Middle East, for example, he says. The Arabs are always complaining that it is unbalanced, biased in Israel's favor, "but they're not doing anything to make the U.S. reconsider its policies, so why should the U.S. reconsider a policy that's working without much of a cost? The Arabs have not shown the United States that this total bias on Israel's behalf carries a price tag." The perception in Washington, he says, is that the Arabs are "incapable of being angry." As a result, neither Israel nor the United States has any incentive to change policy.

The demand that the Palestinians recognize Israel is a diversion from the real issue, "a cop-out," Hallaj feels. What state, he asks, has ever come into being "on the condition that it would not be a threat to its neighbor? Such guarantees have never been demanded of anyone, because it's nonsense. With the Kellogg Pact [the Kellogg-Briand Pact of 1928], they

155

wanted to outlaw wars. Nonsense. And then we had the biggest war, World War II, a few years later. People don't have to recognize each other if they simply find ways to live with each other. The U.S. didn't recognize China for many years, but that doesn't mean they went to war with each other."

The real issue, he believes, echoing Salah Ta'mari and most other Palestinians, is Israel's intentions. "I accept the existence, the reality. There is a reality in the state of Israel. We used to put quotation marks every time we said 'Israel.' We don't do that anymore. We're much more pragmatic and realistic than most people give us credit for." He laughs ironically again. "This is not an issue for us; this is not a problem. You see, this is an Israeli definition of the Arab-Israeli conflict, whether or not the Arabs are willing to accept the state of Israel. Nonsense. The real problem is whether Israelis are willing to accept the reality of Palestinian nationhood."

Hallaj believes that the conflict involves far more than a psychological problem, and he disdains efforts to resolve it by creating greater understanding. Simply sitting down and reaching an understanding, he feels, will not work because for Palestinians, the very existence of Israel has meant the negation of their nationhood, and Israelis fear that the creation of a Palestinian state will mean the negation of Israel. "It's not what the PLO says or the type of leadership it has" that disturbs Israel, he says.

> Yasir Arafat could wear a business suit and a tie and shave three times a day. It's the agenda that bothers them, not how the Palestinians are going about achieving their objectives. I don't think that we're talking about a cosmetic problem here. We're talking about the most basic and fundamental issues, the right to exist. They blamed us for decades, that we caused the problem by refusing their right to exist. I think now things have been reversed. The problem is caused essentially by Israel's refusal to accept the Palestinians' right to exist as a national entity. This is the issue. This is why I'm very pessimistic.

The views of the third person, Emile Sahliyeh, are not markedly different, although he takes a somewhat different approach. Born in Jerusalem and raised in the West Bank village of Taybeh, Sahliyeh, like Hallaj, is a political scientist and taught at Bir Zeit University on the West Bank for several years, from 1978 to 1984. He would have preferred to stay at Bir Zeit but decided to return to the United States, where he had studied for five years in the 1970s, basically because Israel made life too difficult. He cites two major reasons: because the university was so often closed by Israeli officials for weeks and months at a time, which meant closure of all its library and other facilities, his opportunities for research and writing were severely restricted, and because his wife is an American she could not obtain an Israeli identity card and had to leave the country every three months to renew her visitor's permit. Sahliyeh teaches now at the University of North Texas near Dallas.

His emphasis is on the changes in the Palestinian position over the years—from the 1950s and '60s when no Arab entity would deal with Israel at all, to today when only a small minority among Palestinians still advocates dismantling Israel. "You can never ask people to forget the place where they were born and the place where they believe they belong," he says, "but political realities are totally different things," and Palestinian policy has come to be governed by political reality. Sahliyeh is a gentle, soft-spoken man for whom nothing is wholly black or white. He is blind and, by asking anyone he meets to take his arm to guide him to a meeting place, he gives the impression of placing trust in the visitor and thus engenders a reciprocal trust. As he talks about Palestinians who dream of Palestine and those who live by reality, his manner conveys a sense of being able to understand both the dream and the need for realism.

Specifically in answer to the point that Israel regards the Palestinians' dream of a nation as a long-term strategic goal that threatens Israel's existence, Sahliyeh notes that all nations have ideals that they would like to see achieved but would not use force to impose. Speaking a few years before the Soviet Union's dismantlement, he observes that the United States, for instance, "would like to see the rest of the world become more democratic, the Soviets would like to see socialism spread throughout the world. It doesn't mean they would destabilize the rest of the world to do that."

Similarly, he foresees that the Palestinians, having achieved a West Bank-Gaza state, would not jeopardize it by pursuing unrealizable dreams. "Once you establish a state and once you have something tangible, you don't want to destroy your efforts, your struggle for forty years, to destroy it overnight. Because what does it take for Israel to come roll their tanks and overrun the West Bank and reoccupy it again?" For most Palestinians, this fact, this realization of Israel's overwhelming military strength, is the crux of the matter, the reason dreams of retaking all of Palestine have been discarded.

Sahliyeh believes the Palestinians for years hurt themselves by failing to be explicit about what they would accept. Long ago, he notes—well before the PLO formally accepted the two-state solution, recognized Israel, and accepted UN Resolutions 242 and 338 in November 1988—Yasir Arafat and other PLO officials had informally taken these steps, but the acceptance was always couched in "vague terms" or was qualified by subsequent statements. Sahliyeh feels that the PLO's incremental approach diluted the impact of the changes in its position. "The element of surprise is extremely, extremely important in this case," he says, "that you are doing it and you are coming forward with an imaginative initiative." The PLO failed, at least until November 1988, to achieve this impression of making a breakthrough.

On the other hand, he blames Israel and the United States for failing to give Palestinians any expectation that explicit concessions would achieve substantive progress. All the United States ever offered in return for PLO acceptance of Israel, Sahliyeh notes, was the opening of a U.S.-PLO dialogue. "Big deal," he says, with a rare degree of sarcasm. He wonders how the United States could have expected Arafat, under pressure from a constituency unwilling to compromise, to take back to that constituency an offer from the United States merely to talk to the PLO in return for major concessions. In the event, on the strength of the new confidence gained from the *intifada*, the Palestine National Council did endorse a more conciliatory position on the promise only of dialogue with the United States. Nothing productive came of the dialogue, however, and despite the beginning of peace negotiations in 1991, Sahliyeh is not optimistic that real progress can be made toward a solution.

Speaking in November 1988, he said there might be a chance for progress over time if the United States were to work to convene an international conference, if the Israeli people were to become convinced both of the Palestinians' peaceful intentions and of U.S. determination to pursue a peace settlement, and if they then pressed the Israeli government for movement or elected a new, more moderate government. These are a great many "ifs." Even in late 1988, when the Palestinians were experiencing some euphoria as a result of the *intifada*'s progress and the declaration of Palestinian statehood, Sahliyeh was skeptical that his projected scenario would come to be. In 1992, he says that his earlier pessimism "still holds." He blames the Palestinians in part for damaging their own chances, but the principal reason for his pessimism remains Israel's refusal to make compromises and the U.S. failure to press Israel harder.

Apart from being morally wrong, Sahliyeh feels, the PLO's failure to condemn Iraq's invasion of Kuwait more strongly had the effect of seriously undermining its diplomatic maneuverability. Until this point, he says, the PLO conducted diplomacy while Palestinians in the occupied territories, the "insiders," carried on the *intifada*. But the PLO so damaged its position that the West Bankers now have to do both. The insiders' need for a peace settlement has become extremely urgent because of Soviet Jewish immigration and the rapid pace of Israeli settlement construction, but the PLO undercut its bargaining power to such an extent that it could not hold out for representation at the negotiating table and risk delaying the start of talks.

For all his dissatisfaction with the PLO, Sahliyeh is not certain that a different PLO position in the Gulf war would have brought tangible gains. The Israeli government, he is certain, would still refuse to negotiate with the PLO. He believes the Palestinians made substantial public relations gains during the opening conference at Madrid in October 1991, but he is doubtful that this will be translated into "actual political gains" in the form of Palestinian statehood anytime in the foreseeable future. Because of Israel's refusal to make compromises and the U.S. failure to impose on Israel a clear-cut freeze in settlement construction, he feels, "the chances of getting a Palestinian state remain grim."

Will the Palestinians nonetheless persist in their quest for an independent state? He is certain they will. Even those Palestinians in the United States "living an extremely comfortable life always talk about the land and their yearning to have a Palestinian state," he says, "although probably many would not go there. You see, the Palestinian state will be like Israel for the Jews all over the world. Something that we can always point to, something that you could think of as a reference point—an emotional, sentimental thing, more than a tangible reality. It's something to identify with."

A state is particularly important, he believes, for those Palestinians who are less comfortably situated. "My top concern are those Palestinians in the West Bank and Gaza and those Palestinians in the refugee camps in Jordan and Syria and Lebanon. These are the ones that are really suffering, physical suffering. And that's why I want to see a Palestinian state. I want to see it in the West Bank and Gaza. I want to see a quick solution for the sake of these people because it's enough, you know, forty years of misery and tragedy. It's a tragic life."

The common theme among these three men—Salah Ta'mari, Muhammad Hallaj, and Emile Sahliyeh—is that the Palestinians have come around, after forty-plus years, to acceptance of Israel and that it is Israel that now blocks a peace settlement. The Palestinians have not come around willingly, to be sure, but reluctantly, in many respects grudgingly—a fact that they feel makes their conversion all the more convincing. The emphases of these particular men may differ, their tones may vary, but their end point is the same: that the Palestinians must accept something or they will get nothing, that Israel's strength is so overwhelming that it can never be defeated militarily and, probably most important, that too many Palestinians have suffered too long and can only expect to end that suffering through compromise.

The realization of Abdullah Wajeeh, the Palestine National Council member from Detroit, that he can no longer sit comfortably in the United States "having a steak for dinner maybe and some wine" and ask for all of Palestine while the majority of less fortunate Palestinians continue to suffer, expresses the belief of a great many Palestinians, those displaced in 1948 as much as those from the West Bank, that the time has come for Palestinians

159

to stop struggling for a principle that is unlikely to be achieved and begin to look for a compromise that will relieve the plight of Palestinians still in refugee camps and living under Israeli occupation.

The 1982 Israeli invasion of Lebanon, although it did not accomplish Israel's goal of eliminating the Palestinian national movement, did bring the Palestinian leadership to the realization that no part of Palestine will be retaken by military means. The events growing out of the invasion—the Sabra and Shatila massacre in 1982 and the "camps war" from 1985-1988 in which Shiite militiamen sporadically held Palestinian refugee camps in the Beirut area under long siege, once for as much as a year—also forced the leadership, as it had never done earlier when it lived among the refugees and was able to protect them to some degree, to focus on the camp residents' intense need for a peace settlement that would end their vulnerability. Furthermore, to the extent that the *intifada* has been a protest by West Bankers and Gazans against the PLO leadership, it has said to them that those living under occupation are no longer willing to bear the physical brunt of the struggle while the leadership sits in Tunis devising theoretical plans and formulating dreams of the impossible.

The Palestinian people realize this as well as, and perhaps better than, the Palestinian leadership. Repeatedly, when asked how the two-state solution can satisfy their aspirations for national identity when it will not allow for Palestinian sovereignty over their birthplaces, refugees from 1948 living in the United States say that the issue is no longer the pursuit of their own personal aspirations but how to ensure the greater good of the whole Palestinian people. When refugees in camps and residents of the occupied territories are suffering physically, these people have come to realize, pursuit of maximum goals has become a luxury.

Elie Khoury, a Detroit physician who fled Jerusalem as a ten-year-old and grew up in Syria, feels that "satisfaction is my least concern, to be satisfied or not. The problem is for those who are in most urgent need of a home. What needs to be satisfied, if there is a solution, is a peace for those who are homeless." For Rajai Abu-Khadra, the Washington economist and petroleum analyst who fled Jaffa as a teenager, accepting a small Palestinian state is "not something I like, but I have to accept some things. It's not Rajai Abu-Khadra, it's the whole people. I'm not thinking of myself, I'm thinking of these people under Israeli occupation. In the final analysis, we have to have somewhere, you know, someplace where we can say, 'This is my country.' We have to be practical. We're living in a world that if one doesn't accept what is available, then he is going to lose another chance."

Readiness to accept the two-state solution, to "accept what is available," is so pervasive among Palestinians that one finds it among those of all social and economic strata, among the educated and the uneducated, among activists as well as the politically inactive, among 1948 refugees as well as West Bankers and Gazans. The point bears repeating with a sampling of the views of Palestinians who are either refugees or the children of refugees from 1948.

MONA SAHOUM: Sahoum was born in Jerusalem to a father who had left Nazareth in 1948 and a mother whose family remained in Nazareth but who herself left Israel in 1958 to marry: "I hate to say yes [to giving up claims to Palestinian land in Israel] because [I don't like] to think of my family not being included—they are suffering and not to be included in the treaty—but I guess we have no choice. If you're starving to death, I don't think you can refuse a banana if it's offered to you." Her husband, a West Banker, adds that "right now, Israel is a reality, there are around four, five million Jews in Palestine. What you want to do with them? Same thing, the Palestinians are a reality in the world. What you want to do with them? So you can't eliminate the Jews from Palestine, and you can't eliminate the Palestinians from Palestine. I think they should have equal rights to live in that land."

NORMA SAYAGE: Sayage is a San Francisco real estate broker whose parents left Jaffa in 1948: "I think we can't deny that the Israelis have become, over the past forty years, Israelis. Before, we couldn't accept the fact that there were something called Israelis because we considered them Germans and Europeans and Americans. I think over the past forty years they have become a nation. And just like they are denying us a right to exist as Palestinians, I think we would be denying them the right to exist as Israelis if we denied them the right to statehood. It's a concession, [but] half of Palestine is better than none."

HASAN KHALIL: Born in the village of Qaloniya near Jerusalem, Khalil fled with his family at the age of four when the village was destroyed during the Israeli effort to secure the road from Tel Aviv to Jerusalem. Could he accept a Palestinian state that did not include Qaloniya? "Oh, yeah. They [Israel] exist, we accept it. Give us a homeland, give us something. You don't know how it feels when you don't have a homeland. It's the worst thing that could happen to a person, losing his identity and no homeland. If they give us a state in the West Bank, we would deal with Israel, with the Jews, like we been doing for twenty years, but at least we are Palestinian, not occupied....What can we do to prove to them that we want peace?"

MUJID KAZIMI: Now an MIT professor of nuclear engineering, Kazimi was taken from Jerusalem as an infant in 1948: "To ignore that Israel has been now in existence for so many years and the Israelis feel strongly about their country means that you are not dealing with the problem in realistic terms. So I am supportive of the idea that a good solution to the existence of the Palestinians and the Israelis in that part of the world can be the two-state solution. I have to say that my preference would have been for the one-state, two-nation solution, but I think realistically this is not going to be acceptable to the Israelis."

IBTISAM N.: Ibtisam's parents left Jaffa in 1948, and she was born in the al-Amari refugee camp near Ramallah on the West Bank. She is one of fourteen children and grew up living with the entire family in one room of a house shared with her grandparents and several uncles and their children. When she married a man from the West Bank village of Beitunia, she was overwhelmed by the size of the houses in the small town. She lives now in a crowded walk-up flat on the south side of Chicago with her husband and four children. Her husband works the night shift as a gas station attendant, and both complain that they cannot earn enough money to live comfortably. They would rather be back home but feel it is important to stay in the United States to give their children a better opportunity for education and democratic freedoms.

Ibtisam remembers first becoming aware of her refugee status when, just starting school, she took in a birth certificate that said she had been born in Jordan (that is, the West Bank when it was under Jordanian control), when in fact she "knew" that she was from Jaffa. Ibtisam is a simple woman, not inclined to talk at great length; she lets her husband answer when asked if she could be satisfied with a state in only the West Bank and Gaza and nods in agreement when he says this is acceptable. When asked if she agrees with this, she says that Jaffa is more important to her parents than to her because they knew it. What is important, she says, is that everyone live in peace rather than fight constantly. Asked specifically if she and her parents could accept Israel or if they are so angry that they want to destroy Israel, she says, "No, not destroy" and goes on to speak again about the importance of peace instead of continual fighting.

FATIMA HOREISH: Horeish was born in Lebanon of parents who left the town of Safad in 1948. She has been in the United States since she was a young teenager and works as a secretary at the United Holy Land Fund offices in Chicago. The PLO, she says, should have recognized Israel a long time ago. Even though with a two-state solution her parents' hometown would remain under Israeli control, "at least we would have half of it [Palestine]. Better than nothing. Oh, yeah, it's better than nothing. At least this way people would recognize there would be a state of Palestine, you could see on the map 'Palestine,' and you would have passports."

U.S. policy has made Palestinian recognition of Israel's "right" to exist, as opposed simply to recognition of its existence, a centerpiece of its Middle East peacemaking strategy. For over a decade—from 1975, when then-Secretary of State Henry Kissinger pledged to Israel as part of the second disengagement agreement between Egypt and Israel that the United States would not negotiate with the PLO unless it recognized Israel's right to exist, until December 1988 when Yasir Arafat finally pronounced the magic formula—no U.S. administration would hold formal talks with the PLO. Yet for Palestinians, the question of Israel's right to exist goes to the very heart of the conflict. All Palestinians distinguish carefully between recognizing the right to exist and recognizing existence, and most who now have no difficulty accepting and living with the fact of Israel's existence are still uneasy, despite Arafat's pronouncement, about granting Israel's right to exist. To Palestinians, this has the effect of according legitimacy to Israel's actions in 1948. This is an intensely personal thing with Palestinians, for it is tantamount, in the minds of most, to recognizing Israel's right to have dispossessed them: the right of Israelis to live in their homes, farm their land, possess their property.

Karim Dajani, the San Francisco graduate student whose parents were displaced from Palestine in 1948, believes Palestinians should move beyond such preoccupation with "rights," but this sentiment is rare among Palestinians. Dajani has been willing to declare himself publicly on the issue on several occasions. During the Gulf war in 1991, when he was a student in Santa Fe, New Mexico, he appeared in several public forums to discuss the Palestinian situation. Although strongly criticizing Israel, he made a point in each talk of asserting his belief in its right to exist. Noting on one occasion that he believes the land of Palestine belongs to neither Israelis nor Palestinians but that both peoples belong to the land, he said, "As a Palestinian, I say that I absolutely believe in Israel's right to exist." He affirms in private as well that he has no problem recognizing this right. "They're human beings and they have a right to exist. I'm not about to start pretending that the Israelis who are living in Israel don't have as great a tie to Israel as I do."

Although most Palestinians are not as magnanimous as Dajani, most do say they could now recognize Israeli legitimacy if Israel would reciprocate by recognizing the right of Palestinians to exist as a nation. The PLO's formal acceptance in late 1988 of Israel's right to exist was in fact couched in these terms: Yasir Arafat accepted the right to exist of "all parties," including Israel and "the state of Palestine."[10] But Palestinians know that such recognition will not come from either Israel or the United States without a further struggle, and many are uneasy at having conceded a major bargaining point without reciprocation from Israel.

The chief problem for Palestinians in accepting Israel's right to exist involves a simple question of principle—whether, without receiving any acknowledgement from Israel of their own right of possession, they can affirm Israel's right, in their words, to have "stolen" their land and their birthright. Palestinians often speak of this issue using the analogy of stolen possessions, most often a house.

For Stanford linguistics lecturer Khalil Barhoum, for instance, it is as though someone had come into his house with a machinegun and said, "Get the hell out of here. This is my house now and I want you to stay there behind that fence, and before I even talk to you, much less let you back in, you have to acknowledge that this is my property." This attitude, Barhoum believes, preempts the entire negotiating process. Because possession of the land is the issue that is to be negotiated, demanding prior Palestinian acknowledgement that Israelis have a right to possess the land is like asking the Palestinians to concede the main element of their case before even going to court. "What Israel and the U.S. are saying practically is, 'Concede your right to the whole of Palestine, once and for all, and then maybe, maybe we'll be tolerant enough and patient enough to let some of you stay there under Israeli rule.'"

Abdur-Rahim Jaouni, the Berkeley geochemist, makes his case using the analogy of a stolen watch. "What if somebody comes and robs your watch," he says, "and the police come and say, 'Look, this man took your watch, so it's his, and all you need to do now is go with him to the court and give him the right, the legal possession of it.' Now for me as a Palestinian, rationally I say, 'All right, Israel is there,' but emotionally I'm not going to legalize it. I cannot accept the legality of Israel."

Hashem O., an attorney in Chicago, takes a different tack. As a third-generation American from a West Bank family, he is wholly committed to this country and, although he has relatives still in the West Bank, has no intention of living in a Palestinian state. He regards his activism on behalf of the Palestinian cause as something he does as an American. For that reason, he feels he can speak more forthrightly than immigrant Palestinians, whose loyalty to the United States is often suspect and whose views are labeled radical simply because they are immigrants with a dedication to the Palestinian cause.

"I consider myself very moderate," he says, "but my idea of moderation is not that you compromise your position in advance of negotiations." For him, recognizing Israeli legitimacy as a precondition to negotiations constitutes compromising the Palestinian position in advance. "If the Palestinians are given the full opportunity to represent their interests and then they negotiate away all of Palestine, that's their problem," he goes on.

> But when they are denied that opportunity, then I don't apologize for saying their first position is all of Palestine, just like the Israeli first position is all of Israel. I tell American Zionist organizations there is no reason the Palestinians should accept any of Israel now; you have not accepted any of Palestine. If you want the Palestinians to negotiate at a starting point where they've given up sixty percent of Palestine, then I feel like maybe you should start at a point where

you've given up sixty percent of what you call Israel. I have friends whose ancestral homeland is in Israel proper, and I don't think I should apologize to say that's their home. But that doesn't mean that I would then be against a compromise solution. A just and peaceful settlement requires compromise and negotiation. There are other people [Israelis] living there now who are also human beings, who can't simply be removed.

A demand for reciprocity from Israel, involving a reciprocal Israeli recognition of Palestinian legitimacy—of the Palestinian right to exist—is an integral part of the Palestinian position. Full reciprocity, as far as the Palestinians are concerned, would require that Israel give some acknowledgement, through granting compensation for lost property or allowing some agreed number of Palestinians to return to lost lands in Israel, that Israel was established on Palestinian land. One encounters, however, a kind of circularity here that prevents even the most basic understanding between the two sides. Palestinians say they cannot, in the absence of Israeli acceptance of Palestinian legitimacy, accept Israel's legitimacy because this would sanctify Israel's seizure of Palestinian land. At the same time, Israel has difficulty recognizing the existence of Palestinians as a nation and granting Palestinian demands for compensation or the right of return because this would constitute an admission that Israel did indeed take land belonging to another people.

Thus, Palestinians fail or refuse to understand that the Israeli demand for recognition of its "right" to exist is a plea for acceptance as a nation like any other, as a member in good standing of the Middle East community, and Israelis fail or refuse to understand why the issue of its right to exist is so bitter a pill for Palestinians to swallow. As a consequence, when the PLO did finally recognize Israel's right to exist, the Israeli government repudiated the gesture, saying that it exists and has the right to exist whether "Palestinian terrorists" recognize this or not. Even Israelis on the left who support establishment of a Palestinian state in the West Bank and Gaza refuse to consider allowing Palestinians any right of return to areas within pre-1967 Israel. For Israelis of all political colorations, the image of masses of Palestinian refugees flooding into Israel is a frightening specter, something that not only would constitute an open admission of Israeli culpability in 1948 but would as a practical matter negate the Jewish character of the state by overwhelming Jewish numbers with Palestinians.

Palestinians, on the other hand, generally seem to see the demand for a right of return more in abstract than in concrete terms—as a moral symbol, an acknowledgement by Israel of Palestinian rights, more than an open-ended practical commitment actually to admit millions of refugees. In the Palestinian view, it is an issue whose details should be left open for negotiation. Some say they believe large numbers of Palestinian refugees would return, to live under Israeli sovereignty, if allowed the chance to regain their lost property in Israel, but most seem to be aware of the practical difficulties for Israel. If Israel is willing to negotiate the issue in good faith, they are prepared to limit their demands. Palestinians in the United States who are 1948 refugees or the children of refugees generally say they do not themselves envision going back to live in their old homes—although some would go to a West Bank state—and do not expect that the majority of those displaced in 1948 would exercise a right of return. Too much has changed over four decades: they would have to live under Israeli sovereignty, and most of the old towns and homes no longer even exist.

Whatever the practical realities, the abstract moral question of the right of return, whether exercised in fact or not, is of critical importance to all Palestinians as a sign that Israel recognizes Palestinian rights. Dr. Anthony Sahyoun, a Boston surgeon, considers the issue a matter of self-respect. Displaced from Haifa, he has no intention of returning to any part of Palestine, but he demands that Israel recognize his right to do so. Acknowledge that you stole my house, he says, and you can have most of it.

Sahyoun is the director of the organ transplant division of New England Deaconess Hospital in Boston. He is an outgoing, almost jolly man, anxious to talk about his experiences. He was studying medicine in England, intending to return to Haifa following a surgery residency, when Haifa fell and his family fled in 1948. Sahyoun accepts Israel's existence, but he is angered by what he calls its arrogance and its refusal to "open up" to the area in which it lives. The Palestinians, he believes, are Israel's only entree to good relations with its neighbors, but it must grant them legitimacy before it can expect peace with its other neighbors or recognition of its own legitimacy. "I am the person. It's not Egypt, it is not Jordan, or Syria. It's me. I am the person, Tony Sahyoun, who has been humiliated, his country taken, his house taken, his personality taken. And I am never going to forgive them until they give me my self-respect back again. Never."

What would give him that self-respect? "Recognition of my presence." Would a West Bank-Gaza state be satisfactory recognition? "That would satisfy me at least in the sense that they have acknowledged me. Just take an example. This is my house, they came and took my house. I cannot get them out because they are stronger than I am. Well, at least give me one part—you live there and I live here, let's live together. If I cannot get you out—I don't want to throw you out—at least give me my part, and acknowledge that this is my house, acknowledge that this is my house!" He is excited now, sitting forward in his chair, his eyes flashing, his voice intense. "Somebody comes from Russia or Poland or something and takes my house," he goes on, "and tells me this is not my house and that I should tell him it's his right to take my house—I cannot do that. I cannot tell him,

'It's your right, congratulate you, kiss you on both cheeks.' It's inhuman. [But] I can say, 'You have it, I cannot take it. Fine, let's live in peace."

In the late 1960s, the PLO's position evolved from demanding the "total liberation" of all Palestine to calling for establishment of a "democratic secular state" in Palestine in which Jews, Christians, and Muslims would live together in harmony in a truly non-sectarian state based on majority rule. The policy change was only an evolution, a refinement, for it was still intended to effect the liberation of Palestine from Zionism. The expectation was that, however truly democratic, Palestinians would so outnumber Jews that the state would effectively be a Palestinian Arab rather than a Jewish state.

Israelis and their supporters have from the beginning interpreted the concept of democratic secularism as merely shorthand for the destruction of Israel and of Israelis, a nicely worded way of advocating "throwing Jews into the sea." To the extent that a democratic secular state would mean the end of Zionism and of Israel as an exclusively Jewish state, Jewish fears were properly focused. But even as conceived in the PLO's more militant period when armed struggle was seen as the only way to achieve Palestinian goals, the idea never involved destruction of Jews as human beings. In theory, the concept is faultless: a state based on democracy in its purest form— a state indeed which many Palestinians say would be modeled on the United States and its principles of majority rule and separation of church and state—in which members of all religions, including Jews, would participate on an equal basis, not because they are members of a particular religion but because they are residents and citizens of the state, and in which nonsectarianism would promote harmony by avoiding particularism.

The hard realists among Palestinians now dismiss the possibility of establishing a democratic secular state as an unrealistic dream that will never work, and the PLO has dropped this as a serious goal. One Palestinian has said she believes democratic secularism was never more than a theory put forth for propaganda purposes to counter Zionism's exclusivity—a means of showing that whereas Jews wanted only an exclusive state, Palestinians were ready to live in peace with all religions. But, she says, the propaganda move backfired when Israel's supporters portrayed the concept as aimed at killing Jews.

Some Palestinians, however, still cling to the dream of a democratic secular state as the only truly just solution. A small minority, generally those who tend to follow a more principled and less compromising position, feel that because a two-state solution does not do justice to those Palestinians displaced in 1948, ultimate creation of a democratic secular state, following after a period in which two states exist side by side, is the only way to avoid future conflict. Others, in larger numbers but still a minority, are not bothered by the two-state formula as a permanent solution but believe that a unitary Palestinian-Jewish state will inevitably result, decades and perhaps generations hence, from two peoples who each have an emotional attachment to the whole land of Palestine coexisting in peaceful daily commerce. Both of these schools of thought envision the creation of a single democratic state as something that would come about not through force but through an evolutionary process involving the consent and support of both peoples.

One has to listen to the dreamers to appreciate the genuinely peaceful intent of those who hope for a democratic secular state as the real embodiment of peace between the Jewish and the Palestinian peoples. A cynic, or an Israeli, might call Salam Khalili a good actor, but his sincerity is undeniable. What is most striking about him is his remarkable faith in man's capacity for good will.

He likes to call himself simply Salam, because this is the Arabic word for "peace." So many people know him by this name, in fact, that few Palestinians in the San Francisco Bay area where he lives even recognize his full name. He is a writer, poet, and artist and in the early 1970s was the editor of *al-Fajr*, then a weekly Arabic-language newspaper published in Jerusalem. *Al-Fajr* is now Jerusalem's leading Arabic-language daily. Salam was arrested in 1973 for not submitting an article to Israeli censors and was imprisoned for four years without a formal charge. After his release he continued to write and was held under house arrest, alternating with brief periods of imprisonment, for two years before Israeli authorities offered him the choice of returning to prison indefinitely or being expelled. He chose expulsion, along with his Jewish Israeli wife, and came to the United States in 1979.

Salam is not bitter about his imprisonment. When asked about his treatment, he says off-handedly, "I went through a heavy torture period," but then he moves on quickly to a story of establishing rapport with a Russian Jewish prison guard who worked such long hours that he felt as much a prisoner as Salam. Salam is readier to talk about such things as having raised a small bird in prison or his pleasure at seeing one of his own poems scrawled on a prison wall by an earlier inmate than he is to discuss the negative aspects of imprisonment.

Salam finds the Israeli occupation totally unacceptable—"for one nation to occupy another nation, that's refused, even if they feed you on a golden plate"—but in a situation in which an Israeli state and a Palestinian state lived side by side in mutual respect and equality, he can foresee a day when the two peoples achieve such understanding that they become one. Nationalism, he believes, is a poison used by human beings to kill each other. He calls himself a nationalist now, "because I have this problem" with the occupation: "In a period where a nation is trying to liberate itself, nationalism is very important." For this reason, he supports establishment of a West Bank-Gaza Palestinian state. But he hopes for a future in which Jews and Palestinians live together in a single democratic state. Right now, he says,

we are fighting to live in dignity, in peace, in just normal human conditions. Peace will provide that for both sides, and the human relationship will rise over political and national feelings, always. For example, I married a Jewish woman in '77. [They are now divorced.] We are demonstrating together, we fall in love, it's wonderful. So that will happen. The way I see it in my mind, if I can visualize it for the long term, I really see one society, one state, one people. With time, the human relationships will be stronger than any other considerations.

Salam does not foresee this degree of harmony in the near future; there is too much pain and bitterness between the two sides now. "You see, our problem with the Israelis," he says, "and their problem with the Palestinians, most of the time, is that neither one of them is really, really listening to what the other is saying. Our minds are occupied in proving that the other side is wrong. We judge what the other person is saying in advance. But you owe it to yourself to listen, and maybe this person is making sense somewhat."

He is impatient both with Israel's constant concern for security—"Israel's security is not geographical; the Israelis will realize that the real security is not to conquer your enemy, but not to have an enemy at all, because you cannot be strong and alert all the time"—and with the Palestinians' tendency to nitpick over who was in the land of Palestine first. "What difference does it make?" he wonders. "This historic argument doesn't make sense to me. If God Himself came and testified, 'Okay, the Arabs were here first,' would the Israelis leave? They won't. So why argue that point? Israel is there, it's strong, there are generations of Israelis born there, they consider it their homeland. We have to deal with it from this point of view."

Over the longer term, Salam thinks all of these problems will disappear. "Hatred between nations cannot go on forever." He has a deep faith in man's ability to forget bitterness and adjust to compromise. "There are always lots of emotions blocking you from accepting something," he notes, "until it happens and you deal with it and it becomes a fact and you get used to it."

As prospects for establishment of a separate Palestinian state even in the small area of the West Bank and Gaza any time in the near future begin to appear more and more problematic, Palestinians are reaching for imaginative alternative solutions that might at once accommodate their own perceived desperate need for an end to Israel's occupation and Israel's reluctance to cede total control of the land. The solutions may be unrealistic; they do not carry the weight of approval by the Palestinian leadership or enjoy widespread support in the Palestinian community. But they are more imaginative than any plans put forward by the leadership, and they demonstrate the serious intent of the Palestinians' search for peace, as well as the diligence with which many Palestinians are working for a solution.

One Palestinian, for instance, put forward a plan after the Gulf war in 1991 that calls for partitioning Palestine into two separate states but uniting the territories into one homeland. Operating on the assumption that neither Israelis nor Palestinians will wish to concede their right to live anywhere in Palestine, this proposal would allow each people to exercise its political rights only within its respective state, but individuals who so chose could live and work in the other state if this satisfied their emotional needs.[11]

Bayan F. has become so certain that any West Bank-Gaza Palestinian state that Israel is likely to agree to will be so geographically insignificant and so helpless that he is ready to propose that Israel annex the occupied territories so that West Bankers and Gazans will have to be made citizens of Israel and will thus be relieved of the oppression they now endure under occupation. Bayan's plan is not favored by most Palestinians, although some prominent West Bankers have discussed such an idea in the past. Nor is the idea favored by most Israelis, for the addition of almost two million non-Jewish citizens would risk altering the national character of Israel as a Jewish state.

The plan, however, is a striking indication of how much some Palestinians are prepared to compromise in order to achieve a peace settlement that relieves the suffering of those under occupation. The plan is proposed in a large sense from a feeling of hopelessness. "Who in the world," Bayan asks, "believes that Israel is going to remove its settlements in the West Bank to give us this land? Who in the world believes that Israel will negotiate on the status of Jerusalem? Who in the world believes in the possibility of Israel allowing us to exist without trying to destroy us, whether it's economically, whether it's water, whatever it is?"

He does not believe Israel would ever permit the establishment of a Palestinian state large enough and with enough natural resources to be viable. He is convinced the Palestinians would at most obtain only "sectors, little segments of the West Bank" and perhaps the Gaza Strip for a state. "You cannot make a country this way," he says heatedly. "You cannot make a country without an economy. You cannot make a country without water, for God's sake; they've taken our water, they're not going to give it back to us. What if they decided they're not going to give us any water anymore one day because we misbehaved? I mean, it's not a deal. It's not that I don't

170

want to make compromise; there's no compromise to be made with Israel [that is, that Israel would accept]."

The idea of annexation and citizenship is not an alternative Bayan likes, but he feels it is the only way. Palestinians in the occupied territories are treated, he says, "like cattle," and he believes there would be a qualitative improvement in their lives if they were made citizens. They might still live like second-class citizens, as Israeli Palestinians do, but they would no longer experience what he calls that "low-down oppression where I [meaning the Israelis] can kill you on the street and nothing will ever happen to me, I can beat your mother and rape your sister right in front of your eyes and the international community will not be able to touch me."

There is a great deal of desperation in Bayan's impassioned monologue. "My Palestine is gone," he says. "My concern now is for the quality of the human life. I totally believe in struggle, and I totally believe in paying with your own blood, with your soul, for your own liberty, but I don't think it's going to work, and I think that we should have the wisdom of recognizing that and dealing with the situation alternatively."

He believes his proposal would not mean giving up the struggle— "who's going to take away my Palestinianism? Is an Israeli passport going to take that?" The proposal would only transform the struggle from a political to a social struggle. "I want to create the situation where I can transform my struggle from [that of] an oppressed people with absolutely no rights, with absolutely no powers whatsoever, to [that of] an oppressed people with some rights and some power under a seemingly democratic system that I will attempt to exploit to the best of my ability in order to create some kind of social justice." The struggle now, he feels, has become not how to challenge Israel but how to challenge Israel's democracy.

Palestinians are not optimistic about achieving an equitable peace settlement with Israel, but they continue to believe that the effort must be made. The Palestinian mainstream still talked about peace—about starting negotiations and coexisting with Israel—even during the Gulf war, and they do not see their support for Saddam Hussein as a negation of their desire for a peace settlement. Peace, they continue to feel, is their only possible salvation from an increasingly oppressive, confiscatory Israeli occupation.

It is impossible to overemphasize the widespread sense among Palestinians that over the last decade they have offered Israel compromise after compromise, only to have these turned aside by Israel and ignored by the United States. Palestinians may perhaps be too ready to dismiss their own actions (or inaction)—the ambiguity in their positions, the missed opportunities, the failure to pursue initiatives—as a factor in the Israeli-U.S. failure to take their compromises seriously, but their frustration at their inability even to make an impression on, even to evoke a reaction from, virtually anyone in Israel or the United States is profoundly felt.

Palestinian scholar and intellectual Walid Khalidi, who himself came to a publicly enunciated acceptance of the two-state formula and coexistence with Israel a decade before the PLO formally accepted this position, describes the changes in the Palestinian and the Arab stance toward Israel since the early 1980s as "little short of revolutionary." The change was first spelled out at the Arab summit at Fez, Morocco, in September 1982, when the PLO and every Arab state except Libya endorsed a plan calling for establishment of a Palestinian state in the West Bank and Gaza with East Jerusalem as its capital and for UN Security Council guarantees of the peace settlement. Although not wholly acceptable to Israel and not explicit in its acceptance of Israel's existence, the essence of the plan, Khalidi notes, was the kind of guaranteed acceptance by the Arabs that Israel had demanded for so long. "Nothing like this plan," he points out, "had appeared before from the Arab side at such a collective authoritative level."[12]

Six years later, at the November 1988 Palestine National Council meeting in Algiers at which the PLO explicitly endorsed the two-state formula, the Palestinians completed what Khalidi calls a 180-degree shift from exclusive reliance on armed struggle to exclusive reliance on diplomacy and compromise as the way to resolve the conflict with Israel.[13] The 1988 Algiers initiative, Khalidi says, demonstrated the Palestinians' "unmistakable readiness to compromise and a clear willingness to accommodate the central core value of Israel: survival, existence, acceptance, and recognition." At the same time, by formally ceding claim to three-quarters of original Palestine, he believes the PLO "made towards Israel a concession of historic proportions in the interests of preserving their core value of survival, existence, acceptance, and recognition."[14]

Palestinians almost universally refer to the Algiers declaration as a "peace initiative" and as an "historic breakthrough" or an "historic compromise." They think of it as a good-faith grant to Israel of the major portion of their most prized possession, the land of Palestine. The fact that the United States barely even acknowledged the Fez Plan, barely acknowledged several initiatives put forth in the years after the Fez summit, and responded only tepidly to the Algiers declaration has deeply stung all Palestinians. The disinterest in Tel Aviv and Washington after the Palestinians "gave away the store," as one man describes it, is a measure, as far as Palestinians are concerned, of Israeli-U.S. lack of seriousness about pursuing a real peace settlement. Cynics among the Palestinians are not surprised, but they are deeply resentful. Those who thought something might result from compromises of this magnitude express angry disappointment.

"It makes absolutely no sense to approach a Palestinian," notes one man bitterly, reflecting the chagrin of most Palestinians in the aftermath of the

Gulf war, "and say, 'What more can you offer?' We have nothing left to offer except to disappear altogether. We've already offered all there is to offer." All Palestinians ask for is to share Palestine with Israel. And, notes another man, the division Palestinians are asking for "is not even 50-50, for heaven's sake."

NOTES

[1] Hanan Ashrawi, keynote speech to the ADC National Convention, Arlington, VA, April 14, 1989.

[2] For the text of the Declaration of Independence and the Political Communiqué, see *Journal of Palestine Studies* 70 (Winter 1989): 213-223.

[3] "Arafat's Statement on Plans for Peace in the Middle East," *New York Times* (December 15, 1988).

[4] "Words of Yasir Arafat: 'Offering My Hand,'" *New York Times* (December 14, 1988).

[5] Philip Mattar, "The Critical Moment for Peace," *Foreign Policy* 76 (Fall 1989): 143.

[6] See Amalia and Aharon Barnea, *Mine Enemy*, trans. By Chaya Amir (New York: Grove Press, 1988) for background Ta'mari's life and his imprisonment after the Lebanon invasion.

[7] Ibid., pp. 107-108.

[8] Ibid., pp. 6-7.

[9] Ibid., p. 46.

[10] "Arafat's Statement," *New York Times*.

[11] Mohamed Rabie, "Arab-Israeli Peace: A New Vision for a Transformed Middle East," *American-Arab Affairs* 36 (Spring 1991): 73-86.

[12] Walid Khalidi, *The Middle East Postwar Environment*, pp. 24-26.

[13] Walid Khalidi, "The Palestine Problem: An Overview," *Journal of Palestine Studies* 81 (Autumn 1991): 12.

[14] Walid Khalidi, *The Middle East Postwar Environment*, pp. 27-28.

8   Israel's Palestinians
The Bridge

> *I'm not an Israeli in any meaningful*
> *sense, simply because Israel is a Jewish*
> *state. I can't say I am an Israeli; I*
> *could say I'm trying to be, I want to be,*
> *but not that I am an Israeli right*
> *now....Eventually, [Israeli Palestinians]*
> *would like to see a bridge built. They*
> *know the Jews as individuals, as human*
> *beings, and in a situation of peace they*
> *can contribute to changing the Jewish*
> *image among the Arabs.*
>
> Muhammad Siddiq
> UC Berkeley professor
> born in Palestine,
> raised in Israel

Anton Shammas is an Israeli Palestinian writer born in the Christian Arab village of Fassuta in Galilee several years after the establishment of Israel. He grew up speaking Hebrew as well as Arabic, living as an Israeli citizen but not, obviously, as a Jew in the Jewish state, and when in 1986 he published a novel, *Arabesques*,[1] written in Hebrew, he aroused a firestorm of debate in the Israeli intellectual community centering on just how Israeli a Palestinian can be without diluting the state's Jewish identity. "To write a novel in Hebrew when you are an Arab," he told an interviewer, "is a political act that borders on subversion. It awakens the specter of Palestinian nationalism within the Jews' linguistic fortress, and it puts up a mirror to the very concept of an Israeli Jewish state."[2]

The effect of the debate has been to force Israeli Jews to confront their own position on the Israeliness of those Palestinians who live in Israel, and most have unapologetically come out as opposed to any truly Israeli identity for their Arab citizens. The Israeli author A. B. Yehoshua, who is otherwise sympathetic to the Palestinian cause and has expressed support for the establishment of a Palestinian state in the West Bank and Gaza with East Jerusalem as its capital, nonetheless draws the line at Palestinians identifying themselves as Israelis. "I don't want Shammas calling himself an Israeli, a full Israeli," he says, "as only a Jew can be."[3]

The debate between Shammas and Yehoshua reveals a basic difference in how Jews and Palestinians view national identity, a difference that goes to the very essence of why Palestinians have such difficulty accepting Zionism as a legitimate political system. Yehoshua believes that Shammas should identify with his ethnic background, as a Palestinian, rather than with his country, which is Israel, and he says dismissively, "Shammas will have to accept the burden of his identity, just as we do ours."[4] But Shammas and most Palestinians would contend that it is Jews if anyone whose identity is confused. Israel, Shammas says, is not a state like any other in the Western world for the very reason that it identifies its people by something other than their citizenship. Israel, he notes "does not belong to its citizens, as does every state in the Western world, of which Israel considers itself to be a part; rather it belongs to the Jewish people wherever they are."[5]

The United States, as many Palestinians point out, is not a state of Jews or Christians or Anglo-Saxons; it is a state belonging to all of its citizens, native-born and naturalized, regardless of religion or national origin. Israel, on the other hand, is unabashedly a state of Jews, which happens to have a Palestinian minority. This leads to an anomalous and untenable situation for that minority. As Shammas has written, "The State of Israel demands that its Arab citizens take their citizenship seriously; but when they try to do so it promptly informs them that their participation in the state is merely social, and that for the political fulfillment of their identity they must look somewhere else (i.e., to the Palestinian nation)." This is essentially what Yehoshua is advocating. "When they do look elsewhere for their national identity," Shammas goes on, "the state at once charges them with subversion; and—needless to say—as subversives they cannot be accepted as Israelis. Back to square one."[6]

Because of this pull to identify both within and without the state, Israeli Palestinians have a unique perspective on Israel and on the Jewish relation to Israel. The perspective has two aspects. They believe on the one hand that, because they daily experience the real meaning of living in a state created for Jews, they can view Zionism and the question of Jewish identity with more honesty than can most Jews, who are so concerned to portray Israel as a democracy and Zionism as a humanistic political system, and so concerned to preserve an exclusive haven for Jews, that they do not recognize the innately discriminatory character of both the state and the ideology. At the same time, because they have lived among Jews, Israeli Palestinians also believe that they can view Jews with a clearer eye than can most other Palestinians—that is, as human beings rather than as demons or hated enemies—and that they are in a better position to see not only Israel's weaknesses but its strengths and to recognize the signs of change, away from Jewish exclusivity, in Israeli society.

Palestinian Americans who came from Israel reflect this dichotomy. They are on the one hand universally harsh in their judgment of Israel's treatment of its Palestinian minority; they say they came to the United States because they could not tolerate living as second- or third-class citizens in the Jewish state. On the other hand, they also generally tend to speak in more hopeful terms of arriving at the day when Palestinians can live as equal members of the Israeli state. More than other Palestinians, they talk of wanting to feel an active loyalty to the state if Israel would reciprocate and of serving as a bridge between Israeli Jews and the Arab world. Repeatedly, almost as if on cue, one hears the view from Israeli Palestinians, no matter how bitter they are over their treatment by Israeli society, that there are "voices"—this seems consistently to be the word used—in Israel speaking of equality for Palestinians, a fringe on the left working against Israel's exclusivism and toward equal treatment for its non-Jewish citizens.

Adam Nassar, a Washington, D.C., consultant, provides an example of this dual approach. He left Israel while a student at Hebrew University in the early 1970s because, he says, "I felt like I was in prison," and he feels no loyalty to Israel because he "has no identification with the Zionist ideals of Israel; I don't feel like I have a stake in it at all." But still he feels that his interaction with Jews, particularly while in high school, where he says Israeli Jewish youngsters have not yet experienced the indoctrination of the Israeli army, was entirely different from and more favorable than the relationship Palestinians in the occupied territories have with Israelis. As a result, he says, "I learned that with Jews and Arabs it's not like a biological tendency to hate each other, it's just a political thing. Both sides get indoctrinated and they get politicized to hate each other like they are taught. But when there is an opportunity, they can interact with each other on a more human level."

Being a bridge is not a role all Israeli Palestinians welcome; Anton Shammas notes that in a war, "the first to be burned are the bridges."[7] But it is a task most feel they can and must perform. Only they, of all Middle Eastern peoples, know both Jews and Palestinians. Only they are in a position to act as a bridge, whenever the two sides are ready for reconciliation.

Israeli Palestinians almost all express bitterness at their treatment in Israel and particularly at their sense that they are unwelcome in their own homeland. Nadim Kassem was born seventeen years before Israel was created, and he sternly corrects a visitor who refers to his having grown up in Israel. "I grew up in Palestine," he says pointedly. Now a physician in New Jersey, Kassem has been in the United States since the mid-1960s. He is a member of the Druze religious sect, one of fewer than a dozen Palestinian Druze living in the United States. Although a U.S. citizen, he still carries an Israeli passport and visits his native village in Galilee every year to be sure that his wife, an American-born Lebanese Druze, and their four children are familiar with his roots. He considers himself a strong Palestinian nationalist and, unlike many of his Druze co-religionists in Israel, he deeply resents the fact that Israel has appeared to favor the Druze over Christian and Muslim Palestinians.

The Druze are a small religious sect that broke off from Islam in the eleventh century. Concentrated in the mountains of Lebanon, Syria, and Galilee, they closely guard the secrecy of their religious beliefs and do not admit converts. Although often thought of and occasionally treated in Israel as non-Arab, the Druze are in fact ethnically and culturally no different from Arabs of other religious sects. They speak Arabic, and their religious books are written in Arabic. During the 1948 struggle and before, many Druze favored the Zionist forces and as a result gained a reputation, promoted by Israel, as collaborators. In 1956 Israel made all Druze, but no Christian or Muslim Palestinians, subject to conscription, which had the effect of further solidifying Druze relations with the state and further alienating the Druze from other Palestinians. The Druze in Israel have, however, been subject to discrimination, have had land confiscated, and have been denied development monies like all other Palestinians, so that in the words of one Israeli Druze, many have the feeling that they are Jews when it comes to obligations and Arabs when it comes to rights.[8]

Nadim Kassem and his family were among those who from the start resisted being co-opted by Israel. Raised in the mixed Christian-Muslim-Druze village of Ramah in Galilee, he and his family left for Lebanon in 1948 when Israel captured western Galilee—one of only three Druze families from the town to leave. Because two brothers had remained in Ramah, the family was allowed to return to Israel on the basis of family reunification three years later. Kassem had already once been arrested and spent seventeen days in an Acre jail for smuggling himself back into Israel in 1949 to visit his brothers.

In the mid-1950s, when the Druze first became subject to the draft, Kassem, then too old to be drafted but subject to reserve military duty, joined with a group of other Druze in a lawsuit contesting the conscription law, saying that they did not want to be treated differently from other Palestinians, that they were willing to be drafted if others were but would not agree to be selected out especially as Druze. They lost the case, which went to the Israeli Supreme Court, but for the next decade, until he left Israel, Kassem was a conscientious objector. Asked if his objection was to carrying a gun in any cause or only in an Israeli cause, Kassem answers that today he opposes using a weapon in any cause but that he cannot honestly say that was his only reason thirty years ago. "At the time, definitely it was mixed," he says. "They could not understand that as an Arab I was not ready to carry a gun against my people. So I had to resort to the other part of me, which is also true."

Being a part of the Palestinian people is vitally important for Kassem, but he feels that it was not his nationalism or his initial resistance to Israel's takeover so much as it was Israel's own ethnocentrism that prevented him from becoming also a part of the Israeli state. He tells of always hearing Jews describe any poorly done piece of work as *avoda aravit*, Arab work, and of myriad other instances, large and small, of discrimination because he is not a Jew.

"I feel I am a stranger in my own country, my own home," he says, echoing the feelings of most other Israeli Palestinians. "It is not nationalistic feeling only. I am made to feel that, I am forced to feel that. When my land is confiscated to have a Jew settle in it, how am I going to feel nationalistic toward this state?" The feeling of exclusion affects daily life and career choices as well. "I tried to get into chemical engineering before I went into medicine, or petroleum engineering," he explains. "I could not. They would let me take physics, chemistry, biology, but definitely not for a major in chemical engineering or in petroleum engineering. Anything in aviation, in technology, radar systems, and so on—no Arab can get in. Maybe I don't blame them, maybe I understand that, but I want the others [Israelis] to understand that I cannot feel a part of this state when I don't have the liberty of choice like anybody else."

He believes that Israelis harbor "fear and repulsion and hate" against Palestinians and are taught to be suspicious of Gentiles in general. He has a story to illustrate his point. While in medical school at Hebrew University, he became close friends with a Jewish fellow student—someone whom "I considered in my dictionary as a real friend," who visited Kassem's home in Ramah and stayed with his family, often even when Kassem was not there himself. In their sixth and last year in medical school, the friend's mother had a frank discussion with Kassem. "We were discussing the situation of the Arabs in Israel," he recalls,

> and suddenly his mother, God bless her soul, said to me in Hebrew, "Listen my son, I really hate to see you get hurt in life. I would like you to know the reality. We are breast fed that with a goy, a Gentile, [one should] 'respect him and suspect him.' Don't ever believe any Jew who tells you otherwise. You are a Gentile and will always remain a Gentile." And her son said, "*Imma!*" [mother]. She told him, "If you really love Nadim, you have to tell him the honest truth." I mean, for a highly educated woman to say that takes guts, and it takes real love. I got confused—definitely my feelings were

hurt—but then the more I thought about it, the more I assured myself that really if she did not care for my welfare, my future as an Arab in Israel, she would not have said that. She really did not want me to go on a tangent, these flights of ideas, of dreams, and get hurt.

She did not, he believes, want him to expect that he could ever accomplish as much in Israel as a Jew could. Kassem had initially intended to stay in Israel nonetheless, but an experience with another Israeli changed his mind. He came to the United States initially to be with a sister who was undergoing heart bypass surgery and while here met and married his wife and worked for a year or two. When an Israeli physician came to the Bronx hospital where he worked recruiting for positions in Israel, Kassem applied. Although he had been preceded in the interview process by several Jewish physicians who received appointments in Israel, in his own interview the recruiter first said there were no jobs available and then, when he discovered Kassem was a Druze, suddenly found an opening in a Haifa hospital. "That insulted me much more than his previous refusal," Kassem remembers. "You are taking me just for a show-off, that here we brought the Druze doctor." He refused the position and has lived in the United States ever since.

Every Israeli Palestinian has similar stories to tell of discrimination, limited opportunities, non-acceptance—of having poor work always labeled Arab ("Arab becomes synonymous with bad, with underdeveloped, with primitive, with stupid," in the words of one Israeli Palestinian), conversely of doing good work in school and being held up as an example to Jewish students of what "even an Arab can do," of being threatened with physical harm for dating a Jewish girl, of having friendships with Jewish fellow students or co-workers that somehow rarely seem to involve being invited into a Jewish home, of being excluded from a technical or scientific field of study at university level.

The Israeli Palestinian poet Fouzi El-Asmar, who lives in Washington and writes a column on Israel for a Saudi newspaper, describes incidents like these in his book *To Be an Arab in Israel*, written in Hebrew in 1971 while he was under house arrest in Israel following a two-year imprisonment during which no charges were ever brought. The incidents El-Asmar outlines describe a pervasive hostility toward Arabs based on the notion that Israel is Jewish and that only Jews matter in the Jewish state. In 1986, El-Asmar also published a study of the Arab image as promoted in popular Hebrew-language children's literature in Israel and found a consistent effort to "reduce and destroy the image of the Palestinian Arab." Based on a detailed examination of 205 titles published between 1948 and 1975, El-Asmar concluded that Israeli children are raised on a diet of anti-Arabism. "[A]ll Arabs are corrupt; all are willing to commit any action, including treason, for money; all Arabs swear; all Arabs are physically and mentally filthy; all Arabs dress funnily and cover their heads with a kerchief like women, etc....The Palestinian Arab fighter fights only because he is part of an incited mob. He does not know why and what he is fighting for....At best he fights in order to kill and loot, or in order to appropriate Jewish women."[9]

"I think it's one of the most miserable experiences for a young person," says Ghassan Bishara, the Washington correspondent for *al-Fajr* newspaper whose family stayed in the village of Tarshiha during the 1948 war, "to grow up in a place where he, she is made to feel every second of the day that you're not wanted, that you don't belong here, that we don't want you, that you're different, that you're dirty, that you're filthy, that you're stupid, that you're clumsy. Every negative attitude there is immediately pours over you from all corners. Really, it's bad, just miserable." He can sympathize, he says, with the experiences of other minorities—with Blacks and Hispanics in this country and with Jews in the diaspora, who he realizes suffered more. But for Palestinians in Israel, he believes, there is an added element: "It's not just 'We don't want to deal with you, we don't want to be your neighbors.' It's simply 'We don't want you here, period.'" Bishara attributes this to what he calls Jewish chauvinism—"that everything or anything Jewish is better than."

The system is institutionalized. AbdulSalam Massarueh, who is now a free-lance journalist in Washington, D.C., recalls that Israeli identity cards differentiate by religion. "A, B, C—aleph, bet, gimmel," he says, reciting three letters of the Hebrew alphabet that designate religion on the cards. "Gimmel for the Muslims. If you are Christian I think you are a B class. It's not even second class [for Muslims]; it's third class." First class, A, is for Jews.

The system is also highly politicized. Many Israeli Palestinians tell of being imprisoned by Israeli authorities for expressions of Palestinian nationalism or of solidarity with the Arab cause. Suhail Miari, the director of the Chicago-based Palestinian charitable organization, the United Holy Land Fund, was briefly jailed when he was eighteen for having sung an Arab nationalist song at a wedding. This occurred in the early 1960s in a period when the late Egyptian President Gamal Abdul Nasser was promoting pan-Arab nationalism. His calls for Arab unity, although ultimately futile, inspired a great following in the Arab world and marked the first political awakening among Israeli Palestinians. Miari found himself in jail for two nights, was fined the equivalent of a month's salary for his father, and was placed on probation for three months. "I still carry the papers of the court wherever I go," he says, "because it's the first time really that the Israelis indoctrinated me, unwittingly, that I am really Palestinian. I mean, it hurts the hell out of them, and I was proud of it, because they made me feel that I'm worth it."

He had other subsequent run-ins with the authorities, involving interrogations and middle-of-the-night searches of his house, when he worked for the tobacco marketing board and made a practice of telling Palestinian tobacco farmers that the subsidy paid to them was lower than the subsidy given their Jewish counterparts.

Miari found it frustrating that he could not be pro-Palestinian without Israelis thinking he was anti-Israeli or anti-Jewish. "You don't have to be anti-Israeli to be pro-Palestinian, you know," he says. "I was raised trying to adjust and not be anti-Israeli or anti-Jewish, just to be anti-military governor ordinance [that is, opposed to the special regulations imposed by the military government under which all Palestinians in Israel lived until 1966] and yet to be pro-Palestinian." It was a balancing act that he and most other Israeli Palestinians feel was and is unappreciated by Israel's Jewish people and government. He also feels that, because it was formed specifically as a Jewish state, Israel makes no effort at all to adjust to its Palestinian inhabitants. He and other Israeli Palestinians operate from the starting point that they were living in their country and the Jews came to settle it. Therefore, he says, "the adaptation process should take place from both sides. I should adjust definitely to the newcomer, whether they are ruling me or they are not ruling me. At the same time, I did not feel or sense that there is an adaptation process to my culture. They are the conqueror, the one who came to occupy us, so they should learn our culture too."

The pull that Suhail Miari describes between being Israeli and being Palestinian is something described by most Israeli Palestinians. Many say they would like to be good citizens of Israel, even of an Israel in which Jews predominate, but not of an Israel whose very state institutions are established for the benefit only of Jews, a state that proclaims itself a Jewish state and in which they are therefore automatically something less than first-class citizens. But whatever their bitterness, Israeli Palestinians almost always talk in terms of compromise, of bringing about changes within Israel rather than of eliminating Israel. Because they have lived with Israelis, they seem to have realized well before Palestinians outside Israel that Israel is a reality that will not cease to exist, and that the two peoples must make adjustments to each other if they are to live side by side. They believe they have helped the Palestinian leadership make those adjustments by providing a clearer perspective on Israelis and their strengths and weaknesses, and many believe they can help Jewish Israelis make similar adjustments.

Fouzi El-Asmar, for instance, believes that Israelis still have the mentality of a minority and that, despite being in the majority and possessing a massive military machine, this underdog mentality makes them unreasonably fearful and obsessed with security. He sees signs that some segments of the Israeli population are overcoming the sense of being an isolated minority and the fear that accompanies it.

Holocaust-induced fears and insecurity, he points out, are an Ashkenazi complex. Oriental Jews, who now make up over sixty percent of the Israeli population, do not share the fears and, moreover, do share with Palestinians the Arabic language, an Arab culture, and what El-Asmar calls Arab thinking. Although for political and economic reasons having to do with their lower status under Israel's successive Labor governments, most Oriental Jews now identify with the right-wing Likud party and have taken a generally anti-Arab stance, El-Asmar believes that because they are primarily Arab in culture they will gradually bring about changes in Israeli society that will move it away from being an Ashkenazi Jewish culture and create more tolerance for Palestinians. A Palestinian, he says, can have a heated argument with an Oriental Jew, "but after that you can sit down and have a cup of coffee. With an Ashkenazi, if he says, 'Look, you are this color,' then you are this color, period. If you go to Jerusalem you find all these people [Oriental Jews] sitting with Arabs, playing backgammon and smoking narghilas and enjoying the food and enjoying talking Arabic, enjoying listening to Umm Kalthum," an Egyptian singer popular throughout the Arab world.

"As a Palestinian who grew up in Israel," he says, "I can see a lot of things that other people cannot see. I can see that [future leaders of Israel] will realize that they have no choice except to live in the Middle East, with the Arabs and Palestinians, and if they want to continue being enemies with the Arabs and the Palestinians, I don't know if they can survive." He cites the example of the Arabs who conquered Spain. "They ignored the natives. Eight hundred years, they produced a most beautiful culture, they produced the strongest army, they conquered the West, but when they ignored the natives there, they were out. That's what I think the new generation will start realizing. It's going to take time, but I can see this could happen."

The new generation, he believes, will be less influenced by fear and therefore less influenced by the need to preserve Jewish solidarity and will be more likely to consist of people like a young Oriental Jew whom El-Asmar interviewed in Washington. "He said, 'I grew up speaking Arabic, listening to Arabic music, eating Arabic food, and I'm an Israeli, not a Jew. I'm an Israeli, I have nothing to do with the Jews outside.' Now, from my readings, the Hebrew papers, and knowing the people and visiting the country, this kind of feeling is going to grow more and more."

Muhammad Siddiq speaks of fashioning a "new model" by which Jews and Palestinians can live together, having sovereignty over some part of the land while still satisfying their emotional identification with the whole land. Now a professor of Arab literature at the University of California at Berkeley, Siddiq grew up in the town of Shafa-Amr, one of the largest Arab towns in Israel, and while a student at Hebrew University in 1967 was arrested and imprisoned without charge for two years. In the period immediately following Israel's occupation of the West Bank and Gaza, Siddiq says in explanation of his arrest, "everyone was involved in being an Arab, being a Palestinian, and perhaps the occupation made the Israelis nervous and afraid of any expression of Palestinian identity."

Living in Israel, despite its difficulties, gave Siddiq a sense that one cannot generalize about people, and his own children are growing up with this same outlook. They know, he says, because he and his Israeli-Palestinian wife have Israeli-Jewish friends, "that all Israelis aren't bad. These are human beings; they're not devils." Also as a result of having lived with Israelis, he says, "I start from the point of departure that both the Israelis and the Palestinians will always be there, and some way must be found to guarantee their coexistence. With one on top, which has been Israel so far, that's no solution. Those on the bottom cannot accept this as a permanent solution."

Neither side can have it all because, he says, "absolute justice exists only in poetry." He would like to see some imaginative thinking on the subject, and this is where his "new model" comes in. What about, for instance, a solution that differentiated the concept of a homeland from the formal structure of the state? "For instance, someone in Tel Aviv can consider Nablus [the location of the Jewish Biblical town of Schechem] as part of his homeland without having political sovereignty over it, or someone in the West Bank or Gaza could regard Tel Aviv as part of his homeland but not have political sovereignty over it. Then one can begin to see the possibility of a solution."

Such a solution would require an adjustment in Israeli thinking, Siddiq realizes, to accommodate another nationalism, Palestinian, in the land Israel now controls. This is where most Israeli Palestinians come down: Palestinians, they feel, have made their accommodation to Israeli nationalism, although not to Zionist exclusivism, and only if Israel alters its Zionist ideology and adjusts to the existence on the land of another people can the two peoples live together in true harmony. Indeed, only then, they believe, can Palestinians living in Israel hope to achieve anything like equal rights.

The issue of how Israeli Palestinians will identify if an independent Palestinian state is established in the West Bank and Gaza raises interesting questions about the nature of Palestinian nationalism. If they choose to leave their homes in Israel to live in the Palestinian state, does that not take something away from the argument that Palestinians have a unique attachment to the land and have opposed Israel these many years because it deprived most Palestinians of their presence on that land? On the other hand, if Israeli Palestinians do not go to the Palestinian state but choose to remain on their land inside Israel and continue to live as Israeli citizens, does that not dilute the argument that Palestinians are a separate people with a national identity that must find expression in a separate independent state; does it not, in other words, by indicating that Palestinians can be content living under Israeli control as long as they are on their own land, reinforce Israel's argument that a so-called benign occupation is acceptable to Palestinians?

The first question is in fact not an issue, for Israeli Palestinians in large numbers say they would choose staying in their homes, on their land, over moving to a Palestinian state. When an Israeli polling organization raised this issue in a survey in mid-1989, only twenty-nine percent of Israeli Palestinians polled responded "yes" to the question, "I think that a large segment of the Israeli Arab population would be interested in belonging to a Palestinian state, if established alongside Israel."[10] Emile Sahliyeh, the University of North Texas professor, conducted a similar survey in 1982 and recalls that ninety-eight percent, when asked their own personal preference, said they would opt to stay in Israel on their land. These results conform with the views of Israeli Palestinians in the United States, who generally say that, although they have themselves chosen to leave, their families and, they believe, most Israeli Palestinians would prefer to remain on the land.

Nonetheless—and here the second question enters in—the existence of a Palestinian state somewhere is of vital importance to Israeli Palestinians as a symbol of national identity. To those who would argue that any foreign occupation, benign or otherwise, is acceptable to Palestinians, Israeli Palestinians would point in answer to the *intifada*. And to those who would argue that the decision of Israeli Palestinians not to move to a Palestinian state undermines the Palestinian demand for independence, most Israeli Palestinians would answer that, much as the existence of Israel fulfills a need for identification among most American and other Jews remaining in the diaspora, the existence of a Palestinian state somewhere would be absolutely essential to give them a sense of national fulfillment—the sense of national identity that is denied them in a Jewish state.

A Palestinian state in the West Bank and Gaza would not be wholly satisfactory from the Israeli Palestinian standpoint because it would leave unresolved the problem they face inside Israel of living as non-Jews in a declared Jewish state and because it would not give them direct experience of living in a more or less homogeneous Palestinian state. Nonetheless, many expect that in a situation of peace, the existence side by side of an Israeli and a Palestinian state would give them a better opportunity to fight for equality inside Israel and would allow Israel the luxury, in an atmosphere free of war, to examine and perhaps change its exclusivist ideology.

AbdulSalam Massarueh, the Washington, D.C., journalist, believes that, by recognizing the existence of a Palestinian people, the establishment of a Palestinian state will tend to demonstrate how unworkable an exclusive Jewish state is. In peacetime, the Berkeley professor Muhammad Siddiq believes, "Israel will have to define what it wants in a state, whether it wants to truly integrate its citizens or be a theocracy, a religious state— whether it wants to be a state of its citizens or a state in becoming; that is, a state waiting for the Jews of the world to come, that regards the Jews of the world as only 'temporarily' abroad."

Whatever the shortcomings of a solution that creates a West Bank-Gaza state, whatever the struggle still ahead for them in its aftermath, most Israeli Palestinians would welcome a neighboring Palestinian state as the fulfillment of at least some part of their need for national identity and as a kind of haven where they could go if life in the United States or life in Israel became intolerable for any reason.

It would mean, says Ghassan Bishara, the Washington correspondent for *al-Fajr*,

I am not a stateless person. An Israeli writer, talking actually about the Jews, once said it, stateless people are the scum of the earth. The attachment to the land is a means for national identity, and Palestine—the West Bank or Galilee or the Triangle [an area in central Palestine that was bisected by the 1949 armistice lines]—to most Palestinians it's all the land of Palestine. If, for political reasons, for realistic reasons right now, Israel is there and the national consensus within the Palestinian community is to establish a Palestinian state, it does not really necessarily make a difference if it is on the West Bank, the Galilee, or the Triangle. It will have to be on part of historic land Palestine.

As for his own personal aspirations, Bishara defines a Palestinian state, even though he would not go there to live and it would not encompass his family's land, as "a satisfaction to our psyche, a spiritual satisfaction. I think what needs to be satisfied is the missing national aspiration of the rest of my people, a people I like to identify with and which I am part of." There is something else that a Palestinian state would accomplish for him emotionally and psychologically:

I think there is also the individual battle of a person. That is, the truth is Palestinians were kicked out of Palestine. Simple as that. Even many Israelis now don't argue the point. There is to many Palestinians, there is to me—I see it as a personal defeat, a personal failure of my father's generation, of my generation. The establish-

185

ment of a Palestinian state may actually answer that part of me that is my failure, my inability to deal. I was defeated, I was made to accept what I don't want to accept because I was weak and they are strong. I think we all blame that generation that lost the country, but I blame my generation for not doing something about it—efficiently, faster, sooner, enough.

NOTES

[1] The book was published in English translation in 1988. Anton Shammas, *Arabesques*, trans. by Vivian Eden (New York: Harper & Row, 1988).

[2] Victor Perera, "Anton Shammas, Israeli," *Present Tense* (May/June 1989): 34-39.

[3] Ibid.

[4] Ibid.

[5] Shammas, "A Stone's Throw," *New York Review of Books* (March 31, 1988): 9-10.

[6] Ibid.

[7] Perera, "Anton Shammas."

[8] For a description of the Druze and a first-person account of their situation in Israel, see Rafik Halabi, *The West Bank Story*, trans. by Ina Friedman (New York: Harcourt Brace Jovanovich, 1985), p. 5-18. Halabi, an Israeli Druze, is an Israeli television correspondent for the West Bank. The citation from the Israeli Druze appears on p. 11.

[9] El-Asmar, *Through the Hebrew looking-Glass: Arab Stereotypes in Children's Literature* (Brattleboro, VT: Amana Books, 1986), pp. 123-125.

[10] Poll conducted by the Guttman Israel Institute of Applied Social Research in July 1989, cited in Yitzhak Reiter, "Forming Their Identity," *Israeli Democracy* (A Supplement to the *Jerusalem Post International Edition*) (Fall 1989): 31.

9 Palestinian Politics
The PLO, Yasir Arafat, and the Question of Terrorism

> *Who are the PLO? Every Palestinian is the PLO. If I do not support the PLO, I'm denying my identity; that means I'm telling you I'm not a Palestinian.*
>
> Fuad Ateyeh
> San Francisco businessman

> *Of course I condemn terrorism. You can't justify it. However, you can explain it. All I want is for the Western world to use the same measurement. When they talk about Palestinian terrorism, it should be equated with Israeli state terrorism.*
>
> Khalil Barhoum
> Stanford University
> lecturer

Although the three letters PLO are probably the most electrifying in the American diplomatic vocabulary, producing automatic revulsion and conjuring up images of terrorists and moral depravity, to Palestinians the PLO is far more than a terrorist or a military organization, far more even than the sum of its constituent parts. To Palestinians it is the embodiment of Palestinian nationhood, a sign of their separateness and a source of identity. It is virtually impossible to find a Palestinian anywhere who does not support the PLO and regard it as the legitimate representative of the Palestinian people. Palestinians see the organization as a system that represents their interests, much the way any people regards its government and constitutional system. This support does not preclude criticism, often severe criticism, of PLO policies or PLO leaders. Palestinians give their loyalty to what the PLO represents.

The PLO is an idea, a symbol and a focus of nationalism, more than it is a tangible body. "There is no such thing as a card-carrying member of the PLO," says Raja S., the Washington intellectual. "Other than the specific individuals who actually represent the PLO, there is no PLO. That's the irony of it. Most people identify with it, but there is no such thing as a party with people paying dues and carrying cards."

Rami Khouri, a Palestinian writer and journalist in Jordan, describes the PLO as a kind of rallying point that gives a national coherence to the memories Palestinians cling to and the symbols of exile like house keys and land deeds that remain for many the only tangible reminders of Palestine. "The PLO today," he says, "is a movement of national reconstitution, seeking to reunite identity, people, memories, and land into a coherent national entity in Palestine itself....In the face of those who deny our existence, it affirms it. In response to those who would ignore us as a national community, it forces them to see us. As such, the PLO transcends the realm of ideology, and enters the realm of political biology. It is the primordial political expression of the gut feeling of being a Palestinian, with all of its pains and pride, its humiliations and its honor."[1]

For a revolutionary organization, the PLO is a relatively representative body. Perhaps the truest test of an organization's representativeness is the readiness with which those it claims to represent express loyalty to it. Both in the United States and elsewhere in the worldwide Palestinian community, Palestinians are virtually unanimous in expressing their view that the PLO, and only the PLO, represents the Palestinian people. Some few Palestinians in the United States say the organization does not represent them personally because they are loyal first to the United States government, but these same individuals nonetheless express their support for the PLO as the only legitimate representative of the Palestinian people as a whole.

Many Israelis and Israeli supporters claim that Palestinians express support for the PLO only because they are intimidated into doing so. This clearly does not seem to be the case among any major elements of the Palestinian community, and it is certainly not the case in the United States, where Palestinians are free to criticize the PLO, and do so openly while still expressing loyalty to it. "The idea became deeply entrenched in this country," says the Washington, D.C., intellectual Muhammad Hallaj, "that the PLO is an imposed thing on the Palestinians. And because a guy doesn't shave, Palestinians who seem to be sort of decent people and clever and educated can't possibly voluntarily accept that kind of leadership, so it has to be imposed. But it's not a question of fear. It's a question of broad agreement, born out of a shared conception, a shared problem, shared views. A lot of times people don't quite realize that." He mentions Israel's hope that by invading Lebanon in 1982 and destroying the PLO it could free West Bankers and Gazans of their supposed enslavement to the PLO. "So," he says, "they hit the PLO in Lebanon, and then the *intifada* comes around to say to them that you can kill the whole PLO and you haven't solved the problem; you're going to hear the same thing you used to hear from Palestinians. Because to Palestinians, the issues are crystal clear, and there's not much room for disagreement on fundamentals among Palestinians."

For Palestinians, those fundamentals involve obtaining recognition of their existence as a distinct people and redress for the loss of their land and their birthright, and this essentially is what the PLO has represented. For most Palestinians, as the San Francisco businessman Fuad Ateyeh says, denial of the PLO's legitimacy would mean denial of their own identity as a people. By standing for Palestinians throughout the world, the PLO serves as a unifying factor and gives Palestinians a focus and direction they lacked before the organization's formation. American-born Essa Sackllah, a delicatessen owner in Houston, says he learned this from a Palestinian in the occupied territories during a year that he spent in the West Bank teaching in the 1970s. When he asked this Palestinian why he supported the PLO since it had such a bad image, the Palestinian replied that because there are Palestinians all over the world he had no right to sit in the occupied territories and decide for everyone else what the solution should be, whereas the PLO represented the wishes and interests of the 1948 refugees and those in the occupied territories, of those living in the Arab world and those living in the West, of those in Israel and those outside.

Susan Ziadeh, the AMIDEAST project director and an American-born Palestinian, describes what the PLO has done not only for Palestinians in general but specifically for those born in the United States. "Before the PLO was formed," she says,

> Palestinians did not really have any institution that they felt represented their interests. Not only that, Palestinians could easily have been diluted into other Arab entities. It could have been an identity that over time and generations could have disappeared. I think why Israel hates the PLO so much is the fact that not only institutionally they were representing Palestinians, but the organization has embodied the identity of the Palestinian people, and they [the Israelis] cannot stand that. In that sense, as a Palestinian American I am grateful that the PLO was able to serve a function. Make no mistake: I am an American, I live here, I was born here, my loyalty is as an American. But by the same token, I can't forget my roots.

What the PLO has succeeded in doing, Palestinians say, is to put the Palestinian problem on the map, as it were. Whatever its faults, whatever Yasir Arafat's own shortcomings, whatever divisiveness there has been in the organization, most Palestinians believe that without the PLO no one today would be aware of the Palestinian problem. "The Palestinian leadership did a historical achievement," notes Abdur-Rahim Jaouni, the Berkeley geochemist, "by at least trying to put back the Palestinian problem on the

189

international agenda. This is very important. I remember when I was a kid the Palestinian problem was completely forgotten, for almost twenty years. If that continued, it would have been for us by now a disaster."

Formation of the PLO had a "tremendous" impact on Palestinians here and throughout the diaspora, says Abdullah Wajeeh, the Detroit mathematics professor who sits on the Palestine National Council. "When we were in this country before the Palestinian revolution, we didn't dare say we were Palestinian, we were ashamed of ourselves." His friend Elie Khoury, the physician who fled Jerusalem in 1948, breaks in to say Palestinians were not ashamed but had a great deal of difficulty before there was a PLO in explaining who they were and where they were from. "If you told them I am Palestinian, nobody knew," he remembers. "We would have to give them geography and history in order to tell where Palestine was." Wajeeh agrees. The PLO gave the Palestinians pride, stopped their absorption into the other Arab countries, and brought them to international attention.

Their identification with the only organization that speaks for Palestinian interests is so automatic for Palestinians that they all express amazement that anyone would question the right of the PLO to negotiate on behalf of Palestinians. They universally regard the Israeli and U.S. refusal to deal with the PLO as a refusal to face the fact that there is a separate Palestinian people and as an effort to avoid the hard issues that will inevitably be involved in any serious negotiations on the Palestinian issue, whether the body negotiating with Israel is called the PLO or something else.

Osama Doumani, the former political organizer now living in Sacramento, echoes many Palestinians when he says that whether they agree with specific PLO policies and leaders or not, it has become a "matter of political principle" to identify with the organization. "What it means," he says, "essentially is, I don't want you to choose my own leadership. The reason they say we support the PLO has nothing to do with the structures of the PLO, with how they function, with who they are personally, whether you'd like to have them to dinner at your house or not. It's become a point of principle for a Palestinian." Doumani says that when he spoke to groups as an official of the American-Arab Anti-Discrimination Committee he was often asked why Palestinians support the PLO. "For a Palestinian," he says, "they don't need reasons. They know the PLO represents them."

Whatever their support for the PLO, Palestinians do not hesitate to criticize specific PLO policies and PLO leaders. This has been particularly true since the Gulf crisis. Although most Palestinians defend the PLO's support for Saddam Hussein, the leadership's misjudgment on this issue has become the focus for criticism of a quarter century of failure by the leadership. There is perceived to be widespread corruption within the upper echelons of the organization, something generally ignored when it was believed the

PLO was accomplishing something for the Palestinians. But the Gulf crisis, which caused a loss of international stature for the PLO and, with it, a loss of leverage for the Palestinians generally, appears to have brought home to Palestinians at all levels—the man in the street in the West Bank equally with the intellectual elite—a sense that the PLO has accomplished virtually nothing since its early days. "The people are disillusioned, and they're frustrated," notes one highly critical man. The PLO succeeded in reasserting the Palestinian position in the international arena and among the Arabs, "which is I think quite an accomplishment," he concedes, but this occurred in the organization's first five or ten years and "nothing of substance has been really accomplished" since then.

The leadership is often criticized for having become bureaucratically fat and indolent and for having lost the sleekness that a revolutionary organization should have. Palestinians say that the PLO has often even forgotten the plight of its people and lost sight of its ultimate goals in its efforts to preserve itself and guarantee its sinecures in Beirut or Tunis. "Any revolution," says one young man, "is supposedly something that revolts, hits, either succeeds or doesn't succeed, and then dissipates. Any revolution that lasts twenty years is something where the revolution has transformed into an institution, a corporation. We've suffered from that greatly." Some say they would like to see a new, younger and fresher leadership. The present leadership is too much an "old boy network"; there is no headroom for younger men and younger ideas, and the old guard is out of touch and has gone stale arguing the same old arguments over tactics and strategy.

This view perhaps does not do justice to the subtleties in Palestinian thinking about the PLO. Although affection for Yasir Arafat has begun to diminish sharply, many Palestinians have a special regard for him and the group of older leaders around him because of the role they played in the 1960s in organizing and galvanizing the Palestinian national movement. Even those who criticize the PLO for ineffectiveness and for becoming too soft and too bureaucratic do so from within the system, from a position of loyalty to what the PLO represents and to the PLO itself as the only organization that represents Palestinians as a whole.

There is, nonetheless, a wider relevance to the argument that the PLO has wasted time substituting rhetoric for action and arguing fruitlessly over tactics. Some Palestinians criticize Yasir Arafat for trying too hard to please all factions within the PLO and for failing as a result to devise a clear and consistent strategy; others, believing that making concessions has long been inevitable, criticize the hardliners for making it so difficult for Arafat and those willing to compromise. Some few, who are hardliners themselves, believe Arafat has all along been willing to give away too much.

Those who say they want a leaner, purer revolution tend to be the ones who think the PLO has prostituted itself by accommodating to the Arab states. This is where the revolution has gone wrong, the Vermont publisher Samir Abed-Rabbo believes. The lesson of the *intifada*, he says, is that the Palestinians must rely on themselves and, most important, that the revolution seems to betray those who live in misery in refugee camps or under occupation when it consorts with the Arab states, "the worst despotry in the world." How, he wonders,

> can we justify to our coming generation our collaboration with all of these reactionary Arab governments, whether it's in Syria, whether it's in Iraq, whether it's in Saudi Arabia, Jordan—name them, all of them, with no exception? How can you justify that? Can you justify it to them by saying, "I went to them because I needed money"? How can you? A lot of people will respond to what I am saying and say, "But we need to survive." But the choice is either you survive as a free person or you survive as a slave. Then what's the difference [between surviving as a slave and not surviving]? In our situation now, what's the difference? When the Palestinian revolution started it was only dependent on the people in the refugee camps, in the cities and the towns. It did not depend on the treasury of anybody. It was the revolutionary way for a mother to sell her gold bracelets in order to buy a gun for her husband or children. It did not depend on a fat check coming from a fat treasury somewhere. Today, Palestinian leaders think by throwing money at things, we'll solve it. But here, look at the *intifada*. Most of the people who are involved don't get help from anybody. But their active participation in the struggle is changing things, mainly by restoring respect to our cause.

Abed-Rabbo's views are probably stronger than those of most Palestinians, and he acknowledges that many disagree with him, but he does reflect a more general concern that the PLO has not been clear and decisive enough or true to itself. The feeling that the PLO needlessly prostituted itself by taking money from Arab states has become much more widespread since the Gulf crisis, which has resulted in a serious estrangement between the PLO and the Gulf states, particularly its two largest benefactors, Saudi Arabia and Kuwait. Both of these states have terminated financial assistance, and Kuwait, which had had the third largest expatriate Palestinian community in the Arab world, after Jordan and Lebanon, has managed to whittle down a pre-war Palestinian population of more than 350,000 to about 50,000-80,000 by not allowing those who left during the Gulf crisis to return and refusing to renew the work permits of those who remained.

Palestinian Americans are particularly concerned about the image the PLO projects in the United States, which they regard as the critical arena where

Palestinian goals will be either achieved or thwarted. Many of these Palestinians fear that the PLO is too ignorant of American society to know how to address an American audience and that as a result it is continuing to lose the public relations battle to more clever pro-Israeli propagandists.

In an interview with a correspondent for two Arabic-language newspapers, Kuwaiti and Lebanese, in October 1989, Edward Said, the most prominent Palestinian in the United States, expressed his "total disgust" with the PLO's U.S. public relations operation for its "negligence, corruption, and incompetence." The PLO, Said charged, has essentially left the public relations field to Israel and the United States. It has failed to speak out on its own behalf and has failed to mobilize the Palestinian community in this country or the many groups that support the Palestinian cause. It has made no effort, he said, to counter the still prevalent impression that it is a terrorist organization, no effort to explain its position, and no effort to portray the *intifada* as a just struggle against a repressive occupation. As a result, too many Americans still "believe we are a stubborn and silent people who have nothing to say. I believe that this is a horrible distortion of the Palestinian stand."

Americans also do not understand, Said charged—because Palestinians do not tell them—that the occupation is an unjust occupation paid for by U.S. tax dollars. Only when this is widely understood in the United States, he said, can Palestinians hope to win their battle for self-determination. He challenged the PLO to work for the day when it is as impossible for anyone to write an article in the *New York Times* supporting the occupation as it now is for anyone to write in support of South African apartheid.[2]

Other Palestinian intellectuals echoed Said's criticisms. Ibrahim Abu-Lughod, another well known Palestinian intellectual in the United States, followed Said's interview with a similar complaint, noting that he had not seen "even one English-language handbook published by any organ in the United States directly or indirectly affiliated with the PLO to express the Palestinian orientation toward peace." He challenged the PLO no longer to allow "history [to be] written by the enemy."[3]

Many Palestinians share the intellectuals' concern that PLO has little feel for what is necessary to win U.S. support and overcome negative stereotypes about Palestinians and the PLO. Ahmad S. was working on a graduate degree in management at California State University at Long Beach until he returned to his home on the West Bank in 1990. He has very strong opinions on the PLO's need, if it expects to win American support, to speak to Americans in a language they can understand. He criticizes Yasir Arafat specifically for relying too much on rhetoric. The old ways, he says—"all this shouting—don't work anymore." He mentions an appearance by Arafat on the ABC program *Nightline* in early 1988 and says that a leader who knew how to talk to Americans would have made a greater impact. "Thirty minutes on *Nightline* can change a lot," he notes, but he believes Arafat is not accustomed to answering hard questions. "Arab leaders are not used to hot seats"; Arab reporters shy away from tough questions and ask only what they know the leader wants to answer. The problem, Ahmad says, is that the *intifada* can win the Palestinians a great deal of sympathy, but "nobody is listening to you if you don't explain yourself."

Arafat's inability to explain himself as they think he should disturbs a great many Palestinian Americans, who seem generally to believe that he creates a poor image for the Palestinians in the West and particularly in the United States. Even those Palestinians who consider Arafat an effective leader regard him as a poor spokesman because of his imperfect English and a poor image-maker because of his personal appearance. Some, like the Berkeley geochemist Abdur-Rahim Jaouni, believe that the media deliberately paint Arafat as a bogeyman because it is U.S. policy to do so and that, were Arafat in favor with policymakers, the U.S. media would give him a good press: "It's policy. The moment the United States policy changes toward the PLO, the media will immediately shift 180 degrees and portray Arafat as a human again. Look at Mao Zedong. He didn't look very handsome and attractive, but the moment the whole United States policy changed, his image changed."

The majority of Palestinian Americans, however, seem to feel that the problem is Arafat himself and the way he comes across to Americans, rather than whatever the media have done with him. "God, I wish he'd shave!" exclaims one man. Another complains that he makes himself look alien to Americans by always wearing a *khaffiyah*. "We need some charisma," says one woman, "somebody that everybody respects and really looks good. It makes a big difference if Arafat speaks well, if his looks are appealing. All the ladies will like him. This country is for the young, the beautiful, and the strong. If you are not like that, you don't survive in this country."

The most frequently heard complaint, and probably the most serious, is that Arafat too often speaks in English rather than through an interpreter and makes a poor impression. This too is often a matter of appearances. Qassem Khalil, a young physician in Los Angeles, believes that Arabic is something to be proud of, a matter of identity, and that it demeans the Palestinian cause for its leaders to speak in any foreign language when addressing the issue. Even if they know English well, he feels, they should speak only through interpreters.

The problem is more fundamental than mere appearances, however. Thinking in Arabic is a different process from thinking in English, and most Palestinian Americans, who know what Arafat means to say because they too think in Arabic, are better able than he to think in English as well and know that the kind of literal translation he performs in his head is not enough to convey the same idea in English. "I'm not troubled by the way he dresses or by his beard, frankly," says Mujid Kazimi, the MIT professor, but he is troubled by the fact that Arafat seems to be addressing an Arab audience when on American television. "The Arabs are more interested," Kazimi says, "in somebody who perhaps is poetic in his language when he explains something, whereas I think in America what you want is somebody who speaks to the issues in the minimum amount of words. That tends to be much more effective in communicating the case in an American culture than it is in an Arab culture. In fact, in an Arab culture, they will say, 'Well, he's incapable of explaining himself,' if he was so short and direct and to the point."

Palestinian Americans have a unique perspective on Arafat that arises from their dual ability, which Palestinians elsewhere in the world do not share, to reside in both an American and a Palestinian context—to think like Americans as well as like Palestinians. Palestinians elsewhere in the diaspora and in the West Bank and Gaza are not so acutely attuned to U.S. public opinion and therefore tend not to be so critical of Arafat on this score. There is, however, a growing discontent with Arafat personally, particularly in the wake of the Gulf crisis, that reaches around the globe to Palestinian communities everywhere. This seems to emerge as a kind of ambivalence about his person and his style—on the one hand, a lingering affection for him and reluctance to criticize him directly, along with, on the other hand, an increasing resentment that his chameleon-like tactics have hurt the Palestinians over the years.

Arafat has always been regarded with some affection, as the leader who brought the Palestinian people and the Palestinian problem to world prominence, and Palestinians have always quite literally felt they owe their survival to him. He has also always had for many Palestinians the kind of charisma that he lacks with Americans. But much of this affection seems to be waning after the setbacks of recent years. There is a growing sense that, whatever good Arafat did for the Palestinian cause early on, he is now a detriment to the cause. In private, many Palestinians speak with deep bitterness of the harm he has done, using words like "pimp," "thug," "jackass." One man notes cynically that Arafat is ready to play either side of the street on peace negotiations, depending on their outcome. "If the negotiating process yields something of substance," he says, "Arafat will be the first to take credit. This would do injustice to the people negotiating, but that's Arafat. He plays with these people like chess pieces. On the other hand, the minute the whole thing shatters or fails, he's going to be quick to say, 'Oh, I told you so, I thought it wouldn't do any good.'" Some Palestinians even resent the fact that Arafat finally married in 1992, as if he had betrayed the revolution by showing he has a private life.

A few years ago, Palestinians able to see Arafat's strengths as well as his weaknesses tried to put the best face on his foibles and on the state of the movement he created. One man's description of him—he "is not the Messiah, but he's what we have"—accurately reflected the widespread acceptance of this old-line leader and his style of leadership. The mood today, however, is far less accepting.

Discussion of the question of terrorism with Palestinians usually produces a similar mixed viewpoint; there is an "on-the-one-hand, on-the-other-hand" approach that prevents most Palestinians from either endorsing terrorism or condemning it outright. Most are well aware of the damage terrorism has done to the Palestinian image, but they also recall that the terrorism of the late 1960s and early 1970s—the hijacking spectaculars, the attacks at Olympic games and at various airports, and the much publicized attacks inside Israel—are what brought the Palestinian issue to public attention. Most are also acutely conscious of the moral questions involved in terrorism, but they will seldom discuss this without raising the issue of Israeli terrorism; Israel too, Palestinians note, kills civilians—in bombing raids on refugee camps in Lebanon, in attacks by Israeli settlers on West Bank villages, in the past in massacres of Palestinian villagers. These things too, they believe, are terrorism. One thus does not find among Palestinians the kind of moral outrage that Americans or Israelis say they feel about terrorism, largely because Palestinians feel that the Israeli/American outrage is hypocritical and selective, directed at Palestinian but not at Israeli atrocities.

The view that terrorism made the world sit up and take notice of the Palestinian plight is widespread. Riyad A., a Los Angeles merchant, calls it "a bloody commercial." He recalls Israeli actions such as the Irgun's bombing of the King David Hotel in Jerusalem in 1946 and the massacre at the village of Deir Yassin in 1948 and says, "For twenty years [after 1948] we did nothing, behaved ourselves. We were good kids, and nobody paid attention." College student Karim Dajani is more expansive on the subject. From 1948 until 1967, he says, Palestinians lived quietly in refugee camps and "nobody wanted to hear them. At that time, Palestinians had never ever taken any violent steps whatsoever. They waited nineteen years and nothing happened. Nobody was interested. So they resorted to what is known as terrorism." And suddenly the world noticed. "It seemed that the only way we could have people listen is by kidnapping your plane. [People wanted to know], 'Who is the blank who kidnapped my plane?' 'He's a Palestinian.' 'What's a Palestinian?' At least now you sit here with me today, acknowledge me as a Palestinian, and listen to what I have to say." Dajani adds that he believes terrorism is morally wrong and that today it is the worst thing the Palestinians could do, but in the situation of twenty years ago it was the only way to get the world to "acknowledge our presence on the face of this planet."

The Houston delicatessen owner Essa Sackllah says that terrorism was a factor in increasing his own understanding of the Palestinian situation. When PLO-led Black September terrorists took hostage and later killed eleven Israeli Olympic athletes at Munich in 1972, the American-born Sackllah was revolted. "There's no way I could condone the killing of those athletes," he says, "because the Olympics to me is very sacred, when [everyone] should lay down their arms and compete athletically." Sackllah was himself a wrestler in high school and college and felt a great respect for athletes. But, he says, the incident made him think more deeply about the reasons for terrorism, particularly the desperation that often induces it. "Terrorists are created," he believes. "They just don't come out of thin air."

There is, probably not surprisingly, a great deal of this understanding among Palestinians for the kind of hopelessness and despair that lead to terrorism. One often encounters Palestinians in the United States who say they are repelled by terrorism but cannot sit comfortably in an American living room and condemn those desperate enough to carry it out. "You can't condemn a refugee camp inhabitant who has no hope," says one woman, or "Any animal will lash out at you if you corner him," says a man. The Washington, D.C., psychologist Nuha Abudabbeh, looks at it from a psychological perspective. "If you block somebody from expressing themselves positively," she says "—and Palestinians were never given a chance to really express themselves in a positive fashion—they have no choice. It always depends on how you treat people. The Palestinians were mistreated. I cannot say we were the most mistreated people, no. But the difference is that we were just about the only minority that nobody seemed to understand nor care about the depth of our feelings or our frustrations."

Many Palestinians refuse to discuss the issue of terrorism unless the terms are defined. How do you define terrorism? Why do you ask me, a Palestinian, about terrorism when no one discusses Israel's terrorism? Is it terrorism if a Palestinian throws a bomb on a bus carrying two Israeli soldiers, as well as civilians? Is it terrorism if a Palestinian attacks an Israeli military installation manned only by military personnel? Is it terrorism if a Palestinian attacks civilian workers at the facility where Israel builds nuclear weapons? Why is it not considered terrorism if Israel bombs a civilian refugee camp or beats a civilian to death on the West Bank, or the United States stations a warship off the coast of Lebanon and shells areas it knows to be civilian targets with sixteen-inch guns?

It is inequitable to discuss Palestinian terrorism in isolation, most Palestinians believe, because one first of all becomes tied up in selective definitions that place all the onus on Palestinians and because, secondly, Israel is always somehow excluded from the discussion except as a victim.* Mu-

---

* The U.S. State Department defines terrorism as "premeditated, politically motivated violence perpetrated against noncombatant targets by subna-

197

hammad Hallaj, the Washington, D.C., intellectual, will not discuss the issue at all because the discussion is always intended, he feels, to put Palestinians on the defensive. "I refuse to be put in the role of the accused," he says. "I get called by these radio stations and other media things for interviews sometimes, and I always refuse to come in and discuss terrorism. I say, 'Look, your definition is that terrorism is a big deal. To me, it's a byproduct of a problem. I'm interested in discussing the problem.' I've always refused to do this [discuss terrorism in isolation] because I feel that the Palestinians are the accusers, not the accused. We don't have to be defensive about anything."

Palestinians are put on the defensive in such discussions, they believe, because Israel and many Americans define terrorism in such a way as to include any attack against any Israeli as a terrorist act. Israel, the Chicago attorney Hashem O. notes, is "the only country in the world that defines terrorism as an act against military personnel by an indigenous population in their own home state. Israel considers it a terrorist incident when an Israeli soldier is attacked by a Lebanese civilian in Lebanon."

Still more serious, Palestinians feel, is that Israel manages to escape blame itself for conducting terrorism. The theme that Israel conducts terrorist acts, but because it is a state receives no international opprobrium, is an oft-reiterated one in discussions of this issue with Palestinians—and a source of considerable frustration. Many Palestinians are willing to condemn terrorism across the board, including that perpetrated by Palestinians, if Israel is equally condemned. "The killing of civilians is wrong in general," says Rafiq T., a San Francisco grocer, echoing a widespread Palestinian view, "but it has to be condemned from two sides. For a government to kill just because it has a border and a national anthem, that is illegal too." Palestinians feel that the fact that Israel has, as one woman says, "a regular army in a regular state"—that Israel conducts violence with airplanes and several-ton bombs rather than with small arms and home-made bombs—does not make terrorism into something respectable.

Palestinians point to Irgun and Stern Gang terrorism in Palestine before Israel was created; to the massacre at the village of Deir Yassin; to another well documented massacre in 1948 at a village called Dawayima, west of Hebron;[4] to the shooting of forty-seven villagers at the Israeli-Palestinian town of Kfar Kassem in 1956.[5] When the Palestinian capture of a school and the killing of twenty-one children in the Israeli town of Ma'alot in 1974 is mentioned as a terrorist act, Palestinians respond that Israelis bombed a

---

tional groups or clandestine state agents, usually intended to influence an audience"—a definition that automatically exempts states as perpetrators of terrorism. See U.S. Department of State, *Patterns of Global Terrorism: 1988* (Washington: Department of State, 1989), p. v.

school at Bahr al-Baqr in Egypt, in a known civilian area, during the War of Attrition in 1970 and killed over forty children. When Palestinian bombs planted on Israeli civilian buses are mentioned as terrorism, Palestinians respond with tales of Stern Gang bombs on buses in pre-Israel Palestine or of Israeli bombs dropped on Palestinian refugee camps inhabited by civilians. When something like the incident in March 1978, when Palestinian infiltrators captured a bus on the coastal road in Israel and killed over thirty Israelis, is mentioned as a terrorist act, Palestinians recall the massacre of at least eight hundred men, women, and children at the Beirut refugee camps of Sabra and Shatila in September 1982, carried out by Lebanese Christian militiamen allied with Israel and in an area of Beirut controlled and supervised by Israeli military forces.

Omar Kader, who did his doctoral dissertation on terrorism, has a theory that any nation defines how it will be treated by how it treats others, and he believes that, by using intimidation with the Palestinians from the beginning, Israel "defined the medium" by which the Palestinians must communicate with them. Had the early Zionists when they came to Palestine or the Israelis when they established a state used compassion, he believes, "had they picked compromise and mercy and justice, had they picked debate and dialogue and diplomacy and politics," instead of ignoring the Palestinians, using force with them, and expelling them, "we'd have had a whole different relationship. But the relationship is based on how the Israelis treated us. The Palestinians had to reciprocate, because wars of words don't work with Israelis." Kader distinguishes between the airport bombings and hijackings that constitute international terrorism, which is carried out by what he calls a criminal element, and attacks directed at Israelis—"the only edge, the only weapon for survival that the Palestinian has against attempts to grind him out of existence."

Terrorism, he says, is a war of psychology that every state uses to some extent. As a tactic, it can be very effective; "that's how Israel has been able to wage war as a tiny nation so effectively, is to terrorize." But as an overall strategy, it is counterproductive because it can be turned around on its practitioners and becomes a point of vulnerability. "In Israel," he says, "because terrorism is its method, only terrorism makes it vulnerable. Only force and war and violence make it vulnerable."

The effectiveness of terrorism is a matter of psychology. "If you fundamentally believe the Israelis are afraid and that fear motivates them," he says, you will use the weapon that most induces fear. What he is saying, Kader emphasizes, "is not advocacy; this is description." The one thing Palestinians can do effectively, he says, "is inflict fear on every Israeli and make them think that every one of them is a target. 'Until you change your mind and start talking nice to me, you all are a target.' And that's the whole idea with terrorism." He cites the example of the IRA assassination of Lord Mountbatten in 1979, which he says was not an act directed primarily at Mountbatten but at inducing fear in every Briton. "They sent a message to every Brit, including the royal family, that you're all a target. That's the whole psychology of terrorism."

Palestinians occasionally devise their own definitions when discussing terrorism. The question, for instance, of who is a military person and who a civilian in Israel, and therefore who is or is not a legitimate target for attack, is for some Palestinians decided by the fact that most Israelis serve in the military reserve and carry weapons when off duty. "What is a civilian and what is not?" asks Rafiq T., the San Francisco grocer. "One-third of Israelis are reservists, they receive military training, they are allowed to bear arms. Where do we separate the civilian from the not civilian? Tomorrow he will be patrolling the streets or flying an airplane and bombing refugee camps. Settlers are the government, and the government is the settlers. There can't be a differentiation between the two." His wife Amal notes that the press rarely reports the frequent attacks by Israeli settlers on refugee camps on the West Bank. "There's a war between *civilians* and us there," she says, emphasizing the word civilians, "not just with the government." In any case, Rafiq notes, the Israeli settlements on the West Bank "are supposed to be military outposts, even according to their propaganda."

The notion that Israeli settlers on the West Bank are in any way defenseless civilians who should be immune from attack arouses the scorn of many Palestinians. "Israeli settlers, I think if they get killed it doesn't bother me," says the San Francisco librarian Samira F., "because they are aggressively there. I think they are illegally there. And they're armed, how can you call them civilians? They're all running around with Uzis, including the women. In my opinion, they're not civilians, they're aggressive colonialists. If they want to put themselves in that situation, then I have no sympathy. I don't approve of killing, but if something happens, I'm not going to worry too much about that." She draws the line at children. "I don't like to see children killed, no matter who they are."

Quite a few Palestinian Americans condemn terrorism unequivocally, making no excuses for it morally or tactically. "I disagree with terrorism on two grounds," says the former activist Osama Doumani. "One is a moral ground, and the other is a political ground. The moral ground is you don't kill innocent people." He mentions both Israeli actions and Palestinian actions in this regard. "I do not approve. I do not accept this morally. Politically, it is also very destructive, from an organizational point of view. The most stable political structures are, at least in my opinion, those that are built by political action, which means people make decisions about their lives politically. If a small elitist group takes it upon themselves to do that for you, then they are preventing you from achieving political ends, and they are eliminating the political process itself."

But it is more common to hear some kind of ambivalence. Nabil Khoury, the Detroit medical school graduate, thinks that attacks on civilians are not a "fair way to fight" and laments that terrorism has contaminated "a very pure and noble cause with the blood of innocent people," but at the same time he notes that Palestinians "don't have the tools to fight fairly" and cannot be expected to forgo any struggle at all. For Soraya Deifallah Hammad, a young woman born in the United States of a non-Arab mother and a Palestinian father who left the town of Acre in 1948, terrorism has been a dilemma. It is, she says flatly, "unacceptable—no matter who's doing it or what the reason is. I do not see that it ever caused people to look at the Palestinians in any positive way. I mean, we have an honorable struggle, and why taint it with taking defenseless people? How does that help you?" But at the same time, she says, "there've been moments when I was young and I defended it, simply because I had to defend it; everybody was against it, and you found yourself defending it."

Defending it because, for Palestinians, it appears to be the only weapon available against Israel's tanks and airplanes, or because it has been the only way to get attention, or simply because when one's people are besieged one always defends their actions—much as large numbers of Israelis and American Jews defend Israel's need to kill children in suppressing the *intifada*, or to kill civilians in air strikes on camps in Lebanon, or to kill villagers in the heat of battle.

NOTES

[1] Rami Khouri, "Who Represents the Palestinians?" *The Palestinians After the Gulf War: The Critical Questions* (Washington: Center for Policy Analysis on Palestine, 1991), p. 16.

[2] Hisham Milhim, "Edward Said on PLO Dealings With United States," Kuwait *Al-Qabas* (October 7, 1989), in FBIS-NES-89-201 (October 19, 1989): 1-6.

[3] Milhim, "Abu Lughod on U.S.-PLO Dialogue," Kuwait *Al-Qabas* (October 25, 1989), in FBIS-NES-89-209 (October 31, 1989): 2-7.

[4] See Morris, *The Birth of the Palestinian Refugee Problem*, pp. 222-223, for a description of the Israeli army's killing of 80-100 villagers.

[5] The villagers, returning home from work unaware that the Israeli military had imposed a curfew, were shot by Israeli soldiers under orders to "shoot to kill at all curfew-breakers." See Shipler, *Arab and Jew*, pp. 43-45, for a description of the shootings, the initial attempt at a cover up, and the eventual sentencing of eight Israeli military personnel.

10   Palestinian Pride

The Intifada

You can hit a cat one, two, three times,
but one time it will fight back.
           Ahmad S.
           Student

What those kids are saying is, "We were
born under occupation. Our father suf-
fered, our grandfather suffered from the
same deal. So it's our turn to do some-
thing about it in a way nobody else
did."...I think [a solution] will [result].
I think it will eventually, but after more
and more sacrifices. This is only the
beginning.
           Fuad Ateyeh
           San Francisco busi-
           nessman

[After visiting her old school during a
trip to the West Bank at the height of the
intifada in 1988] my French teacher
said to me, "Pray for us in English.
Maybe God will listen in English."
           Terry Ahwal
           Detroit activist

Mohammed Abu Aker was a month short of his seventeenth birthday in August 1988 when an Israeli bullet, fired from a rooftop near his home in the Dhaishe refugee camp outside Bethlehem, tore up his insides. Abu Aker said he had just left his home to visit friends and was walking along the street when an Israeli soldier firing on demonstrators nearby shot him in the abdomen. After several surgeries involving the removal of metal fragments from his abdomen and intestines and, when they turned gangrenous, the removal of his entire small intestine and three-quarters of his large intestine, doctors at the Palestinian-run al-Maqassed Hospital in Jerusalem gave him up for dead, and his family began preparing for his funeral. But when he stubbornly refused to die, his doctors began to investigate other possibilities for him, particularly the idea of a small-bowel transplant.

Dr. Anthony Sahyoun, himself a Palestinian originally from Haifa, is the director of the organ transplant division of the New England Deaconess Hospital in Boston and has performed experimental bowel transplants on animals, although never on humans. The surgery had been attempted elsewhere on humans but never with success. Sahyoun had been working with al-Maqassed Hospital on kidney transplants, however, and he and Deaconess decided to bring Abu Aker to Boston to evaluate the possibility of doing the experimental surgery, since he seemed to have no other chance. Abu Aker arrived in Boston in October 1988, two months after the shooting, weighing eighty-two pounds and looking, according to Sahyoun, "as if he has come from one of the concentration camps."

During surgery Sahyoun unexpectedly found that Abu Aker still had a short section of his small intestine, enough to enable him to take small amounts of nourishment by mouth. The transplant surgery was postponed, and before long, Sahyoun says, he began to drink small amounts and even, "against our advice," to eat some solids. By January 1989, Abu Aker was well enough to return home without the experimental surgery. He continued to improve for a few years after this, taking food by mouth during the day and hooking himself up to an intravenous feeding system at night. The surgery remained as an alternative if problems arose.

But the opportunity never arose. Abu Aker developed an infection in 1991 that doctors could not combat, and no funds could be raised to bring him to the United States for Sahyoun's transplant surgery. He died in the late fall.

Because of his long refusal against all odds to succumb to his injuries, Abu Aker became for Palestinians a living symbol of the *intifada*—"the concept of the resistance," Sahyoun said; "he refused to die, in spite of the bullets of the Israelis."[1]

His death at the *intifada*'s low point was also symbolic—this time of the Palestinians' diminished optimism.

Ghada Talhami, the Lake Forest College political science professor, recalls being called "an idiot" by her Israeli-Palestinian brother-in-law when she expressed confidence in the early 1980s, shortly before Israel's 1982 invasion of Lebanon, that the PLO had a military option against Israel because of its strong presence in Lebanon. "My brother-in-law [who lived in Israel and was visiting the United States] just laughed," Talhami remembers. "He said, 'You must be an idiot to believe that. You know what kind of arsenal the Israelis have?' He literally said I'm an idiot."

Talhami recalls this incident as the beginning of her own realization, which she believes also became widespread among Palestinians at about this time, that there would be no military resolution of the Palestinian problem. The Palestinians were militarily too weak and Israel too strong, and the Soviet Union, whatever its lip service to the Palestinian cause, would not provide significant military or diplomatic help, leaving the United States, as Talhami puts it, holding "all the cards in the game."

The realization of Palestinian military impotence was brought home more dramatically after the PLO was routed from Lebanon during Israel's invasion in 1982. The realization, Talhami says, "doesn't mean you give up on your cause. It means you try different methods. You see, that's what the *intifada* has done; it has resolved the dilemma of military impotency. Because you cannot deal with Israel as a regular army, face to face, they'll clobber you. But an uprising is a lethal weapon."

In several ways the *intifada*, which began in December 1987, was a direct outgrowth of the PLO's expulsion from Lebanon five years earlier. In several ways also, the PLO peace initiative—its explicit acceptance in late 1988 of the two-state solution and of UN Resolutions 242 and 338, as well as its renunciation of terrorism—was a direct outgrowth of the *intifada*. If the PLO had still been in Lebanon, a leading PLO strategist told an interviewer in 1989, "there would never have been an *intifada*. Before we left [Lebanon], people in the Occupied Territories believed that a solution would come from outside, because we were in Beirut with our weapons. But when we left Beirut in 1982, that dream died." The *intifada* in turn, he said, and the phenomenon of "[s]eeing children risk their lives imposed on us the need to achieve a realistic peace."[2] Nabil Shaath, chairman of the Palestine National Council's political committee, told a 1989 gathering of Arab Americans that the *intifada* was the "mother of the peace plan" put forward by the PLO.[3]

With the loss of the Lebanon front, the PLO, according to one scholar, began to build up what it called the "western front" in the West Bank and Gaza by strengthening Palestinian grassroots organizations. The buildup became the pet project of one of Yasir Arafat's leading deputies, Khalil Wazir—known as Abu Jihad, whom the Israelis assassinated in April 1988. Money was channeled to the local organizations through a joint PLO-Jordanian committee set up during a period of PLO-Jordanian cooperation in the mid-1980s with funds from the Arab states specifically to promote *sumud*, the steadfastness of Palestinians living under occupation.[4]

Palestinians say that the PLO never lacked a presence and popular support in the West Bank and Gaza, even before this new organizational effort began. The PLO, says the Washington intellectual and Palestine National Council member Muhammad Hallaj, "is not an extraneous body outside the occupied territories. The PLO is in the occupied territories. It's illegal to be overt about it, yes, but everybody who's lived in the occupied territories, who knows anything about the occupied territories, can name people to you—can say, 'This guy's Fatah, this guy's Popular Front, this guy's Democratic Front.' The PLO is very deeply entrenched in the occupied territories." Salam, the San Francisco Bay area graphic designer who was imprisoned and later expelled by Israeli authorities in the 1970s because of his writings, confirms the pervasive presence of the PLO throughout the West Bank and Gaza, even well before its expulsion from Lebanon. "The PLO is not a strange, foreign existence sitting somewhere isolated from the people. Even when we were in prison, we had our own ways to communicate. It's really a very well woven relationship between all the people."

It is clearly in the interest of Palestinians to claim widespread support for the PLO throughout the occupied territories, but the weight of evidence supports the claim. A poll conducted on the West Bank in 1986, co-sponsored by the East Jerusalem daily *al-Fajr*, the New York newspaper *Newsday*, and the Australian Broadcasting Corporation, showed that 93.5 percent of those surveyed supported the PLO as the "sole and legitimate representative" of the Palestinian people.[5] Although the *intifada* that began a year later was a spontaneous outburst not directed from the outside by the PLO, the strength of the PLO's grassroots organization is what made it possible to sustain the rebellion for so long. There is considerable evidence that popular committees with a PLO affiliation in towns and villages and refugee camps throughout the West Bank and Gaza quickly took over to organize demonstrations and commercial strikes and establish medical relief committees, agricultural production initiatives, and other efforts to compensate local residents for the loss of services.[6]

The *intifada* was probably an outgrowth of the PLO's expulsion from Lebanon in another sense as well. Although it has clearly been carried out in the name of the PLO, the uprising has to some extent been a protest against the PLO for its failure, after Lebanon destroyed any possibility of employing a military option, to do anything to move the Palestinian situation off dead center. The *intifada* was a message to the PLO leadership that, while they sat in Tunis endlessly debating, their constituents in the occupied territories were living on the front lines enduring Israeli occupation and desperately in need of a solution that would give them a respite.

Although the euphoria induced by the *intifada* during its first few years has waned as the uprising has diminished in intensity and as the Palestinians have suffered repeated diplomatic setbacks, the uprising has nonetheless been a source of immense pride to Palestinians everywhere, in diaspora communities around the world as well as in the occupied territories themselves. In the United States, because many Palestinians have relatives in the West Bank and Gaza and because they have often had direct experience themselves with Israel's occupation policies, the *intifada* has been regarded with a kind of proprietary air, as their own battle. Palestinians everywhere look on it as giving the Palestinian cause a dignity that decades of dependence on empty rhetoric and the empty promises of the Arab states never achieved. "For a while," says Adam Nassar, the Washington, D.C., consultant who grew up in Israel, "people were wondering if the Palestinians had the dignity, had the honor to resist occupation, resist oppression. [The *intifada* is] an indication that they will not tolerate oppression."

Jameel Shihadeh, a San Francisco Bay area resident who came to this country from Ramallah as a child and would like to return after finishing graduate school, describes the solidarity that Palestinian Americans feel with those fighting the *intifada*. "We are not only involved in it emotionally," he says. "We are part of it. We are in the United States, but we still consider ourselves as part of this uprising. We are making all efforts, trying to raise money for them, providing medical assistance, humanitarian assistance, trying to be not just sympathizing with [them], but also trying to be a part of this historical moment. Because we consider it to be historical. It is for the first time that every Palestinian—children, women, old people—are involved in this uprising."

Few Palestinian Americans are unaffected by the *intifada* in some direct way. One man's seventeen-year-old brother in Beit Hanina was taken off his school bus by Israeli soldiers and beaten. Another man's mother was hit in the head by a rubber bullet and, because it was fired from a distance, only stunned. His sister has had two miscarriages after being teargassed, and a brother-in-law was beaten and hospitalized for two weeks when he refused an Israeli soldier's demand that he pull down a Palestinian flag from an electric pole. A New York man was shocked to telephone his mother on the West Bank and find that she had just been teargassed. "I said, 'My God, what are you doing, Mom?'" he recalls. "She said, 'Well, I can't just let the Israelis come around and beat the kids, so I go out. If I have to, I throw rocks. I always carry a bucket of water with me so if they throw teargas, I'm there to douse it with water, so I put it out.'" Many other diaspora Palestinians have similar stories.

Asad Asad, the business manager of the Jerusalem Arabic-language newspaper *al-Fajr*, divides his time between Brooklyn and the Jerusalem/Beit Hanina area, even though his wife and children live permanently in the United States. Asad describes the tactics Israeli military officials have used to confiscate the paper since the *intifada* began. Knowing the routes the drivers take to deliver the paper throughout the West Bank and Gaza every morning, Asad says, the Israelis establish roadblocks and confiscate the papers. Finally, in late afternoon, they call Asad and tell him that he can come and pick up the papers. He has pointed out to the military governor's office, he says, that distributing the paper at four o'clock in the afternoon does no good when merchants have been closing their offices and stores during the *intifada* at noon. "The name of the game here," Asad says the military official responded, "is to give you a dead paper. It's dead today."

A few Palestinian Americans have spent time in Israeli jails, and more have had relatives imprisoned. As noted earlier, Mike Hazem Monsour, the Albuquerque jeweler, was arrested by Israeli authorities when he returned to visit his elderly mother in 1984 and was held without charges for three weeks until U.S. officials intervened to secure his release. Samir Abed-Rabbo's older brother was jailed in 1968 when he was "almost fourteen years old." Held with two other young teenagers for two and a half years "for being a member of, whatever," Abed-Rabbo says sarcastically, the youngster was never formally charged. Imprisonment by Israeli authorities for security and political offenses is generally regarded as a kind of badge of honor among Palestinians in the West Bank and Gaza and, far from thwarting opposition to Israeli occupation and retarding the growth of Palestinian nationalism, the prison system is seen as a breeding ground for nationalism.

"The basic graduate school for Palestinian political consciousness has been the Israeli prison system, at least the ones in the occupied territories," says Rashid Khalidi, Director of the Center for Middle East Studies at the University of Chicago, who is a leading Palestinian intellectual and an adviser to the Palestinian negotiating delegation. Those who become the activists in the West Bank and Gaza and those who are leading the uprising, "go to elementary school and high school and college, and then at some stage they go sideways into prison, and that's really where they complete their education. And the organizations are strongest inside the prisons. They task the people, they train the people, they indoctrinate the people, they organize them, they see their capabilities, and by the time they get out, they're full-fledged members in a way that they never were when they went in." Khalidi adds, laughing, "I mean, the Israelis would do themselves an enormous favor if they emptied the prisons."

The impact of imprisonment, in terms of arousing nationalistic feelings, is almost as strong on family members outside the occupied territories as on the prisoners themselves. Mohamed Odetalla, the young Detroit grocery and liquor store owner from Beit Hanina, remembers going with his mother to visit a cousin in a prison in the Negev desert. "We went in the Red Cross buses," he says,

> and when the prisoners came out—you know at weddings and celebrations how the Palestinian women make that noise [ululation, a high-pitched wailing or trilling by which many Middle Eastern women express both joy and grief]?—and when all the prisoners come and all the women all at once they do that, it just grips you.

And tears came down my eyes, and I had goose bumps all over me. And, oh my God, I am a Palestinian, you know! And those people, their sons have been beat up, and you should see the welts on their heads, places where their hair doesn't grow anymore, people had their noses broken, disfigured, and they're steadfast, they're Palestinians, you know, one hundred percent Palestinians. And not one woman cries for her son being in jail; she celebrates the fact he didn't go to jail because he was a drug dealer or because he stole something. He went to jail for his country, for his cause. They [the Israelis] don't know that for everybody they arrest, it's like a diploma from school; they actually have a party for them.

The Israeli harassing tactic that is probably most often mentioned as a source of anger and humiliation for Palestinians is the search process for those entering the West Bank across the Allenby Bridge from Jordan. This is an experience that Palestinian Americans probably encounter more frequently than others because it is usually possible for Palestinians to visit the West Bank only if they have an American passport. Joe A., a Los Angeles businessman from the West Bank, takes up almost an hour of an interview describing in angry tones the thorough and often degrading search. He begins by saying that he is not political; he is not active in political causes, and he has never been to a political meeting. His strenuous attempts to avoid political discussion make his fierce anger over the search process at the bridge all the more dramatic.

It begins, he says, when all passengers are frisked upon disembarking from the Israeli bus that has brought them across the bridge; this is an external but thorough search—to the point, Joe says, that with each woman "they run their hands over her boobs right there while everybody watches." Luggage is inspected minutely—this is a security search, not a customs inspection, which comes later—and passengers are then seated on a bench outside and relieved of their shoes and, if a man is wearing a *khaffiyah*, of the *agal* or rope that holds the headdress on. Shoes and *agals* are sent to be x-rayed and, Joe says—emphasizing the particular humiliation of being shoeless—"we sit, all these men, all these women, barefooted."

At this point, each passenger is taken individually to be strip-searched. The search includes running a metal detector over the Palestinian's naked body—"because maybe you got bombs in your lungs and heart," Joe says with derision. He describes the entire process, which can take as long as eight hours, as a "hell day." Non-Palestinian passengers arriving on the same bus from Jordan do not endure the searches and are passed through quickly. No non-Palestinian, Joe says, has ever witnessed the process, and the press never reports on it. "If they would strangle us there," he says, almost shouting, "no one in the world would know."

No Palestinian is immune from the search. Emile Sahliyeh, the University of North Texas professor, traveled across the bridge in 1980 carrying Braille notes taken over a summer spent in the United States and taped readings made here, and all the materials were confiscated. "It was really awful," he says, "because it was books that I recorded here and I wanted to use in my courses [at Bir Zeit University] when I went back." After hiring a lawyer to retrieve the tapes and notes, Sahliyeh received a letter in Hebrew saying that the tapes had been destroyed in the name of a 1940s security law.

An American passport sometimes serves as a red flag to Israeli inspectors. Omar Kader, even though born in the United States, describes having his passport thrown on the ground and stepped on during a trip in 1986. The Israeli security official at the bridge said, "You're a Palestinian as far as we're concerned," Kader remembers, and he was strip-searched and some computer disks he was carrying were confiscated. The entire process took four hours. "I went as an American with ethnic Palestinian identity, and they treated me like I was one of their subjects," he says bitterly. When he returned to the United States, he gave the story to Dale Van Atta, assistant to Jack Anderson, who wrote a column about it, and the next time Kader crossed the bridge, with copies of the column strewn throughout his luggage, he was passed through in twenty minutes.[7]

The stories are endless, and diaspora Palestinians have a deep and intimate understanding of why West Bankers and Gazans launched and sustained the *intifada* for so long. "We've tried many ways" to end the occupation, the San Francisco businessman Fuad Ateyeh says, speaking from the perspective of a refugee camp resident, "and none of them work because the Israelis only believe in military might. There are no signs that they are going to do anything in a peaceful way. So, when you see hundreds of our people getting killed and thousands injured and thousands arrested, it's not because those people really have nothing else to do. No, it's because they reached the point that there is no other way to do it but force."

Palestinians say repeatedly that what their compatriots are telling Israel through the *intifada* is that its so-called "benevolent" occupation is unacceptable because it is a foreign occupation. Before the uprising, Israel boasted that Palestinians were better off economically and even politically under Israeli occupation than they had been under Jordanian and Egyptian control and better off than the citizens of any neighboring Arab state. But the uprising has shown, Palestinians say, that the occupation was never wholly benign and that whatever economic benefits might have accompanied it were not enough without freedom.

"The uprising has shown," says one man, "that refrigerators and TVs are not what's on people's minds. Nationalism comes first, not Kit-Kats." Kit Kats are the candy that, more than Coke or any other Western product, has become the symbol of Westernism on the West Bank. "What do you do with a refrigerator if you don't have the right to speak out," asks Khalil Barhoum, the Stanford linguistics lecturer, "if you don't have the right to write, if you don't have the right to go to school, if you don't have the right to plant your own tree on your own lot, if you don't have the right to dig a well on your own piece of land? It doesn't mean much. The economic argument has certainly been used before by all occupiers and colonizers—unconvincingly, I might add."

Because it became the symbol for Palestinian self-sufficiency, the *intifada* provided a release for deeply felt and very widespread hostility to the Arab states. This hostility has intensified in recent years, fueled by the Palestinian feeling of abandonment by most of the Arab states, particularly the most powerful countries, during the Gulf war. Palestinians have almost nothing good to say about any Arab country or any Arab leader. The other Arabs are called "bastards," "despicable," "fools," "despots," "stupid," and are almost unanimously condemned for corruption and the dictatorial rule they impose on their own countries, as well as for their cynical handling of the Palestinian question. One of the proximate causes of the uprising in fact was the almost total absence of any mention of the Palestinian issue at an Arab summit held in Jordan the month before the *intifada* began in December 1987. Yasir Arafat was snubbed by the summit's host, King Hussein, and the summit proceedings were devoted almost entirely to the then-ongoing Iran-Iraq war. The summit was heralded throughout the world as signaling the Arab states' disengagement from the Palestinian issue.

Palestinians have no illusions about the Arab countries and their accomplishments. The Arab governments, says one man, "oppress their own citizens, they don't allow their own citizens to operate freely, and they're basically raising robots. I think it's because of the political system they have that the Arab peoples have not been able to utilize their intellectual and scientific abilities. I think if there were democracies in the Arab countries, they would be in much better shape economically, politically, and culturally. I feel like oppression kills creativity." Even Iraq's Saddam Hussein, whom Palestinians hailed for his championship of the Palestinian cause during the Gulf crisis, usually comes in for scathing criticism for stifling freedom in Iraq. In an interesting separation of issues, Palestinians who praise Saddam for trying to help their cause also denounce him as a vicious dictator who disgraces the Arab world.

Nor do Palestinians have any illusions about Arab support for the Palestinian cause. "I think the PLO and the Palestinian people have been hurt by the Arabs more than [by] any other group of people that I can think of," says one man. "More so than the Israelis. The Arab kings and sheikhs, they want to stay kings and sheikhs, and who are the Palestinians? 'Oh yeah [they say], they're our brothers and we love 'em—here's some money, leave me alone.'" It took the Palestinians forty years, says another man, "to realize that the Arab governments are liars, they can't deliver." Palestinians believe the reason the Arab countries don't deliver is that they have too much at stake with the United States. The states are not strong enough, singly or collectively, to wage war effectively against Israel, and many of them have tied themselves so closely to the United States economically and financially that they are unwilling to risk damaging their bilateral relations by pressuring the U.S. on Palestinian behalf. Egypt is so dependent on U.S. economic and military aid that it is in thrall to Washington, Palestinians feel. In addition, since well before the Gulf crisis but particularly since then, Saudi Arabia has regarded the United States as its protector and is unwilling to risk this shield for the Palestinians.

Palestinians are also bitter because so many Arab states have prevented cross-border guerrilla raids into Israel from their territory. Beginning in the 1950s, Israel's retaliatory strikes made such cross-border operations so costly for the sponsoring countries, primarily in those days Egypt and Jordan, that these states, as well as Syria, have virtually sealed their borders ever since. Largely because it has never had a government or an army capable of controlling the Palestinians, Lebanon was always the only Arab country from which Palestinian guerrillas could operate with relative impunity.

The stories here too are myriad. Many Palestinians tell of being made to feel foreign in Egypt or Lebanon or the Gulf countries. One woman talks about the Kuwaiti government's refusal to issue a visa for her grandmother, dying of cancer in Lebanon, to join the family living in Kuwait for her last months. "They said she was a Palestinian, and she might be a terrorist." This was at a time well before the Gulf crisis when more than 350,000 Palestinians lived in Kuwait, providing the backbone of Kuwait's professional class and civil service. A man tells of traveling on a Jordanian passport to Morocco on his honeymoon and being refused a visa, even though his American-born wife was granted one. "We really don't have anything against the Jordanians," he reports the Moroccan airport official as saying, thinking he was a Jordanian. "It's just those Palestinians that we are trying to guard against."

Far more serious than the individual cases of harassment or the Arab states' faint hearts with regard to providing substantial support is the history of Palestinian slaughter at Arab hands. Palestinians remember with intense bitterness Black September in 1970, during which King Hussein's Bedouin army killed thousands of Palestinians and eventually expelled the PLO from Jordan; Tel Za'atar in 1976, a Palestinian refugee camp in the heart of Beirut where Lebanese Christian militiamen in cooperation with Syria held a civilian population under siege for weeks and ultimately massacred hundreds; Sabra and Shatila in 1982, two other Beirut refugee camps where Lebanese Christians operating in an area controlled by Israel slaughtered hundreds of Palestinian civilians; and the "camps war" of 1985-1988 in Beirut, when Lebanese Shiite forces held Palestinian refugee camps under siege.

Palestinians tend to forget their own culpability in the Jordan/Black September situation—the fact that the PLO had grown so strong in Jordan that it had become a law unto itself and had several times attempted to assassinate King Hussein. But the wholesale slaughter and expulsion of Palestinians from an Arab country have stood in the minds of Palestinians for two decades as a symbol of their plight, strengthening the frustration they feel over their exile, homelessness, and abandonment by their Arab brethren.

Palestinians probably look on Jordan, in fact, with more hostility than on any other Arab country, although during the Gulf crisis most Palestinians supported King Hussein's position opposing both Iraq's invasion of Kuwait and the U.S. intervention. Few Palestinians are unaware of Jordan's long record of cooperation with Israel, beginning in the 1920s when Emir Abdullah, grandfather of King Hussein, began an erratic but enduring relationship with the Zionist leadership that ultimately led to an agreement to cooperate in preventing the formation of the Palestinian Arab state when Palestine was partitioned into an Arab and a Jewish state in 1947. Thus was Abdullah able after the 1948 war to annex the West Bank to Jordan.[8]

Throughout the succeeding nineteen years of Jordanian control, until Israel's capture of the West Bank in 1967, Jordan smothered any expression of separate Palestinian nationalism. Some Palestinians from the West Bank say they grew up more or less unaware of their Palestinian identity. "This is one virtue that Jordanians gave to the Israelis," says one man who was two years old when Jordan took control of his East Jerusalem home, "is that they let us forget about Palestine between '48 and '67. We were not taught that in school. I was calling myself Jordanian at that time." Pan-Arabism and Gamal Abdul Nasser's visions of one Arab nation were in vogue on the West Bank at the time, he says, but Jordan tried to suppress even these trends. "In the West Bank you could not be politically active in any way. Any political activity before '67 was on the secretive, underground level." He remembers King Hussein with bitterness. "Politically, he oppressed us, repressed us. He played on the other side. He didn't want the Israelis to invade Jordan, so he killed us."

Palestinians were not wholly quiescent as a result of Jordanian suppression, and not all Palestinians by any means forgot their Palestinian identity. Demonstrations on the West Bank against Jordan were common, and several Palestinians report having been imprisoned themselves or had relatives imprisoned for their political activism and friends shot in demonstrations. In answer to Israel's charge that Palestinians never demanded a separate

212

Palestinian state when the West Bank was under Arab control, Palestinians counter with descriptions of the high level of anti-Jordanian activism.

Economically and culturally as well, West Bank Palestinians suffered from their association with Jordan. "I think the Palestinians as a group were suspect," says one West Banker. "Palestinians possessed many of the skills that Jordanians didn't have to begin with, and they were needed in many ways. [But] the discrimination came in several ways." With the exception of a few notable West Bank families who tied their fortunes to the Jordanian regime, few Palestinians gained access to positions of real power in Jordan. Economically, the West Bank became the poor sister of Jordan proper. It had a primitive, agriculture-based economy with virtually no industry and was left by Jordan to stagnate while resources were invested in Jordan proper. As a result, large numbers of West Bank men and men from refugee camps on the West Bank emigrated to find work on Jordan's East Bank or in other Arab countries.

Extreme bitterness toward King Hussein is widespread among Palestinians who had a direct experience of his rule over the West Bank. The personal rancor continues to the present, despite Jordan's stance during the Gulf war and official Jordanian-Palestinian cooperation in negotiations. Many members of families known for their pro-Jordanian sympathies now say they are embarrassed by their families' support for Hussein and are at pains to give evidence of their own support for the PLO.

Palestinians have also suffered keenly in Lebanon, where the vast majority who live in refugee camps throughout the country have not been permitted to become citizens and where anti-Palestinian hostility has been acute. At the same time, however, there is among a great many Palestinians a special appreciation for Lebanon's role in providing the Palestinians a haven. In some sense this appreciation is odd, given Palestinian travails in Lebanon, but it seems to grow out of the Palestinians' recognition of the unique problems their huge and often disruptive presence has caused for Lebanon and out of a recognition of the fact that Lebanon itself has suffered immeasurably because of the Palestinians.

What is commonly known about the Palestinian presence in Lebanon is that with several hundred thousand people, primarily refugees, it has been an overwhelmingly large presence. Also well known is the fact that the PLO, until it was expelled during Israel's 1982 invasion, had established what Israel came to call "a state within a state" in southern Lebanon. PLO overlordship in the south was heavy-handed, and the Palestinian presence was one, although not by any means the only, spark that set off the civil war that raged in Lebanon for a decade and a half after 1975. Palestinians, however, emphasize other, less well known aspects of the Palestinian presence. They point out that, if the Palestinians played a part in Lebanon's destruction, they also played a large part in its initial growth as a business center. The economic boom Lebanon experienced from the 1950s until 1975—a boom fueled by American investment money and an attractive investment climate—was, they believe, made possible in large measure because of the Palestinian presence in Lebanon.

"Lebanon's boom in a sense came because of the destruction of Palestine" as an Arab country, says Raja S., the Washington intellectual, who himself grew up in Beirut after fleeing Palestine in 1948. Palestine had been the business outlet and banking center for the other territories Britain controlled in Jordan and Iraq, and Haifa was both a major terminus for oil pipeline shipments from Iraq and a port for transshipment of goods inland to Jordan, Iraq, and Saudi Arabia. In 1948 the British pipeline terminals in Haifa and many British banking operations were moved to Lebanon. In addition, American oil interests redirected certain of their own activities to Lebanon. The American-built Trans-Arabian Pipeline from Saudi Arabia, completed in 1949, had to be routed the long way around Israel through Jordan and Syria to a Mediterranean outlet in Lebanon.

"All of that created a real boom in Lebanon," says Raja. "It started slowly in the '50s, but by the late '50s it picked up and in the '60s just took off. It sucked in everybody in terms of work." Those sucked in initially were largely Palestinian Christians, according to Raja; unlike the French-educated Lebanese, they were more likely to be English-speaking because they had been educated in a British system and were better able in the early years, until the Lebanese began to pick up English, to work with the British and particularly the American companies that came into Lebanon.

These Christian Palestinians were far more likely than their Muslim refugee compatriots to be given Lebanese citizenship, according to Raja. But whatever relatively comfortable niche some of them found in Lebanon and whatever role they played in fueling Lebanon's economic boom, the Palestinians as a whole were never truly accepted by the Lebanese. It was easy to spot a Palestinian by his dialect, Palestinians tended to make themselves obvious by not assimilating and clustering in Palestinian neighborhoods, they took jobs from Lebanese, and the refugee camps were considered a blight and a drain on the economy. As the years went on, and particularly after the PLO moved its base of operations from Jordan to Lebanon in 1971, the situation went from bad to worse.

Lebanon has stood as a symbol to the Palestinians of their vulnerability—clear evidence that they will never be accepted by and can never be integrated in other Arab countries and that the only solution to their problem therefore lies in having a state of their own. Israel and its supporters have always taken the position that the Palestinians should become integrated in the other Arab countries, that there are a score Arab countries and only one Israel and the Palestinians should seek satisfaction for their national aspirations with their Arab brethren. But the Palestinian experience in Lebanon above all, though in other Arab countries as well, has demonstrated for Palestinians that, even if they wanted to forget their claims on Palestine, they would never be welcome anywhere else. Lebanon above all—Lebanon's own hostility, the failure of any Arab state to come to the Palestinians' aid during Israel's 1982 attack, and the particular vulnerability of Palestinian refugees in Lebanon to attack by all comers, whether Arab or Israeli—has also convinced Palestinians that they can depend only on themselves to accomplish their goals. This need for self-sufficiency, and the urgency of the need for a solution, Palestinians believe, constitute the principal message of the *intifada*.

The degree and type of violence occurring in the *intifada* are much discussed among Palestinians. Should firearms rather than stones and Molotov cocktails be used against Israelis? Do Palestinians have a right to use any type of violence against Palestinians who collaborate with Israel?

Although weapons, primarily knives, have begun to be used increasingly in attacks against Israelis in the occupied territories, it remains the official policy of the PLO and the *intifada* leadership to discourage armed attacks. The majority of Palestinians appear to recognize the benefits—from a public relations standpoint as well as a practical standpoint, given Israel's military strength—of not using arms against Israelis. "Israelis are pushing us to resort to arms," says Abdul Hamid Salem, the Washington, D.C., publisher of the weekly WAFA Palestine News Agency newsletter. "They have the upper hand. They will crush us [if we use guns], and nobody's going to regret that....[Not using arms] is the only way that we can capture the American imagination and public opinion."

But some few Palestinians are so frustrated at Israel's failure to respond positively to the *intifada* or to the PLO peace initiative, and so convinced of the PLO's military capabilities, that they advocate a step-up in military activity. It is interesting to listen in on a debate between two Palestinians on this issue. The men are members of two prominent Jerusalem families of long standing. Nasib Nuseibeh is from the Muslim family that has since the seventh century held the key to the Church of the Holy Sepulchre in Jerusalem. Nasib left the city with his family at the age of twelve in 1948, and grew up in Lebanon. Although he worked in Kuwait until the Gulf crisis, he is a U.S. citizen with a family in Albuquerque, New Mexico, and when working in Kuwait spent large parts of the year in the United States. Hazem Husseini is a member of one of Jerusalem's leading religious and nationalist families. He left Jerusalem when he was thirteen during the 1967 war and grew up in Saudi Arabia. He is now a businessman in Albuquerque.

Nuseibeh begins by saying he is disappointed that the PLO has foresworn the use of weapons and essentially given up on armed struggle as an aspect of its strategy. He supports the two-state solution, he says, but he fears that the Palestinians gave too much away without obtaining assurances of a response. "The Jews," he says, "won't make any concessions unless really they are hurt and they know they are losing a lot of their people. You know, Arafat should really, as he said in the United Nations [in a 1974 speech], have the olive branch in one hand, in the other hand the weapon. But he's using the olive branch so far, and so far the Jews, why should they be afraid? They didn't lose anything." He has no faith that the United States will move, and he fears that the *intifada* will not last. Only military struggle, he believes, will have any effect.

Husseini breaks in at this point. "Mr. Nuseibeh, maybe I disagree with you on that. I think the *intifada* has proved to us and to the Arab countries and to the world that it is a more effective weapon in our struggle for independence than any other means, including all Arab armies and Arab power and Arab wealth and Arab economic strength and so forth."

"I am not against the *intifada*, don't get me wrong," Nuseibeh interjects. "I am with the *intifada* one hundred percent." He is simply worried, he says, that the benefits gained by the uprising will somehow be turned against the Palestinians. It has happened before, he says.

"Right, absolutely," says Husseini, "so we have to look to our own interests. Every time we pick up the gun and we shoot one bullet, the whole world is looking at us as terrorists, as no good people, as bloodthirsty people. One bullet, okay? And we need the support of the international community. We need to tell the international community that we are a peaceful people and all that we are asking for is our basic human rights and our independent state."

But, Nuseibeh says, after years of suffering in the *intifada*, the Palestinians have gained nothing substantial. "All we have is sympathy." The conversation weaves back and forth inconclusively until Husseini asks Nuseibeh what other alternatives the Palestinians have. "All the Palestinian people should fight" in an underground war using weapons, Nuseibeh answers. "What I'm saying, when they start feeling that hundreds of them are wounded, the Jews, and many cities are burned and they are losing a lot— from inside, they don't see an army which they could kill it—then they start thinking, 'All right, we are losing all the country, we are in trouble, we are losing people.' Then they start thinking."

"Mr. Nuseibeh, we want to prevent the killings from both sides," Husseini says.

But, Nuseibeh rejoins, "we are killed, we are wounded, we are demolished."

"Maybe this is the price we have to pay to get where we're going," Husseini finishes. "The second we fire the first bullet in the *intifada*, we have lost all kinds of wars, and we have lost what we have been working for."

The question of violence by Palestinians against those who collaborate with Israel is a less black-and-white issue for most Palestinians. By the end of the third year of the *intifada*, over 300 Palestinians said to be collaborators had been killed by compatriots,[9] and the internecine warfare has been held up by Israelis and their supporters as another example of the Palestinians' inherent immorality.

The issue is difficult for most Palestinians. They condemn the violence and particularly the fact that much of the Palestinian-on-Palestinian violence has consisted of attacks on innocent people by West Bank street gangs. They agree that the violence reflects badly on the Palestinians. At the same time, they understand the reasons for attacks on collaborators. In over two decades of occupation, Israel has established a network of collaborators who inform on their compatriots and intimidate them, often becoming laws unto themselves. Unlike any other Palestinians in the occupied territories, collaborators are provided with arms by Israel.[10] The collaborators help perpetuate an intolerable occupation, according to Khalil Barhoum, doing Israel's bidding by oppressing the people politically, culturally, and economically. Because they are able to penetrate deep into Palestinian society, they are more damaging, he feels, than Israel could ever hope to be.

Barhoum can see both sides of this issue. "Although the fate meted out to collaborators is deplorable," he acknowledges, "it should be emphasized nevertheless that the population under occupation has no recourse to the law and has no prisons in which to jail them. Unlike sovereign nations who have an established system to try and imprison enemy collaborators amongst them, Palestinians, because of the occupation under which they live, have no judicial system through which to mete out justice. Whatever law enforcement exists is in the service of the Israeli occupiers."

During its first few years, the *intifada* had a remarkable effect on Palestinian Americans. Some people who had more or less dropped out reported a dramatic renewal of their interest in the issue. Fadi Zanayed, a Chicago attorney from Ramallah, says that one Arab-American organization in Chicago that once drew two or three hundred people to its events began drawing as many as 3,000 after the uprising began. "It's lifted the spirits of the Palestinians here," he said in 1989. The San Francisco businessman Fuad Mogannam says of himself, "Before the uprising, I didn't think much about what was happening there because it was like an issue that's almost dying, and nobody seemed to care." He used to downplay his Palestinian heritage because he felt it impolitic to advertise it in the United States, but since the uprising, he says, "I've been a tiger."

The mood has changed dramatically with the repeated setbacks of recent years in Palestinian fortunes. Although people like Mogannam, for whom the *intifada* was a spur to greater interest and participation in Palestinian affairs, have maintained their activism, the sense of real euphoria that the uprising engendered in its first few years has been transformed to pessimism and discouragement.

This is evident in the changing atmosphere at Arab-American gatherings. At the annual conference of the American-Arab Anti-Discrimination Committee, for instance—a three-day convention held in the Washington, D.C., area that usually draws about 2,000-3,000 Arab Americans from throughout the United States—the mood in recent years has grown increasingly somber. In the spring of 1989, at the height of the *intifada* and only months after the PLO declared an independent state and formally agreed to coexist with Israel, the convention was a massive celebration. Keynote speakers from the Palestine National Council and from the West Bank drew thunderous applause; the singing of the Palestinian anthem, *"Biladi, Biladi"* ("My Country, My Country"), brought emotional cheers and foot-stomping from Palestinians and other Arabs. A year later, after the U.S.-PLO dialogue had stagnated, the *intifada* had begun to lose steam, and Israel had failed to respond to Palestinian concessions, the mood at the convention was noticeably more restrained, with none of the elation or the optimism of the previous year. In 1991, after the Gulf war, the convention was totally cheerless; inter-Arab differences over the war prompted bickering among many Arab delegates and booing of some speakers, and calls for Palestinian statehood evoked little elation.

Despite the melancholy mood, the *intifada* and the continued hardships of those living under occupation do still have a strong impact on Palestinians in the diaspora. The acute awareness that the *intifada* brought to Palestinians outside the occupied territories of the urgent need for a peace settlement to free West Bankers and Gazans from the occupation continues to motivate Palestinians everywhere.

Whatever the recent setbacks, Palestinians still link the *intifada* inextricably with the Palestinian desire, individual as well as official, for a peaceful settlement to this conflict. "Now we are ready, we're very ready" for peace with Israel, says Samia C., a West Banker who has been living in the United States since the 1970s but still feels she "needs to get what I call my fix and indulge in things Palestinian" by returning home once or twice a year. "Was the *intifada* the result of the readiness, or was the readiness the result of the *intifada*?" she muses. "I really cannot answer, but I know that people are ready. And I'll tell you something, when I go home, I talk to my parents, who are both elderly and suffering from it [the *intifada*]. I talk to my relatives; they all have very, very strong feelings that this is the right thing, the *intifada*. Everybody is really ready to sacrifice so that the world will know about the cause, and that's remarkable."

NOTES

[1] For further details on Abu Aker's injury and treatment before coming to Boston, see Rev. Don Wagner, "A Living Martyr," *The Return* (November 1988): 4-8.

[2] Jim Hoagland, "Will the PLO Break With Its Past?" *Washington Post* (November 16, 1989).

[3] Nabil Shaath, banquet speech at ADC National Convention, Arlington, VA, April 15, 1989.

[4] Michel Jubran, "'Not Planned But Not Spontaneous': The Intifada, Its Leadership and the PLO," *Washington Report on Middle East Affairs* (December 1989): 10-11.

[5] "The *al-Fajr* Public Opinion Survey, Washington, D.C., 8 September 1986," *Journal of Palestine Studies* 62 (Winter 1987): 196-207.

[6] Jubran, "'Not Planned But Not Spontaneous,'" and Rashid I. Khalidi, "The Uprising and the Palestine Question: New Forces and Old Constraints," *World Policy Journal* (Summer 1988): 497-517.

[7] The article appeared in the Jack Anderson column of November 5, 1986.

[8] See Avi Shlaim, *Collusion Across the Jordan: King Abdullah, the Zionist Movement, and the Partition of Palestine* (New York: Columbia University Press, 1988), for a description of Zionist-Jordanian contacts and their cooperation in preventing the formation of a Palestinian state.

[9] Figures cited in *New Outlook* (December 1990).

[10] See Frank Collins, "Why Palestinians Kill Palestinians in Israeli-Occupied Territories," *Washington Report on Middle East Affairs* (November 1989): 13.

11   Palestinian Intellectuals

The intellectuals of any community are at once its "front men" and its social conscience. They are the shapers of the community's political theories as well as of its moral tone, in many ways molding whatever is unique in its identity. Because of the singular moral overtones that surround the Palestinian-Israeli conflict—arising out of the common perception of Judaism as a humanistic system of high moral values—Palestinian intellectuals have faced a hostile challenge to prove themselves and their community worthy of moral approbation. And because their antagonists, in the eyes of many, have captured the moral high ground, their own challenge to the legitimacy of Zionism as a moral political ideology has received little credence.

Palestinian intellectuals are widely perceived to have failed in the task of building and strengthening their community's moral fiber. They are repeatedly accused of failing to examine the collective Palestinian conscience—of failing or refusing to criticize their own system for its moral laxity and of seeming to condone terrorism by not condemning it. They are often accused of being cold-bloodedly insensitive to Jewish suffering and indeed of egging their community on to greater anti-Jewish malice.

Palestinian intellectuals themselves use a different yardstick and, as on so many other issues involved in this conflict, they begin from a different starting point. They do not accept their accusers' premises. In the interviews that follow, several of the leading intellectuals address this question and others.

Walid Khalidi is perhaps the dean of the Palestinian intellectual community. Son of a leading Jerusalem family noted for centuries for its scholarship, Khalidi has devoted his adult life to the study of the Palestine question. During the Madrid peace conference in October 1991 and the first two rounds of bilateral negotiations in Washington, he served as one of two Palestinians on the Jordanian negotiating delegation. He is a quiet although not unassuming man, a scholar who would rather avoid the limelight but who in a public appearance conveys the kind of assurance that comes with an intimate knowledge of his subject matter. His writing is filled with factual evidence of his people's dispersion, and he writes as if to convince, as though he is making debating points that he knows cannot be challenged because of the evidence he has marshaled.

In both writing and speech, he exhibits a wry, understated humor that comes at unexpected moments. In a serious scholarly quarterly he writes of the Arab states having "their political pudenda appropriately covered";[1] in conversation he brings down the house by saying, with proper British inflections and rolled r's, that Yitzhak Shamir in a recent American television appearance had come across as so forthcoming that "you'd think he was Mother Theresa, you know." He looks the part of a scholar, like a British don with an almost expressionless face and lank gray hair falling across his forehead. In fact, he graduated from Oxford and was a lecturer there. But his lack of facial expression belies his passion; the Palestine question is no mere academic exercise for him.

Khalidi has never felt wholly at home in the United States. He was a young man away from his Jerusalem home when the 1948 war began, and he lived in Beirut thereafter until 1982, when life in Lebanon became all but impossible. In that year he was named a research fellow at Harvard, having for the four previous years been a visiting scholar commuting between Harvard and the American University of Beirut. He feels acutely that there is political hostility toward Arabs in the United States and that he would be more comfortable in a Middle Eastern setting. He once planned to retire to a home he and his wife rented in the mountains of Lebanon, and he says that, were there an independent Palestinian state, he would go there to live.

Although he maintains a strict independence from the PLO, Khalidi has been a kind of pacesetter of Palestinian policy, publicly advocating positions that the Palestinian leadership has not yet officially come to. In 1978, he published an article in *Foreign Affairs* calling for establishment of a Palestinian state in the West Bank and Gaza. Called "Thinking the Unthinkable,"[2] the article was addressed to those Israelis and Americans for whom such a state was and remains unthinkable. His proposal preceded by a decade PLO willingness explicitly to limit Palestinian statehood to the occupied territories.

Khalidi strenuously disagrees with the notion that Palestinian intellectuals have not engaged in self-criticism. "Actually, there is a whole literature of Palestinian self-criticism," he says, "particularly after 1948. In fact, it was almost masochistic—how rotten society is, responsibilities of the leaders, collapse of morals, collapse of the leadership. Tremendous, tremendous amount of self-criticism." He points out that, although it did not live up to its promise, the movement toward military control that swept so much of the Arab world in the 1950s—in Egypt, in Syria, in Iraq, and elsewhere— began as a well intentioned attempt to end the corruption, despotism, and moral laxity of the old regimes.

The critical literature to which Khalidi refers was entirely in Arabic, which accounts in large measure for the fact that Israeli and Jewish intellectual critics of the Palestinians are unaware of it. Khalidi is himself not hesitant to criticize Palestinian policies, but he feels that the forums in which Palestinians are allowed to speak and write in the United States are extremely limited. He has personally found it quite difficult to publish in mainstream American media.

Khalidi is one of few Palestinians who has publicly criticized the Palestine national charter or covenant, which calls among other things for "elimination of the Zionist presence in Palestine." (This is variously translated as "liquidation" or "destruction" of the Zionist "entity" or simply of "Zionism" in Palestine.) As early as 1981, he wrote in *Foreign Affairs*: "One way of looking at the Covenant is to view it as a gratuitous tract of hate against an altogether innocent party. Another is to see it in relation to the evolution of the Palestine problem and the tribulations of Palestinian disinheritance and statelessness. Nevertheless, whatever its background the Covenant is maximalist, unrealistic and no basis for a settlement."[3] Over lunch in a Washington restaurant, he says that the phrase "destruction of the Zionist entity" was "stupid and unnecessary, stupid and provocative and obviously in a sense indefensible. On the other hand, it is not genocide. [But] it's a very badly phrased statement, and we could have done without it. If I had been involved, I would not have supported this. I wasn't."

Khalidi has also written in highly critical terms about PLO policy during the Gulf crisis. Himself condemning Iraq's invasion of Kuwait as "a violation of the central humane values of the Islamic Arab heritage and of the accepted norms of international behavior," he has criticized the PLO and Yasir Arafat for failing "to come out publicly, repeatedly, and forcefully" against the invasion. Whatever the support of the Palestinian people for Saddam Hussein and however understandable the Palestinians' alienation from the U.S.-led coalition confronting Iraq, Khalidi feels, Arafat made a grave moral and strategic blunder by not distancing himself from Saddam. The invasion of Kuwait, he notes, violated "the very principles from which the Palestinian cause drew its moral strength"—that is, opposition to foreign occupation—and Arafat undermined that strength by associating himself with Saddam.

Musing during a luncheon conversation on the general topic of self-criticism, Khalidi arrives at the central difference between Jewish perceptions of what Palestinian self-criticism should entail and the reality of Palestinian perceptions; he addresses the reason that Jews think the Palestinian examination of conscience is not morally adequate, even while Palestinians believe they are examining the central moral question of this conflict. "What is the scope of criticism?" Khalidi asks rhetorically. "Of course, if one doesn't criticize oneself, one would be in terrible trouble, but if one asks me, 'Do you accept the moral basis of the Zionist state?' I say, 'No, I don't.' I do not. I do not accept that the process by which it was established was moral. I don't think any people have the right to seek out their salvation at the cost of another."

This is where Khalidi's passion begins to emerge. He has an intense, disarming stare that challenges the interlocutor to know the facts or keep quiet, and his voice conveys a genteel anger that is somewhat intimidating.

He makes a fascinating aside at this point, which reveals the depth of his own conscience. "I think we've fallen into that trap ourselves in Lebanon"—of seeking one's own salvation at another's expense. Like so many other Palestinians who recognize the problems Lebanon has endured because of the Palestinian presence, Khalidi says, "In a way, we have subjected Lebanon so much to our own interests—put our own interests so much ahead of the interests of the Lebanese—that we've forgotten that this is precisely what our case is. I've told this to our leaders in Lebanon, that we are doing to the Lebanese precisely what the Zionists did to us."

When asked if he can understand the impulse behind Zionism, can sympathize with the reasons Jews "sought their salvation" in Palestine, Khalidi answers, "Well, what I know is that Zionism preceded the Holocaust by some sixty years." When it is noted that there had been pogroms in eastern Europe and Russia well before the Holocaust, he answers, "Oh, one is not denying the persecution of Jews or the reality of anti-Semitism—the two variants of anti-Semitism, the religious and the secular versions." With an historian's precision, he adds, "Religious anti-Semitism goes back all the way to pre-medieval times and the perception of the role of the Jews in the Crucifixion. And, of course, the secular one is connected with the racist concepts that flourished in Europe in the nineteenth century as a result of the establishment of the nation states. How can one deny this?" He has no trouble acknowledging Jewish suffering, but this is not the point as far as the Palestinian-Israeli conflict is concerned. Neither the Arab world nor Islam, he says, had anything to do with either kind of anti-Semitism. "Our struggle," he points out,

> is not against the Jews because they are Jews; our struggle is against them because they are invaders, the same as our struggle against the Italians in Libya, against the British in Iraq or Egypt, the French in Algiers and Tunis, Morocco. It has nothing to do with the fact that they're Jews. I mean, if they'd been Confucians, we'd have fought them, as we fought the British. So, of course, you admit the fact of the Holocaust and the horror of it, but we're not responsible for it, and we don't see why we should make amends for the conscience of the West and of Germany and Christendom. At the same time, we say, given what has happened, given the regional, international, and local realities, we are willing to accept an injustice and to settle on the basis of twenty-three to seventy-seven [percent—i.e., settling for the one-quarter of Palestine in the West Bank and Gaza and giving Israel three-quarters].

The question of Israel's "right" to exist troubles Khalidi as it does most Palestinians. "Accepting Israel as a fact and willingness to settle on the basis of this fact is one thing," he notes, "but if by 'legitimacy' it is meant that the process by which Israel was established is morally right, you're saying my delegitimization is morally right. You're saying my expulsion is also right. You're saying my dispossession is also right. I'm not going to say that." He dismisses the demand for recognition of Israel's right to exist as a "joker" thrown into the negotiating process to make it more difficult for Palestinians to come to the table. Likud leaders like the late Menachem Begin and Yitzhak Shamir, he notes, have never cared whether the Palestinians recognize anything about Israel, and he does not agree that leaders of the Labor party, which was in power when the phrase "right to exist" was coined, genuinely felt any kind of need to be accepted by Palestinians.

"They know that if you raise the issue of rights," he says, "you are raising the issue of the historical interpretation of the genesis and evolution of the problem, and they know that we cannot agree to that." The Palestinians do not accept the very premises on which Zionism rests, the legal foundation by which it established a foothold in Palestine. "They know that our position is that the Mandate was illegal because it was imposed on us by force and because it was in contravention of Article 22 of the Covenant of the League of Nations; self-determination and independence derive from Article 22. We did not and could not accept the Balfour Declaration, which we had nothing to do with. What people would agree to being described as the 'non-Jewish population' of the country?" This is how the Balfour Declaration labeled the Arab inhabitants of Palestine, who at the time constituted well over ninety percent of the population.

The intensity of Khalidi's discourse at this point is powerful, and it is clear that the notion that one people might be so overlooked in the course of another people's quest for sanctuary, and overlooked with the approval of a major world power, is to him a gross misplacement of justice. Few people, he believes, take into account the true reasons for the Palestinians' opposition to Zionism. "The way they present the issue," he says, "is always designed to make the listener think that the Arabs are basically hostile to the Jewish people as a people, for atavistic, irrational considerations that have nothing to do with the Palestine problem. And, of course, this is the exact opposite of the truth. It involves a tremendous, a monumental distortion."

He taps his finger on the table with each of the last few words. His presentation is forceful, his voice barely controlled, and with this statement he brings the interview to an end.

People often don't know what to make of Edward Said. Some, who apparently regard the terms "intellectual" and "Palestinian" or "PLO" as inherently contradictory, call him a paradox because he is an intellectual who speaks and writes on behalf of the Palestinian cause.[4] Israelis and Israeli supporters have trouble dealing with him because he is well spoken and articulate and a moderate. An Israeli embassy spokesman has called him a media manipulator, able to distort true PLO goals because he "puts on a very nice face" and speaks English without an accent.[5] American Jewish spokesmen comment not on what he says about coexistence and acceptance of Israel but on what they feel he does not say: he does not condemn terrorism enough (Rabbi Arthur Hertzberg),[6] he does not criticize the PLO charter enough (Morris Abram),[7] he does not say enough about the horrors of the Holocaust (Leon Wieseltier),[8] he does not tone down his anger enough (Mark Krupnick in *Tikkun* magazine).[9]

Said is actually not a difficult man to figure out. More than many public figures, he says what he means in a straightforward manner, whether he is writing in angry defense of his people's cause, or triumphantly commenting for PBS's MacNeil-Lehrer program on the PLO peace initiative, or speaking out in criticism of the PLO leadership, or simply having a relaxed chat in his office. Although he conveys the impression of being angry in much of his writing and often in his television appearances, this is not a fixed part of his persona. Anger serves a purpose for him: "I think of myself as angry," he says; "I still feel a very important capacity for an intellectual is to be able to feel anger." But he is able to turn it off when he chooses.

During a meeting in his Columbia University office, he comes across as easygoing, the opposite of his public personality. He has a relaxed, wholly self-confident way of engaging the interviewer in a friendly exchange of views, as if he is more comfortable this way than in a more structured interview. He and his assistant are in the process of moving his office from one building to another on the Columbia campus, and there is considerable confusion about where his office chairs have gone and where to find a quiet spot away from movers and stacks of book boxes. He jokes about the bookshelves in the new office and how he will reach them; his assistant had told the university construction staff that they needed shelves for many books, and they have arrived in the new office to find shelves built all the way up to the sixteen-foot-high ceiling. Said's own desk has been moved into its new place and, with considerable pleasure, he invites a visitor around behind the desk to share the lovely view of the Columbia campus from his vantage point.

Said teaches comparative literature and is an award-winning literary critic. His 1975 book *Beginnings: Intention and Method* was awarded Columbia's Lionel Trilling Prize, and his 1983 book *The World, the Text, and the Critic* won the American Comparative Literature Association's Rene Wellek Prize. He is also a music-lover and is the music critic for the *Nation* magazine.

But Said has made activism in behalf of the Palestinian cause an avocation for the last quarter century. He came late to a full consciousness of his Palestinian identity, at least in a political sense. His early life, he says, was "too confusing." Born in 1935 in Jerusalem, he knew he was a Palestinian, but many other identities impinged. His family lived much of the time in Cairo, they left their Jerusalem home shortly after partition was declared and fighting began in late 1947, his mother is half Lebanese, his father was Palestinian but an American citizen, and he came to the United States on his own at the age of fifteen. The Arab world, Said says, was a place he went to for vacations, but it did not provide a political identity. "It wasn't until '67 really that the change came," he recalls. "I was in New York during the '67 war, and it was a shattering experience for me. Then, with the reemergence of a Palestinian national movement, I began to identify."

His early upbringing and his long separation from his birthplace have made the Palestine question an intellectual, although still very emotional, one for Said rather than a strict issue of nationalism. Nationalism makes him uncomfortable, he told one interviewer; his principal interest in struggling for the Palestinian cause is to gain world acknowledgement for what he sees as a huge injustice to a people of whom he is a part.[10] But for Said, justice—which he believes would be achieved by establishment of a Palestinian state in the West Bank and Gaza alongside Israel, something he has advocated publicly for years—would only be intellectually and emotionally satisfying. He feels no particular affinity himself for the West Bank and Gaza and would not go there to live if a state were established. "My Palestine is in fact Israel," he says a bit wistfully, "and in recent months, since November [1988] when we made the historical compromise, it's been very hard for me to think that in some ways that's it." There is no possibility of ever recovering his own home.

He would like to teach on the West Bank for a period; he has never taught Palestinian students, and it would fulfill something in him to teach, for instance, at Bir Zeit University for a while. But he says the idea of moving at his age and after being in the United States for forty years does not attract him. "The idea of transplanting myself out of New York—actually the idea of leaving New York to go anywhere in this country is already kind of daunting," he says, laughing. For that reason, he does not think he would take any position in a Palestinian government or parliament, even though he was a member of the Palestine National Council from 1977 to 1991.

Exile for Said has been an experience of such duration and such pain that in many ways it can never be fully redressed. He writes eloquently of the pain in his 1986 book *After the Last Sky*—of the exclusion and the sense of not belonging—and he often speaks of an uncertainty about where he should be. Belonging is obviously very important to him. On some days he speaks of not belonging anywhere, of always feeling incomplete, even as a Palestinian; on this particular day, he says he likes the United States precisely because its diversity allows him to fit in.

Asked if he ever wishes his family had never left Palestine, he says, "I can't answer that. Because my history and my being here are so present in my mind that I can't imagine another course that my life might have taken. But I do sometimes feel cut off from it. Certainly *After the Last Sky* was a book that comes out of that sense, of wanting to be connected in various ways. I must tell you this, it's sort of very important for me." He pauses; it obviously is very important to him, and he speaks with an evident pleasure at having discovered this side of himself. "In the last fifteen or twenty years, I have discovered ways in which I have been connected to the, shall we say, the general experience of the Palestinians, without being aware of it. My identity had been so largely focused on being a scholar of English literature and being Western and all that sort of thing, but it finally caught up with me that I was certainly those things, but I was also a Palestinian."

The criticisms from the Jewish community that he and his fellow intellectuals do not do enough searching of the Palestinian soul and do not set a high enough moral standard for the Palestinians irritate Said, but he has grown accustomed to them. "It's just that we don't do it in the pages of the *Times*," he says with the slightest sarcasm. "But we certainly do. I think we're much more critical, I think we have a much more nihilistic sense of the world we live in, a much more cynical and skeptical view, than people think." But because of the situation the Palestinians are in—as the underdogs, vastly outnumbered in terms of size and public relations capacity in this country—he believes the role of the Palestinian intellectual is to defend and explain the Palestinian position rather than criticize tactics.

As for the oft-repeated charge that Palestinians use a moderate voice when speaking in English and another, more radical voice when speaking Arabic, Said denies that he personally speaks with more than one voice and cites a recent trip to Cairo in which, speaking in Arabic to members of an Islamic movement, he condemned the Ayatollah Khomeini's death threat against the author Salman Rushdie.

Does he criticize terrorism when speaking to Arab audiences? "Yes, of course. Yes, absolutely. I've always criticized terrorism." Would it be helpful if the PLO issued more conciliatory statements such as the one put out in mid-1988 by PLO spokesman Bassam Abu Sharif expressing understanding for the Israeli people's desire to live in peace? "We've said that many times," he responds. But, he says, "it has to be heard." That particular statement was ignored by Israel and the United States and received very little American press play. "The problem," he says, "is that a lot of us feel, I certainly feel, that we're the ones who require conciliatory statements.

We're not the ones who are occupying Israeli territory, we're not the ones who are killing kids."

But, it is noted, most audiences do not look at it that way. "I think we have to educate people to the realities. I don't think the issue is making conciliatory statements," Said responds. "I think my role is to tell the truth. I think Israelis frequently have to be told—and American Jews have to be told—what is being done in the name of the Jews and of the Israeli people to Palestinians. That has to be registered. I think that's our major role at the moment. But it certainly can be done from a position of relative conciliation. I mean, I have no stake in a state of permanent war."

Does he think he would get a better hearing if whenever there was a terrorist incident he or another Palestinian intellectual wrote an op-ed article criticizing the incident? "No. I think that's a form of hypocrisy," he says unhesitatingly, "taking one regrettable or unfortunate or unforgivable incident and elevating it into the subject of an op-ed piece for obviously cynical and tactical reasons. I think in the amount of time that I have, there's much more demand for testifying to the sufferings of Palestinians, you see. I'm not going to give in to this tactical view that you should try and seduce them by saying this, that, and the other thing that will please people. I'm not a PR person."

He notes that he does, in the course of writing about the Palestinians, condemn terrorism, and in fact a year after this discussion he wrote a letter to the editor in the *New York Times* with a scathing criticism of Abul Abbas, a renegade PLO executive committee member whose Iraqi-supported faction conducted an abortive terrorist attack on a Tel Aviv beach in May 1990. Said called Abbas "appalling," the action "stupid and immoral." At the same time, in keeping with his mission of testifying to the suffering of the Palestinians, he decried the immorality of the U.S. and Israeli tendency to determine the fate of all Palestinians according to the acts of a few terrorists, while Palestinian deaths at Israeli hands in the *intifada* go unnoticed.[11]

The discussion comes around to Said's view of Zionism and his understanding of the Zionist impulse. Yes, he says, he can understand the urge Zionists felt to give Jews a homeland as a haven from persecution. "I can certainly sympathize with the need somehow to do something about the scourge of anti-Semitism. But where I part company with them, I cannot imagine being a part of it at all. The idea of liberating myself at the expense of the dispossession and enslavement of another people is just—I just can't do it. I don't know whether they thought they were doing that or not. That doesn't seem to me my problem."

He pauses, but then makes it obvious that he thinks this is indeed his problem. "They must have known what they were doing. I've spent a lot of time trying to figure it out. The blinders were very powerful. I'm against blinders, let's put it that way, and that's really what I'm about. I mean, I certainly understand and sympathize and appreciate the achievements of Zionism, but they always seem to impinge on Palestinians. Every Palestinian house that's destroyed is, I suppose," he says pointedly, "part of the achievements of Zionism."

Like most Palestinians, Said cannot contemplate the achievements of Zionism, or even the sufferings of Jews, without considering how these impinge on Palestinians. To look at one but not at the other is to wear the blinders he opposes. Israelis, he has written,

> have a history of suffering and of persecution that has made the state of Israel a compellingly attractive resolution for that history, with its amazing longevity and duration, despite genocidal attempts, exile, and dispersion. Yet none of this, in my opinion, can lessen the truth of what all this has meant for the Palestinians....The question to be asked therefore is how long can the history of anti-Semitism and the Holocaust in particular be used as a fence to exempt Israel from arguments and sanctions against it for its behavior toward the Palestinians....How long are we going to deny that the cries of the people of Gaza...are directly connected to the policies of the Israeli government and not to the cries of the victims of Nazism?[12]

At the same time, unlike many Palestinians, Said feels no desire, once there is a Palestinian state, to alter the character of Zionism. He opposes the "imposition of alternatives to Zionism on Jews," he says. "It doesn't seem to be my job to do that. I feel the whole point of self-determination is that you have to allow people to exercise their self-determination in their own way." He regards the idea of a democratic secular state in which Jews and Palestinians would live together in a single non-sectarian state as "a noble idea." But, he says, "if the large majority of Jews in Israel, which is a state and is a society, feel that they want to exercise their own self-determination separately, then it's not for me to deny them. I feel quite strongly about that."

There is no anger in Said's voice at any point in his long discussion. Even his bitter comment about destroying Palestinian houses as an "achievement of Zionism," so characteristic of the pithy anger in much of his writing, is spoken with only a resigned shrug. He recognizes the change in himself. Speaking in 1989 at the height of the *intifada*, he says he still thinks anger has a purpose, but at this point he feels, thanks to the *intifada*, "a confident sense of the alternatives to anger." He is smiling broadly as he discusses this new aspect of himself and of the Palestinian cause. "People who have been angry and suffering have created another state for themselves which is a form of independence, a reorganization of social relations. For me, the *intifada* is not just throwing stones, it's the creation of an emergent and alternative formation. A lot more of my energy is involved in that than simply crying over misfortunes and the deprivations of the past. It's a shift in emphasis. I'm now more drawn to the alternatives to anger."

Three years later, Said again has every reason for anger and sadness. Iraq's invasion of Kuwait and what he has called the "remorseless Arab propensity to violence and extremism" caused him much anguish, an anguish he has voiced repeatedly and publicly in American as well as in Arab forums.[13] Although he also opposed the U.S. response and has expressed sadness at the American ignorance of and failure to support the best aspects of Arab nationalism, he has been vocal in expressing his disappointment at the Palestinian people's support for Saddam Hussein ("why would a victim identify with the oppressor?...[T]his is a matter of principle. Invasion is invasion"), at Yasir Arafat's alignment with Saddam in response to his people's pro-Saddam sentiments ("One of the things that leaders do is lead. Many of us failed in this role"), and at the lack of accountability of Arab leaders and the sterility of the critical process in the Arab world.

Yet for all his distress, Said still places great hope in the Palestinian people. "We have no strategic ally, the Arab environment is deeply hostile, Israel has an almost complete monopoly on the means of violence and coercion." But, he says, Palestinians are "resourceful and unendingly courageous." Above all,

> we have a more just and, I think, a truer picture than our enemies of a future built on reconciliation and peace....What is left to Palestinians today is the moral force of the argument that says a) there is no military option, and b) you have to live with us, we have to live together as Israelis and as Palestinians, and we have to discover modes of sharing.[14]

Hisham Sharabi has a reputation for sternness and unsmiling seriousness, with the dour countenance that one somehow expects in a philosopher and intellectual. But there is a softer side to him, which emerges without much probing. One interviewer got him to reminisce fondly about the German Jewish nanny his family employed when he was a child in Jaffa.[15] At another meeting in his Georgetown University office in Washington, D.C., two unexpected interruptions show him to be a man of warmth. The first is by his daughter, a Georgetown student, who has come asking for money. Sharabi laughs at how she brings him down to earth. The second comes while he is on the phone arranging a speaking engagement. A man enters the room, and when Sharabi sees him, his entire face changes, suffused with a large smile of obvious affection. He takes the man's hand and they embrace, with the phone still at his ear, and when he hangs up they speak intently in Arabic for a few moments. They both apologize for the interruption, explaining that the visitor is traveling "between continents" and has only this moment to see his old friend.

Sharabi has been deeply involved in matters Palestinian throughout his professional career. He is a professor of both European intellectual history and Arab culture at Georgetown, was a founder and served for many years as director of Georgetown's Center for Contemporary Arab Studies, and in 1990 helped found and now chairs the Center for Policy Analysis on Palestine, a Washington-based think tank.

Sharabi found himself caught in the United States, a university student in Chicago, when Israel took his hometown of Jaffa in 1948. He has made the adjustment comfortably, but being in the United States for over forty years has taken nothing away from his feeling of being Palestinian or his dedication to the cause. He says he is devoted to this country—to the American people rather than to their administration—and "cannot carry an American citizenship and say I'm nothing but a Palestinian." On the other hand, he notes, "I am here only because I am a Palestinian. I was going back, and there was no place to go back. Whether I want to go back to Palestine when there is a state in Palestine is another issue. The fact is, my whole life revolves around this issue. My whole life has been molded by what's happened to my people, my family, and to me and to my friends. This is the kind of circumstance that makes me feel attached irretrievably to that land, to that people, to that culture, wherever I am."

When Sharabi discusses the Jewish demand that Palestinian intellectuals be more self-critical and raise the moral standard for Palestinians, he is quick to turn the argument around. It is the Palestinians, he says, who make moral demands on Jews. He equates the demands to those Israel has made of Germany on behalf of the Jewish people—the moral, political, and compensatory demands that Israel required as some redress for the Holocaust. "What is mostly involved around this issue," Sharabi says,

> is, objectively, who is the victim and who is the victimizer. It's an asymmetrical situation. It is for the occupier, for the aggressor, for the one who has caused suffering, to search his conscience and define for himself his moral position. The Palestinians are portrayed as terrorists, as fanatics, their whole case has been distorted in the West, and the source of the distortion is the one who is presumably searching his conscience. The Holocaust for the Jews is now an instrument of political penetration, of making people feel guilty. The Palestinians do not feel guilty.

Most Palestinians, he says, knew nothing about the Holocaust as a reason for Jewish immigration to Palestine; he himself never heard of it until he came to the United States. He accuses the Zionists of never explaining themselves to the Palestinians, never engaging in any kind of debate or give-and-take over the Jewish drive to establish a state in Palestine. Palestinians judge the Zionists by their behavior, he says, "and their behavior has been one of total ruthlessness."

His blunt defense of Palestinians against Jewish accusations of failed morality has never prevented Sharabi from harshly calling the Palestinian leadership and the leaders of the rest of the Arab world to account for their political, social, and moral shortcomings. His 1988 book, *Neopatriarchy*,[16] is an indictment of the Arab states for their authoritarian rule, their oppression of their own peoples and disregard for human rights.

In conversation, he speaks of the PLO leadership as short-sighted and corrupt and politically paralyzed. The *intifada*, he says, although not specifically directed against the PLO, has signified "a certain despair about the PLO liberating the West Bank and Gaza politically or through armed struggle. If [those in the occupied territories] had had the faith that the PLO was able to do something, they wouldn't have paid such a heavy price as the uprising." He finds that there is too little room for free discussion in the higher echelons of the PLO. As an institution, it is very closed, he charges, "composed of groups and elites and sustained by balances of power, balances of money, interpersonal relations, and so forth. It's like any other Arab regime." Even more serious, he says heatedly, is the PLO's penchant for speaking in many voices. "Any of these so-called leaders is willing to make all sorts of declarations, give any kind of interview on the most sensitive subjects, on his own! You see it constantly happening. And they contradict one another and thereby play right into the hands of the Israelis by rendering the PLO as an organization totally lacking in credibility."

Like most other Palestinian intellectuals in the United States, Sharabi has been well ahead of the PLO in openly advocating that for practical reasons the Palestinians must limit their goal to statehood in the West Bank and Gaza. "It's the only solution; there is no other solution," he says positively some weeks before the PLO makes this policy explicit. There is a personal issue for him here, however, as for so many other Palestinians, for his hometown of Jaffa would not be included in the Palestinian state. He could nonetheless accept such a state, he says, "if the Palestinian people want it. I'm one of the lucky few who really got away. I can make my life anywhere. My roots to Jaffa, to Palestine, are deep, and I feel profound nostalgia, but my survival does not depend upon it anymore. The survival of vast tracts of the Palestinian people does depend on a solution, and the modality of that solution is for them to decide. If they decide on what I think is the only practical solution, then I'll back it completely."

Over the last four decades, he says, "the wheel has turned past the most traumatic points, and I think the considerable majority, if not the vast majority, will swallow the knife, as we say in Arabic," and accept the two-state solution. The problem now, Sharabi believes, lies with the Israelis, who he accurately predicted in 1988 were "going to push and to bite and to kick and to dissemble" in order to keep the Palestinians from gaining statehood.

In the aftermath of the Gulf war and the uncertain start of peace negotiations, Sharabi still has faith that the Palestinian people harbor a vision of peace and are ready to seize any opportunity for a genuine peace settlement that arises, but he fears that the war sparked a seething resentment in the majority of the Arab people that will be touched off if the peace process fails or stagnates. In this eventuality, he foresees not a return to the status quo ante, but "a new, dark and bloody phase of the struggle between Palestinians and Israelis, between Arabs and Jews, between Islam and the West."[17]

Ibrahim Abu-Lughod is an habitual optimist. Speaking in January 1989, in the initial wave of euphoria following the PLO's acceptance of the two-state formula and the opening of the U.S.-PLO dialogue, Abu-Lughod had perhaps every reason for optimism. But he has always been optimistic, and even three years later, with the *intifada* in decline and virtually no prospect that negotiations will produce an independent state for the Palestinians in the foreseeable future, he feels little of the pessimism that most other Palestinians do.

Speaking in 1989 in New York city, where he is spending a year on sabbatical from his professorship at Northwestern University, Abu-Lughod says he believes it is "inevitable for people who are deprived of their right to self-determination to achieve it. It may take a long time, but the history of the world is the history of liberation. You can't keep people suppressed forever. Everybody becomes free." Speaking in 1992, he still feels this inevitability. He is so encouraged by the Palestinians' refusal to bow to Israel's occupation that he is convinced that ultimately they will win the right to live "a free life of their own in their own national homeland."

Abu-Lughod is a distinguished looking man; a dark beret atop his full head of gray hair and slanting down to his bushy eyebrows adds a European air. He speaks with a smile in an enthusiastic tone of voice that draws the listener in and tends to persuade by the sheer force of his will.

Abu-Lughod was in his last year of high school in Jaffa in 1948. Because of the situation, the schedule for the matriculation exam was accelerated so that the test could be given in April, before the May 15 date when partition would take effect. The night before the exam, an artillery shell fired by Jewish forces came through the roof of the school, but Abu-Lughod remembers that the students were so intent on taking the exam that they paid little attention to the damage. As the situation worsened, he and an older brother sent their widowed mother and the rest of the family by truck inland to Nablus, intending to stay in Jaffa themselves, but they finally had to flee by boat to Beirut. Abu-Lughod did not return to Palestine until he paid a brief visit to the West Bank in 1991. He has been in the United States since 1949.

His optimism about the long-term outlook for the Palestinians is based on many factors, perhaps chief among them the simple fact that "we have not vanished, and Israel's task is to make us vanish. The reality is that we are much stronger today than we were in '48. We are more competent. The world is more aware of our grievance than it was in '48." This greater knowledge particularly encourages Abu-Lughod. "Today there is an alternative system of information about the Palestinian question that didn't exist in '48. It is legitimate today to study the Palestinian question. American scholars didn't study the Palestine question before. They were afraid."

Thanks to this increased study and wider knowledge, he says, the reality has now become too well known that it is not the Palestinians who are attempting to push Jews into the sea but "that it is the Israelis who have been pushing the Palestinians into the desert, and in my case I was pushed into the sea. That has become clear now." It will become even more widely known, he believes, because it is ultimately impossible to dispossess an entire people and offer them no alternative and expect not to be detected.

The Palestinians themselves, Abu-Lughod feels, will not let their suppression go undetected. Asked if, after the Gulf crisis and the setbacks in the *intifada* and in the peace process, he still believes this, he responds that he is "more persuaded now. I am more persuaded of that outcome because I have seen our people under occupation, and I think their resistance is simply remarkable." Such an occupation, he believes, is abnormal and "simply cannot perpetuate itself forever." The Palestinians are unbowed, and Israel knows this. The Israelis, he says, are "fully conscious of the fact that the people whom they have occupied refuse the fate envisaged for them."

He feels that Palestinians under occupation have shown themselves to be morally superior to Israel because, although physically oppressed, they have remained psychologically and intellectually free. This superiority, he believes, has enabled them to offer options for peace to Israel. Neither Israel nor the United States, he says, has ever offered the Palestinians an acceptable alternative. "Therefore, we as the victims have been offering the alternatives, and every alternative that we have offered is based on coexistence." Palestinians are able to endure precisely because they "envision a future of peace for themselves and for their adversary."

This last point is Abu-Lughod's counter to the Israeli/Jewish challenge to Palestinian intellectuals on the question of morality. The refrain "where is the Palestinian Peace Now?"—that is, where is the Palestinian equivalent of the Israeli peace movement—was frequently heard from Jewish spokesmen before the Palestinian peace initiative of late 1988. Abu-Lughod contends that it is in fact Palestinian intellectuals who led the Palestinian movement toward peace. "All peace programs that have been offered by the Palestinians were discussed [first] by Palestinian intellectuals," he says. "So what you have is a fringe on the Zionist side that is so-called searching constructively for peace—a fringe. And the mainstream of the Palestinian people, led by their intellectuals, is in fact a peace movement. You see?"

He recalls that an eighty-two percent majority of the Palestine National Council, of which he was a member at the time, voted in November 1988 to accept coexistence with Israel. "I have told them publicly in discussions that what I expect from the Jews today is to have a counterpart to the Palestinian mainstream that is calling for peace. I want eighty percent of the Knesset to vote for peace—in the same way, use the same language: coexistence, acceptance of [Resolution] 242, renunciation of terrorism, all that. Eighty percent."

Like many Palestinians, Abu-Lughod is unwilling explicitly to grant Israel's "right" to exist until Israel reciprocates with a recognition of the right of a Palestinian state to exist. Yasir Arafat's statement during a news conference in Geneva in December 1988 that the PLO recognizes Israel's right to exist implied mutual recognition, Abu-Lughod points out; Arafat affirmed "the right of all parties concerned in the Middle East conflict to exist in peace and security...including the state of Palestine, Israel and other neighbors." Nothing is set in concrete until negotiations are concluded, Abu-Lughod feels. "The basic premise of our political program has been the coexistence of the two people on the same piece of land. The political modality of the coexistence is to be determined freely by both people."

He begins to dance around the issue a bit here, fully aware that he is being somewhat cagey and clearly enjoying it. He is asked if a Palestinian state in the West Bank and Gaza that does not include his hometown of Jaffa could satisfy his national aspirations. "Well, I have no idea," he responds. "This is a question that I cannot answer because the only state that I will accept is a state that I can arrive at peacefully in a process of negotiation. If I agree to it, then I accept it. Am I making myself clear?" he asks with a large, significant smile.

What precisely does the PLO demand for a right of return mean, he is asked—does it mean that, for instance, a Jaffan granted such a right would be willing to live in Jaffa under Israeli sovereignty? "Sure," he says, again smiling. "If I am willing to live in peace with Israel, and Israel is willing to accept me, why not? Sure. If Israel can accept a Jew, it can accept an Arab." But such acceptance is by no means certain. "That's part of the negotiating process," he says. "You see, that's why I don't like the questions posed, 'Do you accept the West Bank state?' That has nothing to do with it. We are going to settle a conflict, and the conflict has many dimensions. One is the right of return, [also] the borders, Jerusalem. All of these issues are part of the complex, and that's what we negotiate." He will not commit himself further.

Optimism is so much a part of Abu-Lughod's makeup that he can even put a favorable spin on the concessions the Palestinians accepted to secure a place at the negotiating table in 1991. He refuses to acknowledge even that they were concessions, emphasizing instead the point that agreeing to negotiate for autonomy does not preclude negotiating for statehood at a future stage and the fact that the United States, Israel, and the Palestinians all know that, even if the PLO is not sitting at the table, it approved the negotiating delegation and authorizes everything the delegation does.

He has no faith that either Israel or the United States will concede anything in this round of negotiations—"the Israelis are not interested in it, and the United States will not push enough"—but he does not believe stagnation now will mean the end of the process. Although the United States has always been and remains opposed to Palestinian statehood, its primary interest in the Middle East now is in maintaining stability, he believes, and it recognizes that stability requires that the Palestinian problem be addressed. Abu-Lughod attributes this to a new U.S. realization of three things: that it, along with Israel, stands condemned in international opinion by the *intifada* because it underwrites Israel's oppression; that it cannot evoke international law against Iraq's invasion and occupation of Kuwait and ignore the same international law with respect to Israel's occupation of the West Bank and Gaza; and that it must accommodate those Arab states whose support it needs in the Middle East. "The one issue that will explode this region will be Palestine," he says, and so long as this issue is unresolved the Arab regimes are in danger. "As long as it lasts, every single Arab country can be destabilized."

Abu-Lughod foresees a future in which Jews and Palestinians live in harmony. He finds Zionism's exclusivity particularly repellent because he believes that Palestinian society is and always has been open to a multiplicity of peoples and religions. He raises the Zionism-is-racism resolution passed by the UN General Assembly in 1975 and rescinded in 1991. Although the resolution was interpreted by Israel as negating its existence, Abu-Lughod contends that, on the contrary, it was not a denial of Israel's existence but "a denial of apartheid. Zionism is a form of apartheid. There cannot be a democratic state in Israel for Gentiles and for Jews if Zionism is the dominant ideology. It's a contradiction in terms. Any fool can go to Israel and know the distinction, the eternal chasm between Jew and Gentile. That's what apartheid does, that's what racism is: that is, if your chances in life are directly related to your birth, whether in color or in religion or in whatever form."

Far from being the exclusive domain of any one people, Palestine has always been, Abu-Lughod says, "a land with a tremendous mixture of people, from ancient times to the moment. One of the peculiarities of Palestine is that historically it has rejected exclusivism. It rejected the exclusivism of the Crusaders, and it rejects the exclusivism of the Zionists." Palestinian Arab society has always consisted, he says, of Christians, Muslims, and Jews—the last defined as those indigenous, culturally Arab Jews who were in Palestine before the advent of Zionism. Except for the Crusader period and the period since Zionism's arrival in Palestine, the area has been relatively free of intercommunal conflict, he says. "That's what Palestine since the seventh century is, an Arab community made up of three faiths." Abu-Lughod is enunciating the dream of many Palestinians who view Judaism as purely a religion, not a race or a nationality, and who look toward the day when Israelis will fully integrate themselves in their Middle Eastern surroundings, becoming, if not politically indistinct, at least culturally one with their Arab neighbors.

Naseer Aruri epitomizes the almost complete political and cultural identification with Palestine, and the alienation from the United States, that many Palestinians living in the U.S. feel. Forced from his Jerusalem home as a young teenager in 1948 and never content under Jordan's oppressive rule over the West Bank, Aruri is in the United States because it has been politically impossible for him to identify as a Palestinian in any part of his original homeland. Although he has been in this country since the mid-1950s, with a professorship in political science at the University of Massachusetts at Dartmouth for over two decades, he remains uncomfortable with the country's political conservatism and intensely bitter at what he sees as its deep hostility toward Arabs and Palestinians.

Aruri is a tall, slender man with quiet good looks and a soft-spoken manner that gives no hint, on first meeting, of the anger and discontent that lie beneath the surface. But a brief conversation reveals the depths of his alienation. "It's a struggle [here] because I can't say that for one day I have felt I can be part of the system in which I live," he says, "even though I've lived here much longer than I have in Palestine. Here, you see your character assassinated several times a day, depending on how often you watch television, listen to the radio, or read the press. Anti-Arab racism seems to be the last form of permissible prejudice in this country."

Aruri feels that the struggle in this country for Arab and Palestinian rights is a struggle no other Third World peoples face. There is a constituency in the United States, he notes, for the Central American people and for South African blacks that is able to offer unequivocal support for their struggles. "And yet the work of our constituents," he says, "and that of impartial human rights organizations is so often challenged to show even-handedness that the end result is rendered superfluous. It is rather absurd to require any group advocating fairness and justice in Palestine to give an equal hearing to the Israeli regime, which commits crimes at the level of Chile under Pinochet or El Salvador or South Africa. No one says, 'Let's give Chile or the South African government an equal hearing.'"

As a human rights activist himself, Aruri is well aware of Israeli practices in the occupied territories. He served three terms on the board of directors of Amnesty International from 1984 to 1990 and is currently a board member of Middle East Watch, an affiliate of Human Rights Watch in New York. As a Palestinian, Aruri is particularly disturbed about U.S. sponsorship of Israeli "colonization, repression, and rejectionism," and the fact that as an American citizen he is paying for Israel's occupation practices is, for him, "a travesty, and particularly agonizing." U.S. complicity in Israel's "transgressions," he says, places every American in the position of "aiding and abetting crimes against humanity—crimes in the Nuremberg sense."

Aruri does make a distinction between the U.S. political establishment and American civil society, which tends, he says, "to be open to all sorts of ideas, even the notion that Israel can do wrong things." He sees some signs, for instance, of greater popular American support for the notion of Palestinian self-determination. He also cites his own efforts to obtain publicity for Israel's attempt to expel Palestinians from the occupied territories, including a cousin of his, Bir Zeit University physics and mathematics professor Taysir Aruri, who now serves as an adviser to the Palestinian negotiating team. Israeli authorities issued expulsion orders for Taysir Aruri and several others in August 1988 on charges, which Aruri denied and for which the Israelis never produced evidence, of "disturbing the public order." Taysir Aruri had two months earlier signed a symbolic peace treaty with several Israeli and Palestinian writers and artists.[18]

Naseer Aruri was able to enlist the support of *New York Times* columnist Anthony Lewis and *Village Voice* writer Nat Hentoff in the campaign against the expulsions. Former President Carter and several senators and congressmen also intervened, and the American scientific community provided massive support to Taysir Aruri as a fellow physicist. Some 1,600 scientists, including fifteen Nobel laureates, signed a petition initiated by physicist Edward Wittin of the Princeton Center for Advanced Study demanding Aruri's release, and several scientific organizations took up his cause. Despite the support, however, Aruri was eventually expelled, along with four other West Bankers, in August 1989.

In his concern for human rights, Naseer Aruri has never shied away from criticizing Arab rights violations, calling the Arab countries a "disaster area" on this question. He helped to organize a conference on the human rights situation in the Arab world held in the summer of 1988 at Oxford University.[19] In an Arab-American quarterly, he has written, "Irrespective of the type of government, ideological coloration or foreign policy orientation: whether pro-West or pro-Soviet, conservative or 'progressive,' theocratic or secular, the regimes in the Arab world have displayed a general disregard for the human rights of the individual."[20]

Aruri comes by his low opinion of Arab freedoms through experience. He spent six years living under Jordanian control on the West Bank after 1948. In 1960, returning from graduate school in the United States to a West Bank still under Jordan's control, he was arrested and spent a night in jail because a textbook on the Soviet Union that he was carrying had a hammer and sickle on the cover.

With regard to the American Jewish charge that Palestinian intellectuals fail to examine the Palestinian conscience while Jews endlessly search the Jewish soul, Aruri questions the very premise of the Jewish argument. Some Jewish intellectuals, he says, criticize excesses perpetrated by an expansionist right-wing Israeli government, whereas Palestinian excesses are not committed by the leadership, but by a dwindling radical minority fringe outside the Palestinian consensus. "If they want us to criticize for the sake of criticizing, then it does not really make sense, it's hypocritical. So, if we had someone like Shamir in high office, we would not only criticize him but would actively seek his overthrow, since he follows a right-wing fascist ideology, Revisionist Zionism, which calls for the expulsion of an entire nation." Like most Palestinians, Aruri feels that the moral argument so often used by Zionists should be turned around on them. He is an advocate of democratic secularism as a just alternative to Zionism's exclusivism and anti-Arab bias.[21] What the Zionists did, he says, "caused the dispossession and dispersal of my people and made our lives abnormal. Certainly I can sympathize with the plight of Jews, but I can't sympathize with the remedy that was selected for redress. It created an injustice against my people."

Because of that injustice, still not itself redressed, Aruri is reluctant to grant Israel's right to exist. He feels this should be the end of a process of negotiations. The Palestinian Declaration of Independence and the political statement issued with it in November 1988, he says, put the Palestinians in a morally ascendant position that should obviate the need for such recognition. The documents represent, he says, "a recognition of international and regional realities and reflect our maturity and hence our ability to absorb historical processes, regardless of questions of justice and morality. The fact that Israel exists on conquered Palestinian territory has not been altered; the Palestinian perception and ability to cope with the injustice was instead transformed. The recognition of Israel as a fact certainly precludes, to my mind, a recognition of its inherent right to exist on my land."

He believes that, in explicitly accepting coexistence with Israel, the PLO paid a "high price" to achieve nothing more than a promise of dialogue with the United States. One gets the impression in fact that Aruri is concerned and somewhat ambivalent about the direction PLO policy took in 1988—about the unrequited concessions and the relinquishment of bargaining points. But he insists not; the PLO's concessions, he says, were morally and tactically appropriate because they were based on a demand for "symmetry, parity, and reciprocity" from Israel—part of a process of "bargaining and compromising, not a process of surrender."

Now, however, Aruri, who has recently been appointed to the Palestine National Council, is deeply concerned that in the aftermath of the Gulf war, the PLO has surrendered too much in order to secure the Palestinians a place in peace negotiations that will gain them nothing. There has been no reciprocity from Israel, no symmetry in U.S. pressures on Israel and on the Palestinians, and the hard-won gains of the *intifada* have been traded, he feels, for nothing—"on the altar of an innocuous diplomatic process" designed to produce nothing. The present period, Aruri believes, is the worst the Palestinians have experienced in his lifetime.

Aruri is bitter about the war and what has happened to the Palestinians as a result. He resents the fact that Palestinians are perceived to have been on the "wrong" side and to be somehow deserving of punishment. Human rights, he says, "are inviolable and cannot be forfeited as a result of a certain political stance." In any event, the notion that the Palestinians must be punished by foregoing diplomatic progress or abandoning their right to choose their own representatives at peace negotiations presupposes that diplomatic progress was being made before the war. On the contrary, Aruri notes, diplomacy had stagnated because the United States, then as always, "ignored and marginalized Palestinian rights." What Aruri characterizes as the Bush administration's "three no's"—no to an international peace conference, no to PLO representation at negotiations, no to a Palestinian state—were policy before the Gulf war and remain policy today. Under such constraints, he says, the Palestinians have no hope of ever exercising self-determination.

In answer to this attempt to bypass them, Aruri believes, Palestinians should have insisted that the UN, not the United States, broker peace talks and should have seized the initiative with a new vision and a bold new proposal of their own that would have redefined the terms of discussion. Only in this way would Palestinians have been able to overcome the constraints facing them. Instead of innovation and boldness, however, he believes Palestinians have surrendered, allowing others to dictate the removal of their national rights from the diplomatic agenda.[22]

Fouad Moughrabi can trace his Palestinian ancestry and his family's presence in Palestine back 900 years on his mother's side. That long heritage ended abruptly one night in late May or early June 1948 when Moughrabi's family and many others from the village of Ayn Karim on the western outskirts of Jerusalem fled the village in fear of attack by Jewish forces. Only two months before, a combined force from Irgun and the Stern Gang, the pre-state Jewish underground groups, had killed over one hundred civilians at the nearby village of Deir Yassin, less than two miles away.

Moughrabi, who was almost six years old at the time, recalls the middle-of-the-night flight as a very frightening experience. He remembers hearing shooting and then being warned by a village guard that Jewish forces were nearby and that the village could not be defended. In the darkness, everyone gathered up what belongings they could carry and fled the village on foot. Moughrabi's extended family spent the night in a field listening to shooting nearby and watching tracers overhead, thinking they would be able to return to the village the next day. When this proved to be impossible, they continued to walk eastward. Moughrabi most vividly recalls coming upon the devastation of a bomb or shell detonated apparently among a group of refugees on the road. Bodies lay about unburied, some without limbs. He tells his story matter-of-factly, giving little hint of its impact on him until, asked if the experience frightened him, he tells of having nightmares for years afterwards about trying to escape from a monster in his house but being unable to run.

The family lived in a tent in Dhaishe refugee camp outside Bethlehem for three months and eventually settled in a house in Bethlehem, where Moughrabi grew up. The village of Ayn Karim, which was finally emptied of all its Palestinian inhabitants in July 1948 during an Israeli military attack, was given the Hebrew name Ein Kerem, populated with Jewish immigrants, and incorporated into the Jerusalem city limits.[23] The Moughrabi house still stands, inhabited now by Moroccan Jews. He has visited once, but now only drives by whenever he is in Jerusalem. Moughrabi's mother, who lives now in the United States, still has the key to the house and the deed. The key hangs on a wall in her home.

Moughrabi teaches Middle East affairs at the University of Tennessee in Chattanooga. Except for a few years earning his doctorate in France, he has been in the United States since 1960, when he arrived as an undergraduate at Duke University. He lives easily in American society and is married to a non-Arab woman, but he would rather be in Palestine. He thinks he would most likely not have remained here after schooling had his life in Ayn Karim not been disrupted, and he says unhesitatingly that, if a Palestinian state is ever established, he will go there "to help build, do good in some way, do something concrete." It does not bother him that such a state would not include his native village, so long as he had the opportunity to contribute to rebuilding the nation.

Moughrabi is a witty, somewhat irreverent man, almost a free spirit, quick with banter and repartee and wholly without affectation. He laughs easily. But he has an intensely serious aspect as well that emerges in discussions about the Palestinian situation. He is passionate about explaining the Palestinian perspective and can be quite impatient with interlocutors who repeat the conventional wisdom about the Palestinian-Israeli conflict without knowing its real history.

Growing up in exile has been a fragmented experience for Moughrabi. "I've lived with segmentation all my life," he says. He went to a French Catholic school in Bethlehem, where the nuns tried to turn him into a Frenchman, "and yet I knew I was an Arab and a Muslim." Jordan, which controlled the West Bank after 1948, tried to turn him into a Jordanian, but he knew this was not his identity either. Asked if there was ever a period when he was not particularly interested in the Palestinian cause, he responds with a flat "no." He and his schoolmates, he says, "were fiercely nationalist, Palestinian nationalist, and anti-Jordanian—very strongly."

It was impossible for anyone growing up on the West Bank in that period to be unaware of the Palestinian situation, he feels. Not only were there frequent Israeli cross-border raids, but "we were always involved in [anti-Jordanian] demonstrations, throwing rocks at Jordanian soldiers before the kids of the *intifada* were throwing them at Israeli soldiers. And we hurt some of them," he adds, laughing. Schools were closed for months at a time, and young demonstrators were killed by Jordanian soldiers. "We were always aware of the difference between us and the Jordanians," he says, "and we wanted to run our own affairs. Even as kids."

Living in the United States has added to the segmentation. Although still identifying himself as a Palestinian, Moughrabi also identifies as an American—despite having felt during much of the last thirty years that he was living in "enemy territory"—and says he has become so accustomed to "living in limbo" that he has no problem with this dual identity. In some ways, he feels, it has been an advantage being an exile, "because I can look at the United States and at American society as an outsider. I can look at my own, my Palestinian Arab cultural background also as an outsider. It's a kind of unique position to be able to look from the outside in. Although you are a part of both, you are able to look at them critically."

He is indeed critical of both. He has been a student of public opinion in the United States for the last decade and is struck by the significant gap between the views of the informed American public and those of the U.S. government. Whereas poll after poll since the late 1970s has shown the American public favoring establishment of an independent Palestinian state by at least a plurality and often a majority, U.S. policy, he says, is responsive only to the narrow pressures of pro-Israeli interests. Like most Palestinians, Moughrabi defines the United States as part of the problem in the Middle East, rather than part of the solution. Because massive U.S. aid to Israel sustains Israeli intransigence, he believes, the United States is actually a party to the conflict and cannot act as a truly honest broker in peace negotiations. He is highly critical of the U.S. tendency always to demand more concessions from the Arabs whenever Israel refuses to compromise and says U.S. helplessness in the face of Israeli firmness "doesn't wash."

Moughrabi is not hesitant about also criticizing the PLO. Like many intellectuals, he lobbied the PLO for a decade before the 1988 initiative to adopt an explicit, unambiguous position advocating a two-state solution and coexistence with Israel. Since that position became PLO policy in 1988, he feels, the PLO has done a poor job of explaining and clarifying and convincing public opinion that it truly wants coexistence. "We should be able quite clearly to spell out the fact that we are in favor of coexistence," he says, "and to try to give flesh and bone to what we mean by a Palestinian state and how that state can coexist with Israel and others." The PLO leadership has acted "as if when we adopted these positions the world would recognize and see what we had done and would come around. But things don't happen that way. You have to mount a campaign, you have to be energetic and keep pushing, clarifying, repeating and repeating over and over again until people become convinced." He adds with some cynicism that such an effort would not produce "magical results"; the Israeli government would be no more willing to make compromises. "But I think we should do it anyhow," primarily to convince the Israeli people.

Rather than simply "adopt positions and wait for the world to take notice," he believes the PLO should talk directly to American and particularly Israeli public opinion. He has a rare ability to recognize Israeli fears despite the objective reality of Israel's strength. "I can understand," he says, "based on their history, that they have legitimate fears and concerns, just like us." He believes that Palestinians must make the effort to reassure.

But at the same time, confronted with someone who sees things only the other way around, who sees Israeli victimization but fails to recognize that Israelis have hurt Palestinians, Moughrabi can be roused to anger. During a Middle East forum in Santa Fe, New Mexico, in the spring of 1991, a woman asks Moughrabi how Israelis can be expected to believe that Palestinians are ready to make peace when they have been threatening Israel for more than forty years. Moughrabi responds sharply. "I can't relate to what you're saying," he begins. Accusing the woman of arguing on the basis of myths, not facts, he gives her a list of books by Israeli historians that lay out the facts of the 1948 Palestinian exodus and then describes the Deir Yassin massacre, giving it a personal aspect by noting his own flight at age five from a neighboring village. "And after the establishment of the state of Israel," he goes on with increased fire,

> every other day [there was] an attack across the frontier: the destruction of Qalqilya, the destruction of Nahalin [two West Bank towns raided by Israeli forces], the killing of this, the blowing of this, the blowing of that. Now, it's very difficult for me to relate to your

characterization of Israel as a victim, as a helpless victim, when in fact at the moment and for many, many years Israel has been the most awesome political and military power in the region. So don't keep telling me Israel is the victim. We are the victim.

Moments later, his anger quickly fading, he is talking about his vision of a future shared by Israelis and Palestinians working together as equals. If a peace settlement is ever reached and a Palestinian state established, he believes cooperation with Israel will be absolutely necessary. "We have an opportunity," he says, again with intensity, "to really achieve something of historical importance—together—if we can get beyond the question of political identity, security issues, etcetera, etcetera—and I think we can. We can achieve *incredible* things."

Moughrabi is deeply pessimistic, however, about ever seeing that day. He believes the Palestinians had no choice but to make the concessions forced on them as a condition for entering peace negotiations and that they must make this good faith effort to achieve a peace settlement, but he is not optimistic that a settlement will result. Although he condemns the PLO's failure to distance itself from Saddam Hussein to a greater extent during the Gulf crisis, he does not believe a different PLO policy would have produced a different balance at the negotiating table. "I think that insistence by the Israelis on the conditions would not have been any different," he says. "The fact that the American government agreed with them would not have been any different. The exclusion of the PLO would not have been any different."

His grim assessment that in twenty to thirty years the Middle East will be ruled by uncompromising Islamic republics begins with the West Bank and Gaza, where he foresees that the next stage of the resistance to Israel's occupation will be led by Islamic groups and will be characterized by much more violence. If Israel and the United States offer the Palestinians no hope through peaceful means, they are likely to turn in frustration to violence as the only other alternative and to Islam as the only force capable of mobilizing people.

Rashid Khalidi is one of the youngest among Palestinian intellectuals and the only one born in the United States. He calls his birth here and the fact that he was raised in the United States an "accident"; his father was here attending graduate school when, in 1948, the year Rashid was born, it became clear that the family could not return to Jerusalem. Khalidi, a member of the Jerusalem Khalidi family and a cousin of Walid Khalidi, grew up in New York getting into fights whenever he called himself a Palestinian. He has obviously learned how to defend himself, at least verbally. A professor of Middle East history and director of the Center for Middle East Studies at the University of Chicago, he has become a leading commentator on the Palestinian issue, in writing as well as in public addresses and television appearances. He serves on the advisory delegation to the Palestinian negotiating team.

Khalidi has an historian's objectivity, a virtually emotionless manner of speaking and writing that makes it difficult to discern whether he has a point of view. Anger rarely shows in his speech or writings, passion never, and his utter self-possession conveys an impression of expertise that brooks little opposition. He is a hyperactive person, fast talking, always in a hurry, always seemingly in motion—his manner resembling more a brusque young business executive's than a deliberate academic's.

Like so many other Palestinians, Khalidi dates his political awakening to the 1967 war, which he says "galvanized" him. He believes the same thing has happened to another generation because of the *intifada*. "For one thing," he notes, "it's brought a lot of your faint hearts back, it's wakened up a whole generation." He whistles at the scope of the change that he has observed. The *intifada* has also changed the American public's perceptions of Palestinians; "until the *intifada*, it was really a negative thing to be a Palestinian in this country." Now, he says, "for the first time you can appear to ordinary people to be a Palestinian without incurring an enormous cost." He thinks this remains generally true despite the poor image Palestinians projected during the Gulf crisis.

The *intifada* also had a much more far-reaching impact, Khalidi feels, in terms of PLO policy and strategy, for it gave the PLO leadership the impetus to move toward compromise and toward the explicit acceptance of coexistence with Israel enunciated in 1988. West Bankers and Gazans, as one generation in the occupied territories, were fed up, he says, "with another generation outside, which they perceive as out of touch—on the one hand predisposed to compromise, on the other hand too inflexible—in other words, [who] don't know quite when to be flexible, quite when to be hardline." He sees the 1988 initiative, including the recognition of Israel, as "a response to a set of political cues coming for the first time from the occupied territories. They're demanding a political initiative, saying, 'For God's sake, you're going to do these things anyway. Do them now and get us some leverage.' So for the first time I think that what the PLO leadership has done is to leap from responding exclusively to the cues that come from people on the outside, who had a very strong feeling of resistance to these things, to responding to cues from people on the inside."

Khalidi believes that there is no left or radical alternative to the strategy Yasir Arafat and the PLO mainstream have been pursuing for the last several years, despite some divisions over negotiating strategy. Those Palestinians who remain completely unreconciled to coexistence with Israel are simply, Khalidi says, not part of the Palestinian polity. They represent "point zero one two of the Palestinian polity," have no popular appeal among Palestinians and, unlike the mainstream organizations of the PLO, have no foothold in the West Bank and Gaza. Their different viewpoint on Israel, he says, is "not a difference within the family. I see the polity as essentially excluding those people."

George Habash and Naif Hawatmeh, leaders respectively of the Popular Front for the Liberation of Palestine and the Democratic Front, who are often regarded as uncompromising radicals and who have opposed the PLO's decision to enter peace negotiations on the terms laid down, differ from Yasir Arafat and his Fatah organization essentially only on tactics and have been within the "family," acting as "friendly enemies," for decades. They had no choice, Khalidi believes, but to go along with the PLO's 1988 initiative; their own people in the occupied territories forced Habash and Hawatmeh to go along with the two-state solution because they did not want to break ranks with the mainstream. Khalidi sees them today as skeptics, not as real opponents. They are skeptical about the PLO's negotiating tactics and about whether negotiations on these terms will work. But, Khalidi says, "the skeptics know that there doesn't seem to be an alternative. Now, the moment there is an alternative, we're not talking about skeptics, we're talking about opposition. But I don't think you can talk about real opposition now."

For these reasons, Khalidi does not believe there is a time limit on the PLO's moderation or on Arafat's mandate to pursue diplomatic compromise. "I don't think we're talking about a matter of days or weeks or months. I really don't; in fact, I'm positive of that." Greater pressure, he feels, is being exerted on the West Bank-Gaza leaders, who "have their eyes over their shoulder all the time," looking back at the increasing strength of hardlining Islamic fundamentalists who oppose negotiations. The PLO itself does not have a challenger, he believes, and whatever dissatisfaction exists over the negotiating policy within the PLO's exile constituency outside the occupied territories has very little focus. "I don't think," he says, "that it in any way threatens the strategy in the medium term. I don't think Arafat is under that kind of direct, immediate pressure."

This does not mean he foresees real progress toward a solution anytime soon. Although he perceives real changes in the American public's view of Israel's policies and believes public opinion "will not tolerate Israeli behavior of the sort that it has tolerated" since 1967, he feels no optimism about the prospects for peace negotiations. The Israelis, he says, have shown no seriousness about the peace process from the beginning, and the United States has been so anxious to accommodate Israeli demands that he has little expectation that it will even live up to "the very tepid and limited and weak and hesitant pledges and commitments" contained in the terms of reference for the negotiations and the U.S. letter of assurances. Khalidi speaks forcefully on this point, and for the first time emotion begins to show in his voice. "I don't disagree with this idea that process is everything," he says, "and that ultimately people are inextricably bound to this. Yeah, that's true if there's progress. But I see no reason to assume that there's going to be progress."

He talks with even more intensity of what has been expected of the Palestinians. If the "tepid" American commitments to the Palestinians are not kept, he says, the process probably will break down because the Palestinians cannot be squeezed anymore. "All the squeezing that's been done has pretty much squeezed the Palestinians dry," he says with much feeling. "They can't make any more concessions." Khalidi is not sure the United States fully understands how much the Palestinians have conceded, "that this is pretty much below the minimum and if you go any lower than this, the deal won't be sellable to the Palestinians."

Although recognizing the pro-Israeli pressures U.S. policymakers are under, and the fact that "it's always easier to squeeze the Palestinians than to squeeze the Israelis because the Israelis squeeze back hard," Khalidi feels that Washington's readiness to accommodate Israel is short-sighted, not only because the Israeli government's refusal to compromise does not reflect majority popular sentiment in Israel, but also because constantly accommodating Israeli demands only leads to more demands. "I don't know if that was terribly wise of the secretary of state to basically pander shamelessly to the Israelis" on the terms for starting peace negotiations, Khalidi says, his voice again revealing a rare fury, "to give them every outrageous demand that they were able to dream up, and basically give the Palestinians nothing, because it encourages the Israelis to think that they can get [everything], they just have to stonewall. And it certainly has left the Palestinians with very little."

Khalidi readily acknowledges that the Palestinians did not help their own diplomatic position by their stand during the Gulf crisis. "I think Arafat made a grave mistake," he says, "and I think Palestinians were blind in their position during the Gulf war." It would have been impossible, he believes, for the Palestinians to side with the United States in a war that destroyed an Arab country, and he regards the war as "a stupid and an unjust war." But, he says quite vehemently, "Saddam is an evil and stupid man who has never wished the Palestinians well and has never done them anything but harm." The Iraqi regime "never paid any attention to the Palestine cause, they never will. The little bit of money and diplomatic support that the PLO got from them was worthless compared to the harm incurred by lining up with Saddam. So it was a foolish strategy from the very beginning. It was politically easy and politically understandable for any politician, but in terms of statesmanship and strategy, I would say it was a mistake."

In terms of its practical effect, the PLO's failure to condemn Iraq more strongly has, Khalidi believes, impeded its ability to play a more open role in the negotiations. Israel would have been no readier to permit a PLO presence at the negotiating table had the PLO sided with the U.S.-led coalition, but he feels that the United States would have been more willing to deal directly and openly with PLO representatives sitting on the sidelines. "I'm saying that the PLO could have talked to Washington, even if it couldn't have talked to the Israelis directly." The PLO is running the Palestinian strategy in the negotiations from the background, but as it is now, the fact that the organization is officially ostracized "attenuates the lines of communication and responsibility, the lines of legitimacy, that you're going to have to have for a proper negotiation and for a proper settlement." However cynical and opportunistic it is that the United States is using the PLO's Gulf crisis position to manipulate it out of a direct role in the negotiations, Khalidi says, it is the PLO that handed the United States this lever on a silver platter.

NOTES

[1] Khalidi, "Thinking the Unthinkable: A Sovereign Palestinian State," *Foreign Affairs* (July 1978): 698.

[2] Ibid., pp. 695-713.

[3] Khalidi, "Regiopolitics: Toward a U.S. Policy on the Palestine Problem," *Foreign Affairs* (Summer 1981): 1050-1063.

[4] For example: "Perhaps the greatest paradox of all is that Edward Said is an academic, living and working in the world of ideas, while serving as a spokesman for a militant cause sometimes associated with terrorism." Dinita Smith, "Arafat's Man in New York: The Divided Life of Columbia's Edward Said," *New York* (January 23, 1989): 40-46.

[5] Ibid., p. 42.

[6] Ibid.

[7] Ibid.

[8] Leon Wieseltier, "Palestinian Perversion of the Holocaust," *New York Times* (June 12, 1988).

[9] Mark Krupnick, "Edward Said: Discourse and Palestinian Rage," *Tikkun* (November/December 1989): 21-24.

[10] Smith, "Arafat's Man in New York," p. 46.

[11] Letter to the Editor, *New York Times* (June 15, 1990).

[12] Said, *Peace in the Middle East* (Westfield, NJ: Open Magazine Pamphlet Series #13, 1991), p. 19.

[13] See, for instance, "Many Prominent Americans Support the President's Action in the Gulf," *New York Times* (August 13, 1990); Said, "Shattering Effects of Saddam's Invasion," *Arab News* (September 5, 1990), reprinted in *Washington Report on Middle East Affairs* (November 1990): 48-49; Said, "A Tragic Convergence," *New York Times* (January 11, 1991); Joe Getlin, "Forever an Exile," *Los Angeles Times* (February 3, 1991); and "The Intellectuals and the War: Edward Said," interview in *Middle East Report* (July-August 1991): 15-20.

[14] Said, *Peace in the Middle East*, p. 21.

[15] Orfalea, *Before the Flames*, p. 160.

[16] Hisham Sharabi, *Neopatriarchy: A Theory of Distorted Change in Arab Society* (New York: Oxford University Press, 1988).

[17] Sharabi, "What Next? The Question of Procedure and Substance," The Palestinians After the Gulf War, pp. 33-37; and Sharabi, "Introduction," *A Palestinian Perspective on the Peace Process* (Washington: Center for Policy Analysis on Palestine, 1991), p. 3.

[18] See Anthony Lewis, "Before It Is Too Late," *New York Times* (September 18, 1988), and Nat Hentoff, "Israel as Her Own Worst Enemy," *Village Voice* (September 20, 1988): 34.

[19] Hentoff, "Israel as Her Own Worst Enemy."

[20] Naseer H. Aruri, "The Recolonization of the Arab World," *Arab Studies Quarterly* (Spring/Summer 1989): 276. See also Aruri, "Disaster Area: Human Rights in the Arab World," *Middle East Report* (November-December 1987): 7-16.

[21] See his "Anti-Zionism: A Democratic Alternative," in Tekiner etal., eds., *Anti-Zionism*.

[22] In addition to interviews and correspondence with Aruri, portions of this section are taken from Aruri, "The Palestinians After the Gulf War: What Options?" *The Palestinians After the Gulf War*, pp. 3-11.

[23] Morris, *The Birth of the Palestinian Refugee Problem*, pp. 192, 212.

12   A Story With No End

My son has never been to Palestine. He doesn't know Palestine. But he is as attached to Palestine as I am attached to Palestine. Probably more. And I think this is applicable to all the new generations. So this is a story with no end.

Ghanem Dajani
Beirut broadcaster

In his book *From Beirut to Jerusalem, New York Times* correspondent Thomas Friedman describes an encounter with a young man in a West Bank refugee camp that captures the essence of the Palestinians' struggle. "With his physique," Friedman writes,

> he would have been an elite commando in any Palestinian army. But when I asked him whether he was trying to hurt Israelis when he threw a stone, he answered in a way that made me realize how much the stone was really meant for him—meant to liberate him from his own sense of impotence and humiliation.
>
> "A woman is being raped," said Jameel, "and while she is being raped she uses her nails to scratch the body of the rapist. Is that violence? We have been raped for years, but instead of our brothers helping us, they stood around and watched."
>
> And now that you have taken your destiny into your own hands [by launching the *intifada*]?
>
> "The wounds of the rape are starting to heal," he said. "The woman is combing her hair and looking in the mirror again."[1]

This story highlights one of the most salient facts about Palestinians: their almost total self-absorption. Like the young man who throws stones at Israelis less to hurt Israelis than to restore his own dignity, Palestinians in general are concerned primarily for themselves and for easing their own plight, rather than for seeking vengeance against Jews or Israelis. Palestinians do not spend their time brooding about how to destroy Jews or devising schemes to seek retribution from Israel; they do spend their time, and a major portion of it, thinking about how to obtain justice for themselves—

about surviving as a distinct people and attaining the same national independence that other distinct peoples enjoy. They have a keen sense of themselves as having been deprived of the basic national rights that other peoples throughout the world have long since been granted. Today, forty-plus years after what they regard as their great national tragedy, what has become important to Palestinians is not that Jews and Israelis be made to pay for taking Palestine but simply that Palestinians be given some kind of equal status in that land. What is important in terms of international opinion is not so much that the world be made aware that Jews have been the Palestinians' victimizers as that all these years Palestinians have been victims.

The Palestinians' world view is very self-centered. This is particularly evident in Palestinian literature, which is filled not with attacks on Israel but with introspective treatises on the anguish of exile, or probing analyses of Palestinian shortcomings, or painful recountings of the process by which Palestinians were denied a homeland and an identity. The 1988 PLO initiative itself demonstrates this, showing a readiness to relinquish decades-old claims in the interests of easing the homelessness of Palestinians in exile and the oppression of Palestinians living under occupation. Faisal Husseini, a prominent Jerusalem Palestinian who has been closely involved in developing the Palestinian peace platform and serves as the principal adviser to the Palestinian negotiating delegation, has noted that the message of the peace initiative and of the *intifada* has been that the Palestinians "struggle for the liberation of our people, not to dominate any other people; we struggle in order to establish our own state, not to destroy any other state; we struggle in order to guarantee and secure a safe future for our coming generations and not to threaten the coming generations of any other people in the area."[2]

The fact that Palestinians did not arrive at this position for several decades is still a cause for reprobation among probably most Israelis and many, if not most, Americans. The Palestinians' first reaction to their forcible displacement from a land they had inhabited for centuries was anger and a desire not only to regain what they had lost but to take revenge on Israelis. Anger remains, but the fact that the desire for revenge has diminished is an indication as much of Palestinian self-absorption as of a realization of Israel's strength.

Palestinians have been portrayed for over forty years as wild-eyed peasant savages with no national identity, no ethnic pride, no skills, whose land was sparsely populated and poorly cared for, and who had no particular attachment to or love for it. Their essential baseness is proved, according to the conventional wisdom, by their refusal to welcome into their midst and give haven to a persecuted people whose only desire was to save their own ethnic and religious uniqueness. According to this conventional wisdom, the Palestinians hated Jews merely because they were Jews. In the end, it is said, their flight from Palestine was their own fault; they were ordered by their leadership to leave temporarily while Arab armies cleaned up, pushing the Jews into the sea and leaving the way clear for Palestinians to return safely to their homes.

Israeli historians have recently performed an important task in correcting some of the historical distortions in this conventional wisdom: in showing that Palestinians objected to the partition of Palestine because it gave away over half the land to a people who owned only seven percent of it; in showing that the Zionist leadership and Transjordan cooperated to prevent the formation of a Palestinian state after partition was decreed; in showing that Palestinians did not leave Palestine willingly but from a combination of fear of advancing Israeli forces and in many specific instances outright expulsion by the Israeli military.[3] It is often fruitless to rehash history, but for Palestinians the importance of bringing the world to an awareness of the facts of their dispersal forty-plus years ago lies in their belief—a further indication of their self-absorption—that only through this awareness can they hope to obtain justice for themselves.

Many people, including most Israelis and many American policymakers, still fundamentally misunderstand the essential elements of the Palestinian struggle. It is well understood, thanks in large measure to the *intifada*, that Palestinians are struggling against the Israeli occupation of the West Bank and Gaza, which has continued since 1967, but it is not understood that this struggle is part and parcel, and only the most urgent and immediate aspect, of a problem that has its origins in the Palestinians' dispossession in 1948. From the Palestinian perspective, their collective national and societal existence was destroyed in 1948; 1967 was only the final step in a tragedy that had begun long before.

If much of the world has forgotten the original dispossession and what it has meant for the collective psyche of Palestinians, Palestinians themselves have not. They see themselves as having been deprived not only of a national locus but of the safety and security of their homes, of land that had nurtured them for centuries, even of an identity. The problem for Palestinians goes far deeper than the oppression of an occupier; it goes to the very heart of Palestinian existence.

Exile, that condition of exclusion and deprivation and longing that has been the Palestinian condition since 1948—that most central reality of Palestinian existence—is a phenomenon that affects all Palestinians in some measure, whether they are the fifty percent of Palestinians who are exiles themselves or they are West Bankers, Gazans, and Israeli Palestinians who have never left their ancestral homes. Even those Palestinians who remain within the original area of Palestine feel a solidarity and a common bond with their exiled compatriots arising from their shared lack of a national homeland and their common experience of dislocation.

One can thus understand the true impulse behind Palestinian nationalism only if one understands that exile—the "wound of dispossession"—is what primarily motivates all Palestinians, whether in the United States or in the Arab world, whether 1948 refugees or resident in the occupied territories. One can understand Palestinians only if one recognizes why, for instance, Palestinians care that every patch of tall prickly pear cactus seemingly in the middle of nowhere marks the site of a destroyed Palestinian village; or why it matters to Palestinians when they cannot be buried in the land where they were born; or why families retain the keys and the deeds to homes they have not seen for forty years and that often no longer exist; or why it is important for Palestinians to have it known that falafel is an Arab dish, that Palestinians ate it before there was such a thing as Zionism or Israelis; or why at every Arab-American gathering in the United States sweatshirts and T-shirts are sold that spell out the names of Palestinian villages in stylized Arabic, and why countless American youngsters who have never seen their parents' homeland wear these symbols of their lost birthright; or why it is important for Palestinians to have it known that the exquisitely embroidered dresses and pillows that are often shown off as Israeli handicrafts are in fact the visible symbols of a Palestinian culture that Zionism contends never existed.

Exile is inextricably linked in the minds of Palestinians with what they would term the denial or theft of their identity, with the humiliation of belonging nowhere and the pain of exclusion, whether physically from the land or practically from a meaningful role in determining their own affairs. But at the same time, the common experience of exile binds Palestinians into a distinct people; the common yearning for their lost homeland has meant that they have maintained an identity.

Every event of the last forty years has strengthened Palestinian consciousness. The experiences of 1948 gave Palestinians a common national aspiration, and the formation of the PLO in 1964 gave them a common sense of the need to act for themselves. Israel's occupation of the West Bank and Gaza in 1967 galvanized new levels of political awareness among Palestinians everywhere. The Israeli invasion of Lebanon in 1982 and the severe military and political defeat inflicted on the PLO served to create a new kind of determination and unity, forged in adversity. The *intifada* and both the peace initiative and the declaration of statehood that grew out of it have raised Palestinian consciousness still more, bringing laggards back to the fold and for the first time instilling real pride in Palestinian accomplishments. The failure of these initiatives and the dramatic weakening in the Palestinian position in the aftermath of the Gulf crisis have brought near despair and a concern among many Palestinians that they are in the worst crisis in their history. But, like all past crises, this one has had the effect of heightening rather than diminishing the Palestinians' sense of themselves as a distinct people.

Palestinians take pride in pointing out that, despite all efforts to deny their uniqueness as a people, they have not vanished. The poet and writer Fouzi El-Asmar believes the Palestinian issue transcends all the obstacles and roadblocks sent up to frustrate its resolution. Every obstacle is a setback, he acknowledges, but nothing can destroy the Palestinian people or their demand for justice. Israeli settlements, he says, "are really an obstacle, but not something that can demolish Palestinian rights or Palestinian demands. I know a lot of Palestinians are worried about the settlements; they think that's it, if this continues, the whole thing will be finished. Nothing can be finished. The Palestinians were kicked out of their own country and nothing was finished." Palestinians cannot give up, he believes. "There is no way they can give up because this is part of their life. Nobody is offering them a substitute. Nobody is offering them a passport or a piece of land or even to be part of Arab society—nothing that could challenge their demand for their own state. There is nothing offered to them, so this has to continue."

A story with no end.

NOTES

[1] Friedman, *From Beirut to Jerusalem*, p. 383.

[2] Faisal Husseini, "A New Face to the Middle East," *New Outlook* (November/December 1989): 14.

[3] See Morris, *The Birth of the Palestinian Refugee Problem*; Shlaim, *Collusion Across the Jordan*; Flapan, *The Birth of Israel*; Segev, *1949*; and, by a non-Israeli historian, Michael Palumbo, *The Palestinian Catastrophe: The 1948 Expulsion of a People from Their Homeland* (London: Quartet Books, 1987).

Interviewees

(This list includes more names than are formally counted among the 124 interviewees. Some are listed because they sat in on interviews and contributed to them in some way but did not participate enough to be counted among formal interviewees. Where interview dates and places are not listed, this is to protect confidentiality.)

George (lnu) – Would not provide his last name. Husband of Karimi (lnu). Born in Ramallah. Interviewed in Houston, Texas, February 24, 1988.

Karimi (lnu) – Would not provide her last name. Wife of George (lnu). Born in Ramallah. Interviewed in Houston, Texas, February 24, 1988.

Joe A. – Businessman in Los Angeles. Brother of Riyad A. Born in West Bank. Interviewed in Downey, California, January 27, 1988.

Kamal A. – Taxi driver in San Francisco. Born near Jerusalem. Interviewed in San Francisco, April 18, 1988.

Riyad A. – Businessman in Los Angeles. Brother of Joe A. Born in West Bank. Interviewed in Downey, California, January 27, 1988.

Hilmi Abdulrahim – Businessman in San Francisco. Husband of Nawal Abdulrahim. Born in Jaffa, left in 1948 at age eleven. Interviewed in Millbrae, California, April 22, 1988.

Nawal Abdulrahim – Wife of Hilmi Abdulrahim. Born in Silwan, now part of East Jerusalem. Interviewed in Millbrae, California, April 22, 1988.

Adeeb Abed – Runs a cultural center in Brooklyn. Former regional director of the American-Arab Anti-Discrimination Committee in Brooklyn. Born in Bir Nabala, West Bank. Interviewed in Brooklyn, New York, January 11, 1989.

Samir Abed-Rabbo – Publisher of Amana Books in Brattleboro, Vermont. Born in Qalandiya refugee camp near Jerusalem; family originally from Yasour, destroyed in 1948. Interviewed in Brattleboro, Vermont, January 16, 1989, and by telephone January 22, 1992.

Mona Abid – Wife of Nael Abid. Born in Deir Dibwan, West Bank. Interviewed in Daly City, California, April 21, 1988.

Nael Abid – Grocery store owner in San Francisco. Husband of Mona Abid. Born in New Jersey to a family from Deir Dibwan, West Bank. Interviewed in Daly City, California, April 21, 1988.

Nuha Abudabbeh – Psychologist in Washington, D.C. Born in Jaffa, left before 1948 as an infant, grew up in Turkey. Interviewed in Washington, D.C., April 18, 1989.

Rajai Abu-Khadra – Petroleum economist at the Center for Strategic and

International Studies in Washington, D.C. Born in Jaffa, left in 1948 at age sixteen. Interviewed in Washington, D.C., October 19, 1988.

Ibrahim Abu-Lughod – Professor of political science at Northwestern University. Former member of Palestine National Council. Born in Jaffa, left in 1948 at age eighteen. Interviewed in New York, New York, January 10, 1989, and by telephone February 18, 1992.

Freddie Ahmad – Pharmacist in Brooklyn. Son of Asad Asad, nephew of Norman Assed. Born in Dearborn, Michigan to a family from Beit Hanina, West Bank. Interviewed in Brooklyn, January 12, 1989.

Terry Ahwal – Works for Wayne County government, Detroit. Former regional director of the American-Arab Anti-Discrimination Committee in Detroit. Born in Ramallah. Interviewed in Detroit, Michigan, March 27, 1989.

Anis Ajluni – Physician in Detroit. Husband of Clare Ajluni. Born in Ramallah. President, American Federation of Ramallah Palestine, 1989-90. Interviewed in Birmingham, Michigan, March 23, 1989.

Clare Ajluni – Wife of Anis Ajluni. Born in Ramallah. Interviewed in Birmingham, Michigan, March 23, 1989.

Hala Ajluni – Wife of Hanna Ajluni. Born in Jerusalem, left in 1948 as a young woman. Interviewed in Birmingham, Michigan, March 23, 1989.

Hanna Ajluni – Retired businessman in Detroit. Member of Palestine National Council. Executive editor of *Hathihe Ramallah* magazine published in Detroit. Husband of Hala Ajluni. Born in Ramallah. Interviewed in Birmingham, Michigan, March 23, 1989.

Judy Ajluni – Accountant in Detroit. Wife of Maher Ajluni. Born in San Diego to a Ramallah family. Interviewed in Birmingham, Michigan, March 27, 1989.

Karim Ajluni – Immigration attorney in Detroit. Husband of Suheila Ajluni. Born in Ramallah. Interviewed in Birmingham, Michigan, March 27, 1989.

Maher Ajluni – Broadcaster and real estate developer. Husband of Judy Ajluni, son of Suheila and Karim Ajluni. Born in Detroit to a Ramallah family. Interviewed in Birmingham, Michigan, March 27, 1989.

Sameer Ajluni – High school student. Son of Suheila and Karim Ajluni. Born in Detroit to a Ramallah family. Interviewed in Birmingham, Michigan, March 27, 1989.

Suheila Ajluni – Wife of Karim Ajluni. Born in Ramallah. Interviewed in Birmingham, Michigan, March 27, 1989.

Amer Anabtawi – Graduate student in Los Angeles area. Son of Husnieh and Jamal Anabtawi. Born in Kuwait to a West Bank family. Interviewed in Rowland Heights, California, June 6, 1988.

Aseel Anabtawi – Daughter of Husnieh and Jamal Anabtawi. Born in Kuwait to a West Bank family. Interviewed in Rowland Heights, California, June 6, 1988.

Husnieh Anabtawi – Wife of Jamal Anabtawi. Born in Tulkarm, West Bank. Interviewed in Rowland Heights, California, June 6, 1988.

Jamal Anabtawi – Real estate developer in Los Angeles area. Husband of Husnieh Anabtawi, brother of Yousef Anabtawi. Born in Zeita, West Bank. Interviewed in Rowland Heights, California, June 6, 1988.

Nancy Anabtawi – Daughter of Husnieh and Jamal Anabtawi. Born in Kuwait to a West Bank family. Interviewed in Rowland Heights, California, June 6, 1988.

Yousef Anabtawi – Grocery store owner in Los Angeles. Brother of Jamal Anabtawi. Born in Zeita, West Bank. Interviewed in Rowland Heights, California, June 6, 1988.

Naseer Aruri – Professor of political science at the University of Massachusetts at Dartmouth. Member of the Palestine National Council. Born in Jerusalem, left in 1948 as a teenager. Interviewed in North Dartmouth, Massachusetts, January 19, 1989, and by telephone February 15, 1992.

Asad Asad – Business manager of al-Fajr newspaper in Jerusalem. Father of Freddie Ahmad, brother-in-law of Norman Assed. Family lives in Brooklyn, where he spends half the year. Born in Beit Hanina, West Bank. Interviewed in Brooklyn, New York, January 12, 1989.

Samir Ashrawi – Chemist with Texaco in Austin, Texas. Born in East Jerusalem to a family that left west Jerusalem in 1948. Interviewed in Houston, Texas, February 22, 1988 and by telephone October 8, 1988.

Norman (Naim) Assed – Jeweler in Albuquerque. Uncle of Freddie Ahmad, brother-in-law of Asad Asad. National board member of the American-Arab Anti-Discrimination Committee. Born in Beit Hanina, West Bank. Interviewed in Albuquerque, New Mexico, August 9, 1988.

Fuad Ateyeh – Grocery store owner and food distributor in San Francisco. Born in Qalandiya refugee camp near Jerusalem to a family from Saris, destroyed in 1948. Interviewed in San Francisco, April 19, 1988.

Jawad B. – Physician in Detroit. Born in Gaza. Interviewed in Birmingham, Michigan, March 23, 1989.

Rasmiyeh B. – Dentist. Born in West Bank.

Consuelo Saah Baehr – Novelist. Born in El Salvador to a French-Spanish mother and a father from Ramallah. Interviewed in Alexandria, Virginia, April 15, 1989.

Khalil Barhoum – Lecturer in linguistics at Stanford University. Born in Bethlehem, West Bank, to a family from al-Malha, destroyed in 1948. Interviewed in Menlo Park, California, April 24, 1988; by telephone

December 13, 1989; in Palo Alto, California, March 4, 1991; and by telephone, January 24, 1992.

Albert Batshoun – Food distributor in Detroit. Born in Jaffa, left in 1948 at age seventeen. Interviewed in Redford, Michigan, March 29, 1989.

Peter Belmont – Husband of Sibyl Belmont. Interviewed in Lexington, Massachusetts, January 17, 1989.

Sibyl Belmont – Music teacher in Lexington, Massachusetts. Wife of Peter Belmont. Born in Whittier, California to an American mother and a father from Ramallah. Interviewed in Lexington, Massachusetts, January 17, 1989.

Ghassan Bishara – Washington correspondent for Jerusalem newspaper *al-Fajr*. Born in Tarshiha, Palestine, remained in Israel after 1948. Interviewed in Washington, D.C., October 26, 1988.

Mohammad Busailah – Retired Reynolds Tobacco executive. Born in Lydda, Palestine, left in 1948 at age ten. Interviewed in Glendale, California, June 9, 1988.

Samia C. – Born in Haifa, left in 1948 at age two. Interviewed in Santa Fe, New Mexico, May 22, 1989.

Faris D. – Restaurant owner. Born in Haifa, left in 1948 at age five.

Khalil D. – Liquor store owner in Los Angeles. Born in West Bank. Interviewed in Walnut, California, December 14, 1987.

Ghanem Dajani – Former broadcaster in Beirut. Husband of Nahida Fadli Dajani. Born in Jaffa, left in 1948 as a young man. Interviewed in Annandale, Virginia, October 21, 1988.

Karim Dajani – University student. Son of Nahida and Ghanem Dajani. Born in Beirut to parents from Jaffa and Jerusalem. Interviewed in Santa Fe, New Mexico, May 23, 1988, and by telephone, February 7, 1992.

Nahida Fadli Dajani – Poet. Wife of Ghanem Dajani, sister of Samir Fadli. Born in Jerusalem, left in 1948 as a young teenager after her father was killed. Interviewed in Annandale, Virginia, October 21, 1988.

Wafa Darwazeh – Businessman in San Rafael, California. Born in Nablus, West Bank. Interviewed in San Rafael, California, March 16, 1988.

Osama Doumani – Businessman in Sacramento. Former regional director of the American-Arab Anti-Discrimination Committee in Berkeley. Born in Acre, left in 1948 at age nine. Interviewed in Berkeley, California, April 21, 1988.

Fouzi El-Asmar – Poet, newspaper editor in Washington, D.C. Born in Haifa, remained in Israel after 1948. Interviewed in Washington, D.C., October 20, 1988, and by telephone, February 6, 1992.

Bayan F. – Psychologist. Born in Lebanon.

Samira F. – Librarian in San Francisco. Born in Jerusalem; family left in 1948 while she was out of the country in college. Interviewed in San Francisco, April 20, 1988 and March 4, 1991.

Samir Fadli – Businessman in Maryland. Brother of Nahida Dajani. Born in Jerusalem, left in 1948 at age three after his father was killed. Interviewed in Annandale, Virginia, October 21, 1988.

Rafeek Farah – Physician in Detroit. Born in al-Birah, West Bank. Interviewed in Trenton, Michigan, March 30, 1989.

Osama Fawzi – Editor of the Arabic-language newspaper *Arab Houston Times*, a satirical political biweekly distributed throughout the United States. Born in Jordan to a family that left the Galilee town of Tarshiha in 1948. Interviewed in Houston, Texas, February 24, 1988.

Maha H. – Secretary in Chicago. Born in al-Am'ari refugee camp near Ramallah to a family from Lifta, destroyed in 1948. Interviewed in Chicago, Illinois, February 17, 1989.

Mahmoud H. – Engineer in Berkeley. Born in West Bank. Interviewed in Berkeley, California, March 15, 1988.

Wadi H. – Businessman in Houston. Born in West Bank. Interviewed in Houston, Texas, February 24, 1988.

Amal Halawa – Accountant. Wife of Walid Shafi. Born in Cairo, Egypt, to a family from Gaza. Interviewed in Houston, Texas, February 22, 1988. Now living in Cairo.

Muhammad Hallaj – Director, Center for Policy Analysis on Palestine, Washington, D.C. Member of the Palestine National Council. Born in Qalqiliya, West Bank. Interviewed in Fairfax, Virginia, October 21, 1988, and by telephone February 3, 1992.

Nawal Hamad – Bank vice president in Arlington, Virginia. Born in al-Birah, West Bank. Interviewed in Fairfax, Virginia, October 22, 1988.

Ronnie Hammad – Former regional director of the American-Arab Anti-Discrimination Committee. Husband of Soraya Deifallah Hammad. Born in Lebanon of Syrian-Lebanese parents. Interviewed in Houston, Texas, February 22, 1988.

Soraya Deifallah Hammad – Wife of Ronnie Hammad. Born in Texas to an American mother and a father from Acre who left in 1948 as a child. Interviewed in Chevy Chase, Maryland, April 16, 1989.

Fadwa Hasan – Daughter of Nawal Hamad. Born in United States to a West Bank family. Interviewed in Fairfax, Virginia, October 22, 1988.

Nader Hasan – Son of Nawal Hamad. Born in United States to a West Bank family. Interviewed in Fairfax, Virginia, October 22, 1988.

Nael Hasan – Son of Nawal Hamad. Born in United States to a West Bank family. Interviewed in Fairfax, Virginia, October 22, 1988.

Raif Hijab – Electrical engineer in Santa Clara, California. Born in West Bank. Interviewed in Berkeley, California, March 15, 1988.

George Hishmeh – Senior editor at U.S. Information Agency in Washington, D.C. Born in Haifa, left in 1948 at age twelve. Interviewed in Washington, D.C., April 13, 1989.

Fatima Horeish – Secretary at United Holy Land Fund in Chicago. Born in Lebanon to a family that left Safad, captured by Israel in 1948. Interviewed in Chicago, Illinois, February 17, 1989.

Hazem Husseini – Owns a landscaping business in Albuquerque. Born in East Jerusalem, left in 1967 at age thirteen. Interviewed in Rio Rancho, New Mexico, May 15, 1989.

Abdur-Rahim Jaouni – Geochemist with Lawrence Berkeley Laboratory in Berkeley. Born in west Jerusalem, moved to East Jerusalem in 1948 at age two. Interviewed in Berkeley, California, March 15, 1988 and March 6, 1991.

Bahjat K. – University professor.

Omar Kader – Security systems expert. Former executive director of the American-Arab Anti-Discrimination Committee. Born in Utah to a family from Shufat, now part of East Jerusalem. Interviewed in Alexandria, Virginia, October 25, 1988, and by telephone February 1, 1992.

Nadim Kassem – Physician in New Jersey. Born in Ramah, Palestine, left in 1948 at age seventeen, returned in 1951. Interviewed in Roseland, New Jersey, January 12, 1989.

Mujid Kazimi – Professor of nuclear engineering at MIT. Born in Jerusalem, left in 1948 as an infant. Interviewed in Cambridge, Massachusetts, January 17, 1989.

Mary Kempker – Born in East Jerusalem, of Armenian descent. Interviewed in Grand Rapids, Michigan, March 28, 1989.

Diana Khabbaz – Digital Equipment Corp. manager in Boston. Born in Beit Jala, West Bank. Interviewed in Winchester, Massachusetts, January 15, 1989.

Rashid Khalidi – Professor of modern Middle East history and director, Center for Middle Eastern Studies at the University of Chicago. Cousin of Walid Khalidi. Born in New York of a Lebanese mother and a father from Jerusalem. Interviewed in Chicago, Illinois, February 14, 1989, and by telephone February 19, 1992.

Walid Khalidi – Research fellow at Harvard. Cousin of Rashid Khalidi. Born in Jerusalem, unable to return after 1948. Interviewed in Washington, D.C., April 17, 1989.

Hasan Khalil – Businessman in Los Angeles. Born in Qaloniya, left in 1948 at age four when the town was destroyed. Interviewed in Los Angeles, California, June 8, 1988.

Qassem Khalil – Physician in Los Angeles. Nephew of Hasan Khalil. Born in Kuwait to a family from Qaloniya, destroyed in 1948. Interviewed in Los Angeles, June 8, 1988.

Salam Khalili – Called Salam. Graphic designer in San Francisco Bay area. Born in Jordan to a family from Hebron, West Bank. Former newspaper editor in Jerusalem, imprisoned and expelled by Israel. Interviewed in San Rafael, California, March 14, 1988.

Najat Arafat Khelil – Nuclear physicist and activist in Washington, D.C. Born in Nablus, West Bank. Interviewed in Potomac, Maryland, October 17, 1988, and by telephone February 12, 1992.

Dina Khoury – College student. Daughter of Elie and Farideh Khoury. Born in Detroit. Interviewed in Birmingham, Michigan, March 26, 1989.

Elie Khoury – Physician in Detroit. Husband of Farideh Khoury. Born in Jerusalem, left in 1948 at age ten. Interviewed in Birmingham, Michigan, March 23, 1989.

Farideh Khoury – Pharmacist in Detroit. Wife of Elie Khoury. Born in Syria. Interviewed in Birmingham, Michigan, March 26, 1989.

Nabil Khoury – Physician in residency in Detroit. Son of Elie and Farideh Khoury. Born in Detroit. Interviewed in Birmingham, Michigan, March 26, 1989.

Ibrahim M. – Physician in Los Angeles. Born in West Bank. Interviewed in Los Angeles, California, December 12, 1987.

Yacoub Jamil (Jack) Mahshi – Landscape architect in Berkeley. Born in Jerusalem, left in 1948 as a young man. Interviewed in Berkeley, California, April 19, 1988.

AbdulSalam Massarueh – Journalist in Washington, D.C. Born in Taiyba, Palestine, remained in Israel after 1948. Interviewed in Annandale, Virginia, October 26, 1988, and by telephone February 11, 1992.

Suhail Miari – Director of United Holy Land Fund in Chicago. Born in Haifa, remained in Israel after 1948. Interviewed in Chicago, Illinois, February 14, 1989.

Fuad Mogannam – Real estate developer in San Francisco. Born in Ramallah. Interviewed in San Francisco, California, April 15, 1988.

Mike Hazem Monsour – Jeweler in Albuquerque. Born in Deir Dibwan, West Bank. Interviewed in Albuquerque, New Mexico, October 22, 1987.

Fouad Moughrabi – Professor of Middle East affairs, University of Tennessee at Chattanooga. Interviewed by telephone, January 16, 1992 and March 24, 1992.

Amneh Mustafa – Activist in Chicago. Born in Beitunia, West Bank. Interviewed in Chicago, Illinois, February 9, 1989.

Bayan N. – Gas station attendant in Chicago. Husband of Ibtisam N. Born in Beitunia, West Bank. Interviewed in Chicago, Illinois, February 15, 1989.

Ibtisam N. – Wife of Bayan N. Born in al-Am'ari refugee camp near Ramallah to a family that left Jaffa in 1948. Interviewed in Chicago, Illinois, February 15, 1989.

Nuha Nafal – Poet and travel agent in San Francisco. Born in Bir Zeit, West Bank. Interviewed in San Francisco, April 23, 1988 and March 5, 1991.

Adam Nassar – Consultant in Washington, D.C. Born in Arraba, Israel and grew up in Israel. Interviewed in Albuquerque, New Mexico, June 29, 1988.

Nasib Nuseibeh – Highway expert formerly living in Kuwait. Family lives in Albuquerque. Born in Jerusalem, left in 1948 at age twelve. Interviewed in Rio Rancho, New Mexico, May 15, 1989.

Hashem O. – Attorney in Chicago. Born in Chicago to American-born parents from Beitunia, West Bank. Interviewed in Chicago, Illinois, February 16, 1989.

Mohamed Odetalla – Co-owns grocery and liquor store in Detroit area. Husband of Sana Odetalla. Born in Beit Hanina, West Bank. Interviewed in Canton, Michigan, March 23, 1989.

Sana Odetalla – Wife of Mohamed Odetalla. Born in Beit Hanina, West Bank, to a family that left Lifta, destroyed in 1948. Interviewed in Canton, Michigan, March 23, 1989.

Mohammad Rajab – Video store owner in Houston. Born in Haifa, left in 1948 at age six. Interviewed in Houston, Texas, February 24, 1988.

Awni Rayyis – Former waste disposal supervisor for Los Angeles County. Killed in robbery attempt May 1988. Born in Gaza. Interviewed in La Crescenta, California, December 11, 1987.

Faizeh Rayyis – Wife of Bayan Shafi. Cousin of Awni Rayyis. Born in Gaza. Interviewed in Houston, Texas, February 22, 1988.

Ahmad S. – Former student in Long Beach. Born in West Bank, now living again in West Bank. Interviewed in Long Beach, California, January 27, 1988.

Raja S. – Intellectual in Washington, D.C. Interviewed in Washington, D.C., April 13 and 18, 1989.

Sami S. – Computer store owner in Los Angeles. Born in Bir Zeit, West Bank. Interviewed in Los Angeles, January 28, 1988.

Essa Sackllah – Delicatessen owner in Houston. Born in Dearborn, Michigan, to a family from Ramallah. Interviewed in Houston, Texas, February 23, 1988.

Emile Sahliyeh – Professor of political science at North Texas University. Born in Jerusalem, left in 1948 at age two. Interviewed in Beverly

Hills, California, November 5, 1988, and by telephone February 11, 1992.

Mona Sahoum – Housewife in Los Angeles. Born in Ramallah to a family that left Nazareth in 1948. Interviewed in Los Angeles, December 14, 1987.

Anthony Sahyoun – Surgeon in Boston. Born in Haifa; family left in 1948 while he was out of the country in medical school. Interviewed in Boston, Massachusetts, January 17, 1989, and by telephone February 6, 1992.

Edward Said – Professor of comparative literature at Columbia University. Former member of Palestine National Council. Born in Jerusalem, left in late 1947 at age twelve. Interviewed in New York, New York, April 11, 1989.

Asad Salameh – Former bookstore owner in San Francisco, now living in Syria. Born in Deir Dibwan, West Bank. Interviewed in San Francisco, March 14, 1988.

Abdul Hamid Salem – Journalist in Washington, D.C. Born in Dura, West Bank. Interviewed in Alexandria, Virginia, April 15, 1989.

George Salem – Attorney in Washington, D.C. Brother-in-law of Susan Ziadeh. Born in Jacksonville, Florida to a family from Ramallah. Interviewed by telephone October 29, 1988 and January 23, 1989.

Norma Sayage – Real estate agent in San Francisco. Born in Chicago to a family that left Jaffa in 1948. Interviewed in Daly City, California, April 21, 1988.

Adli Shafi – Businessman in Houston. Brother of Walid Shafi, nephew of Bayan Shafi. Born in Gaza. Interviewed in Houston, Texas, February 22, 1988.

Bayan Shafi – Businessman in Houston. Born in Gaza. Husband of Faizeh Rayyis, uncle of Walid and Adli Shafi. Interviewed in Houston, Texas, February 22, 1988.

Samira Shafi – Daughter of Faizeh Rayyis and Bayan Shafi. Born in Jordan to a family from Gaza. Interviewed in Houston, Texas, February 22, 1988.

Walid Shafi – Former businessman in Houston, now living in Cairo. Husband of Amal Halawa, brother of Adli Shafi, nephew of Bayan Shafi. Born in Gaza. Interviewed in Houston, Texas, February 22, 1988.

Riyad Shalabi – Student in Long Beach. Born in Jordan to a family from the West Bank. Interviewed in Long Beach, California, January 27, 1988.

Hisham Sharabi – Director, Center for Contemporary Arab Studies, Georgetown University, Washington, D.C. Born in Jaffa; family left in 1948 while he was out of the country in college. Interviewed in Washington, D.C., October 20, 1988, and by telephone February 14, 1992.

Jameel Shihadeh – Graduate student in San Francisco. Born in Ramallah. Interviewed in Daly City, California, April 21, 1988.

Muhammad Siddiq – Professor of Arabic literature at the University of California at Berkeley. Born in Shafa-Amr, Palestine, remained in Israel after 1948. Interviewed in Beverly Hills, California, November 4, 1988 and March 6, 1991.

Amal T. – Teacher of English as a second language in San Francisco. Wife of Rafiq T. Born in Bethlehem, West Bank. Interviewed in San Francisco, California, April 17, 1988 and March 5, 1991.

Hanan T. – Daughter of Amal and Rafiq T. Born in San Francisco to a family from the West Bank. Interviewed in San Francisco, California, April 17, 1988 and March 5, 1991.

Rafiq T. – Grocery store owner in San Francisco. Husband of Amal T. Born in Nablus, West Bank. Interviewed in San Francisco, California, April 17, 1988 and March 5, 1991.

Ghada Talhami – Professor of political science at Lake Forest College. Born in Nablus, West Bank. Interviewed in Skokie, Illinois, February 10, 1989, and by telephone February 11, 1992.

Salah Ta'mari – Director of Roots organization in Washington, D.C. Former Fatah military commander. Born in Bethlehem, West Bank. Interviewed in Washington, D.C., April 18, 1989.

Abdullah Wajeeh – Professor of mathematics in Detroit. Member of Palestine National Council. Born in a Galilee village, remained in Israel after 1948. Interviewed in Birmingham, Michigan, March 23, 1989 and by telephone February 3, 1992.

Fadi Zanayed – Attorney in Chicago. Nephew of Salameh Zanayed. Born in Ramallah. Interviewed in Chicago, Illinois, February 15, 1989.

Salameh Zanayed – Owns a travel agency in Chicago. Member of the Palestine National Council. Uncle of Fadi Zanayed. Born in Ramallah. Interviewed in Chicago, Illinois, Februry 13, 1989.

Susan Ziadeh – AMIDEAST project director in Washington, D.C. Sister-in-law of George Salem. Daughter of Islamic scholar Farhat Ziadeh. Born in Seattle, Washington; family originally from Ramallah. Interviewed in Washington, D.C., October 19, 1988.

Selected Bibliography

Abraham, Sameer Y. and Nabeel Abraham, eds. *Arabs in the New World: Studies on Arab-American Communities.* Detroit: Wayne State University, 1983.

Abu-Laban, Baha and Michael W. Suleiman, guest eds., "Arab Americans: Continuity and Change," *Arab Studies Quarterly* 11, nos. 2 & 3 (Spring/Summer 1989).

Abu-Laban, Baha and Faith T. Zeadey, eds. *Arabs in America: Myths and Realities.* Wilmette, IL: The Medina University Press International, 1975.

Abu-Lughod, Ibrahim, ed. *The Transformation of Palestine: Essays on the Origin and Development of the Arab-Israeli Conflict.* Evanston, IL: Northwestern University Press, 1987.

Ajami, Fouad. *Beirut: City of Regrets.* New York: W. W. Norton & Company, 1988.

"Arafat's Statement on Plans for Peace in the Middle East," *New York Times* (December 15, 1988).

Aruri, Naseer. "Anti-Zionism: A Democratic Alternative," in Roselle Tekiner, Samir Abed-Rabbo, and Norton Mezvinsky, eds. *Anti-Zionism: Analytical Reflections.* Brattleboro, VT: Amana Books, 1988.

-----. "Disaster Area: Human Rights in the Arab World," *Middle East Report* (November-December 1987): 7-16.

-----, ed. *Occupation: Israel Over Palestine,* 2nd edition. Belmont, MA: Association of Arab-American University Graduates, Inc., 1989.

-----. "The Recolonization of the Arab World," *Arab Studies Quarterly* 11, nos. 2 & 3 (Spring/Summer 1989): 273-286.

Baehr, Consuelo Saah. *Daughters.* New York: Delacorte Press, 1988.

Barnea, Amalia and Aharon Barnea. *Mine Enemy,* trans. Chaya Amir. New York: Grove Press, 1988.

Baris, Michael. "Personality: George Salem," *Washington Report on Middle East Affairs* (March 18, 1985): 7.

Bishara, Ghassan. "Yesterday's Fighters Are Today's Peace Seekers," *Al-Fajr* (Weekly English-language edition) (May 8, 1989): 4.

Brand, Laurie. *Palestinians in the Arab World: Institution Building and the Search for a State.* New York: Columbia University Press, 1988.

Busailah, Reja-e. "The Fall of Lydda, 1948: Impressions and Reminiscences," *Arab Studies Quarterly* 3, no. 2 (Spring 1981): 123-151.

Cainkar, Louise. "Palestinian Women in the United States: Coping with

Tradition, Change, and Alienation." Ph.D. diss., Northwestern University, 1988.

Cattan, Henry. *Palestine, The Arabs and Israel: The Search for Justice.* London: Longmans, Green and Co., Ltd., 1969.

Center for Policy Analysis on Palestine. *The Palestinians After the Gulf War: The Critical Questions.* Washington: Center for Policy Analysis on Palestine, 1991.

-----. *A Palestinian Perspective on the Peace Process.* Washington: Center for Policy Analysis on Palestine, 1991.

-----. *The Palestinians and the War in the Gulf.* Washington: Center for Policy Analysis on Palestine, 1991.

Christison, Kathleen. "The American Experience: Palestinians in the U.S.," *Journal of Palestine Studies* 72 (Summer 1989): 18-36.

-----. "Of Grasshoppers and Supermen: The Palestinian View of Zionist Ideology," *New Outlook* (April/May 1991): 26-28.

-----. "Palestinian Americans Lament Life in Exile," *Christian Science Monitor* (October 14, 1988).

-----. "Palestinians in U.S. Feel Pull of Homeland," *Christian Science Monitor* (October 7, 1988).

-----. "Palestinians in U.S. Grapple with Issue of Israeli State," *Christian Science Monitor* (October 28, 1988).

-----. "Uprising Captivates Palestinians in U.S.," *Christian Science Monitor* (October 21, 1988).

Collins, Larry and Dominique Lapierre. *O Jerusalem!* New York: Simon and Schuster, 1972.

Cobban, Helena. *The Palestinian Liberation Organisation: People, Power and Politics.* Cambridge: Cambridge University Press, 1984.

Egan, John P. "An American Testimony from an Israeli Prison," *Journal of Palestine Studies* 53 (Fall 1984): 118-125.

El-Asmar, Fouzi. *Through the Hebrew Looking Glass: Arab Stereotypes in Children's Literature.* Brattleboro, VT: Amana Books, 1986.

-----. *To Be an Arab in Israel.* Beirut: Institute for Palestine Studies, 1978.

-----. "The Wandering Reed," in A. M. Elmessiri, ed., *The Palestinian Wedding: A Bilingual Anthology of Contemporary Palestinian Resistance Poetry.* Washington: Three Continents Press, 1982.

Elmissiri, A. M., ed. *The Palestinian Wedding: A Bilingual Anthology of Contemporry Palestinian Resistance Poetry.* Washington: Three Continents Press, 1982.

Flapan, Simha. *The Birth of Israel: Myths and Realities.* New York: Pantheon Books, 1987.

Friedman, Robert I. "Did This Man Kill Alex Odeh?," *Village Voice* (July 12, 1988).

-----. "Who Killed Alex Odeh?," *Village Voice* (November 24, 1987).

Friedman, Thomas L. *From Beirut to Jerusalem.* New York: Farrar Straus Giroux, 1989.

Ghabra, Shafeeq N. *Palestinians in Kuwait: The Family and the Politics of Survival.* Boulder, CO: Westview Press, 1987.

Goitein, S. D. *Jews and Arabs: Their Contacts Through the Ages.* New York: Schocken Books, 1964.

Greenberg, Joel. "West Bank U.S.A.," *Jerusalem Post International Edition* (Week Ending April 18, 1987).

Halabi, Rafik. *The West Bank Story*, trans. Ina Friedman. New York: Harcourt Brace Jovanovich, 1985.

Hallaj, Muhammad. *"The Mission of Palestinian Higher Education,"* *Journal* of Palestine Studies 36 (Summer 1980): 75-95.

Harkabi, Yehoshafat. *Israel's Fateful Hour*, trans. Lenn Schramm. New York: Harper & Row, 1988.

Heller, Mark A. and Sari Nusseibeh. *No Trumpets, No Drums: A Two-State Settlement of the Israeli-Palestinian Conflict* New York: Hill and Wang, 1991.

Hentoff, Nat. "A Human Rights Disaster Area," *Village Voice* (September 27, 1988)

-----. "Israel as Her Own Worst Enemy," *Village Voice* (September 20, 1988).

Hicks, Joe R. "Palestinians Battle Deportation and Government Surveillance," *Civil Liberties* 367 (Summer 1989).

Hitti, Philip K. *The Syrians in America.* New York: George H. Doran Company, 1924.

Hooglund, Eric J. *Crossing the Waters: Arabic-Speaking Immigrants to the United States Before 1940.* Washington: Smithsonian Institution Press, 1987.

-----, ed. *Taking Root: Arab-American Community Studies*, Vol. II. Washington: American-Arab Anti-Discrimination Committee, 1985.

Hudson, Michael, ed. *The Palestinians: New Directions.* Washington: Center for Contemporary Arab Studies, 1990.

Husseini, Faisal. "A New Face to the Middle East," *New Outlook* (November/December 1989): 14-15.

"The Intellectuals and the War: Edward Said," interview in *Middle East Report*, no. 171 (July-August 1991): 15-20.

Jiryis, Sabri. *The Arabs in Israel*, trans. Inea Bushnaq. New York: Monthly Review Press, 1976.

Kayal, Philip M. "America's Arabs," in Dennis Laurence Cuddy, ed., *Contemporary American Immigration: Interpretive Essays (Non-European).* Boston: Twayne Publishers, 1982.

Khalidi, Rashid I. "No Peace From Mr. Shamir," *New York Times* (April 4, 1989).

-----. "Observations on the Right of Return," *Journal of Palestine Studies* 82 (Winter 1992): 29-40.

-----. "The Palestinians and the Gulf Crisis," *Current History* 90 (January 1991): 18-20.

-----. "The PLO's Yasser Arafat," in Barbara Kellerman and Jeffrey Rubin, eds., *Leadership and Negotiations in the Middle East.* New York: Praeger, 1988.

-----. "Revisionist Views of the Modern History of Palestine: 1948," *Arab Studies Quarterly* 10, no. 4 (Fall 1988): 427- 432.

-----. *Under Siege: P.L.O. Decisionmaking During the 1982 War.* New York: Columbia University Press, 1986.

-----. "The Uprising and the Palestine Question: New Forces and Old Constraints," *World Policy Journal* 5, no. 3 (Summer 1988): 497-517.

Khalidi, Walid. "The Arab Perspective," in William Roger Louis and Robert W. Stookey, eds., *The End of the Palestine Mandate.* Austin: University of Texas Press, 1986.

-----, ed. *From Haven to Conquest: Readings in Zionism and the Palestine Problem Until 1948.* Washington: Institute for Palestine Studies, 1987.

-----. *The Gulf Crisis: Origins and Consequences.* Washington: Institute for Palestine Studies, 1991.

-----. "A Meeting of Minds on Middle East Peace: An Arab: Talk With Palestinians," *New York Times* (March 9, 1984).

-----. *The Middle East Postwar Environment.* Washington: Institute for Palestine Studies, 1991.

-----. "Plan Dalet: Master Plan for the Conquest of Palestine," *Journal of Palestine Studies* 69 (Autumn 1988): 4-70.

-----. "Regiopolitics: Toward a U.S. Policy on the Palestine Problem," *Foreign Affairs* 59, no. 5 (Summer 1981): 1050-1063.

-----. "Thinking the Unthinkable: A Sovereign Palestinian State," *Foreign Affairs* 56, no. 4 (July 1978): 695-713.

-----. "Toward Peace in the Holy Land," *Foreign Affairs* (Spring 1988): 771-789.

Krupnick, Mark. "Edward Said: Discourse and Palestinian Rage," *Tikkun* 4, no. 6 (November/December 1989): 21-24.

Kuntsel, Marcia and Joseph Albright. *Promised Land: Arab and Jew in History's Cauldron—One Valley in the Jerusalem Hills.* New York: Crown Publishers, Inc., 1990.

Kurzman, Dan. *Genesis 1948: The First Arab-Israeli War.* New York: New American Library, 1972.

Lustick, Ian. *Arabs in the Jewish State: Israel's Control of a National Minority.* Austin: University of Texas Press, 1980.

Massarueh, Abdulsalam Y. "The Fate of Palestinians: The Arabs, Too,

Give Them Second-Class Status," *Washington Post* (August 3, 1986).

Mattar, Philip. "The Critical Moment for Peace," *Foreign Policy* 76 (Fall 1989): 141-159.

McCormick, Eileen M. "Young Pharmacist Achieves 'American Dream' in His Inner-City Pharmacy," *Pharmacy Times* (December 1988): 36-40.

Milhim, Hisham. "Abu Lughod on U.S.-PLO Dialogue," Kuwait *Al- Qabas* (October 25, 1989), in FBIS-NES-89-209 (October 31, 1989):2-7.

-----. "Edward Said on PLO Dealings With United States," Kuwait *Al-Qabas* (October 7, 1989), in FBIS-NES-89-201 (October 19, 1989): 1-6.

Morris, Benny. *The Birth of the Palestinian Refugee Problem, 1947-1949.* Cambridge: Cambridge University Press, 1988.

Moughrabi, Fouad. "American Public Opinion and the Palestine Question," in Elia Zureik and Fouad Moughrabi, eds., *Public Opinion and the Palestine Question.* New York: St. Martin's Press, 1987.

----- and Elia Zureik, Manuel Hassassian, and Aziz Haidar. "Palestinians on the Peace Process," *Journal of Palestine Studies* 81 (Autumn 1991): 36-53.

----- and Pat El-Nazer. "What Do Palestinian Americans Think? Results of a Public Opinion Survey," *Journal of Palestine Studies* 72 (Summer 1989): 91-101.

Naff, Alixa. *Becoming American: The Early Arab Immigrant Experience.* Carbondale, IL: Southern Illinois University Press, 1985.

National Lawyers Guild, *International Human Rights Law and Israel's Efforts to Suppress the Palestinian Uprising: 1988 Report of the National Lawyers Guild.* New York: National Lawyers Guild, 1989.

Orfalea, Gregory. *Before the Flames: A Quest for the History of Arab Americans.* Austin: University of Texas Press, 1988.

Oschinsky, Lawrence. "Islam in Chicago: Being a Study of the Acculturation of a Muslim Palestinian Community in That City." M.A. thesis, University of Chicago, 1947.

Palestine National Council. "Palestinian Declaration of Independence, Algiers, 15 November 1988," *Journal of Palestine Studies* 70 (Winter 1989): 213-216.

-----. "Political Communique, Algiers, 15 November 1988," *Journal of Palestine Studies* 70 (Winter 1989): 216-223.

Palumbo, Michael. *The Palestinian Catastrophe: The 1948 Expulsion of a People from Their Homeland.* London: Quartet Books, 1987.

"A Profile of Chicago's Arab Americans," AAI Notebook, Winter 1986.

Quandt, William B. "The Middle East in 1990," *Foreign Affairs* 70, no. 1, "America and the World 1990/91" special edition (1991): 49-69.

Quandt, William B., Fuad Jabber, and Ann Moseley Lesch. *The Politics of*

Palestinian Nationalism. Berkeley: University of California Press, 1973.

Rabie, Mohamed. "Arab-Israeli Peace: A New Vision for a Transformed Middle East," *American-Arab Affairs* 36 (Spring 1991): 73-86.

Rubinstein, Danny. *The People of Nowhere: The Palestinian Vision of Home.* New York: Times Books, 1991.

Sahliyeh, Emile. *In Search of Leadership: West Bank Politics since 1967.* Washington: Brookings Institution, 1988.

Said, Edward W. *After the Last Sky: Palestinian Lives.* New York: Pantheon Books, 1986.

----- and Christopher Hitchens, eds. *Blaming the Victims: Spurious Scholarship and the Palestinian Question.* London & New York: Verso, 1988.

-----. "How to Answer Palestine's Challenge," *Mother Jones* (September 1988): 16-18.

-----. "The Mind of Winter: Reflections on Life in Exile," *Harper's* (September 1984): 49-55.

-----. *The Question of Palestine.* New York: Vintage Books, 1980.

-----. "Shattering Effects of Saddam's Invasion," *The Arab News* (September 5, 1990), reprinted in *Washington Report on Middle East Affairs* (November 1990) 48-49.

-----. "A Tragic Convergence," *New York Times* (January 11, 1991).

Sarid, Yossi. "A Meeting of Minds on Middle East Peace: An Israeli: Talk With Palestinians," *New York Times* (March 9, 1984).

Sayigh, Rosemary. *Palestinians: From Peasants to Revolutionaries.* London: Zed Books, 1979.

Segev, Tom. *1949: The First Israelis.* New York: The Free Press, 1986.

Shammas, Anton. *Arabesques,* trans. Vivian Eden. New York: Harper & Row, 1988.

-----. "A Stone's Throw," *New York Review of Books* (March 31, 1988).

Sharabi, Hisham. "Creating Palestine," *New York Times* (December 20, 1981).

-----. "The Impact on the Palestinian Diaspora," *Middle East International* (December 15, 1989).

-----. "A Look Ahead: The Future State of Palestine," in Michael Hudson, ed., *The Palestinians: New Directions.* Washington: Center for Contemporary Arab Studies, 1990.

-----. *Neopatriarchy: A Theory of Distorted Change in Arab Society.* New York: Oxford University Press, 1988.

Shipler, David. *Arab and Jew: Wounded Spirits in a Promised Land.* New York: Times Books, 1986.

Shlaim, Avi. *Collusion Across the Jordan: King Abdullah, the Zionist Movement, and the Partition of Palestine.* New York: Columbia University Press, 1988.

Siddiq, Muhammad. *Man Is a Cause: Political Consciousness and the Fiction of Ghassan Kanafani.* Seattle: University of Washington Press, 1984.

Smith, Dinitia. "Arafat's Man in New York: The Divided Life of Columbia's Edward Said," *New York* (January 23, 1989): 40-46.

Stillman, Norman A. *The Jews of Arab Lands: A History and Source Book.* Philadelphia: The Jewish Publication Society of America, 1979.

-----. *The Jews of Arab Lands in Modern Times.* Philadelphia: The Jewish Publication Society of America, 1991.

Suleiman, Michael W. *The Arabs in the Mind of America.* Brattleboro, VT: Amana Books, 1988.

al-Tahir, Abdul Jalil. "The Arab Community in the Chicago Area, A Comparative Study of the Christian-Syrians and the Muslim Palestinians." Ph.D. diss., University of Chicago, 1952.

Talhami, Ghada. "Women of the Intifada," *Chicago Tribune* (December 15, 1989).

Tekiner, Roselle, Samir Abed-Rabbo, and Norton Mezvinksy, eds. *Anti-Zionism: Analytical Reflections.* Brattleboro, VT: Amana Books, 1988.

Teveth, Shabtai. *Ben-Gurion and the Palestinian Arabs: From Peace to War.* New York: Oxford University Press, 1985.

Turki, Fawaz. *The Disinherited: Journal of a Palestinian Exile.* New York: Monthly Review Press, 1972.

-----. *Soul in Exile: Lives of a Palestinian Revolutionary.* New York: Monthly Review Press, 1988.

Wagner, Rev. Don. "A Living Martyr," *The Return* 1, no. 4 (November 1988): 4-8.

Wieseltier, Leon. "Palestinian Perversion of the Holocaust," *New York Times* (June 12, 1988).

Winternitz, Helen. *A Season of Stones: Living in a Palestinian Village.* New York: Atlantic Monthly Press, 1991.

"Words of Yasir Arafat: 'Offering My Hand,'" *New York Times* (December 14, 1988).

Zaghel, Ali. "Changing Patterns of Identification Among Arab Americans: The Palestinian Ramallites." Ph.D. diss., Northwestern University, 1977.

Zogby, James, ed. *Taking Root, Bearing Fruit: The Arab-American Experience.* Washington: American-Arab Anti-Discrimination Committee, 1984.

Index of Names